Labor in Developing Economies

A Publication of the
Institute of Industrial Relations
University of California

Labor in Developing Economies

EDITED BY WALTER GALENSON

Berkeley and Los Angeles, 1963
UNIVERSITY OF CALIFORNIA PRESS

UNIVERSITY OF CALIFORNIA PRESS
BERKELEY AND LOS ANGELES
CALIFORNIA

CAMBRIDGE UNIVERSITY PRESS
LONDON, ENGLAND

SECOND PRINTING, 1963

LIBRARY OF CONGRESS CATALOG CARD NUMBER: 62-8491

Foreword

During the past eight years, the Institute of Industrial Relations has participated in the Inter-University Study of Labor Problems in Economic Development, which has been supported by a generous grant from the Ford Foundation and more recently by a second grant from the Carnegie Corporation. Conducted in coöperation with industrial relations centers at Harvard, Princeton, the Massachusetts Institute of Technology, and the University of Chicago, the project has been directed by Clark Kerr, John T. Dunlop, Frederick H. Harbison, and Charles A. Myers. Their book, *Industrialism and Industrial Man* (1960), includes a list of all the participants in the project and of the numerous publications that have resulted from it.

Included in the plans for the Inter-University Study from an early stage was the preparation of two volumes of essays on the labor movement and industrial relations in selected countries, to be edited by Walter Galenson. Although the more highly industrialized countries were, for the most part, to be excluded, the essays were to deal with countries in various stages of industrialization. An effort was made to include a large enough group of relatively underdeveloped countries to provide a wide range of illustrations of patterns of labor relations likely to emerge in the course of economic development. Another important consideration in the selection of countries was the availability of experts who had acquired substantial firsthand knowledge of their respective countries or areas.

The first of the two volumes, *Labor and Economic Development* (published by John Wiley & Sons, Inc., 1959), included chapters on India, Japan, Egypt, French West Africa, and the British West Indies.

The present volume contains essays on Argentina, Brazil, Chile, Indonesia, Israel, Pakistan, and Turkey. Together, the twelve countries whose labor relations have been analyzed provide examples of stages of economic development ranging all the way from a backward area such as French West Africa to the far more mature economies of such countries as Israel and Japan. The distribution of essays between the two volumes, however, followed no particular pattern and was influenced largely by the writing schedules of the individual authors.

Walter Galenson, the editor, is Professor of Business Administration and Economics at the University of California, Berkeley, and a member of the Institute research staff. He is widely known for his many previous publications on comparative labor movements, labor history, and labor productivity.

Arthur M. Ross, Director,
Institute of Industrial Relations

Contents

Contributors

Robert J. Alexander

Associate Professor of Economics, Rutgers University. Author of *The Perón Era* (1951); *Communism in Latin America* (1957); *The Bolivian National Revolution* (1958); and *The Struggle for Democracy in Latin America* (1961). Worked with the Office of Inter-American Affairs and the International Cooperation Administration.

Walter Galenson

Professor of Industrial Relations and Research Economist, Institute of Industrial Relations, University of California, Berkeley. Author of *Rival Unionism in the United States* (1940); *Labor in Norway* (1949); *The Danish System of Labor Relations* (1952); *Labor Productivity in Soviet and American Industry* (1955); *The CIO Challenge to the AFL* (1960); and *Trade Union Democracy in Western Europe* (1961). Editor of *Comparative Labor Movements* (1952), and *Labor and Economic Development* (1959); co-editor of *Labor and Trade Unionism* (1960).

Everett D. Hawkins

Chairman, Department of Economics and Sociology, Mount Holyoke College. Author of *Dismissal Compensation* (1940); *Labor Practices in Indonesia* (1960). Program Planning Officer, MSA, Djakarta, 1951–1952; Desk Officer for Indonesia, TCA-FOA, Washington, 1952–1953; Visiting Professor of Economics, Gadjah Mada University, Jogjakarta, 1958–1960.

Trade Union Power in Underdeveloped Nations

Trade unionism is not a very hardy flower; it is particularly susceptible to the winds of politics and to economic adversity. One does not need too long a memory to recall the time when collective bargaining was not part of the American way of life. It is small wonder that nations which are unstable politically and struggling desperately to develop their economic resources do not exhibit powerful, well-functioning labor movements. Democracy in the factory usually lags well behind democracy in civil life generally.

In underdeveloped countries, trade unions face the fact that the industrial worker is a minority group, sometimes a very small one. In Pakistan and Turkey, for example, three-quarters of the labor force is engaged in agriculture, and only a small percentage of the remaining quarter consists of wage earners in modern industry, the group most susceptible to organization.

There are exceptional cases where trade unions have participated in the struggle for national independence, and thus gained general public esteem. This is true in Indonesia, where, despite the overwhelmingly agrarian character of the economy, the trade unions have played an important role in the country since the attainment of independence. The Israeli labor movement, the Histadrut, has been in the same position, although there it has also served as colonizer and entrepreneur, and prior to statehood was perhaps the chief rallying point for the aspiring nation.

The Latin American countries considered in Professor Alexander's essay provide interesting examples of the vicissitudes in trade union fortune as economic development proceeds. Brazil, Argentina, and Chile have all had a long history of labor organization, and, given their stages of development, one would expect to find fairly stable unions. But this expectation is fulfilled only in Chile. Argentina, the most highly developed nation of South America, had a Western-style labor movement for many years, but the Perón era seriously weakened it. The situation is even worse in Brazil, where the labor movement is just beginning to recover from the corporate state introduced by Vargas, and is hampered, moreover, by the country's continued inability to move forward economically with any appreciable speed.

It is not only a potentially small constituency that confronts the aspiring labor organizer in an underdeveloped country. Unemployment and underemployment are antithetical to the cause of unionism. Once having secured a job, the worker is extremely reluctant to incur the displeasure of his employer, who, for his part, is generally not averse to using his economic power to keep out what he regards as an alien, radical force. Discrimination, the blacklist, outright force are typically part of the employer's antiunion arsenal. Organizational progress is usually feasible only when the government steps in to provide protection; after all, it required the Wagner Act to pave the way for the unionization of heavy industry in the United States. But the governments of underdeveloped countries are not likely to welcome unions for the new recruits to industry. At best, they constitute annoying pressure groups for higher real wages and more advanced social services than the economy can afford at a time when investment is the critical need. At worst, they may be led by political radicals dissatisfied with the existing system of government. The line of least resistance, the one followed in all too many cases, is to deprive the unions of independence of action, if indeed they are permitted to exist at all.

This has been pretty much the story in Pakistan, Turkey, and Brazil. Pakistan inherited a not inconsiderable trade union base when it split from India, but the movement failed to make any progress because of employer hostility and government indifference. When the constitutional government was overthrown in 1958, the military authorities instituted an absolute ban on strikes and made union operation difficult generally. Professor Weatherford observes: "Persons high in planning circles in the government are frank to admit that union encouragement must 'make haste slowly,' only after careful study shows that union growth will not impede economic development." Similarly in Turkey, the activities of unions are so circumscribed by law as to exclude them from any effective role in industrial relations. They do not enjoy the right to strike, or even to handle grievances at the factory level. The Brazilian trade unions became social welfare organizations under the Vargas dictatorship, and, although there has been a great deal of relaxation of government control in recent years, they still tend to be dominated by government officials.

Indonesia seems to be in quite a different category, but it is not inconceivable that things may eventually turn out the same way. The Indonesian government has been prounion since the country gained its independence, not least because so large a part of the entrepreneurial class was foreign. But now that management has become largely Indonesian, and the problem of development has reached so critical a stage, it may not be long before the government finds that the presence of a dozen fiercely competing labor federations is inimical to progress. The military are already playing an important role in industrial relations, and there is always the temptation to take the ultimate step of suppressing unionism altogether, or of incorporating the unions into a national front.

Once a trade union movement becomes really firmly rooted in a society, however, it has a great deal of staying power, as the Argentine experience demonstrates. Perón did not attempt to smash the movement, for that might have imperiled his regime. Instead, he strengthened it and adapted it to his own purposes, achieving an invaluable adjunct to his machinery for political control. Employers were obliged to recognize the unions and bargain with them. Loyal Peronistas were infiltrated into key union positions and could thus control union policies. So successful was this tactic that Peronism outlived Perón in the trade unions, and this remains one of Argentina's chief political problems. The Argentine unions have probably raised labor costs above what they otherwise would have been, and thus hindered development. They have enormously complicated the attainment of a stable price level, and have contributed in no small measure to persistent inflation. But, as Professor Alexander points out, they have "tended to assure the worker that he will not be considered merely a 'factor of production,' but will be treated as an individual, with certain prescribed rights and duties," and the resultant gain in social stability may more than offset the possible loss in investment.

The case of the Histadrut in Israel is a very special one, though several other countries have shown interest in it as a developmental model. The Histadrut generates 25 per cent of the national income and provides 30 per cent of national employment through its industrial, construction, and commercial enterprises. All this is in addition to its collective bargaining function, for the Histadrut is the only labor federation in the country and represents the workers who are employed in private enterprise. In the past there was some question of whether the Histadrut or the Israeli state itself was the more powerful body, but in recent years the Histadrut is becoming increasingly subordinate to the state, though it still remains an important independent center of authority.

Trade Unions and Politics

In a companion volume published several years ago, I made the following observation about the political roles of trade unions in a different set of underdeveloped countries: ". . . it should be apparent that the outlook for nonpolitical unionism in the newly developing countries is not bright. We may expect, rather, a highly political form of unionism, with a radical ideology. Indeed, so strong is the presumption that this will be the prevailing pattern that, when it is absent, we may draw the conclusion that unionism is, in fact, subordinated to the employer or to the state, i.e., that we are dealing either with company unionism or a labor front."[1] Does this generalization hold up against the present set of countries, or are modifications necessary?

Three of the cases with which we are concerned offer no threat to the validity of the thesis. Indonesian trade unions are more aptly described as divisions of political parties than as independent economic organizations. The country's largest federation is under the control of the local Communist party. In Chile, where the Communists also control the major federation, "the intensely political nature of Chilean trade unionism has been a disturbing factor in labor relations for several decades. Strikes are not infrequently called more for the consolidation of the political group in control of a given union than because they are justified economically." Communism is not an issue in Argentina, but the peculiar kind of radicalism represented by Peronism is. Argentine unionism was highly political in character long before Perón, and it remains so to this day.

The Brazilian case is not quite so clear, for unions there have undergone several transmutations. Under Vargas they were essentially a labor front for the government. They are still subject to considerable government influence, but their greater independence now makes them a more attractive target for the political parties. It can hardly be said, however, that they are either independent or politically neutral.

Israel again presents a peculiar situation. The Histadrut is supra-party but not nonparty. All of its governing bodies are elected from slates presented by the various political parties which cater to workers, of which there are half a dozen. Mapai, the party which has been at the head of the government coalition since the achievement of statehood, has a majority in the Histadrut, and this provides a very close government-union link. Policy is made within the Histadrut along party lines, and "even when the party members in Histadrut feel that the decision taken is antithetical to their Histadrut interests, they obey." Surely this would not qualify the Histadrut as a nonpolitical organization. Its dominant ideology is a mild socialism.

There is a clear distinction between Pakistan and Turkey, on the one hand, and all of the foregoing nations on the other. In neither Pakistan nor Turkey is there an alliance between unions and parties, and the unions are not operated by the government. They seem to be genuinely apolitical, with a diversity of views among the leadership, which is quite conservative on the whole. We have here, certainly, an

[1] *Labor and Economic Development* (New York, 1959), p. 8.

exception to the generalization stated above. But whether this situation will continue remains to be seen. The unions in both countries have thus far been so impotent as to make them unattractive for colonization by political parties. Moreover, in Turkey quite consistently, and in Pakistan at least since the institution of martial rule, there has been little scope for parliamentary democracy. The unions could go either way, but they are not likely to remain in the present limbo. If political democracy is restored, and the unions are permitted to grow, they will probably become more highly political. If, on the other hand, the trend is toward authoritarianism, it is not unlikely that they will become part of the government's control mechanism. Professor Rosen has summarized the situation very well: "If decentralization of the decision-making process is not introduced at the appropriate moment, the state will have no alternative but to create a vast bureaucratic apparatus for dealing with industrial disputes; in such a system unions would be little more than appendages of the state. The crucial decision-making period is not far off. Unless it is given the chance and the wings for flight, Turkey's union movement is likely to degenerate and decline. . . ."

Collective Bargaining

A viable system of collective bargaining takes many years to develop. It requires the establishment of attitudes of mutual forbearance, and the realization by employers that they are playing a game rather than seeking the extinction of their opponents. For successful collective bargaining, there must be at least approximate equality of bargaining power, and the willingness of the parties to forget the lacerations caused by the bargaining process. These ingredients are rarely to be found in underdeveloped countries. The bargaining power of trade unions is apt to be political rather than economic; they can cause demonstrations and riots, and alarm the government into action with the urgency of their demands, but they lack the ability to run sustained work stoppages. Discrimination and blacklisting are facilitated by the existence of pools of strikebreakers from among the unemployed or the rural underemployed.

Nor is the weight of government influence likely to be thrown on the side of the trade unions, even in the most favorable of circumstances. Wage determination is too closely geared to growth potentialities to be left to bilateral settlement. Labor market negotiations will be closely supervised, and agreements scrutinized for their impact on the economy. Even in the United States, we are beginning to realize that bilateral bargaining on a sectional basis may endanger national objectives. The amount of slack in an underdeveloped country is much less, and tolerance accordingly quite narrow.

By and large, these observations are borne out by our sample of seven countries. Very few Pakistani employers are willing to recognize unions, and where collective bargaining has been accepted, government officials control the outcome, either informally or through compulsory arbitration tribunals. Turkish employers display an even greater hostility to the idea of collective bargaining. Prevailing legislation, moreover, allows unions to raise demands only on wages, and these must be resolved through compulsory arbitration. In Brazil, the prevailing pattern is for unions to present wage claims to labor courts, which hand down final decisions, although collective bargaining is beginning to find its way into the picture as the spirit of corporatism recedes.

In Indonesia, it is not the strength but the weakness of employers which necessitates government intervention. There is also the fact that the government itself supplies a substantial proportion of available employment. Professor Hawkins describes the situation in that country as follows: ". . . a few pieces of labor legislation have been adopted, the most important of which provides for tripartite arbitration of labor disputes. This system has tended to be a substitute for free union-management negotiations. . . . It is unlikely in the near future that the government will take its hands off labor relations or give up its power to arbitrate disputes or to declare strikes illegal in times of emergency."

A collective bargaining system appears to have become fairly well stabilized in Argentina and Chile, by virtue of a longer industrial experience in these countries. However, there has been repeated government intervention (apart from the Perón experience in Argentina, where bargaining was completely centralized under government direction) in the interest of price stability. The Chilean government in 1956 limited the maximum wage increase in any year to 50 per cent of the previous year's price rise, and has taken other steps to cope with mounting inflation. Determination of relative wages and prices has been a thorny political problem for every Argentine government since the downfall of Perón.

Finally, the close intertwining of government, political parties, trade unions, and management that characterizes the Israeli scene makes the unions more sensitive to the national welfare than to the sectional interests of wage earners. Wage restraint rather than increase has been the order of the day. According to Professor Sobel, the Histadrut "has been opposed to any general wage increases since governmental economic policy, which Mapai members of the Histadrut Executive must adhere to, has been one of wage restraint so that productivity ultimately will catch up with wage rates and social benefits."

Wage Differentials

It is generally believed that wage differentials, particularly those relating to skill, are large in early stages of industrialization and tend to diminish as development proceeds. Skilled labor, the argument runs, is in short supply initially, so that the price will be bid up by employers attempting to fill their short-run needs, while society will condone the maintenance of a high premium for skill in order to encourage its acquisition. Once training gets under way, and the general level of education is raised, a better balance will be achieved and the differential will narrow.

Not all the essays in this volume deal with this issue, but those that do throw considerable doubt on the validity of this theory. For one reason or another, narrow rather than wide wage differentials seem to prevail in underdeveloped countries. In Pakistan, the skilled-unskilled ratio is about two to one, roughly the United States ratio a quarter of a century ago. The premium for skill in Indonesia is only about 50 per cent, while Israel has one of the most compressed wage and salary structures in the world.

Since the authors are all economists, and the facts fly in the face of their strong preconceptions, they tend to put the blame for what they regard as an uneconomic state of affairs on sociological factors. In Pakistan, it is apparently due to the force of tradition and humanitarian considerations that the wages of unskilled labor exceed marginal productivity. In Indonesia, the importance of payment in kind, again on social grounds, keeps real differentials narrow. In Israel, it has been trade union policy to provide the lowest-paid workers with a Western European standard of living, which has meant that very little is left over for groups with higher productivity. Pakistan has apparently had some skilled labor shortage as a result, though no corresponding problem is noted for Indonesia. Israel started with a surplus of skilled labor as a result of immigration of refugees from Western Europe, but with rapid industrialization and a change in the character of immigration, skill bottlenecks have begun to manifest themselves.

This whole issue calls for much closer scrutiny than is made in this volume, but at least some doubt is thrown on the inevitability of a particular natural history of wages in the course of economic development. There are simply too many other variables, in addition to supply and demand, to permit the drawing of any simple conclusions. Moreover, it is not at all clear that the pure economic variables are the most critical ones, even from the point of view of developmental success. The

Pakistani worker, for example, is as much motivated by traditional values of prestige and honor as by monetary incentives, and if the nonpecuniary incentives can be properly utilized, they may mitigate the severe impact caused by introducing a pure wage incentive system into an economy not yet geared to the generation of a sufficient quantity of consumer goods. The idealism and self-sacrifice that have been the mainsprings of Israeli life may permit the deployment of the labor force on the basis of "uneconomic" wage differentials for some time to come.

I have yet to see a single well-documented case in which the lack of labor skills prevented development, or even provided a serious hindrance. Caution should be exercised in insisting that wide differentials are necessarily correct for underdeveloped countries. At low absolute levels of living, wide differentials may impose severe hardships on the unskilled, and unless they prove absolutely essential, it might be the better part of valor to avoid them.

A Critical Choice

Many other subjects are discussed in the thoughtful and stimulating essays that follow. Among them are the problems involved in the conversion of a backward peasantry into an industrial work force; the manpower aspects of the management cadres; the social service dilemma, i.e., the problem of reconciling adequate welfare minima with the capabilities of an underdeveloped economy; the recruitment of capable trade union leaders; and the financing and structure of unions.

But there is one issue which transcends all the others in importance, and because of their preoccupation with individual cases, the contributors to this volume may not have given it sufficient emphasis. There are, in the final analysis, two great conceptions of labor market organization confronting one another in the world today. One of them, that prevailing in the Communist bloc and in countries with corporate systems, such as Egypt and Spain, regards the interests of labor, as well as of other social groups, as subordinate to the interests of the state, which is conceived of as the only legitimate representative of parochial interests. Trade unions, or similar bodies, are regarded accordingly as administrative arms of the state, charged with the primary responsibility of maintaining discipline and furthering productivity. They are permitted to distribute welfare benefits as a substitute for direct state payments, but their wage function is limited at most to minor individual adjustments. They are not permitted to exert any real pressure for shorter hours or higher wages, since the state is presumably improving these conditions as rapidly as the development of the economy will allow.

The second conception, that which is held in the West, starts with the basic assumption that sectional interests may on occasion diverge from the national interest, and permits the establishment of organizational means by which parochial interests may be furthered. It is recognized that the assertion of individual and group interests may inflict damage on the economy, but the long-run interests of society are regarded as being advanced by the clash of conflicting group desires. Collective bargaining, reinforced by the ultimate right to strike, is the classic *modus operandi* of trade unionism in a society conforming to this conception, though political action may be a complementary means. For this concept to be meaningful, trade unions must be basically independent of state and employer influence, or they cannot function as genuinely representative institutions.

Every country which is now in the process of determining its ultimate institutional arrangements will have to opt for one or the other of these systems. There are many shadings within each, and sometimes it is not even easy to distinguish one from the other. But in any specific case it is usually not too difficult to determine where the line has been drawn. For example, all of the countries in our sample appear thus far to favor the Western concept, though the final balance has not been struck in every case. There is no doubt at all of Chile and Israel. Brazil and Argentina are still recovering from the traumatic experience of native corporatism, but independent unionism seems to have a secure future. Pakistan, Turkey, and Indonesia are the most doubtful cases. They face quite different economic problems and political perils, but the eventual governmentalization of labor organization is by no means an impossibility in any of them.

All of us who have worked on this book, and on the larger project of which it is a part, are convinced that independent trade unionism and satisfactory economic development are by no means antithetical. On the contrary, we believe that independent unions can make a major contribution to development by giving the individual worker a sense of personal dignity and a means of redressing his grievances. It is quite understandable for government leaders who are concentrating on the achievement of economic goals in the face of what must sometimes appear to be impossible odds to be impatient with intractable, "irresponsible" representatives of workers. There is an ever-present temptation to silence them and to substitute paternalism for bargaining and conflict. But the price may be very high indeed: the loss to the nation of the creative energies of free men who feel themselves masters of their own fates rather than cogs in a vast, impersonal machine.

Chapter II | Pakistan

WILLIS D. WEATHERFORD, JR.

Five underlying influences are shaping the current economic development of Pakistan. Some knowledge of these forces is essential for an understanding of contemporary labor problems in this recently independent country.

Background Factors

RECENT EMERGENCE OF PAKISTAN AS A NATION

Since the turn of the century Hindus and Muslims of British India had worked side by side for self-government, but between 1937 and 1940 friction between the two groups mounted to such a pitch that Muslim leaders called for a separate state of Pakistan to be formed when the British granted self-rule. Thus with independence in 1947 came partition, establishing a new state which combined British constitutional processes with an ideology inspired by the Koran. The new state had five provincial governments already operating, but a central government located at Karachi had to be formed *de novo*. Pakistan's planning for economic development and labor utilization has been considerably slowed because many of her able leaders have been so engrossed in establishing the new political entity.

To compound the difficulties of forming a new state, there was a mass migration of seven million Muslims into Pakistan from India, and a similar number of Hindus fled into India from Pakistan, during three months of arson and murder in 1947. Relief of these many unsettled refugees has constituted a major drain on the country's economic resources, which otherwise could have been used for economic development. In addition, the one-tenth of the population which is refugee has had no firm geographic or occupational roots and has tended to unsettle the labor force and placed special strains on industrial relations.

The heritage of Pakistan when the British left India was a difficult one. Pakistan was born as a divided nation with two areas separated by nearly a thousand miles of Indian soil. Both East and West Pakistan were Muslim majority areas; they were united by a strong determination to create a new state based on the principles of Islam, but in other respects they were totally different. In the East, more than half the population lives in one-sixth of the country's total area, crowded into one of the most densely populated alluvial plains in the world. Here jute and rice are the major crops, and drainage of swamps is a major problem. In West Pakistan, less people live in an area five times as large, on land which was arid sand and rocky hills before irrigation schemes made the desert bloom with wheat and cotton. Agriculturalists in the East are desperately poor, while in the West they live on at least a subsistence level. People of the East speak Bengali, while those of the West speak Urdu and several local languages more closely related to Persian. Bengal has for centuries been a seat of Muslim culture and literature, while much of West Pakistan supported only a nomadic population until the advent of irrigation. The differences between East and West Pakistan have made political as well as industrial unity difficult. The old Indian province of Bengal was a cultural unit, but partition divided it between the two emerging nations. East Bengal became the only province of East Pakistan, so the two terms are used interchangeably in this discussion.

Political tensions have created economic difficulties. Ever since partition, Pakistani politicians and parties have been unable to give the nation that political stability needed for economic planning and development. Political life has been a scramble among individuals undisciplined by adherence to established party lines or stable ideology, while corruption within provincial governments has been a byword. Political control has been in the hands of professional politicians in parliamentary parties unresponsive to the voice of the people, since provincial elections had been held but once and national elections not at all up to the declaration of martial law in 1958. Much of Pakistan's ability has been drained into fruitless political bickering instead of being devoted to building the new nation.

Up until 1954, the Muslim League party held undisputed sway among politicians and people. It had fought against British and Hindus for an independent state, and was held by many to be synonymous with

Pakistan. Its platform was independence; but once this was achieved, it had too many divergent elements to last. In the fall of 1956 it lost control of the Central Legislature, and the Premiership passed to another party. The Awami League, standing slightly to the left of the Muslim League but having many elements within its ranks, emerged from the United Front as the strongest party of East Bengal and made a bid for membership in the West. It was the only large party in Pakistan which stressed building up grass-roots support. Since the advent of martial law the activity of political parties has been eclipsed by administrative developments.

HUMAN AND NATURAL RESOURCES

Pakistan with its 94 million people is the seventh most populous country of the world. East and West Pakistan are so different that any discussion of population relative to resources must separate the two areas. River basins have determined population concentration since time immemorial: East Bengal sits astride the lower Ganges and Brahmaputra rivers and has been densely populated for centuries. With 777 persons per square mile, it is one of the most crowded areas of the world. East Bengal, with over one-half the nation's population, must earn its living from only one-sixth of the land area; there is only .55 acre of cultivated land per rural person. Although the alluvial deposits enrich the land annually and the omnipresent waters conspire with the heat to give good growing conditions for paddy and jute, the rice yield is one of the lowest in the world. The overburdened land can support the population only on a bare subsistence basis, and Bengal has always been a food-deficit area, although 83 per cent of her people are agriculturists.[1] Nevertheless, Bengal furnishes Pakistan with its most important export and dollar earner, since it grows most of the world's supply of jute. Perhaps it is a blessing that Bengal, being one of the poorest areas of the subcontinent, has one of the lowest rates of natural increase.[2]

West Pakistan was peopled primarily by wandering herdsmen until irrigation works were introduced around the turn of the century, and large-scale migration from heavily settled areas of India started only after the First World War. The 41 million people of West Pakistan are thinly scattered over a vast area of sandy, rocky soil, but are concen-

---

[1] *Census of Pakistan, 1951*, Vol. 3, Bengal, Table II.

[2] The census of 1951 gives the average annual increase from 1901–1951 as 0.75 per cent, but of course this was upset by the migrations at partition. *Census of Pakistan, 1951*, Vol. 1, Chap. 1. Davis, on the basis of net reproduction rates calculated for each province before partition, found undivided Bengal to have a very low net rate of reproduction (1.26 per cent). Kingsley Davis, *The Population of India and Pakistan* (Princeton: Princeton University Press, 1951), p. 87.

trated mainly around the river Indus, its tributaries, and the canals, which form the most extensive irrigation system in the world. Since over half the cultivated area is irrigated, West Pakistan enjoys a slight food surplus in good years, but not enough to overcome the deficit of East Bengal. Because of irrigation, yields of the principal crops, wheat and cotton, are above those of other areas of the subcontinent, but are low in world comparisons.

Although inadequately fed at present, the population is growing rapidly. The Punjab in particular has for several decades been one of the most prosperous areas, but also has a very high rate of natural increase.[3] The population for the whole of Pakistan is growing at the rate of 2.2 per cent, or about two million people, per year, placing an ever larger strain on the limited land and water resources. To feed this growing population, very little additional land is available in the crowded East, while in the West the bottleneck is water.

The human resources of the nation are abundant, but the low standards of education and health reduce their effectiveness. Although 19 per cent of the people can read, only 4 per cent are effectively literate in being able both to read and write, and only 1 per cent have received more than ten years of schooling. The stamina and strength of the work force is undermined by the inadequate diet and widespread disease, particularly in East Pakistan, where the debilitating effect of malaria is prevalent.

Pakistan's lack of large power and mineral resources places her at a disadvantage, and her development must be planned accordingly. She is particularly deficient in coal, oil, and iron ore.

THE AGRICULTURAL NATURE OF THE ECONOMY

Nine-tenths of Pakistan's population is rural and depends on agriculture directly or indirectly, 76 per cent of the labor force is engaged in agriculture, and 60 per cent of the national income is agricultural in origin. Only 7 per cent of the workers are engaged in mining and manufacturing, while less than a million workers are engaged in modern organized industries.[4] Thus the welfare of the country is dependent on agriculture both for subsistence and for foreign exchange.

---

[3] Davis found the net reproduction rate of undivided Punjab to be 1.63 per cent. *Ibid.*, p. 87. The 1951 census shows West Pakistan growing at the rate of 1.45 per cent per year over 50 years, and 1.82 per cent per year since 1931. *Census of Pakistan, 1951*, Vol. 1, pp. 28–29. The Central Statistical office uses 1.5 per cent per year in estimating population growth for the whole country. Preliminary results of the 1961 population census show a 2.17 per cent increase per year since 1951. *Dawn*, Karachi, March 4, 1961.

[4] Government of Pakistan, Ministry of Labour, *Report of the ILO Labour Survey Mission on Labour Problems in Pakistan* (Karachi, 1953), p. 12.

Pakistan's golden fiber and primary foreign-exchange earner is jute; cotton is a close second. These two cash crops are each found alongside a major food crop; jute and rice are predominant in the wet East Bengal climate, while cotton and wheat abound on the dry plains of the West. Understanding the conditions governing these four crops provides the key to the nation's welfare, since they furnish nine-tenths of the food grains and three-fourths of the country's foreign exchange.

The pattern of land tenure is a basic determinant of income distribution as well as of the possibilities for economic development in an agricultural area. The land tenure pattern is also a very important determinant of the industrial labor force, since an area with large numbers of tenants-at-will and landless agricultural workers will easily furnish industrial workers, whereas cultivating landowners are loath to leave their lands for alternative employment. Among the agricultural workers of Pakistan, 37 per cent own all the lands they cultivate, 50 per cent are renters of all or part of the lands they work under many types of tenure, and 14 per cent are landless laborers who are highly unstable. A brief description of the conditions of these three sorts of farm workers will indicate their susceptibility to becoming part of the industrial labor force.

Owners and occupancy tenants are assured of security on their land and are the most stable part of the agricultural population. Nonetheless, many have such small holdings that they are driven to find additional work, usually within agriculture. One-fifth of the owners of the Punjab own less than one acre. Patel has described the process by which these small owners fall into debt, ultimately lose title to their land, and become tenants or landless laborers, but so long as they have rights in the land they are not likely to be wooed into the industrial labor force.[5]

Tenants-at-will generally pay their rents in kind to the landlord under the *batai* system, the proportion so paid usually being set at half the crop. Their security is precarious, since the tenancy agreement must be renewed each year, and under such a system efficiency suffers because the tenant will never make any capital improvements. In areas where tenants-at-will have fewest rights, such as the *hari* of Sind or the *bargadar* of East Bengal, they come close to being landless laborers in the looseness of the ties which bind them to the soil.

Landless laborers are at the bottom of the labor force hierarchy.

[5] Surendra J. Patel, *Agricultural Laborers in Modern India and Pakistan* (Bombay: Current Book House, 1952). See also Government of Pakistan, Ministry of Labor, *Report on Labor Conditions in Agriculture in Pakistan,* by Sir Malcolm Darling (Karachi, 1954).

Casual laborers are usually employed by the day and have little security, and ordinarily no provision is made by the employer for their housing. Landless laborers and tenants-at-will are particularly prevalent in East Bengal and Sind, while Punjab has a larger proportion of small landowners. Year-round workers in the tea plantations of Bengal get low wages, but receive more medical care and housing than most other laboring groups because of close government protection. They are really halfway toward becoming industrial workers.

THE COMMERCIAL NATURE OF THE INDUSTRIAL SECTOR

At partition, Pakistan had almost no factories and was dependent on India or the outside world for factory products, but her commerce was relatively well developed. The emphasis on commercial development is revealed in the labor force distribution as shown in the 1951 census. Five per cent of the labor force was engaged in trade and commerce, and only 6 per cent was employed in manufacturing (and of these many were handicraft manufacturers).

There is a small but growing number of large and mechanized industrial plants, especially in cotton and jute; about 600,000 workers are employed in establishments hiring more than 100 workers, but far more workers are in small units employing from 10 to 50 men. The small units are individual or family enterprises using family capital and individual direction. Accounting procedures involve little more than a cash box, and cost accounting is unknown. Below these small factories are myriads of individual craftsmen who still eke out their village existence.

CULTURAL FACTORS AFFECTING ECONOMIC DEVELOPMENT

It is difficult to say whether Pakistan is being held together by the positive bonds of unified faith in Islam or by a common desire not to be submerged by the Hindu majority of the subcontinent. Although the common worship of Allah is a strong bond and is recognized in the constitution, this is not enough to make Pakistan an Islamic state. The *ulema* (religious leaders) have hoped that the legal structure of the state would be a direct outgrowth of the Koran, but an influential westernized group continues to administer the machinery of government along lines established by the British. One does not feel that in Pakistan the state and religious community are one, as would be the traditional idea under Islamic law.

The special status of women in Islam has strong economic consequences. Inequality between the sexes, with male dominance, is accepted as natural. *Purdah* is expensive to maintain but enhances the social position of the family, while a career woman is viewed with suspicion. The taboo which is attached to women, and is symbolized by the veil, prevents middle-class women from working outside the home. Poorer women are fully occupied in the home, but the upper strata are gradually becoming less restricted under the leadership of Miss Fatima Jinnah. The result is that, while 67 per cent of the men are in the labor force, only 4 per cent of the women are so occupied, but one must remember that most women are nonetheless occupied in the home. The resulting scarcity of workers is particularly felt in some "traditional" women's occupations such as teaching, nursing, and secretarial work.

The caste system in the strict sense is peculiar to Hinduism, and of course is prevalent among the nine million Hindus of East Bengal. But through long association the Muslims have developed parallel caste-like groups of their own, which, while not so rigid as those found among Hindus, still have considerable economic significance. Islam emphasizes the equality of men, all pray together, and social intercourse is fairly free, yet ". . . there are readily identifiable caste-like groups which carry the connotation of a particular occupation."[6] This reduces somewhat the mobility of the labor force and hence the adaptability of the society.

Although the proportion of joint families is small, to the extent that they do exist they tend to reduce individual incentive but to increase security within the family unit. Saving is reduced, since the ablest members of the family support those who are weaker and so reduce the possibility of investment.

The Koran affords passages to justify both free will and predestination—but in any case, the Pakistani is not filled with a strong sense of being able to control human events. "Allah wills it" is heard on all occasions, and the psychology of progress is absent. This atmosphere is a strong deterrent to innovation, but no more so than in numerous other traditionalistic societies.

Perhaps the chief motivation of most villagers is to maintain or increase their *izzat,* which involves status, honor, prestige, and power. Wealth is only one way to increase one's *izzat,* and occasionally may defeat the purpose. Generosity with consumption goods increases *izzat,* but miserly saving is scorned. Thus the usual Western material reward must be supplemented in order to get maximum effort from most men. We of the West must recognize this as merely a different tradition from our own, certainly not bad and probably good, even though it makes achievement of productive efficiency more difficult.

---

[6] Stanley Maron (ed.), *Pakistan: Society and Culture* (New Haven: Human Relations Area Files, 1957), p. 85.

The Emergence of an Industrial Labor Force

The free industrial labor force in Pakistan has emerged in large part from the disadvantaged groups created by a static society as it has begun to change. Recruits have been landless agricultural laborers who have become underemployed as population grew and village organization changed, or destitute craftsmen robbed of a livelihood by changing tastes and increasing competition.

HISTORICAL DEVELOPMENT

Before the coming of the British, the Indo-Pakistan subcontinent had reached a static form of economic organization in which each person fulfilled a role, changed only with difficulty. The Hindu way of life with its caste system dominated economic organization. The village was the center of economic activity, and here about four-fifths of the workers were agricultural. Land was relatively plentiful, so small-landowning peasants dominated the village. The various craftsmen, such as carpenters and blacksmiths, as well as menials such as washermen, scavengers, and farm laborers, were attached to and dependent upon the farmers of the village. They were not paid a wage in proportion to work done, but were allowed a customary payment in kind from the harvest of each farmer, in return for the customary amount of work it was thought proper to ask. The carpenter's son became a carpenter, and the isolation and self-sufficiency of the village reinforced social structures which assured that this would continue, for one's social standing as well as his standard of living depended on his caste-occupation. This static system pervaded Muslim as well as Hindu villages, since many Muslims brought their socioeconomic customs with them when converted from Hinduism. To be sure, Muslim areas of the subcontinent had somewhat more flexibility in village organization, but the picture of a static society where each family plays a traditional role is a true picture for the forebears of contemporary Pakistanis. So long as the demand for various types of workers is stable and the birth rates of various occupational groups are equal, such a system provides for a rational division of labor. But if tastes, job efficiency, or birth rates change, or if outside influences enter, the system is bound to experience internal tensions.

Around 1850 these tensions began to be felt in the subcontinent with two results for the labor force: (1) a landless but free agricultural work force emerged, not tied to the village and thus available for industrial employment; (2) displaced village and urban craftsmen swelled the ranks of the landless agricultural laborers or turned to industrial employment.

The eighteen fifties and sixties started great changes in India. The 1857 Mutiny resulted in the Crown's taking over direct political control from the East India Company. Road construction was pushed during the 'fifties, and the Grand Trunk Road was opened in 1853. Railroad construction started in 1854 and was rapidly extended from ports to inland centers, permitting much more foreign trade. The completion of the telegraph to England in 1865 tied India closer to England politically, while the opening of the Suez Canal in 1869 tied the two together economically. By 1860 the British had extended their political control, and western commercial and legal influences were beginning to be felt throughout the subcontinent.

In 1871, at the time of the first census, 18 per cent of the agricultural workers were landless laborers, but by 1931 this proportion had increased to 38 per cent.[7] This change is an indication of the disintegration of the old static social organization. Increasing transportation opened the hinterland to trade, and the villages became less self-sufficient and were gradually brought into a money economy. Before British days, farmers could borrow only on security of the standing crop, so debt was limited. But the British introduced the idea of mortgaging the land itself in a contract enforceable in the courts. Peasants began borrowing much larger sums, either for productive purposes or for social occasions. Moneylenders acquired land, and the poorer peasants, unable to repay ill-advised borrowings, lost their land and sank into the condition of landless laborers, dependent on others for employment. This group today is one of the reservoirs of labor available to industry.

A more fundamental force creating this agricultural proletariat has been the great increase in population which has occurred since 1850. The population of the subcontinent is thought to have been rather stable at about 130 million for the fifty years preceding 1850, but to have grown rapidly to 255 million in 1871, the time of the first census, and in 1951 it was 435 million.[8] This rapid population growth is the result of a stable birth rate and a declining death rate, which Kingsley Davis attributes to the elimination of war and banditry following the spread of British rule, the control of famine through irrigation and extension of railroads, and the control of epidemics through public

[7] Much of this paragraph is based on Patel, *op. cit.*, pp. 14ff.

[8] Pakistan, 74 million; India, 361 million. *Census of Pakistan, 1951*, Vol. 1, p. 31; *Hindustan Year Book, 1955* (Calcutta: Sarker & Sons, 1955), p. 11.

health measures. The increasing pressure of population on the land, when coupled with inheritance customs, has caused ever smaller holdings through successive subdivision each generation.[9] As holdings become very small, an increasing proportion of farmers cannot support themselves at any decent level, and become part of the rural proletariat ripe to enter an industrial labor force if jobs are available.

Displaced craftsmen constitute another source of the growing group available to industry. Traditional India had a large group of less skilled craftsmen in the villages, to meet the primary needs of the population, and a smaller group of highly skilled luxury craftsmen in the towns. About 1860 the town craftsmen began to be displaced from their traditional work. The political ambitions of the British had reduced most native courts to shadows, and the loss of court patronage was enough to kill much of the finest craftsmanship.[10] The growing middle class of civil servants imitated foreign tastes for imported goods and did not patronize the dying crafts. With increasing transportation facilities, foreign competition began to make itself felt about the same time, which further reduced the work available to town craftsmen.

The largest group of village artisans were weavers. At first they were untouched by the competition of Lancashire cotton mills, even after the Suez Canal opened in 1869. But as transportation to villages increased, first spinning and then weaving were hard hit by English competition. The progressive removal of the tariff on imported cotton goods and yarn between 1882 and 1894, at the insistence of Lancashire cotton interests, increased the effectiveness of foreign competition and accelerated the displacement of village weavers.[11]

What happened dramatically to weavers was happening to smaller numbers of other craftsmen. Changing local tastes and foreign imports were depriving them of a livelihood and forcing them into an agri-

[9] Hindu custom permits all sons to inherit, so holdings are split up in each generation. Among Muslims this process is accelerated, since daughters also receive a half share. Between 1891 (considerably after the population growth had started) and 1941 the cultivated land per agricultural worker declined from 2.2 to 1.9 acres. Davis, *op. cit.*, p. 207. This tendency is discussed in M. B. Nanavati and J. J. Anjaria, *The Indian Rural Problem* (Bombay: Vora and Company, 1951), Chap. 9; Government of India, *Famine Inquiry Commission Report* (Madras, 1945), pp. 258–261.

[10] Much of this and the following paragraph is based on D. R. Gadgil, *The Industrial Evolution of India* (London: Oxford University Press, 1950), Chap. 3.

[11] By about 1900 weaving was at a very low ebb, particularly among weavers of medium grades of cloth, but seems to have become stabilized since then at this low level. Gadgil, *op. cit.*, p. 168. There has been much dispute over the *cause* of decline in handicrafts. Wadia stresses foreign competition while Gadgil stresses a change of local tastes. Gadgil, *op. cit.*, p. 40; P. A. Wadia and K. T. Merchant, *Our Economic Problem* (Bombay: New Book Company, 1950), p. 260.

cultural wage-worker class or encouraging them to migrate to towns to seek industrial work. As a result, the proportion of the population dependent on agriculture actually increased from 61 per cent in 1872 to 73 per cent in 1921.[12] But many of the village craftsmen thus thrown back on agriculture were underemployed and were available to industry when jobs developed.[13]

SOURCES AND MEANS OF RECRUITMENT OF THE INDUSTRIAL LABOR FORCE

Only 31 per cent of Pakistan's population was in the labor force at the time of the 1951 census. This exceedingly low proportion reflects the youth of the population, with a high death rate and many children. A second explanation is that Muslim women are largely restricted to working within the home, so that their labor is excluded from labor force statistics. Only 25 per cent of the labor force was non-agricultural, and of these, only one-third were urban workers.

TABLE 1

OCCUPATIONS OF THE NONAGRICULTURAL LABOR FORCE, 1951

Nonagricultural labor force	Number of workers (thousands)
Professional and technical	223
Administrative	513
Sales	1,027
Forestry	13
Fishermen	202
Mine and quarry workers	8
Transport operators	191
Skilled manufacturing workers	1,229
Food, drink, and tobacco processors	103
Unskilled laborers	1,229
Domestic servants	353
Other service workers	298
Police, fire, etc.	91
Unclassified	3
Total	5,489

SOURCE: *Census of Pakistan, 1951*, Vol. 1, Table II-A.

[12] Wadia and Merchant, *op. cit.*, p. 293. Some would dispute the validity of this conclusion.

[13] In more recent times, also, urban jobs have not been expanding as rapidly as the labor force. In 1931 only 69 per cent of the labor force in Pakistan areas was agricultural, but this had increased to 76 per cent by 1951. During this period nine-tenths of the increase in the labor force went into agriculture. *Census of Pakistan, 1951*, p. 107.

It is necessary to give a breakdown of the nonagricultural labor force by occupation, as a prelude to consideration of recruitment problems. This is done in table 1, but explanation is needed. It would be an error to assume that this table represents all nonagricultural workers, for an additional 1.6 million agricultural workers follow some nonagricultural occupation as a sideline. It would also be a mistake to conceive of these 5 million workers as employees in organized industry. For of the 449,000 textile manufacturing workers, for example, only 74,000 are employees; the rest are independent workers, primarily cottage craftsmen. Altogether, 3 to 4 million of the nonagricultural workers are self-employed craftsmen or laborers in cottage industries. The workers in organized industry, with which we are primarily concerned, numbered under a million in 1955. Their distribution by industry is shown in table 2.

Most factory laborers are temporary migrants from villages where they maintain homes, and many of them leave their families in the village. The Royal Commission on Labour in India in 1931 found factory workers to be predominantly village migrants, but stressed that they were largely from nonagricultural classes in the village, such as craftsmen and landless laborers. The Labour Investigation Committee of the Government of India made a survey of a number of industrial centers in 1944 and agreed that industrial workers were largely village migrants, but were not primarily from farming classes. In every industrial center sampled they found that at least 80 per cent of the workers were migrants from villages. In some towns they found almost no landowners among factory workers; but in other centers, nearly half the workers owned village land. This weakens their contention that factory labor is nonagricultural.

The only thorough survey of the source of industrial laborers in Pakistan was made for Bengal at the University of Dacca in 1954. It was found that only 4 per cent of the workers considered themselves residents of the town where they were employed, while 84 per cent came from other parts of the same province, and 12 per cent had migrated from other provinces; some 55 per cent of the workers in the sample owned land in their home villages. The previous job of 28 per cent of these workers was farming, while 52 per cent of them had fathers or grandfathers who were farmers and thus belonged to an agricultural tradition. Nearly a seventh of the industrial workers returned to their villages during sowing and harvest seasons. The study concludes that ". . . there is often a far more intimate connection of the industrial worker with agriculture than the Report of the Royal

Commission would suggest."[14] East Pakistan is more agricultural than West Pakistan, and industry is located closer to the rural setting, but the author's interviews with personnel officers of establishments in West Pakistan tend to corroborate the conclusion of the East Bengal study.

Pakistan's industrial workers are thus recent migrants to factory areas. Only a minority have cut their ties with the village and are permanent urban residents, and this group is the lowest rung on the social ladder. The refugees from India constitute a major exception to this generalization. Their village ties were forcibly cut at partition, and those who got no land became permanently settled and dependent upon industry. This group forms a nucleus which may develop into a stable industrial labor force.

TABLE 2

EMPLOYMENT BY INDUSTRY,[a] 1955

	Number of workers (thousands)	Per cent contract workers
Tea gardens, wool, and jute ginning	155	22
Extractive industries, forestry	40	55
Food processing	40	13
Tobacco manufacture	8	1
Textiles	176	7
Paper and printing	17	1
Chemicals	20	8
Cement, clay products, and glass	15	26
Basic metals and metal products	19	1
Machinery manufacture	14	1
Transport equipment manufacture	57	0
Miscellaneous manufacturing	21	0
Construction	115	66
Water, gas, electricity, sanitary services	36	5
Trade	17	9
Finance	14	0
Transport	126	39
Communications	23	0
Welfare, personal services, and education	68	1
Total	979	21

SOURCE: Ministry of Labour, *Interim Manpower Survey Report*, 1955.

[a] Industries arranged into major groups from detailed data. Includes only workers in establishments of 20 workers or over.

Industry uses three main methods for recruiting laborers. One-fifth of the industrial workers are contract laborers. Almost two-thirds of the

[14] A. F. A. Husain, *Human and Social Impact of Technological Change in Pakistan* (Dacca: Oxford University Press, 1956), Vol. 1, pp. 230, 343–347.

industries use some contract laborers, especially for loading and unloading, but these workers are concentrated in a few industries, as seen in table 2. The labor contractor recruits workers and offers them as a gang to the employer. The primary employer deals with the individual workers only indirectly, through the contractor. This system will be discussed in more detail below, in connection with the special recruitment problems of those industries using a high proportion of intermittent laborers.

Where the factory recruits its own workers, it is usually done "at the gate." When a vacancy occurs, word is spread by the workers, whose relations show up at the gate. If the work is unskilled, the *sardar* or foreman is likely to pick a healthy-looking man by sight and put him to work. If greater skill is required, he may interview several, and try out the most likely candidate for a day or so. Where experienced labor is not available, the *sardar* or *mistri* may have several men working with him in on-the-job training for several weeks, during which the trainees may receive little or no wages. The key person in this most prevalent hiring system is the *sardar,* who goes by various names in different areas. The system is obviously open to abuse, since workers may be required to pay a fee to the *sardar* to get or keep a job. The author found one factory of 17,000 workers with no personnel office, where hiring was done by each departmental supervisor at the gate. Hiring at the gate has become possible because of population growth, migration to cities, and refugee populations, which have increased unemployment and made the people job-hungry. It is a great change from the earlier day when industries sent recruiting agents into the villages to entice people into the factories. Better public health practices have had no small part in bringing about this change in hiring procedures, since they lie at the bottom of the swelling urban populations.

Some of the larger factories with personnel offices use a more rational hiring procedure. Generally they also spread the word of vacancies through workers; newspaper advertisements are seldom used, since they bring forth so many workers that screening is difficult. Sometimes personal interviews are allowed, but frequently such factories receive applications only by mail. A few factories are introducing testing for skilled jobs, supplemented by trial on the job. The employment exchanges operating in twenty-three urban centers place only 20,000 to 40,000 workers each year, and not many employers find them useful.

Plantations form a bridge between agriculture and industry, and their unique recruitment practices may be mentioned briefly. As tea plantations are located on isolated hillsides, the labor shortage in early years was acute. This resulted in a *sardar* system of recruitment: an agent was paid on a per capita basis to return to his home area to recruit laborers. These recruits were forwarded to the plantation under an elaborate system of government rules. Tea estates now in Pakistan recruited mostly from Bihar and Orissa, several hundred miles away. Up until 1915, tea laborers worked under a penal system which permitted forceful return of runaway laborers in order to prevent employers from losing on their investment in the expensive recruiting process. Today the settled, highly paternalistic plantations employ workers born on them, and outside recruitment is a minor problem. To maintain this position, however, plantation managers often resist education of workers' children, since schooling makes it more likely that they will leave the plantation and seek urban employment.

Other industries with special recruitment problems are those offering intermittent work and those located in rural areas and needing unskilled laborers. Where work is intermittent, the employees must have alternative employment which supplements the seasonal employment; such industries in Pakistan usually employ agriculturists from nearby villages. These laborers are seldom available at sowing and harvest time, but are glad of work opportunities during slack seasons. Among these intermittent employers are the cotton gins, jute presses, grain mills, sugar factories, railway construction, inland water transport, docks, civil engineering works, and building construction. In addition, several rural and isolated industries, such as coal mining, stone quarrying, forestry, brick kilns, and railway maintenance-of-way work, have similar recruiting problems in that they must recruit from among those close at hand, namely, from the nearby agricultural villages.[15] In these industries, the industrial worker is primarily an agriculturist. He may go each day from his village to the work place, or he may leave the village for several months during slack seasons, but he remains a part of the social fabric of the village, and his conduct is molded by the village mores. His entrance into industry is not likely to upset his social balance; on the contrary, such work, by raising village incomes, probably preserves traditional agrarian life patterns. He has not become a committed member of the industrial labor force; labor turnover is naturally great.

These industries have found a joint solution to their common recruitment problems. They hire large portions of their unskilled work force through labor contractors, who recruit workers from the villages and

[15] The Baluchistan coal miners are migratory shepherds from great distances; the salt miners of the Punjab are more nearly permanent miners, living in agricultural villages right at the pithead. Government of Pakistan, *Report of the Chief Inspector of Mines in Pakistan* (Karachi, 1948), pp. 2–3.

act as gang bosses on the job. Payment is ordinarily on a piece rate system, and the contractor is frequently paid for the work of his whole crew. He in turn pays the crew members, keeping a percentage for himself. This system obviously lends itself to bribery. It also enables the primary employer to escape many provisions of the regulatory labor laws, since he does not directly control his own labor force, and the laws do not apply to the contractors who are in actual control of the laborers. The system was seriously questioned by the Royal Commission on Labour in India (1931), the Labour Investigation Committee (1946) and by the ILO Labour Survey Mission on Labour Problems in Pakistan (1953).[16] It remains because it meets a specialized need; employers universally say contractors can get more work out of a gang than can the primary employer.[17] Intermittent labor, without loyalty to or dependence on the employer, needs close supervision, which the contractor provides. The recruitment problem is obviously a specialized function which many employers hesitate to undertake, since high labor turnover makes it a continual process. The system of contract labor has become less prevalent as the labor supply available at the plant gate has increased, but table 2 shows that one-fifth of all industrial workers are still contract laborers, and much anti-social conduct remains. Contractors sometimes get crew members indebted to them and exploit workers without mercy. This system also loosens the control of managements over their own workers.

Efficient use of the labor force is seriously impeded in Pakistan by the lack of more rational recruitment and screening of workers. Employers overestimate the capacity of some employees, and place others at jobs beneath their ability. Both groups develop into dissatisfied workers, who offer less than their best effort and add to workers' protest movements. More carefully planned hiring procedures would increase efficiency and reduce costs by a considerable margin.

---

[16] Government of India, *Labour Investigation Committee, Main Report* (Delhi, 1946), p. 81; Great Britain, Royal Commission on Labour, *Report of the Royal Commission on Labour in India* (London: His Majesty's Stationery Office, 1931), p. 494; *Report of the ILO Labour Survey Mission,* pp. 22–23.

[17] This answer was given to the author by almost all employers in a large number of interviews. Government public works employers stress this particularly, saying contractors will drive their crews harder than a government department would be allowed to do. On the Karachi docks, the *serang* employs a group of *jemidars* together with their crews in a daily shape-up. These crews are paid on a weight basis by what amounts to a group incentive system. Five men are attached to the industry for each permanent job available, so the effort to increase output and keep the job is tremendous. Employers claim decasualization in Karachi port, with the attendant eradication of the *jemidar* system, would halve the output of workers and double the turn-around time of freight vessels, as has happened in other Eastern ports.

THE SPEED OF LABOR FORCE DEVELOPMENT

Only fragmentary evidence is available on the rapidity with which the industrial labor force is developing. In the decade before the 1951 Census, the population increased at the rate of 1.35 per cent per year, and between 1951 and 1961 the rate of increase was 2.2 per cent per year.[18] Also important is the growing proportion of the population in the work force. In 1931, only 25.2 per cent of the population of the area which is now Pakistan was in the civilian labor force, but by 1951 this proportion had risen to 30.7 per cent, and by 1955 it was 31.8 per cent.[19] All these proportions are extremely low, but this increasing percentage who are working or seeking work is explained in part by the increasing proportion of males in the population, since only 5 per cent of the enumerated work force is female.[20] The increasing urbanization also accounts for a small part of the increase, but the major cause must be related to fundamental economic conditions and a change in the mores of the people.[21]

Between 1931 and 1951, in the area of Pakistan, population increased 1.25 per cent per year, while the civilian labor force grew at the rate of 2.06 per cent. But the nonagricultural labor force expanded at the much slower rate of 1.09 per cent. It is well known that from about 1870 onward an increasing proportion of the population of the subcontinent was forced to depend on agriculture for a living. Although some industry was developing, it was not sufficient to absorb the increasing work force, and the Pakistan area was no exception to this tendency; in 1931, 30 per cent of the labor force was nonagricultural, but by 1951 this had declined to 25 per cent.[22] However by 1955 the nonagricultural portion of the labor force had risen to 35 per cent, showing a remarkably rapid reversal of a trend. This shows that as

[18] Government of Pakistan, *First Five Year Plan*, Vol. 1, p. 211. The rate of increase would be expected to rise after partition, when Pakistan became more nearly a Muslim population, as Muslims have consistently shown a higher fertility rate than the Hindu group. Davis, *op. cit.*, p. 193; *Dawn*, Karachi, March 4, 1961.

[19] *Census of Pakistan, 1951*, Vol. 1, p. 107; Government of Pakistan, *First Five Year Plan*, Vol. 1, p. 215. The civilian labor force includes all persons over 12 years of age who are not in the armed services but are self-supporting, or earning dependents, or seeking work.

[20] There are 112.8 males per 100 enumerated females, and the ratio is increasing. *Census of Pakistan, 1951*, Vol. 1, p. 55.

[21] The age distribution has changed very little over the period, and the shift in the religious communities at partition should have had little effect, since Muslims and Hindus participate in the labor force to about the same extent.

[22] This decreased proportion in industry was aggravated by partition, which brought an influx of Muslim agriculturists, and by the rapidly increasing populations in the canal colonies of Sind and Punjab. *Census of Pakistan, 1951*, Vol. 1, p. 107.

industrial jobs became available the industrial labor force was able to expand with great rapidity, being recruited from the ranks of the underemployed.

THE PROBLEM OF COMMITTING THE LABOR FORCE TO INDUSTRY

If underdeveloped areas are to industrialize, one of their crucial problems is to transform surplus agricultural laborers into efficient and contented industrial workers. This is a problem in Pakistan no less than elsewhere. We have seen that the workers in organized industries number just under a million, but many of even this small group are still villagers at heart and are not committed to being part of a permanent and stable work force. Absenteeism and turnover are high. This presents a picture of workers forced into factories because of necessity, accepting industrial employment only because traditional village work will no longer support them. They are pushed into the factory because of the drabness and poverty of the village, not drawn into industry because of its attractiveness. In 1931 the Royal Commission reported: "Few industrial workers would remain in industry if they could secure sufficient food and clothing in the village; they are pushed, not pulled, to the city." [23] Their motivation and prestige systems are still village-oriented. Until this is changed, and workers feel themselves a part of industrial life, they will not seek to progress within the new system by contributing their ability and increasing their efficiency. The rapidity of industrial development is thus checked by the human factor as well as by the lack of capital. It is a major problem which government and industry must tackle jointly. It is the purpose of this section to state some of the difficulties involved in this process, although it should be realized that some workers, particularly refugees cut off from their home villages, have already made such a commitment to their new way of life.

The beginning of understanding about the human effects from the impact of technological change is to realize that the worker's life is a whole and that a specialized technical change of one segment may have side effects on a people which make the whole of life distasteful. A new way or place of working required by industry may change the complex ties of caste and family, leading to personal disintegration. From a survey in East Pakistan, it was concluded that "a majority of the workers are more or less maladjusted to factory life. To some the degree of maladjustment is so considerable that they are anxious to quit at the earliest opportunity. . . . The most important sources of maladjustment are in matters of working conditions, food, housing, sanitation,

[23] *Report of the Royal Commission on Labour in India,* p. 16.

contact with one's family and treatment by the supervisors." [24] One can hardly expect a committed labor force from such maladjusted workers.

As the worker comes to industry, he leaves the social and economic pattern which has nurtured him and offered security, and at first the industrial scene appears chaotic. In the village, land is the source of economic security for the whole community, even for those who own no land; the land always produces something save in the worst drought, while the worker finds his factory job subject to the caprice of the foreman or perhaps of business conditions. The joint family system assured security even to nonearning members, but factory workers usually separate themselves from the joint family at least physically, and many find themselves in bachelor barracks. Caste and family assure a known social status in the village, but in the town a man must make his own way, since family means little. If the worker leaves his wife and children in his village, he is cut completely adrift from his traditional sources of status and security. He is lonesome and alone. This insecurity militates against a labor force committed to the industrial way of life. The new industrial worker resents his loss of freedom. In the factory he must come and go at a certain time, the pace of work is set by the foreman, and the place of work is determined by others. Furthermore, the Muslim tradition has a strong emphasis on leisure which is difficult to realize within a factory routine. This weakens any attachment the worker might feel for factory work.

Since the majority of factory workers are generally conceded to be personally maladjusted, of low efficiency, and uncommitted to a new mode of existence, one might naturally ask if this antipathy could not be overcome by an increase in wages. Unfortunately the answer is not so simple. In the first place, although wages are low, they are not low relative to productivity, and it is questionable how much they can be raised without raising either prices or productivity. Secondly, workers seem to be reasonably content with their wages, although like most workers they would be grateful for more. Husain found factory workers on the whole satisfied with their wages, which were less than the income of a subsistence farmer owning his own land, but 69 per cent higher than the wages of landless agricultural workers.[25] The nub of the problem is that the effectiveness of wage increases in obtaining a committed labor force depends upon the laborers' having a value system which places monetary return at the top of their hierarchy of values. But this is not true in Pakistan. The chief desire of the villager is to maintain and increase his *izzat:* his prestige, or honor. This does

[24] Husain, *op. cit.*, pp. 310–311.
[25] *Ibid.*, pp. 141, 311.

not necessarily involve money, so that monetary incentives, while not powerless, are not the central motivations for the Pakistani Muslim. Thus, either the workers must accept the primary values of the industrial system, which are largely Western, or industry must learn to approach workers in terms of incentives which fit into their traditional value patterns. In practice, both are happening together.

The ILO Labour Survey Mission, after noting that Pakistani workers seldom take pride in their work or show responsibility for machinery, stated: "The question of raising the status of those who work with their hands is one that is vital to the future of any country that hopes to become an industrial nation." [26] It is only when the people accept the dignity of labor that *izzat* can be achieved through factory labor. Husain found that the best-adjusted workers were those who had accepted many of the new system's values and strove to achieve them by becoming foremen or group leaders; these men frequently were able to remain good Muslims and strong supporters of the joint family and other traditional cultural values. They gave up part of their old cultural values, but retained other traditional values while accepting some incentives from a new system. If this finding is correct, it is highly important and comforting, since it means industrialization can succeed by selective, rather than wholesale, displacement of traditional values.

All are agreed that lack of adequate urban housing is a major reason for Pakistan's unstable industrial work force. Husain found that although the wages of factory workers were higher, their housing, diet, sanitation, and health were poorer than for their village counterparts.[27] Adequate urban housing erected by government or industry would enable the worker to unite his family, thus appealing to a strong traditional value.

Myers has pointed out in discussing Indian labor problems that poverty in villages may push workers toward industry, but these workers will become committed to industrial work as a way of life only if they are properly treated by their employers.[28] This is equally true in Pakistan, and there is no more crying need than to revise supervision and promotion practices. The author's interviews with plant managers disclosed that very few Pakistan factories have any definite promotion system, so that a worker may be at a plant for years with virtually no change in status or pay; the railroads are the major exception to this lack of promotion policy. Supervision of labor is both lax and authori-

---

[26] *Report of the ILO Labour Survey Mission*, p. 18.

[27] Husain, *op. cit.*, pp. 150–172.

[28] Charles A. Myers, *Labor Problems in the Industrialization of India* (Cambridge: Harvard University Press, 1958), p. 50.

tarian. It is lax because of an inadequate number of supervisors; in textiles, for example, a *jemidar* or subforeman is placed over 10 to 15 workers and a foreman over 50 to 70 men. This low ratio of foremen is particularly inadequate, since many workers are new to industry and need extremely close supervision, and since the prevalence of illiteracy demands that all instructions be oral. The supervision is authoritarian in that discipline is too much a matter of the foreman's whim and not enough a matter of rational justice, a practice which was common in the West before personnel departments became widespread. All too many foremen treat their workers with disdain, overlooking their human dignity, and only a few of the largest plants have a personnel department capable of rectifying capricious personnel mistakes of foremen. All these factors make factory life more distasteful to the worker and reduce his commitment to the industrial labor force.

Absenteeism from the job is a good objective indicator of the degree of commitment of the labor force to industry, since many absences are for visits to the worker's home village. Husain, in his intensive study of East Bengal workers, concluded that absenteeism measures the degree of connection with the home village. He found that of the 52 per cent of all workers not living with their families, nine-tenths visited their home villages at least once, two-fifths visited their villages at least three times, and one-fifth paid such visits ten times during a year.[29] Only East Bengal collects statistics on absenteeism in factories, which averaged 9.7 per cent of total work time in 1952–1953, compared to less than 4 per cent in American industry.[30] The interesting aspect of absenteeism is its seasonal nature. It reaches a high point at the two harvest seasons and the sowing season, when workers return to help out on the family lands.

The Development of Labor Organizations

At partition Pakistan inherited the tradition and organizations of labor protest which had grown within the subcontinent for half a century. Although N. M. Lokhandy organized the Bombay Millhands' Association in 1890 as India's first labor union, it was not until World War I

[29] Husain, *op. cit.*, pp. 184, 228.

[30] *Ibid.*, pp. 228, 377; F. S. McElroy and Alexander Moros, "Illness and Absenteeism in Manufacturing Plants, 1947," *Monthly Labor Review*, Vol. 63 (September, 1948), pp. 235–239. Inspection of Bengal absentee figures over the years shows no marked trend, though some industries, such as railway workshops and engineering plants, have higher-than-average absentee rates. Labor turnover figures are not available for Pakistan. Absenteeism figures are printed in issues of the *Eastern Pakistan Labour Journal*, which is an official publication of the Labour Directorate, Government of East Bengal.

that unrest was sufficient to result in widespread labor organization. The first union federation in India, the All-India Trade Union Congress (AITUC), was formed in 1920 during a series of postwar strikes; in its first year the Congress affiliated 64 unions with 140,854 members.[31]

In the early years many unions were formed and led by intellectuals, which helped to orient the union movement toward political activity. The outstanding development of the 'twenties was the growth of Communist strength, which culminated in their winning control of the AITUC in 1929. In 1926 the government passed the Trade Union Act, which permitted unions to register with the government and exempted them from prosecution for conspiracy in restraint of trade.

The 'thirties were years of violent extremism, and moderation of demands was unknown. The movement was split into three ideological groups: on the left were the Communists in the AITUC; the Indian Trades Union Federation was socialist and nationalist in outlook; while on the right the Ahmedabad Textile Labour Association, with Gandhi as its mentor, eschewed politics, rejected the class struggle, and was reformist in outlook.

The worldwide unity move of the Communists, under the threat of German fascism in the late 'thirties, brought about temporary unity in the Indian labor movement, but the changing allegiances of war did not allow this unity to remain undisturbed. In 1942, M. N. Roy led a secession of those unions wishing to back the British war effort, forming the Indian Federation of Labor (IFL) with Roy as its intellectual leader. Naturally the IFL found favor in government eyes, and for a time it was the most representative labor federation in India.

Roy was an ex-Communist as well as an ex-Congressman, and had recently founded his own Radical Humanist party. He could not agree with the Communists on basic ideology, and parted with the Congress Party over the war, which they viewed as an unholy cause. Though a socialist at heart, he held that the proletariat of India was insufficiently differentiated from the peasantry to become the leader in a new social order. He urged unions to be apolitical, leaving social reform to political parties; unions should be reformist, accepting the broad outlines of the economic system, and should stress workers' education. The IFL and its leader are important in that most labor leaders in West Pakistan today were Royists in the 'forties, and still feel a strong attachment to his ideas.

---

[31] S. D. Punekar, *Trade Unionism in India* (Bombay: New Book Company, 1948), p. 71. For other briefer surveys of the Indian labor movement, see Oscar A. Ornati, *Jobs and Workers in India* (Ithaca: Cornell University Press, 1955); Myers, *op. cit.*

Since the Congress party opposed the war effort, many of its leaders were jailed; the union field was left to the Communists and Royists. In 1946 an official government investigation was made to determine the most representative labor organization. Table 3 shows the results for areas now partly in Pakistan.

TABLE 3

UNION MEMBERSHIP IN SELECTED AREAS ON THE EVE OF PARTITION, 1946[a]

	Bengal		Sind and Punjab	
	Unions	Membership	Unions	Membership
AITUC	112	139,000	32	20,000
I.F.L.	41	106,000	23	95,000
Total	153	245,000	55	115,000

SOURCE: Government of India, Central Labour Commissioner, *Report on the Representative Character of the AITUC and IFL*, by S. C. Joshi (Delhi, 1946).

[a] Sind and Punjab figures include most but not all unions in the area now West Pakistan, and Punjab figures include some unions now in East Punjab, India. Bengal figures include a large number of unions in what is now West Bengal, India, which is the more industrialized part of Bengal. But the data give some indication of alignments of labor in the two wings of Pakistan before partition.

Thus at partition there was a strong union movement in Bengal, with a predominance of unions with AITUC background, while the weaker union groups in the West Pakistan area were predominantly Royists.

THE DEVELOPMENT OF THE LABOR MOVEMENT IN WEST PAKISTAN

The unions of Pakistan consist of a large number of local units restricted to workers of an individual employer; these locals have been loosely federated into four major federations in Bengal and three others in West Pakistan. There is nothing which corresponds to the strong national craft unions of Europe or the powerful industrial unions of the United States, although there are some decentralized industrial federations. This section and the one following will deal with the development of the major federations, in which reside the ideological content which transforms a group of disparate local unions into a labor "movement." The two wings of Pakistan are so different economically and culturally that it is no wonder that the union movements have developed differently. Therefore we will consider the development of labor federations and ideas separately for East and West Pakistan.[32]

[32] There is no adequate written account of the development of trade unions in Pakistan. A few government documents, some union reports, a few brief articles, the daily press and a few sporadically issued union journals are available. Much of what follows has been pieced together from many interviews with union leaders and impartial observers in various parts of Pakistan. Every effort has been made to check these reports. The specific interview source is ordinarily not

The early beginning and continuing strength of trade unionism in West Pakistan lie in railroad and port unions. The North Western railroad, which is a government enterprise, is the largest employer in Pakistan, while the Karachi port employs over 10,000 workers in various engineering and stevedore capacities. M. A. Khan, a Punjab stationmaster, had been organizing railroad workers ever since 1919, and his United Union of North West Railway Workers, uniting workers on the lines, shops, and stations of the railroad, had a long history as a staunch member of the All-India Railwaymen's Federation.[33] He led his NWR workers and much of Punjab labor into Roy's IFL in 1942, and at partition claimed a membership of 54,000 railway workers.[34]

The second early source of labor strength was among the dock workers in Karachi port, which was the third largest port of undivided India. In 1928 the Karachi Port Trust Labor Union was formed among engineering employees of the port authority, and by 1934 had monthly sessions with management for the settlemen of grievances, although the control of the union had fallen into the hands of Communists. The Karachi Port Workers Union among the stevedore workers was born in a series of strikes in 1930. Although a member of Roy's IFL, it became one of the most militant unions of the area, perhaps because many of the men had left their families in the villages and were living in bachelor barracks, which made their solidarity and willingness to take risks much greater. Thus at partition there were in West Pakistan two centers of strength where the workers had experienced leadership and a tradition of collective action.

At partition, four-fifths of the organized workers of West Pakistan were members of Roy's Indian Federation of Labour.[35] On August 3, 1947, two weeks before partition became effective, M. A. Khan gathered a group of IFL leaders to establish the Pakistan Federation of Labour, with 22 unions of 50,000 members as charter affiliates.[36] Conspicuous among these were the United Union of NWR Workers and the Karachi Port Trust Labor Union. In an area where three-quarters of the laborers work in agriculture, it was fitting that the Sind Hari

---

given, but is available in the author's field notes. The picture presented here is corroborated by Khalid Mahmud, *Trade Unionism in Pakistan* (Lahore: Punjab University, 1958).

[33] *Annual Report of the General Secretary of the United Union of NWR Workers*, given at Karachi. November, 1955. I am indebted to Mr. S. S. Malik for translating this document from the Urdu.

[34] Government of India, *Report on the Representative Character of the AITUC and the IFL* (Delhi, 1946).

[35] *Ibid.*

[36] Pakistan Federation of Labor, *Report of the First Annual Labor Conference*, Karachi, February 5–6, 1949, p. 5.

Federation among tenant farmers should be one of the influential bodies within the labor federation. M. A. Khatib was elected general secretary, and has remained in this post as the outstanding leader of West Pakistan unions since the death of M. A. Khan in 1949.

The outlook of the Federation was set by the presidential address at the first general conference in 1949: "We do not look upon trade unions as mere agencies for securing economic concessions. We regard them as social organizations calculated to advance workers' economic and other interests and also to teach them the democratic way of life." [37] The demands were for higher wages, health insurance, housing, legal protection for *haris* (tenant-farmers-at-will), ratification of additional ILO conventions, and decasualization of contract labor. The Federation has maintained this practical orientation, and it has continued to dominate the labor movement of West Pakistan.

The Federation prospered, and at its first conference in 1949 reported 47 unions with 90,000 members, with major strength in the transportation field. However, it was not alone in claiming the allegiance of workers. During the war, Roy's backing of the British war effort made his IFL unions unpopular with many nationalist workers; this gave the Communists an opportunity to strengthen their unions, particularly in the railway workshops outside Lahore. From this center, the Communists made rapid progress with a sizable organizing cadre and outside support. In 1948 they established the Pakistan Trade Union Federation (PTUF), which by 1949 claimed 38 unions of 48,000 members.[38] Though the Federation was run by Communists, some of the constituent unions were not. In 1949 the Federation called for nationalization of key industries, increased wages, recognition of the U.S.S.R., and the channeling of trade to Russia.[39] There is little doubt that workers' welfare was primarily a means toward the achievement of political objectives for the PTUF. Nevertheless, some of their unions were exceedingly well run and were particularly strong in processing day-to-day grievances, which was the area in which most Pakistan unions were weakest. Mirza Mohammed Ibrahim and Muhammed Afzal have been the two outstanding leaders of the PTUF, and under their guidance the Federation grew greatly from 1948 to 1951.

---

[37] *Ibid.*, p. 19.

[38] Azizali F. Mohammad, "Prospects for the Growth of the Trade Union Movement in Pakistan," *Pakistan Economist*, June, 1951, p. 70.

[39] United States of America, Department of State, Foreign Service Dispatch No. 1402, Karachi, April, 1949. I greatly appreciate permission given by officers in the Department of State and the Department of Labor to use unclassified dispatches from Pakistan on labor matters. Also see *Civil and Military Gazette*, Lahore, October 19, 1949.

Three events in quick succession reduced Communist strength in the labor field. First, after an investigation of the relative strength of the various federations in 1949, the government and the ruling Muslim League became concerned over Communist union strength, particularly in the Punjab. In subtle ways, government employers made the task of Communist unions difficult.[40] At the same time the Muslim League started a concerted drive in the Punjab to affiliate as many unions as possible to the moderate Punjab Labor League. In 1951 the PLL succeeded in winning 33 unions from PTUF, thus seriously weakening Communist union strength. Second, after the Rawalpindi Conspiracy in 1951, a number of Communists, including Ibrahim and Afzal, were arrested, which removed some of the ablest PTUF leaders from the field of action. The Communist party was banned in 1954, and, without overt activity to occupy its members, lost prestige and strength. Third, a left-wing Socialist group, headed by Malik Fazal Elahi Qurban, withdrew from the PTUF in 1953, taking most of the remaining PTUF unions into a new Socialist alignment, the Pakistan Mazdoor Federation. The PTUF was left with only a few affiliates and was dead by 1957, although some of its activities and interests were carried on by the Mazdoor Federation (PMF).

Paralleling these events, another change of alignments had been brought about from the same causes. Following the 1949 investigation, the concern of the Minister of Labor over Communist union strength caused him to urge the major moderate federations of East and West Pakistan to unite, so that the resulting non-Communist organization would be clearly the most representative labor organization of Pakistan. As a result, the Pakistan Federation of Labour changed its name to the West Pakistan Federation of Labour (WPFL) and united with the East Pakistan Federation of Labour (EPFL) in December, 1949, to form the All-Pakistan Confederation of Labour (APCOL). The WPFL retained its autonomy and most of its powers, surrendering to the APCOL only the functions of conferring with the government on countrywide policies and the appointment of delegates to international meetings.

Since its formation, APCOL has regularly sent delegates to ILO

---

[40] For example, Communist leaders of the NWR Workers Trade Union charged that government refused special leaves for members to attend the annual union conference. Pakistan Labour Publications, *Worker,* January–February, 1953. A charge that the government had transgressed ILO Convention No. 87, protecting the freedom of association, was brought against Pakistan by the WFTU in 1951, but the Committee on Freedom of Association of the ILO exonerated the government, ruling that it had not transgressed trade union rights nor specifically aided non-Communist unions. International Labour Organization, *Seventh Report of the ILO to the United Nations* (Geneva, 1953), Case No. 49, pp. 347–354.

sessions, since it is recognized by government as the most representative labor organization. One of its first actions was to join the ICFTU, and M. A. Khatib was elected a vice-president of that body in 1954. It also participates in discussions on labor policy about twice a year, at meetings bringing together representatives of labor, management, and government. Labor leaders report that these sessions have helped greatly to bridge the gap in outlook between labor and management leaders. By 1958, the APCOL claimed 235 unions with a membership of 350,000 in the two sections of Pakistan.

With the decline of Communist strength after 1951, the WPFL has been the dominant federation in the West, and has been able to devote its energy to organizing new unions. By 1955 the Federation had 13 organizers, although its expenditures were only about Rs.7,000 per year; finances were weak, since the WPFL collects only 2 annas (1/8 rupee, or 2.6 cents) per member per year, and even this small fee is frequently not paid.[41] However, membership has grown from 22 unions with 50,000 members in 1947 to 106 unions with 151,000 members in 1954, and has continued to grow slightly since that time, as shown in table 4. Its most intensive organization drive has been in the rapidly growing textile industry around Karachi, but success was limited, since most textile employers were merchants in outlook, new to the industrial field and violently antiunion. Loose industrial federations have been formed among transport workers, railroad workers, seamen, bank employees, government employees, miners, textile workers, agricultural tenants, and petroleum workers. The strength of the Federation continues to be centered in the Transport Workers Federation, which embraces both port and railway workers and includes a majority of the WPFL membership, as well as many of its outstanding leaders. Government influence has helped the Federation to increase its membership, but has hindered its independence of thought and action. This has prevented the WPFL from appealing to some of the most active groups of workers.

The Socialist labor group, the Pakistan Mazdoor Federation, has enjoyed a modest growth, claiming 44,000 members in 1957. A group around Lahore, the United Trade Union Federation of Pakistan, also claimed 15,000 members, but was restricted in its activity.[42] Thus, since the Communist PTUF was moribund, at least temporarily, the WPFL had no serious rival save the much smaller PMF.

In 1955 West Pakistan had a labor force of 11.7 million, but of these

---

[41] West Pakistan Federation of Labour, *Report of the Annual General Conference*, December 25–27, 1953; WPFL, mimeographed financial report for 1956–57 and 1957–58.

[42] Foreign Service Dispatch No. 704, Karachi, November 8, 1957.

TABLE 4

MEMBERSHIP OF REGISTERED UNIONS AND CLAIMED MEMBERSHIP OF FEDERATIONS, PAKISTAN, SELECTED DATES

	Registered Unions				Claimed Membership of Federations							
	All Pakistan		West Pakistan		APCOL		WPFL		PTUF		PMF	
	Unions	Members (thousands)	Unions	Members (thousands)	Unions	Members (thousands)	Unions	Members (thousands)	Unions	Members (thousands)	Unions	Members (thousands)
August, 1947 [a,b]							22	50				
December, 1948 [b,c]	150	192	88	161			41	90				
December, 1949 [d]							67	154	38	42		
March, 1950 [g,f]	243	193	160	98	180	320	104	196				
December, 1951 [e,h]	309	393	211	284			107	152				
December, 1952 [e,i]	352	394	232	262			135	172				
December, 1953 [e,j]	394	424	249	279			108	153				
December, 1954 [e,k]	382	410	236	272			106	151				
March, 1955 [l,m,n]	406	403	113	213	154	279			2	18	12	19
March, 1957 [m]	560	309	162	100								44
March, 1958 [m]					325	350	135	164				

[a] Pakistan Federation of Labour, *First Annual Labour Conference Addresses and Reports*, p. 5.
[b] A. Q. Bankapur, manuscript of Lectures to Trade Union Institute, Karachi, 1955. WPFL claim as of July, 1948.
[c] Government of Pakistan, Department of Commercial Intelligence and Statistics, *Statistical Digest of Pakistan*, Karachi, 1950, pp. 96–97.
[d] A. F. Mohammad, "Prospects for the Growth of Trade Union Movement in Pakistan," *Pakistan Economist*, June, 1951, pp. 70ff.
[e] *Pakistan Labour Gazette*, March, 1955, p. 119.
[f] All Pakistan Confederation of Labour, *First Annual General Conference, Presidential Address*, 1950, back cover. Labor claims refer to September.
[g] M. Shafi, *Pakistan Labour Yearbook, 1949–50*, pp. 191–205.
[h] WPFL, *Addresses and Reports of 3rd General Conference*, 1951, back cover. Data for union claims refer to May.
[i] WPFL, *Addresses and Reports of 4th Constitution Convention*, 1952, back cover. Union claims refer to August.
[j] WPFL, *Addresses and Reports of 5th General Conference*, 1953, back cover. Union claims refer to August.
[k] WPFL, mimeographed list of union membership as of July, 1954.
[l] Central Labour Commissioner, *Classified List of Registered Trade Unions in Pakistan*, Karachi, 1955.
[m] *Foreign Service Dispatch*, Karachi, October 29, 1957; March 21, 1956; No. 661, January 26, 1959; and No. 704, November 8, 1957.
[n] Membership of unions claimed by PMF assembled by author.

only about 600,000 were in organized industry susceptible to unionization.[43] It seems remarkable that one-third of these workers should be union members, as the figures seem to indicate. However, even union leaders concede that membership claims are considerably exaggerated.

THE DEVELOPMENT OF THE LABOR MOVEMENT IN EAST PAKISTAN

Although Bengal was one of the more industrialized provinces of undivided India, that portion of it which now forms East Pakistan was an agricultural hinterland of the Calcutta trading and industrial complex. Thus there was little scope for industrial unionism. In East Bengal just after partition in 1947 there were only 141 factories operating continuously, and they employed only 28,000 workers.[44] Three-quarters of these workers were employed in transportation and textiles, and it was in these industries that the beginning of unionism was found in East Pakistan.

Before partition there was no center of labor protest in what is now East Pakistan, such as Lahore had been in West Pakistan. The weak unions in eastern Bengal were mere outposts of stronger union groups in Calcutta. The All-India Railwaymen's Federation had local units in eastern Bengal during the 'twenties. Later the All-India Railway Muslim Employee's League was formed, and it is from this group that railroad union leadership emerged at partition. Even stronger was the Bengal Mariners' Union, first registered in 1927, which organized workers on the many steamships plying the inland waterways. At partition two outstanding leaders of this union, Faiz Ahmed and Aftab Ali, moved their base of operations from Calcutta to East Bengal, and their strength among mariners was the nucleus about which the strongest East Pakistan federation has been built. Thus in East as well as in West Pakistan the base of union membership and leadership at partition was found in transportation, since here were found most of the major employers.

In contrast to the Western sector, many East Pakistan labor groups trace their beginnings to AITUC-affiliated unions.[45] It should be re-

---

[43] The 1955 Manpower Survey found 979,000 workers in establishments of over 20 employees, of which 631,000 were in West Pakistan (distributing casual workers in the same proportion as regular workers). *ILO Interim Manpower Survey Report;* Government of Pakistan, Department of Manpower and Employment, *Report of the ILO on Manpower Survey in Pakistan* (Karachi, 1958), p. 15.

[44] Government of Pakistan, Central Labour Commissioner, *Working of the Factories Act During 1948*. This includes only factories of over 20 workers using power machinery; half of these factories were rice mills.

[45] The Bengal National Chamber of Labor, an anti-Communist labor group started in 1938, did not operate to an appreciable extent in eastern Bengal before partition. In all of Bengal, the government reported in 1946 that 112 unions

membered that in the years just before partition, though the AITUC included unions of many shades of opinion, its central leadership was Communist after the government arrested the top Congress leaders following the 1942 Quit India movement. At partition there were only about 30 unions with a total membership of 20,000 members operating in what is now East Bengal, most of these being in transportation and affiliated with the AITUC.[46] We will first recount the growth of the East Pakistan Federation of Labour, which has become the major group in the East, and then outline the development of the three competing federations.

A few weeks after partition, the AITUC decided that its affiliates in Pakistan could establish separate central organizations, but that the working class would stay united across the national boundary. Representatives of its affiliates in East Pakistan met at Narayanganj in September, 1947, to found the East Pakistan Trade Union Federation. The demands of the new organization showed that moderates were in control: reasonable wages, education and health services to be provided by government, full freedom for trade union organization, and equal status for all workers. As in the West, most demands showed both a naïve trust in government intentions and lack of the strength necessary to wrest concessions from employers. Socialist ideas are more deep seated in Bengal than among West Pakistan unions, as is reflected in constitutional objectives calling for nationalization of production and workers' participation in the control of industry.

By 1949 the federation was the largest in all Pakistan. However, the rapid growth of the communist PTUF in the West was disconcerting to members of the Cabinet. Therefore the Minister of Labor, A. M. Malik, urged the widest possible amalgamation of non-communist federations. Since Malik had been one of the founders and a member of the executive committee of the EPFL, his counsel weighed heavily with labor leaders of both West and East. In 1950 the federation changed its name to the East Pakistan Federation of Labour, dropped several unions in West Pakistan from its list of affiliates, transferring them to the WPFL, and united with the WPFL to form the All-Pakistan Confederation of Labour.[47] However, the two constituent federations

of 139,000 members were affiliated with the AITUC, while 41 unions of 106,000 members were affiliated with Roy's Indian Federation of Labour. The AITUC strength was in railways, shipping, and jute, while IFL showed strength only in jute. *Report on the Representative Character of the AITUC and the IFL.*

[46] Richard C. Kriegal, *Labour in East Pakistan 1947–1959*, mimeographed report of USOM/Pakistan, 1959. This is the best written source on labor problems in East Pakistan; it was most useful in preparing this section.

[47] The EPFL did not take its new name until April, 1950, although it had de-

remained autonomous except for international labor contacts and country wide consultation with government. This autonomy was necessary since the eastern group is considerably more socialist and political in its orientation than is the WPFL. As one labor leader put it, the two groups get along well together since they have so little to do with each other.

The provincial government was favorably disposed toward the EPFL, which helped it to grow until in 1950 it claimed the affiliation of 76 unions with a membership of 124,000. This is not to say that the Federation was tied to the ruling Muslim League political party, or that it was not highly critical of the government. However, as a moderate organization directed toward economic objectives, it was looked upon by the government with more favor than were some other groups.

This happy relationship ended temporarily during the brief United Front Government in 1954, which was a landmark in East Pakistan political life. Several political parties united around the idea of more provincial autonomy for East Bengal, to defeat the Muslim League in the March 1954 elections for the provincial Legislative Assembly.

Radical elements, some with political affiliations, capitalizing upon the economic unrest and sectional rivalries among workers, stirred up violent strikes and interworker conflicts in 1934, resulting in several hundred deaths at three major factories. About 300 persons were killed at the Adamjee Jute Mill riots, and smaller numbers at the Chandragona Paper Mill.[48] After being unable for two months to prevent the spread of such riots, the provincial government was removed from office by the central government, which imposed governor's rule, entailing strict

---

cided to join the APCOL in October, 1949. The amalgamation was consummated at the first APCOL General Conference in September, 1950. Malik had tried to include Nurul Huda's "Trade Union Federation, Pakistan" in the merger; with that in view, Huda's group united with the EPFL in April, 1950, but the leaders could not agree, so a rift occurred in October, 1950. In the text we omitted the complicating fact that the EPFL was known for a few months in 1949, as the All-Pakistan Trade Union Federation, and this was its official name at the time it joined the WPFL to form the APCOL. Malik spoke of his part in this during his inaugural address at the first APCOL Conference. A. M. Malik, *Labour Problems and Policy in Pakistan* (Karachi: Pakistan Labour Publications, 1954), p. 25.

[48] The whole affair was hushed up by the government, and a special investigation report was issued only in 1957. The worst riot was at the Adamjee Mills, where Bengali and non-Bengali workers were at odds, the Bengalis claiming that outsiders were given preference by the management, which was also considered to be of "outside" origin. The mill manager and a number of mill officials were killed according to a predetermined plan at the Chandragona Paper Mill. Two mill officials and 44 workers were finally given prison sentences. Government of East Bengal, Labour Directorate, *East Pakistan Labour Journal*, Vol. 7, March, 1954, p. 3; Foreign Service Dispatch No. 119, Karachi, July, 1954, and October 14, 1957.

control of trade union activities. The EPFL was quick to dissociate itself from all of these riots. In July, the Communist party was banned and a number of its leaders imprisoned, including some union leaders.

These developments on the political scene had a considerable influence on the labor federations. During the brief United Front rule, the EPFL lost members rapidly, and rival federations gained. After governor's rule was instituted, the EPFL returned to favor and to an enlarged power. These developments indicate that the EPFL is not as apolitical as the WPFL.[49] In fact, as a result of these experiences Faiz Ahmed seriously considered starting a labor political party in 1955, feeling that unions without political support were at the mercy of changing government alignments. In 1956 Aftab Ali was reported ready to form a political party in alignment with the Awami League, and in 1958 he resigned as vice president of the APCOL in order to enter politics, although he remained as president of the EPFL.[50]

Having weathered this storm, the EPFL has continued to grow and has become by all odds the outstanding labor federation in East Pakistan, claiming 100 unions of 186,000 members in 1958. The backbone of the federation continues to be the Bengal Mariners' Union, which was the nucleus with which Faiz Ahmed and Aftab Ali started. Its 6,000 members work on the large vessels plying the inland waterways, but are faced with layoffs because of the inroads which small motor launches are making on the business of the large carriers. Another bulwark of the EPFL is the East Pakistan Cotton Mill Workers' Union, begun in 1949, which has organized 12,000 workers in 11 major cotton mills and has gained both recognition and a considerable increase in wages. Also the East Pakistan Sugar Mill Workers' Union, whose 9,000 members work for four companies, is a rapidly growing union. These unions taken together are the source of power in the EPFL, since they have stable membership and are solvent financially. They contribute 85 per cent of the modest income of the Federation, which spent only Rs.9,049 in 1954–55.[51] Faiz Ahmed is either president or general secretary of every union in this list, in addition to having been EPFL general secretary since its founding. This brings out the extreme importance of leadership for the unity of the Pakistan labor

[49] The major leaders of the EPFL are not tied to a political party, and Faiz Ahmed has in fact often repeated that trade unions should be kept out of politics and work for economic objectives. However, his unions prospered most in the early years when the Muslim League was in power. *Dawn*, July 12, 1952; Foreign Service Dispatch, Karachi, March 21, 1956.

[50] Foreign Service Dispatch, Karachi, March 21, 1956; *APCOLabor*, Karachi, February 24, 1958.

[51] EPFL, *General Secretary's Report, Fifth Annual Conference*, Dacca, 1955.

movement; one can rely on continued support only so long as one can dominate the group personally.

There are three lesser federations in East Pakistan. Before partition, Nurul Huda had been an officer in the Railway Muslim Employees' League, and soon after partition he organized and became president of the East Pakistan Railway Employees' League, which has since become the largest, though not the most stable, union in East Pakistan.[52] From this center he organized post and telegraph workers and shop assistants, around which the "Trade Union Federation, Pakistan" was formed in 1947. Since this federation catered largely to government enterprises where there were large aggregations of employees, membership grew rapidly until it looked as if it might become the largest federation in Bengal. However, many of its unions were highly unstable and weak, and Huda did not have the experience to remedy this.[53] Huda was primarily a lawyer and did not spend full time on union matters, which reduced his effectiveness.

In the 1949–50 anti-Communist unity effort urged by the minister of labor, Huda was urged to join with the EPFL, which he actually did for six months, but leadership differences soon brought about a split again. Huda's organization, again separate, took the name of "Pakistan Federation of Labour" (PFL), which title it has retained.

M. A. Kissam Choudhary had been organizing among jute workers around Calcutta before partition, but only some time after partition did he begin to take a renewed interest in labor matters. Feeling that he had been slighted by Faiz Ahmed and by the PFL, he assembled in 1951 a group of existent unions into the Mashriqi Pakistan Federation of Labor (MPFL). It was a non-Communist group of unions, mostly Muslim, with a wide variety of ideological outlooks. A basic aspect of Choudhary's policy was to organize rival unions alongside EPFL locals wherever possible, and in this he was relatively successful, partly because he was able to use the name of the popular Hassain Hullah as president.[54] The federation had many small unions of dubious strength, with some concentration among jute mill workers. By 1952 its strength was sufficient to be a menace to EPFL unions, which began to employ strong-arm methods by which they successfully slowed MPFL growth.

Preceding and during the United Front period of 1954, both Nurul

[52] In 1955 it was registered as having 47,000 members. Government of Pakistan, Central Labour Commissioner, *Classified List of Registered Trade Unions in Pakistan* (Karachi, 1955).

[53] The 210,000 members claimed for 1950 is a gross exaggeration; 107,000 of these were in one agricultural union. In 1949, the government estimated that the Federation was smaller than the EPFL or the WPFL.

[54] Hullah was a brother of the Nawab of Dacca, and the family name had an appeal to most workers.

Huda and Kissam Choudhary separately made overtures to the Awami League, one of the parties in the successful United Front. Maulani A. H. K. Bhashani, a leftist and a power in the Awami League, was made president of unions within each federation, notably of the large Eastern Pakistan Railway Employees' League. Both organizations grew rapidly at the expense of the EPFL, as unions shifted their allegiance. During the unsettled 1954 episode, the two groups found they were coöperating in various ventures with Communists, a course they normally would not have pursued. When governor's rule was instituted later that year, both groups lost affiliated unions, while the EPFL gained; after 1955 they declined in importance.[55] Huda became much less active in labor affairs, although in 1959 he was still president of the PFL, which had dwindled to 6,000 members. The MPFL continued on, largely as a paper organization with unions which paid little or no dues; in 1956 its unions were stricken from the government registration list because of nonreporting.

Before partition, Communists had strength in East Bengal among workers on the railroads, on the docks of Chittagong, in electricity supply, and in cotton mills. After 1950 they began organizing among the tea estates of Sylhet; most of their activity has been among Hindu minority groups. It was not until the United Front period in 1954 that they came into prominence, being instrumental in the riots at the Adamjee Jute Mill and Chandragona Paper Mill, as well as in other public disturbances. On the political front a few Communists had been elected to the Legislative Assembly as members of the United Front, and in the labor field they worked through some MPFL and PFL unions as well as in unions they more fully controlled. They became established for the first time in inland water transport, forming the East Pakistan Nabik Union, the 3,000 members of which have since become the nucleus of their labor efforts. As a culmination of their efforts, the East Pakistan Mazdoor Federation was started by a group of Communist unions in February, 1958, with the Nabik Union at its center; political sponsorship came from Communist elements of the National Awami Party. With the advent of martial law in October, 1958, many of its leaders were arrested, and its activities have ceased.

Thus in 1959, East Pakistan was left with the relatively strong and moderate East Pakistan Federation of Labour, and two very weak rivals: the PFL and the MPFL. The Communist group had ceased to function as a federation, although individual unions continued with

[55] In 1955 the PFL and MPFL united to form the United Trade Union Federation, Pakistan, but since both organizations retained their autonomy, unity existed primarily on paper.

difficulty under martial law. In 1955 East Pakistan had 14.4 million persons in the labor force. Of these, only about 350,000 workers were in industry susceptible to organization, yet registered trade unions claimed 157,000 members that year, and 204,000 by 1959. This is certainly a very high proportion in unions, and leads us to remark once again that union claims are considerably exaggerated.

THE NATURE OF LOCAL UNIONS

The unions of Pakistan consist of a large number of local units, usually confined to the workers of one company without regard to skill or occupation. The local union frequently is not related to other unions in the industry, but is loosely associated in the large global federations we have been discussing. Since most unions are too weak to wrest concessions from employers by their own strength, they turn to government for aid, and this throws the federation into a position of prominence, since its leaders are usually better known by government officials. Nevertheless, the local union remains the basic unit which can offer or deny its support to the various federations and has direct contact with the workers.

There are almost no national craft unions and only the bare beginnings of industrywide federations, but they can hardly be compared to the strong and centralized industrial unions of the United States. Each local union stands largely by its own effort, and has little outside support in time of strike; this is a major source of union weakness. Competition among unions is intensified, since several federations may seek locals in the same plant, thus leading to local as well as national rivalry.

Since most industrial establishments are small, unions are also small, which makes it impossible for most of them to support paid officers. In 1955, two-thirds of all registered unions had less than 300 members each, although the presence of a few large groups, including two railroad unions of over 40,000 brought the average size to 833.[56] Most of the large unions are among government employees, while the remaining ones are in textile mills.

The main struggle of unions is for recognition from employers, who are reluctant to see any value in labor unions and usually fight them at every step. Foreign concerns generally are more open to dealing with unions than is local management. Even where the union is recognized, collective bargaining is rudimentary, agreements usually being signed

[56] These figures are based on union claims of membership, and err on the high side. The observations are based on an analysis of union data given in *Classified List of Registered Trade Unions in Pakistan.*

only after the government conciliator has used considerable pressure to bring the parties together.

Very few unions have shop stewards, so essential for the day-to-day operations of an efficient union, although some of the larger shops have shop committees, established by government order, which give an alternative channel of communication between management and the workers. The inability of most unions to help workers meet daily problems and grievances is one of the major weaknesses of Pakistan unions. Because of this, most workers have little respect for the unions and "there is a serious lack of confidence in trade unionism amongst rank and file workers." [57]

Unions which organize among poor workers must expect poverty. In 1955–56, the average annual per capita income among industrial workers' families was Rs.283 in Karachi and Rs.228 in Lahore and Dacca.[58] From average annual industrial wages of Rs.899 (in 1954), most unions ask from 4 to 8 annas (¼ to ½ rupee) per month as dues, but the percentage of collections is poor. In 1953–54 all reporting registered unions spent Rs.277,000, which averaged Rs.1575 per union, or Rs.2.08 per member.[59] The great instability of membership is one cause of this difficulty; members join during strikes, only to drop out when they are asked for dues in a time of tranquility. Irresponsibility in the handling of union funds is fairly widespread, and leakage of funds to officers is particularly serious when the unions have so little financial support. It is inevitable that such poverty-stricken organizations cannot render wide services to their members.

UNION LEADERSHIP

A number of labor leaders have risen from the ranks. For example, the outstanding personalities of the labor movement in East and West Pakistan, Faiz Ahmed and M. A. Khatib, were once a seaman and a docker respectively. However, the salient fact of union leadership is the large number of outsiders, particularly lawyers, who are union officers.[60] This is a natural result of the prevalent fear officeholders have of being fired or discriminated against by employers. Unions find it necessary to seek spokesmen who are free from this pressure.

---

[57] *Report of the ILO Labour Survey Mission*, p. 135.

[58] This is equivalent to 48 to 60 United States dollars. Central Statistical Office, "Family Expenditure Survey 1955–1956," *Statistical Bulletin*, Vol. 6, January–February, 1958, pp. 71–72.

[59] Government of Pakistan, Central Labour Commissioner, *Working of the Trade Union Act During 1953–54*.

[60] Under the Trade Union Act of 1926, at least half the officers of registered unions must be workers in the industry.

Some outsiders use union office as a steppingstone to political prestige, while a very few use it for personal aggrandizement, though the movement is too poor for much of that. Outside leadership is often necessary for effective organization where most workers are illiterate. Moreover, a lawyer as officer can be most helpful where much union activity involves representation before governmental bodies.

In both sections of the country there have grown up a group of professional labor leaders who serve as officers of from 10 to 20 unions. Their attention is thereby so divided that they cannot be very effective; on the other hand, this is probably the only way poor unions can command the services of reasonably able leaders.

Pakistan labor leaders stand out in Asia as being less politically inclined than those of most areas. This is particularly true in West Pakistan. Only a small number of the leaders are primarily politicians, although quite a few in the East have become involved in political parties. These remarks do not apply to the Communist leaders, whose actions and pronouncements have shown that they are interested in workers' welfare primarily as a means to a political objective.

Following Roy's advice, Pakistani federations have placed considerable emphasis on training competent union leadership. Several training institutes have been organized by the WPFL and the EPFL in coöperation with the ILO, the ICFTU, the Pakistan Workers' Education Society, and the Pakistan Institute of Personnel Administration.

IDEOLOGICAL LEANINGS

Enough has been said of the seven major federations to reveal their affiliation or lack of affiliation with national political parties. Certainly the EPFL, the WPFL, and the APCOL are controlled by no political group and are as free from political involvement as one could expect to find in an Asian country.

With regard to economic and social philosophy, Pakistan's union leaders cover a wide spectrum, but can be divided into three groups. The WPFL stands on the economic and social right wing of the movement, as indicated by the moderation of its demands, its willingness to coöperate with government, and the lack of any call for the nationalization of industry in its pronouncements. This is not to say that all its officers are happy with the status quo, but the dominant view is that it is not the business of unions, but rather of political groupings, to reorient social institutions; much of this view comes from Roy's influence. On the extreme left are the two Communist groups, the PTUF in the West and the East Pakistan Mazdoor Federation. Although they never have had great coördination of policies, they have both looked to Indian Communists for leadership, and have resorted to violence when it seemed appropriate.

In the Center stand four federations: the EPFL, the PFL, the MPFL and the PMF, three from the East and one from the West. These groups are radical in that they regard the remaking of economic institutions as the legitimate business of labor unions. They stand for the nationalization of industry and workers' control of industry at the same time. They are Socialists and many, but not all, of their leaders are Marxists, but they are not Communists; most of them condemn the use of violence and have coöperated more often than not with government. This group is also in a central position with relation to the importance attached to political action.

THE INFLUENCE OF UNIONS ON NATIONAL LIFE

Perhaps as important as their social philosophy is the degree of union influence in spreading their views through the broader social and economic life of the country. It must be admitted that in Pakistan this influence is minimal. "Labor unions and labor leaders have had relatively little impact on local or national elections. The degree of personal or party loyalty of union adherents is small, the main force of interest dissipating quickly beyond the confines of labor-management interplay within a specific business or industrial enterprise. Labor in Pakistan has no effective political organisation." [61] Thus labor has had little influence on governmental policy or even upon labor legislation, which is evidenced by the almost complete lack of important labor law amendments between independence and the beginning of martial law.

The labor movement has had little impact on public opinion except perhaps through its strike activities. Financial stringency prevents an active labor press for workers, and little thought is given to public relations relative to the larger population. The APCOL mimeographs a fortnightly *APCOL*, the EPFL has published *Sangram* rather consistently, and the United Union of NWR Workers has published fairly regularly the *Railwaymen's Herald* and, for a number of years, *The Voice of Labor*. Mr. F. E. Qurban, the guiding force of the PMF, publishes the weekly *Mazdoor Dunya*, which is openly Marxist. The circulation of all these papers hase been severely limited.

POTENTIAL DEVELOPMENT

From one viewpoint, the outlook for the labor movement in Pakistan is relatively bright. Industrial employment is growing fairly rapidly,

[61] United States Government, International Coöperation Administration, *The Labor Situation in Pakistan* (Washington, 1956), pp. 33–34.

and it is likely that unions will grow as the working force becomes more committed to an industrial way of life. The major stream of the movement is united, though somewhat tenuously, in the APCOL, and is as apolitical and economic in its outlook as any in Asia. It is beginning to take Roy's advice of emphasizing training of union leadership, which augurs well for the future.

On the other hand, the movement suffers from many maladies which retard healthy development toward the industrial democratic unionism to which the leaders aspire. Employers combat the unions at every turn and frighten off much labor leadership by victimization of officers. Overdependence upon outside leadership slows the growth of internal resources. Inadequate processing of grievances is a major weakness which reduces the loyalty of the membership. The unions' dependence upon government is perhaps inevitable at this stage, but it is a condition which must be outgrown for healthy and independent unionism to develop. Unfortunately, under martial law the unions have become even more dominated by government, and their independence has been seriously impaired.

It has been said that, while unions spring from workers' protest, the particular form and ideology they develop is largely a response to the institutions and culture of the ruling elite of the country.[62] The author would hold that the Pakistan elite is rather authoritarian, but at the same time wishes to retain Western democratic institutions; it is nationalist and anti-colonial but not revolutionary. Nationalist authoritarian elites are held to call forth weak unions, accepting paternalism and using outside intellectual leaders; this seems to fit the Pakistan situation pretty well. On the other hand, there are elements of middle-class, anti-revolutionary, and democratic mentality among the elite which would be expected, according to this theory, to call forth an economically oriented labor movement with rank-and-file leadership; this seems to fit reasonably well also, at least in West Pakistan. My conclusion is that the form which the main stream of the Pakistani labor movement is taking is patterned not only in response to business opposition and government paternalism, but is also an expression of the age-old dependent status of the manual workers of the subcontinent.

The Problems of Management

In 1958–59, the gross national product of Pakistan at constant prices was 21 per cent larger than that of 1949–50, while the index of in-

[62] This thesis was expressed by Dr. John Dunlop in a seminar at the Pakistan Institute of Development Economics, Karachi, March, 1959 (mimeographed report).

dustrial production based on 1950 was 406.[63] This rapid industrial growth was accompanied by a 98 per cent increase of industrial employment between 1951 and 1955. Such a rapid growth of employment poses major problems for management in recruiting, training, and utilizing efficiently the new recruits.

MANAGEMENT'S RECRUITMENT OF LABOR

Earlier we discussed some aspects of the recruitment problem and noted three major recruitment procedures. First, one-fifth of all workers in organized industry are casual contract laborers, hired by *sardars* or gang bosses who act as both recruitment officers and subforemen. Here the employer has little to say about whom he hires or qualifications of workers; rather, he hires the whole group, and his contacts for pay and discipline are through the contractor. Second, most unskilled laborers are hired at the gate by foremen who advertise job openings through present employees, who in turn spread the word to relatives and friends. Such workers are tried out for a few days before more permanent employment is offered. This hiring is haphazard, decentralized in the hands of foremen, and open to bribery; it is no wonder that management complains of lazy and incapable workers when so little care is exercised in selection. Third, a very small but growing number of firms, particularly foreign ones, use centralized hiring through a personnel officer who may or may not use aptitude or mechanical tests as part of his hiring procedure.

Unfortunately, management personnel is chosen almost as irrationally as are common laborers. Nepotism is widespread, and family connections are the main avenue to business opportunity. There are several communities known for business enterprise, such as the Memons and Bohras, and these form a management ingroup; for example, the Jains control practically all port and dock work in Karachi. Recruitment into the ranks of management is thus only very loosely connected with ability.

The mercantile tradition had been to teach one's son to cipher, which constituted the whole of his business training. Firms have not turned to the universities for business leadership, because no real business administration courses were offered until recently, when the Institute of Public and Business Administration was started at the University of Karachi. Three commercial schools were available, but they taught accounting primarily. The 1951 Census listed only 3,300 engineers and architects; business management complained that the three

[63] Information supplied by the Central Statistical Office of the Government of Pakistan, *Statistical Bulletin*, Vol. 7, January, 1959, p. 65.

engineering colleges trained men to be too theoretical, and they neither could nor would work with their hands. The dignity of manual labor is an ideal foreign to the East; its adoption by engineering graduates would go far toward stimulating efficiency. The government and the government-operated railroads are outstanding in their careful selection of able university graduates for management positions. These men are given further formal and in-service training, so that they form a respected elite in the community.

TRAINING THE LABOR FORCE

One of the major problems in Pakistan is the training of a sufficient number of skilled workers to support rapid industrialization. In 1955, the fields of shortest supply included draftsmen, molders, machinists, toolmakers, turners, fitters, mechanics, welders, typesetters, glassmakers, and nurses.[64] Although there is considerable child labor in industry, contrary to law, there are very few apprenticeship schemes, management fearing that their trained apprentices will find employment with a competitor. A first-class apprenticeship program is carried on by the Batala Engineering Company and by the Dhakeswari Cotton Mills, and the defence establishment trains good machinists, but these are notable exceptions. Pakistan had 27 vocational schools in 1948 and has added a few since, but they are inadequate to meet the tremendous need.

A number of business managers indicated in interviews that the most serious impediment to efficiency was the breakdown of communication between management and workers at the crucial link of the foreman. Yet training of supervisors is unusual in Pakistan, the Batala Engineering Company, the Pakistan Ordnance Factory, and the railroads being notable exceptions. "Training Within Industry" programs sponsored by the International Labor Organization have proved helpful in training supervisors.

Of crucial significance in an underdeveloped economy is the need for managerial ability of a high order. Persons with this talent can, like seed corn, multiply their kind. Men of such talent are hard to find and, when found, need training. The British tradition of a broad humanistic education for the elite is the heritage of modern Pakistan. A major policy question for the government is the degree to which the whole educational system, and the universities in particular, should change toward a more practical and professional variety of training. The trend toward a greater emphasis on technical education has been apparent since 1958.

[64] *Report of the ILO on Manpower Survey in Pakistan,* p. 33.

ORGANIZATION OF MANPOWER FOR EFFICIENCY

Because of the shortage of entrepreneurial talent, the managing agency system grew up in the subcontinent long ago and is still important in the management of Pakistan industry. The agency usually supplies a portion of the capital, appoints major operating officers, purchases raw materials, furnishes the accounting service, and sells the goods made by the operating companies under its control. This makes for a high degree of concentration of control and conserves scarce talent, though it has been bitterly criticized for the financial manipulation which concentrated control makes possible. The managing agency is best known for its financial and mercantile successes; it has rendered less conspicuous service in the efficient organization of production and the rational use of manpower. In fact, a preoccupation with finance has diverted attention from the important problems of organizing the work force efficiently.

Capital investment is a major means by which Pakistan has planned her economic development. It has been suggested that increases in capital investment, to be effective, must be accompanied by concomitant increases in managerial and organizational manpower, more foremen, office workers, and idea men. Yet this is precisely where most Pakistan industry falls short; shiny and modern equipment is imported but placed in the old organizational context, and results are often disappointing. There are at least two causes for most entrepreneurs' overlooking the importance of efficient organization of manpower. First, very low wages tend to make management profligate with a cheap resource, but it turns out that while labor is cheap per man-hour, labor costs are not low per unit of output.[65] Second, the psychology and background of the newer entrepreneurs in industry cause them to seek quick returns in buying and selling, but to overlook the need for efficient organization of manpower so as to reduce production costs.

The people who promote and finance industry are primarily traders turned producers, and they retain the trader's psychology. This means that the owner of a cotton mill may see his function as that of buying cotton and selling cloth. He pays very little attention to organizing or supervising production, but leaves that almost entirely to others. This dooms him to a small, high-price market. In one mill I found the owner trying to slip over shorter staple cotton on his own spinning

[65] Pakistan sugar made in modern mills costs three times the landed price of Cuban sugar, and Pakistan ordnance rifles cost twice the foreign price. Seminar at the Pakistan Institute of Development Economics, Karachi, March, 1959 (mimeographed report), p. 98.

master without warning; production costs were high, since the machines continually had to be readjusted to varying staple lengths and the spinning master was left to detect the trouble when threads began to break. Such an outlook is probably most prevalent in the textile industry, but it is not entirely absent elsewhere.

Office management and long-range planning are nearly absent. This is partly because accounting practice is too underdeveloped to become a tool of planning. Records are archaic and, if kept, frequently cannot be found. Most records are in longhand, since the Urdu typewriter is so cumbersome; only larger firms keep English records. The author visited one cotton mill employing 500 workers, where the total office force was the owner and one bookkeeper. On payday the workers were paid in cash, from a box, without record. In effect the owner said: "Let the foreman out in the shed make cloth from my cotton, it's his business how he gets it done." One must add that this was an extreme case, at least for a mill of that size.

A particular instance of high-cost manpower organization is the low foreman-worker ratio. Pakistan, like a umber of other Asian countries, has two or three times as many workers per foreman as is found in the West. Perhaps this was justified so long as processes were simple and skills traditional, but new capital-intensive and complicated processes require closer supervision, especially when many workers are illiterate.

Other problems of efficiency are also related to the foremen. They do not feel themselves to be a part of the management team, and most managements make little attempt to remedy this. The personnel officer of one of the most modern plants in the country, when asked about this, commented: "Why should we waste time convincing foremen of their importance to management? If they don't act as they are told, they are fired." The foreman's response to this insecurity is usually an unduly authoritarian attitude toward the workers under him, which leads to labor unrest and frequently to slowdowns.

Another supervision problem is the lack of an adequate promotion scale in most plants. The author found workers who had been at the same machine for ten years with no offer of change. A particularly alert workman may be made a subforeman, but usually his advancement beyond that is blocked, since the foreman must ordinarily know English. A number of personnel officers still feel that the Anglo-Pakistani makes the ideal foreman, the foreman's economic status being exactly parallel with the social status of the Anglo-Pakistani: neither fish nor fowl. This lack of mobility upward in the management hierarchy means that it is difficult to attract able supervisors, and robs top management of a chance to get earlier experience at the foreman level. Lack of direct contact with workers is perhaps one reason why top management is slow to realize the importance of efficient manpower management and personnel relations.

Another specific problem of manpower organization has to do with the wage structure. In a static society the differential between skilled and unskilled wages is narrow, while a developing economy calls for new skills, and wage differentials are likely to widen. Pakistan's difficulty is that she still retains the traditional narrow differential wage structure in an economy that is struggling to expand. Already severe shortages have developed for skilled personnel, but so far inherited attitudes have prevented the noticeable widening of wage differentials which will be necessary to attract able young people to undertake training for skilled jobs. The ratio between skilled and unskilled wages is only about two to one, in spite of the scarcity of skilled workers and unemployment in the unskilled categories.[66] The productivity of skilled workers is probably greater than their wages, but tradition prevents economic forces from operating to raise wages to attract skill. Productivity of unskilled workers, particularly in agricultural pursuits, is probably even lower than their miserably low wages, but humanitarian considerations and government pressures exercise a buoyant influence on these lower rates. The result is that the wage pattern does not reflect productivity differentials, and misallocation of manpower follows.

Only the very largest plants have a personnel department and the centralized hiring and manpower planning functions which that makes possible. A number of the larger plants have labor welfare officers whose function is to ameliorate the lot of the worker within the existing organizational structure. These men are in the anomalous position of handling welfare programs for the workers and being their friend and counselor; but, at the same time, they are expected by management to be spies and disciplinary officers as well. As one industrialist put it, the labor welfare officer "has to thin down the margin of exploitation between the employers and employees. . . ."[67] Though paid by management, they occupy a position midway between management and

[66] Data assembled by the Employers' Association in Karachi in 1955 showed average wages of Rs.3–15 for skilled and Rs.1–15 for unskilled workers, which gives a ratio of 2.03 to 1. Leibenstein has shown how wages can persist above productivity even in a competitive model where caloric intake is so low as to be influenced by wages. Harvey Leibenstein, "Theory of Underemployment in Backward Countries," *Journal of Political Economy*, Vol. 65, April, 1957, pp. 91–103.

[67] A. Razaak, "The Welfare Officer," in *Employees' Welfare in Pakistan* (Karachi: Pakistan Institute of Personnel Administration, 1955), pp. 41–43.

the workers, and have little to do with the efficient use of labor. Usually they are untrained and are treated as a fifth wheel by both management and workers. Only a few employers have been willing to experiment with basic modifications in the terms and conditions of work as a means of securing happy and productive workers instead of relying on ameliorative welfare measures. In the Bata shoe factory, where such an approach has been taken toward workers' welfare, productivity per worker has been about the same as that of European workers using identical machinery.[68]

DEALING WITH UNIONS

The employers of Pakistan spring from a culture in which the elite was authoritarian and paternalistic, and this pattern has survived in modern industry. Foremen are autocratic, unions are recognized by only a few firms, and workers are seldom consulted, but under law a rather extensive range of welfare services is offered, at least in theory.

Under the Industrial Employment Act of 1946, industrial establishments employing 100 or more workers were required to set forth "standing orders" which included many of the terms of employment normally covered by a collective agreement. These orders were required to define the classification of workers, hours of work, holidays, wage rates, conditions for suspension or dismissal, and means by which workers might gain redress against arbitrary acts.[69] These orders were to be submitted to the Labor Commissioner, and, when certified, were posted where all employees would have access to them.[70] These provisions are modified by the Industrial and Commercial Standing Orders Ordinance of 1960, which extends coverage to commercial firms, reduces to 50 the minimum size of unit which is regulated, and provides that the government, rather than the employer, shall write the standing orders. Management can change these standing orders

[68] Up to 1955, the Bata plant reported that output per man-week was just as good as that in its identical European plants: 58 leather shoes and 130 rubber shoes per week; in 1955, output dropped to 46 and 104 respectively, after a strike in which hard feelings developed.

[69] Perennial factories generally observe a 48-hour week, while seasonal plants work a few hours longer. Small factories frequently work much longer hours. A weekly rest day and 10 days' annual leave is compulsory in those factories coming under the Factories Act, and an additional 8 to 12 days' festival leave is ordinarily granted, so Pakistan's industrial workers are about as well off in this respect as those anywhere. Government of Pakistan, Central Labour Commissioner, *Working of the Factories Act during 1954; Report of the ILO Labour Survey Mission*, pp. 68–69.

[70] The ILO Labour Survey Mission found compliance left much to be desired, and that government was very slow in certifying standing orders even when they were submitted. *Report of the ILO Labour Survey Mission*, pp. 62–63.

only in the direction of greater welfare for the workers, and unions may bargain collectively for such changes. These orders give considerable protection to workers against arbitrary acts of management.

Most dealings with workers and unions are on a company basis, but by 1957 at least fifteen employers' associations had been formed, for which labor relations were a major function. The most important of these were the Federation of Chambers of Commerce, the Employers' Association of West Pakistan, the Employers' Association of East Pakistan, the East Bengal Cotton Mill Owners' Association, and the Pakistan Tea Association. These associations collect wage and other labor data for use of the members, and approach government on matters of joint concern to employers. In November, 1958, the martial-law government announced a policy of registering all employers' associations, uniting and rationalizing their geographic location, and setting up certain standards for officials. Actual labor relations are still largely an internal company matter.

Charles Myers found three major forms of labor management relations in India,[71] and this classification also fits Pakistan, since its background is so similar: (1) negotiations between employers and unions occasionally resulting in collective agreements but usually reaching a settlement only before a conciliation officer or an industrial tribunal; (2) works committees which are established by law in larger factories; (3) the settlement of individual grievances. These three types of labor management relations will be discussed in turn.

UNION-MANAGEMENT NEGOTIATION

In 1960 the government issued the new standing orders ordinance, discussed above, and also required compulsory recognition of "most representative" unions by employers. These ordinances make 1960 a watershed year in union management relations in Pakistan. First, we will discuss these relationships as they existed before the new enactments.

Before 1960 very few employers recognized or bargained collectively with unions. The ILO Labor Survey Mission found that in 1953 only about 30,000 workers were protected by collective bargaining agreements and tribunal awards taken together. In West Pakistan, almost all the agreements which existed were between individual companies and the union in their establishment. Ordinarily, neither unions nor managements would let associations conduct their negotiations, although the stevedoring firms and the lighterage firms of Karachi were exceptions. In East Bengal, agreements between a province wide union

---

[71] Myers, *op. cit.*, pp. 119–132.

and the employers' association were usual in cotton and jute mills and on tea estates.

Two examples of collective agreements may clarify what was usually covered. The Bata Shoe Company posted extensive standing orders covering many subjects in addition to those required by law, including methods to be used by the company for recruitment of new workers, rates of pay for various categories of workers, hours of work, double wages for overtime, a list of 15 offenses leading to dismissal, treatment of absenteeism and lateness, grievance procedure, 20 days' leave per year with full pay, provident fund, bonus, and promotion policy.[72] In this case there was not much left to be covered by the collective agreement with the Bata Mazdoor League, which was one of the better-organized unions in the Punjab. The agreement recognized the League as exclusive bargaining agent, the company agreed not to lock the workers out, and the union agreed not to strike before exhausting the governmental conciliation procedure. The union acknowledged management's prerogatives, and each party agreed it would not intimidate or discriminate against workers because of membership or nonmembership in the union. In this agreement the union had virtually no voice in the welfare of individual workers, but only in their collective relationships.

Quite different was the agreement between the Burmah-Shell Oil Company of Pakistan and the Burmah-Shell Employees Union. Here the Standing Orders covered a much more limited range of subjects, and a wider field was left for union negotiation. The wage scales were a matter of negotiation, and cost-of-living allowance clauses were in the collective agreement, as were clauses on bonus, leave, seniority in layoffs, and grievance procedure.[73]

Most such agreements were in fact reached only after mediation by a government conciliator or by an award of an industrial tribunal under the Industrial Disputes Act of 1947, which formed the framework within which most union-management negotiations took place.[74] The Act provided that the central or provincial government might refer any industrial dispute in its jurisdiction to a conciliation officer, to promote

---

[72] Bata Shoe Company, "Collective Agreement and Standing Orders and Rules." This agreement was dated April 1, 1955, to be effective for three years. In 1958 there were only 175 firms which had issued standing orders in East Bengal, although twice that number were covered by the Industrial Employment (Standing Order) Act of 1946. Kriegal, *op. cit.*, p. 175.

[73] Agreement between Burmah-Shell Oil Storage and Distributing Company of Pakistan and Burmah-Shell Employees' Union, dated July 29, 1955, to run through the end of 1957.

[74] M. Shafi, *Labour Code of Pakistan* (2nd ed., Karachi: Pakistan Labour Publications, 1958). The Industrial Disputes Act of 1947 was amended in 1948, 1956, and 1957.

a settlement, or to an industrial tribunal, which was empowered to award a decision binding on both parties for one year. It was obligatory on government so to refer disputes in public utilities, or where both parties requested such referral. Strikes and lockouts without two weeks' notice were prohibited in public utilities under the original act, and this provision was extended to all factories of over 20 workers by the 1956 amendment.

In practice, most small disputes have been settled amicably by government-appointed conciliators, and the activity of these officers has been markedly successful in keeping industrial peace within a framework of relative justice. They have handled hundreds of cases, usually gaining agreements, although it must be admitted that they sometimes exercised more moral pressure on the parties than would be acceptable in the West. The larger disputes usually went to an industrial tribunal for an award, but the proceedings were kept flexible enough so that the parties could agree on some points during their course, and these points then became part of the award. Up to April, 1954, there had been only 39 such industrial tribunal awards. Thus compulsory arbitration, though infrequently used, was always in the background as a possibility. It prevented the parties from coming to a solution if prospects were good for a more favorable tribunal award, but it did exert some pressure for agreement at the last minute.

There have been many criticisms of the working of the Industrial Disputes Act. Probably the major difficulty has been in the length and delay of proceedings, sometimes extending to two years, which led the ILO Labor Survey Mission to state: "The Act is really being used to smash trade unionism." [75] From reading the awards as well as talking with tribunal officers, one gained the impression of fairness and judiciousness in the awards when handed down.

In 1959 a new Industrial Disputes Ordinance was promulgated by the martial law regime; it repealed the 1947 act, but reinstated the same conciliation provisions. Industrial Tribunals were replaced with tripartite Industrial Courts, to which government was required to submit disputes if requested by either party, after a prescribed period of conciliation efforts had proved fruitless. Public utility cases are so referred after 14 days of unsuccessful conciliation efforts, and other cases after 28 days. The decision of the Court is final, without appeal, but is binding for only one year. Strikes and lockouts are prohibited in public utilities except after six weeks' notice, and are unlawful in all industries during conciliation or industrial court proceedings.[76]

[75] *Report of the ILO Labour Survey Mission*, p. 141.

[76] Government of Pakistan, *Gazette Extraordinary*, October 21, 1959.

The new ordinance introduces no novel features, but assures that more disputes will go to the compulsory arbitration stage. The reason for the change was to give government a greater influence over settlements, and to speed decisions. It was hoped that both these influences would stimulate higher production. Decisions have been speeded up by the new system, but not so decisively as had been hoped.

Legally there are only two parties to these conciliation and court proceedings, but in fact the government is present as a third party in the person of the conciliator or judge. These officers frequently warn the parties that some possible settlements would not be in the best interest of economic advancement in the country, and thus discourage them. The result is that tripartite bargaining has replaced the usual collective bargaining, and labor deals with management through the government. Western observers at first are likely to feel that this robs the primary parties of their freedom, but further experience convinces one that, where unions are weak, the government can perform a service in these proceedings by protecting workers from exploitation, and at the same time protect society from ill-advised private settlements which might hamper economic development. The author concludes that unwarranted as compulsory arbitration is in advanced economies, the developing economy of Pakistan cannot afford the industrial strife which would precede the establishment of mature collective bargaining as it is known in the West. Government participation in labor-management disputes is the inevitable result.

Until 1960 very few employers recognized unions as the legitimate representatives of the workers. The struggle for recognition was as important and caused as much industrial strife as the effort to get better wages and working conditions. The strike was frequently the only way to get management to listen to the union, and it frequently brought the intervention of government which enforced a variety of collective bargaining.

The 1960 Trade Union ordinance requires recognition of the union found to be most representative of the workers, provided the union membership includes ten per cent of the workers; the bargaining unit usually is the company. Management is required to bargain collectively with such recognized unions. Additional provisions of this ordinance will be described later.

By government edict unions have now gained the recognition for which they had struggled with so little success. The hope is that industrial peace and productive efficiency will be encouraged by removing a major cause of strikes and ushering in a period of collective bargaining. It is too early to assess the results of the new ordinance, but government is finding it extremely difficult to enforce its provisions on reluctant employers. A temporary period of industrial strife may erupt in Pakistan, as happened in the United States after passage of the Wagner Act, but the possibility of this is lessened since Pakistani unions are relatively weak, and because the martial law government holds a tight rein on public disturbances and strikes.

WORKS COMMITTEES, GRIEVANCE PROCEDURES, AND STOPPAGES

The Industrial Disputes Act required all factories of over 100 workers (amended to over 50 by the 1959 ordinance) to establish works committees consisting of representatives of management and workmen "to promote measures for securing and preserving amity and good relations between the employer and workmen." These committees exist in a number of factories, but they have been a marked failure. The ILO Labour Survey Mission reported that not a single instance of a live and properly functioning works committee was found in all of Pakistan. Management charges that the workers try to use the committee as a forum for collective bargaining. Unions fear the works committee may replace the union, but this fear was reduced in 1960 when union officers were permitted to serve on these committees. It is true that, in some shops, works committees are used as substitutes for unions, but they have not done much to create "amity and good relations."

The grievance procedure is usually stated very briefly and informally in the standing orders or collective agreement. For example: "Any employee having a grievance should present it to his immediate supervisor and, if not settled to his satisfaction, to the next level of authority and lastly to the Departmental/Divisional Manager. If the employee is still unsatisfied he may represent his case to the Union." [77] Usually the grievance is considered as a case between the individual employee and the company, although it is fairly frequently referred to the works committee as the last procedural step. Only a few strong unions are involved at any point in the grievance machinery, and even then they do not follow the case at each step. A very few agreements include referral to an impartial arbitrator as the last step. Grievance procedures for manual workers in government establishments are only slightly more organized than in private industry.

This brief review indicates that union-management relationships are primarily at the insistence of government. Before the ordinances of 1959 and 1960 unions were not strong enough to force management to

---

[77] Collective agreement between Burmah-Shell of Pakistan and Burmah-Shell Employees' Union, dated July 29, 1955.

negotiate. It should be noted that most labor legislation before 1958 was for the welfare of the individual worker, rather than to protect the union as an organization. No effective control existed against victimization of union officers, and the unions themselves were not strong enough to protect their officers. Victimization continually soured relations between unions and management and was one of the important reasons for the new labor ordinances.

TABLE 5

MANDAYS LOST FROM WORK STOPPAGES IN PAKISTAN, 1948–1959

	West Pakistan (thousands)	East Pakistan [a] (thousands)	Total [b] (thousands)
1948	23	112	135
1949	19	82	101
1950	43	40	83
1951	42	35	77
1952	51	75	126
1953	27	89	116
1954	193	90	283
1955	83	38	121
1956	101	273	374
1957	80	693	773
1958	225	152	377
1959	—	—	47

[a] Richard C. Kriegal, *Labor in East Pakistan, 1947–1959*, mimeographed report of USOM/Pakistan, 1959, p. 80.
[b] *Pakistan Labour Gazette*, July–September, 1956, p. 407, and for each quarter thereafter.

The freedom to strike or lock workers out has gradually been circumscribed. Up until 1956, only lightning strikes (without two weeks' notice) in public utilities were illegal, but in that year the prohibition was extended to all establishments of over 20 workers. During this period, strikes were also illegal during a conciliation or tribunal proceeding. Thus work stoppages could be delayed considerably, but they were not prohibited. With the advent of martial law in October, 1958, all strikes of any nature were prohibited in "public utilities," which was so broadly interpreted that for all practical purposes the right to strike had at least temporarily ceased. In 1959 the right to strike was restored, except during conciliation or industrial court proceedings, but public utility workers can strike only after 6 weeks' notice. Table 5 shows strike experience from 1948 to 1959.

The two peaks of industrial unrest in the West and the three peaks in the East, as measured by workdays lost, all correspond to periods of high and rising prices and political instability occurring simultaneously.

The Role of Government

Pakistan faces a basic dilemma in her labor policy. She is being pushed by world opinion, by ILO conventions, and by her own humanitarian impulses into the modern era of the welfare state with its many social services and protection of workers' rights. But Pakistan is a land where the productivity of men and of land is low, and more than anything else she needs to raise the standard of living and the productivity upon which it is based. Her leaders believe that too rapid an expansion of social services or too rapid an increase in workers' welfare, unaccompanied by corresponding increases in productivity, may stop short the development process. They know they cannot stop the expansion of welfare to the common man, nor do they wish to do so, but the problem is the rate at which the economy can support such an expansion.

This is a particularly serious problem since Pakistan is in the crucial "take-off period" during which investment and income are just beginning to rise above the minimal level of a static society; a false move may return her economy to that drab and static level once again.[78]

THE DEVELOPMENT OF LABOR POLICY

In inaugurating the first tripartite Labour Conference in 1949, the Prime Minister, Liaquat Ali Khan, stated a dual objective in general terms: "We must create conditions which are favorable to labor. My government will take all necessary steps to see that labor gets its due share in all enterprises. . . . Labor must remember that the interest and welfare of Pakistan comes before the interest of any individual or class of individuals and it must not do anything which in any way weakens Pakistan. If Pakistan endures and prospers the problems that labour has can be solved." [79]

Labor had to wait until 1955 for the government to issue a general statement on labor policy. The preamble to this policy statement bears quoting in part because it shows so clearly the government's dilemma in trying to stimulate the labor movement without impeding economic development.

[78] Between 1949–50 and 1958–59, national income rose by 21 per cent from Rs.17.2 billion to Rs.20.8 billion; income generated by manufacturing rose by 118 per cent, but agricultural income increased by only 11 per cent. Per capita income increased by only 5 per cent, from Rs.232 to Rs.243 (all figures in constant 1949–1953 prices). Data supplied by the Central Statistical Office of the Government of Pakistan. Pakistan is finding it difficult to raise her rate of investment much above the 5 per cent level, which is about enough to cover replacement. See W. W. Rostow, "The Take-off into Self-Sustained Growth," *Economic Journal*, Vol. 66, March, 1956, pp. 25–48.

[79] Government of Pakistan, Ministry of Law and Labor, *First Pakistan Labour Conference, Proceedings*, Karachi, 1949, pp. 9–10.

It is the policy of government to encourage growth of genuine and healthy collective bargaining on the part of labour and to enable it to conduct negotiations with due appreciation of the country's economy. The fundamental object of government is to raise living standard. . . . Sound and healthy relationship between the employers and employees is a pre-requisite of increased productivity and efficiency. Economic progress demands industrial peace. In this country where industrialization is in its early stages Government are anxious that, while labour should get its just rights, industry should not be hampered by unnecessary upheavals and strikes. Government therefore believe in promoting the settlement of disputes between employers and employees in the interest of industrial peace through constitutional means . . . For this purpose government desire that genuine Trade Unionism be recognized. At the same time, however, Government must insure that Trade Unionism is not exploited for political purposes. Government are anxious that labor is not victimized for legitimate Trade Union activities.[80]

The above statement includes almost all the problems the government has encountered in its labor policy, which is obviously subservient to its industrial development policy. The policy statement included an ambitious list of specific objectives, some of which were acted upon, but many of which were never carried out before martial rule because the cabinet, and particularly the operating departments of government, which were the nation's largest employers, would not implement them.

It remained for the Martial Law government of General Ayub Khan to enact many of the labor welfare provisions which had remained only as statements of purpose with earlier regimes. His government has reflected the desire for order and central authority which is common to the soldier and bureaucrat. But because of its power and the lack of legislative restraint, the government has had the courage to enact many labor welfare measures. At the same time the government has hedged these welfare measures sufficiently to prevent their disruption of economic growth.

In 1959 a revised labor policy was announced which reasserted the importance of economic development, industrial peace and healthy trade unions. It promised speedy action to establish industrial courts for arbitration of industrial disputes, compulsory recognition of trade unions, a broader social insurance system, a more effective system of welfare officers in factories, and more adequate housing for industrial workers. Most of these promises have become realities, as is shown by the discussion of specific programs elsewhere in this study.

As a member of the International Labour Organization, Pakistan

[80] Government of Pakistan, "Labour Policy and Programme," press release, August 23, 1955.

has ratified twenty-three conventions. Since 1947, she has ratified seven conventions, including Convention 87 on the freedom of association and Convention 98 on the right to organize and bargain collectively. These conventions are policy statements which Pakistan is trying to live up to, although it is hard to do so.

We have said enough to indicate that the salient features of the labor policy of Pakistan both before and after martial law have been: the welfare of labor is desirable but is secondary to industrial development, encouragement of trade unions must stop short of impeding economic growth, work stoppages must be minimized through conciliation and arbitration, and labor unions should be apolitical.

LABOR LEGISLATION

At partition, Pakistan inherited from undivided India a reasonably extensive system of labor legislation, which was reaffirmed. However, from partition to 1958 the outstanding fact of labor legislation was its paucity. Although tripartite labor conferences repeatedly recommended specific action, and government policy statements favored such action, the legislative machinery was largely immobile. The primary reason for this was the political instability of the government and the preoccupation of legislators with staying in power and drawing up a constitution, which was not completed until 1956 (only to be abrogated in 1958). A second cause was the fear of disrupting economic development by welfare or labor legislation. Though there were seven or eight fairly important acts passed in the labor field, only one of them, the East Pakistan Minimum Wages Act of 1957, broke completely new ground.[81] Most labor matters are the subjects of concurrent jurisdiction of the central government and the provinces; most of the important legislation in fact is federal, but implementation is left to the provinces in a number of instances.

The basic act regulating terms and conditions of employment is the Factories Act of 1934, which covers factories employing 20 or more workmen and using power. Hours of work are limited to nine per day and 48 per week in perennial factories, unless double overtime rates are paid. After one year, employees are entitled to 10 days' annual leave with pay, and to one day of rest per week. The minimum work age is 12 years, adolescents' hours of work are limited, and they are

[81] The central and provincial governments inherited 100 labor acts from undivided India; between 1947 and 1958 the central government has passed 20 acts and the provinces 27, but most of them have been minor modifications of existing legislation. Shafi, *op. cit., passim*. The best survey of labor legislation and its implementation is found in the *Report of the ILO Labor Survey Mission*. The texts of the laws may be found in Shafi, *op. cit.*

excluded from certain dangerous occupations. Women are not permitted night work or overtime work, and are excluded from certain dangerous occupations; in factories with over 50 women, nurseries are to be provided for children under six. The ILO Labour Survey Mission found that most of these provisions, save the last, were reasonably well enforced. The Factories Act also provides considerable regulation of safety and hygiene, but the ILO reported much less strict observance in this field. This basic act has not been amended to meet new conditions since partition, although the ILO Mission recommended several changes, particularly in the areas of safety, hygiene, and better inspection.

There are somewhat similar acts for shops and commercial establishments, mines, ports and docks, railways, and ocean-going vessels, all of these being areas of central government jurisdiction, except the first. Altogether these acts apply to only a little more than half a million workers out of a labor force of 26 million.[82] Small establishments and agriculture are not covered. The ILO Mission reported that the labor inspectors hired to enforce these acts were untrained, underpaid, and overworked. Therefore, the acts cover much more than the government is presently able to implement.

In an earlier section we discussed the Industrial Disputes Act of 1947, and the ordinance of 1959, which provide for works committees in factories and establish the machinery for conciliation and arbitration of labor disputes.

The third basic act in the labor field before 1958 was the Trade Unions Act of 1926, which permitted seven or more persons to apply for registration of a union. Registered unions and their officers were exempted from punishment under charges of criminal conspiracy in restraint of trade and from civil suit for interference with trade. They were required to submit annual reports, they might not spend dues receipts for political purposes, and at least one-half their officers were required to be employed in the industry. The benefits of registration were not sufficient to entice all unions to register, and their annual reporting was very lax. This act offered very mild protection indeed for unions, and did not prevent union officers from being victimized by employers, which was the greatest complaint of Pakistani unionists.

The Trade Union ordinance of 1960 amended the previous act by providing for compulsory recognition of trade unions, as has been discussed. It remains to point out several additional provisions of this new

[82] Approximate numbers covered are: factories, 200,000; mines, 10,000; railroads, 150,000; shops and commercial establishments, 20,000; sea-going vessels, 125,000; docks and ports, 20,000. Shafi, *op. cit.*, p. 1652.

ordinance. Unfair labor practices are established for employers and unions, following the example of the Labor Management Relations Act of the United States. Unfair practices by the employer are: (1) to interfere with, restrain, or coerce workers in their right to form and join labor organizations, (2) to interfere with or support a union, (3) to victimize, discriminate against, or dismiss a union officer because of his union responsibilities, (4) to discriminate against a worker giving evidence under the ordinance. Unfair labor practices on the part of unions are: (1) to engage in irregular or illegal strikes, to instigate such, and failure to take action against members who engage in such activities, (2) to coerce a worker to join a union against his will, (3) to cause an untruth to be told in any report required of the union under the ordinance.

If a representative union is not recognized by the employer within three months, it may seek redress in the courts. If a union commits an unfair labor practice, it may be denied the right to recognition. The proportion of union officers who may be outsiders is reduced to one-quarter. Experience under the ordinance is so brief that its results cannot be assessed, but union leaders have hailed the action as the *Magna Charta* of labor.

There are a few other legislative acts which need only be mentioned. A welfare fund has been established for coal miners, financed by a tax on coal. The Workmen's Compensation Act is based on the principle of employer's liability, without enforcement procedure, and the employer's responsibility can be evaded by the use of contract labor. The maternity benefit laws apply primarily to women working on tea estates, so that coverage is quite inadequate. A number of the medium and large factories have provident funds, which are savings funds designed for retirement, but which under certain conditions may be withdrawn earlier. Under the Essential Services Act of 1952, as amended in 1958, the government can prevent any person from leaving his job or locality of work if he is in an essential service as defined by the government. Though not much used, this gives great power to government in limiting freedom of movement.

In 1960 the government appointed a commission to study ways of mobilizing large masses of unemployed and underemployed workers on capital improvement projects for the benefit of the nation. Part of this program involved a registration of all technical personnel on a national roster.

In 1957, East Bengal established the country's first Minimum Wage Board, which was gradually to work out minimum wages for the major industries. The federal government extended this principle after 1958 and is slowly establishing minimum wage rates by industry and by occupations within each industry. The government is in effect establishing the whole wage structure of each industry, but only a few industries have been affected as yet. This measure runs contrary to the philosophy President Ayub Khan has enunciated, of encouraging a free economy to provide for Pakistan's growth.

Inspection and enforcement leave much to be desired in those areas where legislation is not self-enforcing through complaints of the parties protected. Other functions of government are felt to be more crucial for national development, so the labor inspectorate staff has been much too small for its task. In East Bengal, in 1959, the Labor Commissioner had only 13 inspectors and 5 clerks to help him with his multifarious functions in a province of 37 million people. One can hardly blame the commissioner's office for its inability to police so many laws adequately. Yet the economy cannot afford too large an overhead of inspectors. The ability to implement legislation is thus one of the limiting factors on the amount and variety of legislation desirable. Better a few important laws well enforced, than many which only fill the statute books.

RELATIONS WITH TRADE UNIONS AND MANAGEMENT

The Pakistan government has its most direct relationships with unions as an employer. In 1953, government-run factories employed 73,000 workers, or 28 per cent of the workers in registered factories. The two government railroads are the largest employers in Pakistan, employing 120,000 workers in 1954. Some aspects of railway employment policy are excellent: the most complete system of welfare benefits and services for workers in Pakistan; assured security for "permanent" employees; training of workers' children for future skilled employment; and definite, published promotion ladders. But, like any big bureaucracy, railroads receive their full share of criticism. Workers complain that the grievance machinery, while specific, is too cumbersome for justice; the railroads bargain with railway unions only on the most restricted basis, with many subjects "off limits"; and unions charge that management is guilty of discrimination against union officers.

The Pakistan Industrial Development Corporation, which had built 70 factories up to 1959 at a cost of one billion rupees, is a major employer. The PIDC is primarily designed to supply entrepreneurial leadership and risk-bearing to get large new projects underway. It supplies part of the capital, but, once an enterprise is a going concern, tries to sell it to private interests. Under PIDC direction, some of the largest and most modern factories of Pakistan have been successfully launched. The Corporation has led the industrial community in recruiting and training much-needed management talent. Its record in the labor field is less uniform, with both good and bad reports from the unions which have relations with the various PIDC factory managements. For example, the 1954 Adamjee and Chandragona riots in East Bengal were in PIDC factories. The PIDC director frankly questions how far Pakistan can afford to go in encouraging labor unions and expanding social services.

Labor leaders feel government enterprises should be models for other employers, but they charge that government employers are almost as antiunion as private managements. The large number of industrial employees working directly for government agencies, which are expected to pay a return to the treasury, is certainly one reason for the slow development of needed labor legislation up to 1958.

In 1949, the government started a series of tripartite labor consultations, the Standing Labour Committee and the Tripartite Labour Conference, each of which meet about once a year. These meetings bring together 15 to 20 leaders divided about equally among labor, management, and government for two days of frank discussions.[83] Participants in these sessions, advisory in nature, have discussed and recommended to government numerous legislative actions in the labor field, but only a few of these recommendations have been followed. One function of the conference was to lend public support to the Minister's effort to guide the labor policy of the government. These consultations frequently showed government's hesitancy to saddle industry with additional financial burdens, and provide examples of the government's basic dilemma. Another function of these meetings is to discuss the approach Pakistan should take on matters raised by the ILO. However, probably their greatest service is to permit a free and unhurried exchange between outstanding labor and management leaders. Both groups admit the other has become more understanding of its point of view since the meetings began.

The ILO is another agency through which labor, management, and government are brought together in the interest of better understanding. Pakistan has been an active participant in ILO affairs, her Minister of Labor having been President of the ILO governing body. Twenty-three ILO Conventions have been ratified, and the frequency with which they are referred to in labor discussions and the Tripartite

---

[83] Each group has about the same number of delegates, but the Conference has a group of observers and advisors in attendance as well. The Committee is the basic group, determining the agenda for the larger meeting. Proceedings of the meetings are published by the Ministry of Labour.

Labour Conferences shows that these conventions are used as important benchmarks around which labor policy is formed. It is difficult for residents of highly developed countries to realize the great importance of the ILO in underdeveloped areas, both in matters of governmental policy and trade union affairs. On several occasions the ILO has caused Pakistan to redirect its labor policy. Finally, four of the most informative labor reports on Pakistan have been by ILO Technical Assistance Survey Missions.[84]

Up until 1958 the government gave only mild encouragement to trade unions, and did little to protect their members against victimization by employers. The dominant feeling of labor in this period was summed up: "There is a widespread feeling that government support to unionism does not go much beyond lip service." [85] The martial law government has given workers greater protection, and unions more encouragement, but at the same time the effectiveness of the strike weapon has been curbed. Unions are more dependent than ever upon the goodwill of the government. Persons in high planning circles in the government are frank to admit that union encouragement must "make haste slowly," only after it is demonstrated that union growth will not impede economic development.[86]

The government has been particularly cordial in its relations with the West Pakistan Federation of Labour and the East Pakistan Federation of Labour, and in fact the Minister of Labour was instrumental in their joining to form the APCOL as the most representative labor federation. The government even stated in its official 1955 labor policy program: "It is the objective of the Government to encourage the affiliation of the trade unions with the All-Pakistan Confederation of Labour." [87] On the other hand, while maintaining an officially correct position, the government has found ways to discourage Communist unions.

The most important way in which government affects the relations

---

[84] *Report of the ILO Labour Survey Mission;* Ministry of Labour, *Report of the ILO Mission on Social Security in Pakistan,* Karachi, 1954; Ministry of Labour, *Report on Labour Conditions in Agriculture in Pakistan* (Karachi, 1955), *Report of the ILO on Manpower Survey in Pakistan.*

[85] United States Government, International Cöoperation Administration, *Summary of the Labor Situation in Pakistan* (Washington, 1955), p. 8.

[86] The Director of the PIDC and the Chief Economist of the Planning Commission expressed this view in a seminar at the March, 1959, Pakistan Institute of Development Economics (mimeographed report), pp. 45, 56.

[87] Government of Pakistan, "Labor Policy and Programme," press release, August 23, 1955. The East Bengal martial law government was even prepared to require all unions to join the EPFL, but this was changed when the central government pointed out that it violated ILO Convention No. 87. Kriegal, *op. cit.,* pp. 143–147.

between employers and unions is through the machinery for compulsory union recognition and the settlement of labor disputes. Work stoppages have been kept at a minimum, which has blunted labor's major weapon considerably, but strikes have not been completely prohibited. Conciliators and arbitrators have kept in mind the requirements of rapid industrial development, which has had a strong influence on the type of labor agreements which they encourage. Through this process, industry has been persuaded to make considerable, but not crippling, concessions to labor. Young economies today find it more difficult to grow rapidly than did their more individualistic predecessors of the West during the last century, who could exploit labor with little fear of public opinion. Today world opinion and local pride require that Pakistan's workers receive at least a modicum of the protection and amenities which it has taken Western workers over a century to achieve.

Our final conclusion is that the government has sought to provide individual laborers with as much welfare and protection as it thought the economy could stand, but that, when the two were in conflict, this objective had to give way before the more important goal of economic development. In the author's opinion, up to 1958 the encouragement of organized unions stopped considerably short of the point at which it might have impeded economic growth. Union encouragement since 1958 has been much greater. It remains to be seen whether Pakistan can achieve simultaneously responsible unionism, freedom for employers, and adequate economic growth.

Chapter III Indonesia [1]

EVERETT D. HAWKINS

Labor relations in Indonesia, a newly independent country, are still primarily a function of the continuing nationalist revolution against colonial patterns. In both the fighting phase from 1945 to 1949 and the period of economic pressure from 1950 to 1958, Indonesian labor has been in the vanguard—so much so, in fact, that in both periods the government stopped the workers from taking over Dutch plants, and provided instead its own civil or military supervisors. With the end of Dutch political control and economic dominance, but with internal revolts still not fully suppressed, President Sukarno has since 1958 been exhorting his people to "complete the revolution" and to develop their own system of "guided democracy," "functional representation," and "socialism à la Indonesia." Although the trend toward more control is already apparent, until the basic economic and political framework of the nation is established, the patterns of labor relations will also be fluid.

[1] Much of the material was gathered during a field trip to Indonesia during the summer of 1956, made possible by travel grants from the Inter-University Study of Labor Problems in Economic Development and the Center for International Studies of the Massachusetts Institute of Technology. More recent data were gathered in 1958–1960 while the author was Visiting Professor in the Faculty of Economics, Gadjah Mada University, Jogjakarta, under a University of Wisconsin contract financed by the Ford Foundation. The author wishes to express his appreciation not only to the many trade union, management, and government officials in Indonesia who aided in the study, but also to certain members of the Institute of Economic and Social Research of the University of Indonesia and the Faculty of Economics of Gadjah Mada University. The author is also deeply indebted to several American experts, including Robert Kinney, Edgar McVoy, William Taylor, and Vidkunn Ulriksson, who shared so generously their extensive knowledge of Indonesian labor relations.

Unlike the colonial period, when unions had been controlled and strikes suppressed, the new republic freely gave labor the right to organize unions, to strike, and to have political representation. Soon after the granting of sovereignty, however, the Government established in 1951, as amended in 1957, a system of regional and central disputes committees to try to prevent unnecessary strikes. Gradually, through their compulsory arbitration powers, these committees established a system of industrial jurisprudence. When martial law was declared in 1957, strikes were prohibited in essential industries and, as part of the drive for West Irian, a whole series of new functional groups was established by the military, including the Labor-Military Organization (*Badan Kerdja Sama Buruh dan Militer*). As long as the state of war exists, the military will be a factor in the labor field. Furthermore, each of the large political parties, ranging from Moslem to Nationalist to Communist, has tried to form unions to further its own political interests. This has resulted in a multiplicity of unions, including a dozen trade union federations and many unaffiliated national and local unions.

Behind the drive for national political and economic independence stand certain long-run objectives. Indonesia, like a number of other newly independent countries, wants to raise the standard of living of its people by accelerating the process of economic development and industrialization, although the methods and techniques of achieving such change have not been agreed upon. The process of industrialization varies depending on a number of factors, including the source of capital, the supply of labor, the type of management, and the speed of industrialization.

In the colonial period, capital was supplied by the Dutch, by forced labor, and by ploughing back some of the export profits into plantations, mining, and transportation facilities. Management of large business firms was foreign and applied authoritarian methods, supported generally by the colonial government, with a growing layer of paternalistic practices and laws. Part of the revolution was the drive to defeat such controls. Foreign management, however, still ran most of the large firms until the end of 1957 when the New Guinea (West Irian) dispute set off a whole series of actions against the Dutch. This forced an acceleration of the "Indonesianization" of management and staff employees, with the military taking the lead in filling the gap until more Indonesian managers could be trained. Furthermore, although some capital may be raised by foreign loans and from private internal sources, the government will undoubtedly be an increasingly important source of capital.

Although the Parliament finally adopted the first Five-Year Plan

(1956–1960) at the end of 1958, most Indonesian observers agree that the expulsion of the Dutch in 1957 and the rebellions starting in 1958 so adversely affected many aspects of economic life that some parts of this very modest Plan could not be implemented.[2] The new National Planning Council appointed by Sukarno in 1959, in the framework of the "Return to the Constitution of 1945," faced gigantic tasks, including budget deficits, shortages, and inflation,[3] as it tried to develop a realistic Eight-Year Plan for 1961–68. Planning thus far has not affected employment or production enough to have had an appreciable effect on low-wage, job-conscious Indonesian labor. Planning is further complicated by the wide differences (1) in the size of plant, (2) in the oversupply of labor, especially in Java, and the relative shortage of labor in some of the other islands, and (3) the lack of a sufficient number of skilled workers, professionals, and managers with adequate training and experience.

Background Factors

The complexity of labor relations in Indonesia is a product of the rapid transition from colonial to independent status. Labor relations reflect the present stage of economic and social development, in which the basic village life has been modified by some commercialization and industrialization, but low standards of living reflect low productivity and low wages. The different stages of economic development, the variety of cultural patterns, and the varying degrees of political stability in the many islands of the country, make it important to temper generalizations about background factors with frequent reference to the diversity within Indonesia.

AGRICULTURAL SETTING

Indonesia still remains predominantly an agricultural economy, with three-fourths of the labor force engaged in agriculture and related fields as a main or secondary occupation. From 1953–1958, the agricultural sector contributed between 53 and 58 per cent of the national income. Agriculture is carried on not only in big, largely foreign-built estates which produce for export such crops as rubber, tea, coffee, copra, fibers

---

[2] For a report on the first three years of the Plan, see Government of Indonesia, Biro Perantjang Negara (National Planning Bureau), *Laporan Pelaksaan Rentjana Pembangunan Lima Tahun 1956–1960 Mengenai Tahun-Tahun 1956, 1957 dan 1958* (*Report of the Implementation of the Five-Year Plan* [1956–1960] *during the years 1956, 1957, and 1958*) (Djakarta, 1959).

[3] For a discussion of the economic and political problems in Indonesia, 1959, see Willard A. Hanna, *Bung Karno's Indonesia* (New York: American Universities Field Staff Reports Service, 1960).

and spices, but also in many smallholdings operated by Indonesians primarily for domestic food supply, rice being the main crop. In recent years, however, the smallholding production of rubber has exceeded the quantity coming from the estates.

Since agricultural products account for one-half to two-thirds of the total exports, they are also an important factor in the economy of the country. In 1957 total exports had risen to over Rp.11 billion, with agriculture accounting for 60 per cent of the total.[4] In 1958 agricultural exports were valued at over Rp.4.8 billion, out of a greatly reduced total of about Rp.8.6 billion; more than Rp.2.5 billion was paid for small-holder crops and over Rp.2.2 billion came from the estates. Minerals, chiefly petroleum and tin, constituted most of the remaining exports.[5] In 1959, exports had increased to an annual rate of Rp.9.9 billion, with a substantial increase in production from the smallholders and a small increase from the estates.[6]

The estates were fostered by the Dutch as export earners. This has caused a high degree of commercialization in the estate crops, in contrast to the general subsistence farming among the smallholders. On the estates, a majority of the workers now belong to one of a score or more of estate workers' (*buruh*) unions, while a number of farmers' (*tani*) organizations serve the smallholder. The diversity of organizations reflects not only political differences but also the divergent economic interests of the workers and the farmers. Much of the small farmer's earnings are in the form of food consumed by the family, supplemented by money from the sale of some of his crops. Even when outside workers are hired to help with the harvest, the pay usually takes the form of a share of the crop (one-sixth of the rice cut is frequently accepted as a fair share for the harvest worker). To the extent that the farmers sell their crops to the cities, to exporters, or to the estates for distribution to their workers, the smallholders are drawn into the money economy, but not as yet into a modern wage economy. While money wages are infrequently paid by the smallholders, the workers on the estates are employed and paid a monetary wage supplemented by various payments in kind, allowances, and rights.

---

[4] Bank Indonesia, *Report of the Governor of Bank Indonesia for the Financial Year 1957–1958* (Djakarta), pp. 124–129.

[5] Government of Indonesia, Biro Pusat Statistik, *Monthly Survey* (*Statistik Konjunktur*), November–December, 1959, p. 35. For earlier figures, see: Government of Indonesia, Biro Pusat Statistik, *Statistical Pocketbook of Indonesia, 1958;* and Benjamin H. Higgins, *Indonesia's Economic Stabilization and Development* (New York: Institute of Pacific Relations, 1959), pp. 65–68, 157.

[6] Government of Indonesia, Biro Pusat Statistik, *Graphs on the Economic Development of Indonesia, First Half of 1959*, p. 16; *Statistik Konjunktur* (*Monthly Survey*) (October–November, 1960), p. 27.

Since the earnings of many farmers are so low, and since many are fully employed only part of the year, they and their wives and children take on supplementary jobs at low rates of pay. Secondary jobs are the rule in the rural areas around Jogjakarta in Central Java.[7] Many men and women in rural areas have migrated to the cities, and there they have to accept whatever jobs they can find. The large rural overpopulation, especially in Java, Madura, and Bali, therefore contributes to the low wage structure of the country. The various transmigration schemes, discussed below, to transfer people from overcrowded Java to the outer islands, have had no substantial effect on the unequal labor supply of the islands, nor have plans to open up large areas of land by means of heavy machinery greatly increased the supply of food.

Within Indonesia there are great differences in degree of intensity of farming. In Java and parts of Sumatra there is rich volcanic soil which makes possible intensive cultivation of rice and other crops. With an even, warm temperature and a relatively plentiful rainfall, aided by a complex system of irrigation, it is possible to grow paddy (wet-field) rice plus another crop in a year's time. This is not so true in some of the outer islands, where the poor jungle soils are quickly leached of their valuable mineral contents. Here much more primitive methods of "shifting" (*ladang*) agriculture are practiced. A family burns an area to clear the ground, plants crops for several years, and then moves on to another area when the soil is depleted. Such a destructive system is possible only where the population is relatively sparse; on Java, Madura, and Bali, the intensive forms of wet and dry cultivation are used.

Indonesia grows a great variety of vegetables, root crops, and fruits for its own consumption. After independence it made some progress on the road to self-sufficiency in its rice production, but since 1955 rice deficits have been large, making it necessary to secure large quantities of surplus rice from the United States and China as well as the usual rice surplus countries of Southeast Asia. The government, through the Ministry of Agriculture, is pushing a program of better seed selection, increased use of commercial fertilizers, and better methods of cultivation to increase the yields per hectare. To the extent that these programs are successful, foreign exchange will be released for needed imports of capital goods and raw materials.[8]

Up to the electioneering period of 1955, the farmers and the rural

[7] Gadjah Mada University, Bureau of Economic Research, *Consumer Finances in the Region of Jogjakarta: A Preliminary Report on Research Conducted in August,* 1959 (Jogjakarta, January, 1960).

[8] Only a very little cotton, which is the basic material for Indonesian clothing, is produced within the country. Experiments are being started in Bali and in some of the Lesser Sunda Islands to try to grow more cotton.

communities had been somewhat neglected by Djakarta and the politicians. Great efforts were then made to organize the farmers and to secure their votes. With the national and local elections over, there was some tendency to concentrate attention on the cities and on international affairs, although the President endorsed the beginnings of a program for rural community development.[9]

For obvious political reasons the government tended to help the individual smallholders rather than the large estates, then owned primarily by foreigners, but the government now runs the former Dutch estates and needs the revenues which come more easily from taxing estate crops. One cabinet fell because of the difficulty of freeing estate lands from squatters in the North Sumatra area. Furthermore, some estate leases other than those run by the Dutch are coming up for renewal in the near future. Unless the owners are assured that they will be able to renew their leases, they will not make the capital investments necessary to improve the level of production and to pay higher wages. For example, unless rubber trees of high yield are planted, Indonesia will no longer be able to compete with the estate rubber of Malaya.[10] The same problems now face the Indonesian government where its officials have taken over the management of the Dutch estates.

For some time Indonesia will depend on agriculture as the main source of income, both domestic and foreign. Although efforts are being made to eliminate the colonial elements on the estates, there is heavy dependence on their production to supply the necessary foreign exchange. Since estate workers are the largest group of organized workers, the labor movement itself must be concerned with agricultural problems of yields, markets, and fluctuating world prices. It must also consider the vast rural labor supply, most of which is looking for supplementary sources of employment and income.

COMMERCIALIZATION AND INDUSTRIALIZATION

Although Indonesia remains primarily an agricultural economy, a considerable degree of commercialization has taken place in at least part of the economy, and there are some beginnings of industrialization. Just as the agricultural economy is divided into the large commercial

---

[9] Technical experts from India have been consulted. S. K. Dey, "*Gotong Royong* or *Alang-alang?* A draft scheme for a community development programme in Indonesia," *Ekonomi dan Keuangan Indonesia,* Vol. VIII, No. 9 (September, 1955), pp. 528–587.

[10] However, in spite of the many difficulties, a substantial yearly replanting program has been carried out by Goodyear at their Dolak Merangir estate in North Sumatra.

estates and the smallholdings, so commerce has, until recently, been generally divided into the large and middle-sized businesses, which were foreign-owned, and the very small businesses, which were owned by Indonesians, such as market-stall operators, peddlers, carters, and *betjak* drivers.[11] Until the end of 1957, foreigners, including Dutch, British, American, Chinese, Indian, and Arab businessmen, owned and operated most of the large estates, banks, trading firms, and manufacturing companies. Under the Dutch regime, foreign trade had been a monopoly of the Big Five Dutch import and export companies, while the Chinese had been encouraged to engage in internal commerce. Indonesians had little opportunity to become businessmen and entrepreneurs on a large scale. The Indonesian elite, including the newly educated men, chose government positions rather than business careers. The role of savings, investment, and management is, therefore, relatively new to most Indonesians.

There are some exceptions to this rule: for some years Indonesians have been owners and managers of many of the handicraft industries, such as batik and silver work, but even here a large share of the selling of these products at wholesale and retail is still in the hands of the Chinese.[12] The coöperative movement, grown to include by 1958 over 2.2 million members in 13,971 coöperatives, with capital reserves of over RP. 750 million is managed almost exclusively by Indonesians.[13] Management of all regular government services and various public enterprises such as the railways, telephone and telegraph, and estates, is now in Indonesian hands, with only an occasional foreign adviser or management training team.

At the present time the Indonesian government is committed both to providing its people with a higher standard of living, better health facilities, and more education, and to increasing the participation of Indonesians in trade and industry. Even before the take-over from the

---

[11] This dichotomy in the economy is analyzed by Professor J. H. Boeke, *Economics and Economic Policy of Dual Societies as Exemplified by Indonesia* (New York: Institute of Pacific Relations, 1953), and by J. S. Furnivall in *Netherlands India: A Study of a Plural Economy* (London: Cambridge University Press, 1944). See the article by Sadli, "Some Reflections on Professor Boeke's Theory of Dualistic Economies," *Ekonomi dan Keuangan Indonesia,* Vol. X, No. 6 (June, 1957), pp. 363–384. This article also discusses the paper by Benjamin H. Higgins, *The Dualistic Theory of Underdeveloped Areas,* MIT, Economic Development Program, Indonesia Project, A/55-24.

[12] Bintarto Hardjosuwignjo, "The Batik Industry in Central Java," *Ekonomi dan Keuangan Indonesia,* Vol. XI, No. 7 (July, 1958), pp. 345–401, esp. pp. 352–355, 375–377.

[13] Biro Perantjang Negara, p. 415 (cited in note 2). For earlier material see Mohammad Hatta, *The Coöperative Movement in Indonesia* (Ithaca: Cornell University Press, 1957), pp. 108–109.

Dutch in 1957, various "Indonesianization" programs had been started, calling upon foreign firms to train Indonesians for more of the high level positions. The government has, in dealing both with the Dutch and the Chinese since 1957, put its second commitment ahead of the first. Soon after independence the government offered loans to Indonesian firms to enter the export-import field. In 1959, however, eight government firms were given a monopoly in handling nine major classes of imports. Some Indonesian businessmen felt that private business was being limited by the introduction of this and other measures of a "guided economy."

Indonesia has not yet gone so far with over-all planning as India or Communist China. It started with a series of sector plans: various agricultural welfare plans, an industrial urgency program, and a ten-year educational program to wipe out illiteracy. After a National Planning Board of nine Cabinet members and a Planning Bureau of civil servants were established, United Nations experts came in 1952 to work with Bureau personnel to help devise an over-all plan. Early in 1955 Dr. Djuanda, who was then head of the Planning Bureau and who later became Prime Minister, indicated that preliminary planning for the first Five-Year Plan 1956–1960 would require investment in the government sector of about Rp.12.5 billion (more than a billion dollars at the then official rate of exchange) in new investments to be divided as follows:

13 per cent for agriculture, transmigration, and other projects of social improvement
25 per cent for irrigation, power, and multi-purpose projects
25 per cent for industry and mining
25 per cent for transportation and communication
12 per cent for education, health and social projects [14]

These percentages remained firm when the plan was officially submitted by the Cabinet to Parliament in the fall of 1956, and in the law which was finally enacted in November, 1958. The Planning Bureau issued a book taking up in each of the twenty chapters a particular area or part of the plan.[15] Priority was given to those projects which contributed to the country's balance-of-payments position, aided social welfare, or as-

[14] *Indonesian Observer,* March 17, 1955, p. 1.

[15] Government of Indonesia, Biro Perantjang Negara, *Garis-Garis Besar Rentjana Pembangunan Lima Tahun, 1956–1960* (Djakarta, 1957). Another volume included the proposed planning law, and a third, specifications for individual projects. See also Government of Indonesia, National Planning Bureau, "Some Explanations of Indonesia's 1956–1960 Five-Year Development Plan," *Ekonomi dan Keuangan Indonesia,* Vol. IX, No. 11 (November, 1956), pp. 661–682.

sisted key industries. The plan contained a series of proposals rather than a completely integrated program like India's.

The amount of investment contemplated in the first Five-Year Plan was modest, little more than the government had been investing in previous years. In spite of the political-military difficulties of 1957 and 1958, the Planning Bureau found that the government had invested in the three years 1956–1958 some Rp.7.3 billion, while only Rp.6.8 billion had been planned.[16]

Because of the disruption caused by the exodus of the Dutch in 1957 and the rebellions in 1958, the real national income, which had been rising from 1952 to 1957, fell sharply by an estimated 12.8 per cent in 1958. Indications are that real national income in 1959 did not rise significantly, although some sectors had recovered partially from the 1958 lows. Many industrial firms were complaining in 1959 about shortages of imported raw materials, spare parts, transportation, and working capital, the last especially after the monetary purge in August, 1959.

The President gave strong political backing to the new National Planning Council appointed by him in 1959 with 77 members from various geographical regions, functional groups, and political parties, to replace the old National Planning Board and Bureau. It was given the almost impossible job of developing within a year a realistic plan. The Council proposed in 1960 an ambitious Eight-Year Plan for 1961–1968. In order to finance this plan, Rp.240 billion of governmental investment will be needed, on an average of Rp.30 billion a year, which will amount to about 13 per cent of the 1960 income estimated at Rp.236 billion. About half of the required total, 2.7 billion dollars, is needed in foreign exchange. This will be secured largely from greatly expanded exports of oil, rubber, copra, and tin. The other half, or Rp.122 billion, would come from domestic sources: the monetary measures taken on August 25, 1959, capital of state enterprises, savings, sale of government obligations, sale of capital goods, and sale of consumption goods. In order to carry out the 335 proposed projects, a number of so-called "B" projects must be financed at a cost of Rp.39 billion. In essence these "B" projects encourage the exploitation of natural resources for export purposes, in order to finance the foreign exchange component of the plan. Whether or not the country will be able to exploit its own resources sufficiently to carry out such a large plan without serious inflation is still impossible to predict since, although the plan was approved

[16] Government of Indonesia, Biro Perantjang Negara, *Laporan, Report for the Years 1956, 1957 and 1958*, pp. 121–135 (cited in note 2). The real investment was probably less than shown because of price increases.

by the People's Congress at the end of 1960, it was not implemented in the first half of 1961.

Indonesia started out her independence with a heritage of strict Dutch controls, plus her own protective devices, which included old-fashioned infant industry protection and some of the latest twentieth-century exchange controls and licensing provisions. On top of these were placed a modest Five-Year Plan and, more recently, a whole new layer of military rules, "guided economy" regulations, and a new attempt at planning. Although foreign capital and management have played a decisive role in the past, for the time being most of the capital must be supplied directly or indirectly by the government, with public rather than private management being favored. Since the government controls so many phases of economic life, it is not surprising that labor relations are also subject to considerable regulation.

CULTURAL AND POLITICAL FACTORS

The motto "Unity through Diversity" is particularly appropriate for Indonesia, a country of thousands of islands and hundreds of ethnic groups having their own languages, customs, traditions, and *adat* or customary law. The Javanese, being the largest group, tend to play a central role in Indonesian life and are sometimes patronizing toward the people of the outer islands. On the other hand, some of the people in Sumatra look down upon the Javanese who were recruited to work on the estates. The Bataks of North Sumatra have developed rapidly in the field of business and trade,[17] and, since many are Christians, there is sometimes conflict with the Moslem majority. This also applies to some of the Menadonese from Sulawesi and the Ambonese from the Eastern Islands, who are also Christians and usually well educated. The Atjehnese, who live on the northern tip of Sumatra, are known to be fierce fighters; the Balinese have a wide reputation for their artistic ability; and the Minangkabau from Central Sumatra have done very well in government circles. Some Indonesian groups are primitive in relation to the vast bulk of the population—for example, the Dayaks in Kalimantan (Borneo) and the Sakais in Sumatra. Although it is

---

[17] A family relationship often exists between the Batak employer and his Batak workers, since many Bataks still resent being treated as employees. Furthermore, many of the workers actually hold a higher position in the family system than the employer. Strikes among Bataks are, therefore, most unusual. When Bataks move to Java and establish businesses there with Javanese workers, the situation is the more customary one of employer and employee. In Central Java, however, many of the small craft shops also operate under a Javanese family system with traditional rights and duties.

patriotic to stress Indonesian unity, these ethnic differences are sometimes important in political, social, and labor affairs.

The largest group of non-Indonesians consists of over two million Chinese. Although many of them have been in Indonesia for a long time, have intermarried, and no longer speak Chinese, there is a definite feeling against them because they have remained, as in other Asian countries, a group somewhat apart. This was probably accentuated because the Chinese were favored by the Dutch as local traders and money-lenders. Chinese firms and schools, sympathizing with the Kuomintang on Formosa rather than the Peking government recognized by Indonesia, were taken over by the Indonesian government in the fall of 1958. The following year the government ordered aliens (and this meant almost exclusively mainland Chinese) out of trade in rural areas as part of a program to Indonesianize business. Some of these displaced traders moved to urban areas, and some thousands of others early in 1960 returned to Mainland China. In addition, the country has a number of Eurasians whose position is also relatively tenuous at the present time, since under the Dutch they also had a privileged position, being paid at a higher rate than the Indonesians.

Although Indonesia is said to be 90 per cent Moslem, actually this figure is deceptive because there are many nominal Moslems,[18] who are frequently referred to as Red Moslems in comparison with the more orthodox White Moslems. Within the Moslem orthodox group itself there are certain modern progressive Moslems and some who are more traditional in their outlook.[19] The orthodoxy of the Moslems does not appeal to the nominal Moslems in Java, who are influenced more by Hindu-Buddhist culture and animism than by the Koran. The orthodox Moslems feel that they are a strong bulwark against Communism. The evidence seems clear that the Communists have not made inroads in this group, but rather among the less orthodox or nominal Moslems in East and Central Java. The other principal religions in Indonesia are Buddhism, Hinduism, and Christianity, both Protestant and Catholic. Although the government has played down religious differences and stresses religious freedom for all, religion often accentuates regional

[18] One of the author's friends referred to such Moslems as "statistical" Moslems: they are counted as Moslems, married as Moslems, but they do not perform the usual rites of a Moslem.

[19] For an excellent discussion of the role of the Moslem religion in economic activity in Java see the article by Clifford Geertz, "Religious Beliefs and Economic Behavior in a Central Javanese Town: Some Preliminary Considerations," *Economic Development and Cultural Change,* Vol. IV, No. 2 (January, 1956), pp. 134–158.

differences and has been the basis for the formation of several important parties and trade unions.

Caste is not important. In fact, only in Bali are there significant remnants of the system. There are still some class distinctions based on hereditary sultanates, but education is coming to be the new basis for distinction. Although the illiteracy rate was still over 90 per cent at the end of the colonial regime, the Dutch had provided a very thorough classical, continental education for a few Indonesians, some of whom had gone on to universities in the Netherlands for advanced training. Education became a sign of prestige and a way of securing a position in the government, although early in the twentieth century it was limited to those in the higher social brackets who were able to speak Dutch fluently.

Since the revolution, the right to education, to continue in school as long as possible, has become one of the fundamental rights. Considerable progress has been made in reducing the amount of illiteracy, both through adult education programs and by greatly increasing the number of primary schools. Some workers have learned to read and write, and many of their children now have a chance to go to primary schools. Great strides have also been made in teachers' education programs, middle schools, and universities. Technical education has been pushed by a number of specialized schools and training courses.[20] From their colonial experience, Indonesians have associated work with forced labor and, therefore, freedom in some of their minds meant freedom from work. To combat this point of view, government leaders have tried to encourage harder work; but the tradition of leisure and a good life still remains strong in the minds of many people. Among many educated people there is a prejudice against manual labor and a preference for white-collar jobs. Some of the graduates of senior technical high schools, however, are proud of their new positions.

An intense, nationalistic spirit exists in Indonesia as a result of the struggle against the Dutch and the newly won independence. This national feeling takes several forms: the Indonesians are very anxious to preserve their independence and are worried about any new foreign control of their country, their educational system, their unions, and their way of life. In foreign affairs they support an "active, independent" foreign policy and foreign aid from both the East and the West. They are united with other Asian/African countries of the Bandung group in attacking colonialism in any part of the world, and in return

[20] Everett D. Hawkins, "Labor-Management Relations as a Strategic Factor in Indonesia's Development," *Ekonomi dan Keuangan Indonesia,* Vol. XII, No. 4 (April, 1959), esp. pp. 148–151.

expect other countries to support them in their struggle to regain West Irian, the last remnant of Dutch control in the old area of the Netherlands East Indies. The negative unity against the Dutch, the Chinese, and all forms of colonialism and imperialism has not been matched by a positive unity in favor of economic and political programs and objectives. Indonesia is still a land of many islands and languages, many political parties, and many trade union federations. The goal of "Unity through Diversity" has not yet been attained.

The Emergence of an Industrial Labor Force

The long colonial period of feudal and paternal labor relations has left a peculiar mark on the emerging labor force.[21] The Dutch East India Company, with complete autocratic powers, was the instrumentality used from 1602–1799 to open the Indies as the center of the carrying trade and to monopolize the export of spices to Europe. Because of the Napoleonic Wars in Europe, the British under Raffles ruled the Indies for a short period early in the nineteenth century and tried to institute a number of reforms. In 1830 the Dutch government, however, introduced the "culture" or "forced cultivation" system in Java, which required that the Javanese work so many days a month on export crops which were turned over to the colonial government for sale on the world markets. By this method of compulsory labor, the colonial government was able to show a large profit and turn huge previous deficits into substantial surpluses. New crops were introduced from abroad, such as sugar, coffee, and rubber, all of which throve on the rich soils of Java. Furthermore, the Indies were the one large area on the equator, unlike equatorial Africa and South America, where it was easy to ship supplies in and take raw materials out because of the long coastline of the islands and the many rivers flowing to the sea. Slavery was gradually given up in the nineteenth century by the Dutch, but forced labor with government-supplied capital was the method used to exploit the commercial crops of Java. Actually, some of the profits from the sale of these raw materials supplied the capital to be ploughed back into the colonial economy.

Starting gradually with the Agrarian Law of 1870, the Netherlands government introduced the so-called "liberal" system which allowed

[21] For more detailed material on this period, see W. F. Wertheim, *Indonesian Society in Transition* (The Hague: W. van Haeve, Ltd., 1956), pp. 230–273; Amry Vandenbosch, *The Dutch East Indies* (Berkeley: University of California Press, 1942), esp. pp. 284–292; Bruno Lasker, *Human Bondage in Southeast Asia* (Chapel Hill: University of North Carolina Press, 1950); Virginia Thompson, *Labor Problems in Southeast Asia* (New Haven: Yale University Press, 1947), pp. 117–166.

private businessmen rather than the government to develop the export crops. Labor was forcibly recruited by the various Indonesian rulers who were required to supply a given quantity for the estates and for the construction of harbors, highways, and railways. As the labor supply in Java increased, compulsory labor gave way to estate labor which was paid low wages. Compulsory labor service for public works disappeared in the Dutch-ruled areas of Java in the twentieth century, but continued until the 1930's in the outer islands and in the areas under indirect or Javanese rule.

Starting at the end of the nineteenth century, business firms turned to Sumatra and some of the other outer islands for further areas to exploit with export crops. Because of the labor shortages in these areas, plantation owners used all sorts of recruiting devices to secure labor from Java, China, and India. Labor contracts were authorized by the Coolie Ordinance of 1880 which tied the worker to his job for a definite period of years; violations of this contract by a worker were punishable by jail sentences. Because of the fear of losing scarce workers, labor contracts with the penal clause were not discarded in the outer islands until after some pressure had been applied by a convention of the International Labor Organization and by certain provisions in the U.S. Tariff Act of 1930.

In spite of the "ethical" policy (paternalism) which was started in 1901 by the Dutch to provide better conditions for the Indonesians, the latter had a strong feeling that work was something which the Dutch imposed upon them and that the private foreign employers could go to the government to have the labor laws enforced against them. In the revolt against forced work, against employers, and against a government that supported employers, trade unions were formed starting in 1908.

While Indonesia has a surplus of labor in the islands of Java, Madura, and Bali, and a relative shortage in the other islands, there is still an over-all shortage of trained personnel. Many of the major companies in Sumatra and the other islands today still have recruiting campaigns to encourage Javanese to accept jobs away from Java. This is done by urging Javanese workers already in Sumatra to have their families and friends join them. Already there is a second and third generation of Javanese who are staying to work on the plantations or in the oil fields in Sumatra. The public employment offices and the various transmigration schemes encourage Javanese to move to the outer islands, but in no case have the migrations been large enough to reduce substantially the labor surplus in Java.[22]

---

[22] The Department of Transmigration of the Ministry of Social Affairs moved more than 160,000 persons from 1950 to 1957, and the Bureau of Employment

Both the population and the labor force in Indonesia have increased remarkably in the last 140 years. Table 6 shows that, according to census data prepared by the Dutch, the population in the islands of Java and Madura increased almost ten times from 1815 to 1930. Since 1930 there has been no complete census of Indonesia, and the data,

TABLE 6

POPULATION OF INDONESIA, 1815–1960 (IN MILLIONS)

Year	Indonesians Java and Madura	Indonesians Outer Islands	Others	Total
1815 census	4.5	—	—	—
1860 census	12.5	—	—	—
1905 census	30.0	9.7	.7	40.4
1930 census	41.7	18.2	1.6	61.5
1940 estimate	47.5	22.2	1.7	71.4
1950 estimate	49.3	25.6	1.8	76.6
1954 estimate	52.0	27.1	2.0	81.1
1957 projection	—	—	—	84.7–86.0
1960 projection	—	—	—	88.6–91.3

SOURCE: "The Population of Indonesia," *Ekonomi dan Keuangan Indonesia*, Vol. IX, No. 2 (February 1956), Appendix D, I and II.

therefore, are based on estimates. Professor N. Keyfitz estimated that the total population of Indonesia in 1954 was 81.1 million, approximately double that in 1905. The projections for 1960 made by the Planning Bureau show an estimated population of about 90 million.

A substantial increase in the estimated working force is also evident from table 7. The Dutch census showed approximately 20.7 million employed in 1930, and the U.S. Department of Labor estimated about 30 million in 1953. The Planning Bureau used a figure of 33 million gainfully employed workers out of a population of about 85 million in 1956.[23] Of this number, about 8 million are people who are employed for a definite wage or salary. The rest are independent farmers, people engaged in trade or commerce, or unpaid family workers. Even within the wage or salary group the largest number are employed on the estates in essentially agricultural production, although it is well to remember that many of these estates do some processing in connection with rubber, sugar, palm oil, or sisal.

Of the 25,000 firms registered under Law No. 23 of 1953, there were

of the Ministry of Labor reported that about 90,000 people had left Java and Madura in the same period for jobs in the other islands. In addition, some veterans have been moved by the National Bureau for Reconstruction and the Bureau for Rehabilitation of Veterans. *Statistical Pocketbook of Indonesia, 1958*, pp. 16, 243.

[23] *Garis-Garis Besar Rentjana Pembangunan Lima Tahun, 1956–1960*, p. 150 (cited in note 15).

about 575 with over 500 employees and 1,500 more with 100 to 500 workers, mostly estates, tobacco firms, textile plants, and various kinds of transportation concerns. Over one-third of the estates have more than 500 employees, but most industrial firms have fewer than 20

TABLE 7

ESTIMATED OCCUPATIONAL DISTRIBUTION OF THE INDONESIAN LABOR FORCE, 1930 AND 1953 (IN THOUSANDS)

Occupation	1930 [a]	1953 [b]	Per cent increase of 1953 over 1930
Agriculture [c]	12,789	18,200 [d]	28.4
Plantations	1,387		
Mining	161	4,000 [e]	69.5
Manufacturing	2,199		
Transportation	304	800	163.2
Commerce	1,262	3,000	137.7
Professions	157	200	27.4
Government	495	1,800	263.6
Other	1,993	2,000	0.4
Total	20,747	30,000	44.6

[a] ILO, *Report to the Government of Indonesia on Social Security* (ILO/TAP/Indonesia/R.3) (Geneva, 1953), p. 75. From the 1930 Census.
[b] U.S. Department of Labor, Bureau of Labor Statistics, *Summary of the Labor Situation in Indonesia* (Washington, July, 1955), and earlier publications.
[c] Includes farming, forestry, stock breeding, fishing, and hunting.
[d] Production of raw materials.
[e] Industry.

workers. The vast bulk of plants and firms are, therefore, relatively small; family ties are frequently important. More industrial workers are at the handicraft than at the modern factory stage of production.

Starting in 1956, the Ministry of Labor has gathered considerable new and more detailed manpower and labor force data. The manpower survey conducted in June, 1956, indicated that there were only about a million employees in large firms with over 100 workers, and that the employers anticipated considerable seasonal employment, especially on the sugar estates and among the unskilled workers who made up almost 65 per cent of the employees.[24]

The first preliminary figures from the Ministry of Labor sample survey of the labor force in Java and Madura indicated that 27 million,

[24] Government of Indonesia, Ministry of Labor, Manpower Directorate, "Laporan Penjelidikan Tenaga Kerdja (Manpower Survey) Tahun 1956," *Ekonomi dan Keuangan Indonesia,* Vol. XI, No. 1 (January, 1958), pp. 2–44. More detailed information was published for the city and region of Sukabumi in Ministry of Labor, Manpower Directorate, *Laporan Projek Pertjobaan Pasar Kerdja (Pilot Project Employment Information) Dalam Wilajah Kota dan Kabupaten Sukabumi,* January 30, 1957.

or 47.7 per cent of the population of 56.6 million, had worked during 1958, with a great deal higher percentage working in the rural than the urban areas.[25] (See table 8.) Since Java and Madura account for about 65 per cent of the total population, a simplified projection would

TABLE 8

TOTAL POPULATION CLASSIFIED BY THOSE IN THE WORKING FORCE (WORKING AND UNEMPLOYED), THOSE NOT IN THE WORKING FORCE, AND THOSE OF WORKING AGE, IN RURAL AND URBAN AREAS ON JAVA AND MADURA, 1958

	Rural	Urban	Total
Population	48,339,274	8,225,033	56,564,307
Working force			
Working	23,957,545	2,636,415	26,593,960
Fully unemployed	195,294	201,488	396,782
Total	24,152,839	2,837,903	26,990,742
Not in working force	7,728,177	2,716,399	10,444,576
Total of working age	31,881,016	5,554,302	37,435,318

Working Force

Rural	49.9 per cent of the population
Urban	34.5 per cent
Java and Madura	47.7 per cent

SOURCE: Ministry of Labor, Manpower Directorate. Preliminary data.

be about 40 million in the labor force of all Indonesia in 1958. The Ministry was able to cross-classify information for about 24 million people who held jobs when the survey was taken, or about 40 per cent of the population of Java and Madura. Table 9 indicates that in Java and Madura, 68 per cent of those having jobs were engaged in agricultural or related occupations, 11 per cent in trade, 8 per cent in manufacturing, slightly less in services, including the government, and 5 per cent in all other occupations. Classifying the labor force by status, the Ministry found that about 8 per cent of the total were owners who employed other people (but three-fourths of these were engaged in agriculture); 31 per cent were owners without workers; 32 per cent, unpaid family workers; and only 29 per cent, paid workers. The Ministry also reported less than 1 per cent (172,426) in professional and technical positions, and about 1 per cent as managers, directors, and

[25] Data supplied by the Manpower Directorate of the Ministry of Labor. The marked rural-urban differences in the working force were also found in the region of Jogjakarta. In Jogjakarta on the average only 45 per cent of the population was in the labor force. See Gadjah Mada University, Bureau of Economic Research, *op. cit.*, pp. 19–23.

administrative staff. About 44 per cent of the working force were female, with women very important in agriculture, trade (in which they exceeded men), and industry.

TABLE 9

TOTAL NUMBER OF PEOPLE IN JAVA AND MADURA 12 YEARS OF AGE OR OVER WHO HAVE JOBS IN RURAL AREAS, CLASSIFIED ACCORDING TO INDUSTRY AND STATUS, 1958

	Owners with workers	Owners without workers	Workers	Members of a family who work without wages	Total
Agriculture	1,704,930	4,204,849	3,802,224	6,666,437	16,378,440
Mining	2,239	5,429	22,319	5,729	35,766
Industry	79,271	701,528	798,102	416,351	1,995,252
Construction	5,768	33,959	213,489	5,980	259,196
Public utilities	—	—	4,903	—	4,903
Commerce	106,902	2,089,491	129,317	390,218	2,715,928
Transportation	6,868	141,869	104,852	3,740	257,329
Services including government	27,767	287,214	1,463,321	85,178	1,863,480
Other	1,723	2,614	421,829	9,323	435,489
Total	1,935,468	7,466,953	6,960,356	7,583,006	23,945,783

SOURCE: Ministry of Labor, Manpower Directorate. Preliminary data.

The figures on total unemployment in this report were very low, about 1.5 per cent of the total who worked during the year, but in the urban areas the percentage was about 7 per cent of the labor force. A similar figure was found in the sample survey conducted in the city of Bandung in 1957.[26] About 7.2 per cent were unemployed, plus 4.4 per cent who were not actually working when the survey was taken. In addition, 9.3 per cent of those employed were working less than 35 hours a week. Estimates of disguised unemployment of as high as 10 to 15 million have been made for the country as a whole—the great bulk in rural areas.[27] Undoubtedly, Indonesia has a substantial number of partially and totally unemployed and underemployed people, particularly on crowded Java.[28]

[26] *Ekonomi dan Keuangan Indonesia,* Vol. XI, Nos. 3–4 (March–April, 1958), pp. 115–157; and Vol. XI, No. 10 (October, 1958), pp. 581–599.

[27] *Ekonomi dan Keuangan Indonesia,* Vol. VIII, No. 7 (July, 1955), p. 436.

[28] Unfortunately, figures from the 109 public employment offices do not give any real clue to the volume of unemployment, since the number of job placements has been so small, from 18,000 to 35,000 a year, that most of the unemployed have not registered. *Statistical Pocketbook of Indonesia* (1957), pp. 222–223.

The early Dutch experience indicates that it was difficult to hold a labor force on the job, that is, to commit a labor force to continued employment, and, therefore, various forms of force were utilized. Many of the workers who go to Sumatra or the other islands for their first tour of duty still decide they wish to return to Java and their own agricultural villages. Most of the large employers, however, indicated that they have a high percentage of long-service workers; in fact, once an employee gets attached to a firm he tends to stay even if the employer might like to reduce the force. In other words, after a short space of time there is often an overcommitment of the labor force. New Indonesian unionists are very job-conscious and attempt most vigorously to control the total number of jobs and to resist all attempts to reduce the number of positions, even if the amount of work has been reduced. This has been a particular problem for the sugar mills, which needed larger numbers of workers initially to put their fields and mills back into operation at the end of the revolution than they now need for normal operations.

Some employers report a tendency for workers to be irregular in their attendance. Other large employers, who have kept accurate records on absenteeism and enforce discharge rules for frequent absence, find that the rate for all absences, including excused absences, is relatively low. In order to meet the absence problem several devices have been used. Some firms pay a seventh-day wage if the worker has been present continuously for six days. A more difficult problem has been the tendency of workers not to work the full day. To meet this, some firms pay a bonus for those who complete a full day's work. In some areas of Indonesia where attachment to the job is relatively new, there may still be a tendency to work just long enough to earn a specific sum of money and then to enjoy leisure. Inflationary pressures, however, causing a rise in the cost of living, have tended to make workers more regular in their employment, work a full week, and even find supplementary employment.

Moreover, there has been a rapid movement to the cities since the census of 1930, and this movement continued in the '50's. From 1930 to 1956, population in the country as a whole rose about 40 per cent, but 12 out of the 13 principal cities listed by the Bureau of Statistics had more than doubled in population in that period, and six of this group had increased more than 3½ times. This means that the urban areas have an increasing supply of labor which has already given up rural farm life for other forms of employment. Much of this labor force is relatively unskilled and unused to the regular discipline of more industrialized employment. In most urban centers of Java, therefore, the problem is not one of recruitment or commitment of labor, but rather of how to train and energize a productive labor force.

The Development of Labor Organizations

Since their birth in 1908, Indonesian trade unions have been influenced by nationalist aspirations for freedom. Political and ideological considerations have frequently been more important than economic demands. Leadership, whether Moslem, nationalist, Socialist, or Communist, still plays a more important role than the rank-and-file membership. Diversity in leadership has resulted in multiple unions in many plants and in twelve national federations, each with a known political orientation. Because of its role in agitating for freedom and actually fighting for independence, and because of the strength of the unions in key sectors of the economy, labor has been granted a significant role in the Republic of Indonesia. Unions are one of the functional groupings recognized as important in the attempts in 1958–1960 to reorganize the country's political life.

Trade union history in Indonesia can be divided into six major periods:

1. The early beginnings from about 1908 through World War I when the influence of the nationalist *Serikat Islam* was strong.
2. The 1920's, when Communist leadership was most active.
3. The 1930's, when more moderate leadership was in control.
4. The period of suppression during the Japanese occupation, 1942–1945.
5. The growth of unions and the birth of the national federation SOBSI during the revolution, 1945–1949.
6. The struggle among the various labor federations after gaining independence, 1950 to date.

POLITICAL ORIENTATION AND IDEOLOGICAL LEANINGS [29]

Just as the political parties can be divided along ideological lines into four categories—nationalist, religious, Socialist, and Communist—so the unions have been subject to the same forces. Because nationalism and freedom have been overriding considerations since the start of the trade union movement, almost all unions have been motivated by the drive for political and economic independence from Dutch colonialism.

[29] See Iskandar Tedjasukmana, *Political Character of the Indonesian Trade Union Movement* (Southeast Asia Program, Modern Indonesian Project, Monograph Series [Ithaca: Department of Far Eastern Studies, Cornell University, 1959]); J. Henry Richardson, "Indonesian Labor Relations in Their Political Setting," *Industrial and Labor Relations Review*, Vol. XII, No. 1 (October, 1958), pp. 56–78.

Only later did these ideological influences tend to be so strong as to divide labor's drive for national independence.

Until 1921 the most important organization which supported the struggling labor unions was the *Serikat Islam*, a nationalist religious movement, formed in 1912, which grew rapidly by including in its membership intellectuals, religious leaders, merchants, peasants, and laborers. As is frequently the case in colonial and underdeveloped areas, the first Indonesian unions were made up of government and railroad and other transportation workers. Only gradually did unions spread to some of the estates and industries. The first union in Indonesia, the Union of Railway and Tramway Personnel (*Vereeniging van Spoor en Tramweg*), was formed in Semarang, Java, in 1908.[30] Other unions which followed were those of customs officers and teachers in 1911, officials of the state pawnshops in 1913, employees of the State Opium Monopoly in 1916, and officials of the Treasury and Public Works Department in 1917. During the war period several nongovernmental unions were started, the most important of which were the Agricultural Workers in 1915 and the Union of Factory Workers in 1917. "At the end of December, 1919, the *Serikat Islam*'s central leadership managed to unite twenty-two Indonesian trade unions totalling 77,000 members, under one of its leaders, R. M. Soerjopranoto." [31] By August, 1920, the *Persatuan Pergerakan Kaum Buruh* (PPKB), the first Central Federation of Labor in Indonesia, could boast of 150,000 members. It elected Semaun, a railroad worker and a leader of the radical Semarang branch of *Serikat Islam,* as its first president; Soerjopranoto, a moderate, as its vice-president; and Hadji Agus Salim, who was to become the "elder statesman" of the Republic of Indonesia, as its secretary.

At this very first meeting the president, Semaun, who had helped Sneevliet, Bergsma, and other Dutch left-wingers to organize in 1917 a Social Democratic Federation of Indonesia, tried to wrest control of the new federation from *Serikat Islam* leaders. Being unsuccessful in this attempt, Semaun and Tan Malaka, following the lead of the Third International, took a group of fourteen unions out of the Central Federation of Labor and formed a new revolutionary trade union center. This left the Central Federation of Labor under the direction of moderate leaders who favored political representation of labor, social legislation, and adequate wage regulation. In 1922 Semaun was success-

---

[30] An organization for Dutch workers, the National Arbeids Secretariat, dates back to 1890. For more details on the history of trade unions in Indonesia see Government of Indonesia, Ministry of Labor, *Gerakan Buruh Indonesia* (*Indonesian Labor Movement*) by Sandra (Djakarta, 1958) (mimeo).

[31] George McT. Kahin, *Nationalism and Revolution in Indonesia* (Ithaca: Cornell University Press, 1952), p. 75.

ful in forming a new all-embracing federation, the Union of Indian Labor Unions, or *Persatuan Vakbonden Hindia* (PVH). Thus the split between the Socialists and the Communists which rocked European labor after the Russian Revolution and World War I had its counterpart in the unions and labor parties of Indonesia.

During the '20's, after splitting off the branches they controlled from *Serikat Islam*, the Communists were active in organizing political parties and trade unions, in leading many strikes, and finally, in 1926, in trying to organize a revolt against the Dutch. The Dutch government gradually passed tighter antistrike measures and finally outlawed the Communist party of the Indies in 1927. Starting with Sneevliet in 1918 and Tan Malaka in 1922, most of the Communist leaders were jailed, exiled, or expelled from the country. Semaun himself had to leave in 1923 and went to Moscow, where he remained as a teacher of the Indonesian language until 1957. In 1959 Sukarno appointed him one of the five members of the new Supervisory Commission for Government Affairs.

During the '30's Indonesian labor groups turned away from revolutionary Communist leadership and looked to the evolutionary Social Democratic and Christian trade union movements of Europe. Hadji Agus Salim, after attending the International Labor Conference in 1929, organized a National Federation of Public Servants, or *Persatuan Vakbonden Pegawai Negeri* (PVPN), which was made up of fourteen unions and about 30,000 members. In 1931 the PVPN affiliated with the International Federation of Trade Unions. The depression of the '30's and the arrest of many Indonesian leaders slowed up the drive for national independence.

During the period of suppression by the Japanese, many trade union leaders went underground and learned new techniques of organization. Others had opportunities to hold higher political offices than they had had under the Dutch. The Indonesian language was fostered by the Japanese, and in general the Indonesian leaders looked on this period as one of temporary occupation.[32]

The end of the war came sooner than had been anticipated, creating a problem as to what the next step should be. The Japanese had indicated that they would eventually give the Indonesians freedom. Some leaders felt, therefore, that they should wait and take no hasty action;

[32] This belief was fostered by an old legend which said that there would be conquerors from the north for a short period of time, but that soon the Indonesians would be free. This was widely believed and was a factor which encouraged them to plan for eventual freedom.

on the other hand, a group of seventeen young medical students kidnapped Sukarno and Hatta and insisted that they sign an immediate declaration of independence on August 17, 1945.

Labor was one of the first groups to offer its services to the revolution. A revolutionary workers' army was organized, together with a women's corps. Instead of limiting labor, as had the colonial government, the new republic tended to encourage trade unions. The government, however, was worried about workers' groups taking over Dutch plants in syndicalist fashion under the leadership of Tan Malaka, who was an anti-Stalinist Communist. The government wanted the control in its own hands.[33] Iwa Kusuma Sumantri, later president of Padjadjaran University in Bandung, a left-wing labor leader who had been exiled by the Dutch, was appointed the first Minister of Social Affairs, and tried unsuccessfully to organize in September, 1945, one universal federation of labor, the Indonesian Labor Front or *Barisan Buruh Indonesia* (BBI).

Among the groups which were organized soon after the revolution, some out of prewar remnants, were the estate workers, the oil workers, the railroad workers, the gas and electricity workers, seamen, miners, teamsters, longshoremen, pawnshop employees, printers, and teachers. These groups formed several temporary organizations and in November, 1946, the All-Indonesian Central Labor Organization or *Sentral Organisasi Buruh Seluruh Indonesia* (SOBSI) was organized along industrial lines, but with craft unions having full equality. For a short time SOBSI, the first permanent federation in the postwar period, was for all practical purposes the sole federation in Indonesia. Since 1946, SOBSI and its affiliated unions have been in the vanguard of the revolutionary movement in Indonesia and have led the protests against Dutch imperialism, capitalism, and management.

During the early days of the revolution there was a short period of coöperation among most leftist groups. The left-wing coalition, or *Sajap kiri*, was made up of the Socialists (PSI), the Indonesian Labor party (PBI), the Communists (PKI), the Socialist Youth Organization (PESINDO), the Indonesian Peasant Front (BTI), and SOBSI. In 1948, however, Premier Sjarifuddin split the *Sajap kiri* by organizing a left-wing People's Democratic Front (Communist) to oppose the moderate Socialist wing led by Sjahrir, a former Premier. This new Communist front refused to join in a new coalition Cabinet of Socialists and

[33] Kahin, *op. cit.*, p. 474; Selo Soemardjan, "Bureaucratic Organization in a Time of Revolution," *Administrative Science Quarterly*, Vol. II, No. 2 (September, 1957), pp. 182–199.

Moslems (Masjumi) led by Vice-President Hatta. This 1948 split in the party and in the unions has continued to the present time. Even the Trotskyites, led by Tan Malaka, supported the Hatta coalition as opposed to the Communist group. In 1948 Tan Malaka established a rival federation called the Federation of Unions of the Revolutionary Workers of Indonesia, or *Gabungan Serikat Buruh Revolutioner Indonesia* (GASBRI).

SOBSI suffered a much more serious blow when many of its leaders took part with the Communists in the abortive Madiun revolt in September, 1948, against the Indonesian government. The Nationalist government of Indonesia put this revolt down rapidly and firmly. Many of the SOBSI leaders were killed or fled the country. Since 1948 many rival federations have been formed and at times have seemed to be gathering real strength, but SOBSI remains the largest and most important labor federation.

In 1950, after the granting of sovereignty, SOBSI again began a strong organizing campaign and took the leadership in organizing strikes in the estates. Several regional groups opposed the growth of the SOBSI unions, but it was not until after many SOBSI and other left-wing leaders had been jailed in August, 1951, because of a possible coup on Independence Day, that these groups gained much momentum. In 1953, with the foundation of the All-Indonesian Congress of Workers or *Kongres Buruh Seluruh Indonesia* (KBSI), it looked as if there would be a strong second federation. Actually, this organization had a very short honeymoon, because later in 1953 the president of the union, Mr. Kusnan, resigned and took the nationalist-oriented unions out of the federation. It is generally believed that this was done for political reasons, since SOBSI (Communist-oriented) saw a possible threat in KBSI and therefore insisted that the Nationalist party, whose Prime Minister they were supporting, withdraw its unions from the new federation. Since that time other federations have been organized or grown in power, so that at the present time there are twelve national federations of labor in Indonesia.

Most of these federations have a strong political orientation. In fact, many of the trade unions are the labor divisions of a political party. Each of the major political parties operates several branches or divisions: for example, a women's division, a veterans' division, a farmers' division, a youth division, and a labor division. This means that it is impossible to study the trade unions without considering the political parties.

Listed below are the national trade union federations in existence in 1959 and their political affiliation or orientation:

SOBSI	—Communist party	(PKI)
KBSI	—Socialist party *	(PSI)
SBII	—Masjumi party *	(Moslem)
KBKI	—Nationalist party	(PNI)
HISSBI	—Labor party	
SOBRI	—Partai Murbah	(Independent Radical)
SARBUMUSI	—Nadatul Ulamah	(Moslem Teachers' Party)
GOBSII	—PSII	(Orthodox Moslem)
GSBI	—Nationalist party	(PNI)
KBIM	—Masjumi *	(Moslem)
O.B. PANTJASILA	—Catholic party	
SBKI	—Christian party	(PARKINDO)

* Disbanded by government order, 1960.

As the first and leading federation in Indonesia, SOBSI includes many non-Communist members, but its leadership and politics are generally recognized to be Communist-oriented. SOBSI has in recent years trained its own leadership apart from the leaders of the Communist party. Although it is easy to demonstrate [34] that many of the resolutions passed by the various SOBSI unions are politically in line with the views of the Communist party, it is also possible to show that its unions engage in genuine trade union activities. They are interested in and push for higher wages and better working conditions. In fact some employers feel that the Communist unions are better organized and disciplined and, therefore, more responsible than other unions in Indonesia. Other employers, however, used to complain that many of the demands of the Communist unions were so great that they could not possibly hope to win these requests, which were made to harass and disrupt production. Usually the Communist unions have been more active in demanding large increases and in carrying out strikes when a government unfriendly to the Communist party was in office. Since 1957, SOBSI unions have strongly supported the government against the rebels and generally obeyed the no-strike ban for immediate political reasons, while stressing the right to strike as a basic trade union principle.

The KBSI claims that it is not a Socialist trade union, but an independent trade union federation, because Dr. Kusna, the president, is a nonparty man. He also heads the large railroad union, PBKA, which prides itself on being an independent union with many officers who are not Socialists. Mr. Silitonga, who heads a Sumatran union, PERBUPRI, of estate workers affiliated with the KBSI, also claims that his union is

[34] In addition to many publications in Indonesian, SOBSI issues a mimeographed monthly in English, *Indonesian Trade Union News*, which quotes speeches and resolutions and relates the activities of the Federation and its affiliates.

independent. In fact, although Mr. Silitonga himself is a Socialist, he refused to allow the Socialists to use his union in the national elections, with the result that two definitely Socialist-oriented groups were split off from his union.

In 1959 the KBKI broke its formal connections with the Nationalist party[35] and moved into offices in separate buildings. Ideologically, however, the KBKI leans on the Nationalist party (PNI), which subscribes to a doctrine called Marhaenism, an indigenous philosophy opposed to the foreign ideologies of capitalism and Marxism. It favors group action by Indonesians and their government. Some would think of it as a sort of state socialism, or "socialism à la Indonesia." President Sukarno and other nationalist leaders talk a great deal about their five principles (*Pantjasila*): divine omnipotence, international humanitarianism, nationalism, democracy, and social justice. The first, belief in God, runs counter to Marxism, but this is not stressed by SOBSI.

It is no secret that the Masjumi party before it was ordered to disband fostered the SBII, even if there have been suggestions by SBII officials that the union should be separated from the party, since some of the Masjumi leaders supported the revolution in Sumatra in 1958.[36] So far the Nadatul Ulamah has done relatively little with its new Moslem federation, but in a few centers SARBUMUSI is recognized by the employers. GOBSII, another Moslem federation, supported by the PSII party, seemed to be little more than a paper organization by 1960. SBII, however, became worried by this spate of new Moslem federations, including KBIM, which split off from SBII, feeling that by and large these new confederations would draw from the Moslem unions rather than struggle to take members away from SOBSI. For this reason the then Secretary-General of SBII proposed in 1956 that there be an agreement among Moslem unions not to proselytize from their own membership but to concentrate on winning new members for their group. By 1959 a constitution was drawn up for a Moslem confederation to which all four Moslem unions would belong, while each would keep its own identity.

The difference in ideology between the Communists, who stress the class struggle, and the Moslems, who talk about the principle of sharing the wealth with the poor,[37] is significant in labor relations in Indonesia.

---

[35] The GSBI also claimed to be independent, but most of its membership was made up of government workers, a large percentage of them oriented to the Nationalist party. It recently affiliated with the KBKI.

[36] Wibisono, the President of SBII and a former Masjumi leader and Minister of Finance, was appointed as a labor representative in the 1960 Parliament.

[37] Rich Moslems have a general responsibility toward their workers and a particular duty to make an annual contribution or bonus to them.

Since some of the Moslem unions tend to talk in terms of the Islamic faith instead of the class struggle, they sometimes refuse to join in certain strikes and are considered more "moderate." On the other hand, since they are in competition for members, they frequently must ask for and get the same things as the Communist unions.[38]

These ideological differences have their counterparts in the international affiliations of various Indonesian unions. In 1947, at the Party Congress in Malang, SOBSI decided to affiliate with the World Federation of Trade Unions. It sent its new president to the WFTU conference at Prague in June, 1947, and since that time there has been a close affiliation between SOBSI and the WFTU. Because the WFTU helped support the revolution against Dutch colonialism, workers have been willing to be affiliated with this Communist-oriented international group in spite of the so-called "independent" foreign policy of their government. After the death of Stalin, the small Trotskyite federation SOBRI also joined the WFTU. Several SOBSI unions are affiliated with the respective Communist-oriented trade secretariats.

On the other hand, there was until 1957 a great reluctance on the part of the non-Communist unions to affiliate with the International Confederation of Free Trade Unions (ICFTU). The WFTU and SOBSI have attacked this organization as procolonial in its outlook, since many of the unions and their leaders come from the so-called European colonial powers. Gradually in recent years there has been a tendency for some of the non-Communist unions to be interested in the ICFTU.[39]

In 1957, SBII applied for membership in the ICFTU and, after being investigated by a committee of unionists from other countries, was accepted and has subsequently participated in various international and regional meetings and congresses. Efforts were made at the second congress of the *Serikat Sekerdja PTT* (an independent union of postal, telephone, and telegraph employees) at Solo in 1958 to urge it to join the trade secretariat for this group of workers located in Berne, Switzerland. The Railroad Workers (PBKA) joined the international secretariat of the non-Communist Transport Workers Union. In spite of these growing relationships and the various training programs for labor lead-

[38] Just as there was some tendency in the political field for the Masjumi and Socialist parties to work together before they were ordered to disband, so there has been a tendency among the Moslem and Socialist unions to join forces in opposing SOBSI.

[39] The ICFTU sent to Indonesia first a Swedish trade union leader for about a year and a half, 1955–56, and second, a representative of the Malayan plantation union in 1959. For more information about their activities see their monthly publication *Dunia Buruh Merdeka* or the ICFTU *Asian Bulletin.*

ers supported by the technical assistance program of the United States government, the Colombo Plan, and private foundations,[40] the links between the non-Communist unions in Indonesia and their counterparts in the rest of the world are less strong and less formal than those of the Communists.

Undoubtedly Indonesian unions, or at least their leaders, have been influenced by foreign ideologies. However, the beliefs of Islam and the nationalistic ideas of Marhaenism play a role in the labor movement. As long as many parties based on various ideologies and religions remain, and as long as they are active in supporting labor groups, it will be difficult to attain a single labor movement or even a few federations. On the other hand, President Sukarno has for several years been trying to reduce the role of the political parties, and he has also indicated that he wished to reduce the number of trade union federations. A story was circulating in Djakarta at the end of 1959 that SOBSI wanted this number reduced to one, since it undoubtedly would be that one organization, while the Nationalists wanted two organizations, one SOBSI and the other Nationalist-oriented, including all the other federations. The Moslems were said to have wanted three federations, one Communist-, one Nationalist-, and one Moslem-oriented.

LEADERSHIP

Leadership is an especially important factor in trade unionism in Indonesia. Some leaders play a dominant role, setting the pattern for the workers to follow. Furthermore, the rank-and-file have less power than in some American and European unions. This reflects the scarcity of trained leaders and the low standard of education and living of the majority of the workers.

As has been indicated, leadership in Indonesia has frequently come from political groups; many of the union leaders are lawyers or politicians or both. In many cases men have served as both union and party leaders. The SOBSI unions since the early days of the revolution have had representatives in the appointed or elected parliaments. Although in former times functionaries of the Communist party served as key leaders of the SOBSI unions, an attempt was made recently to separate the party and the union leadership. This reflects the fact that the SOBSI unions have a much greater depth and strength in leadership than the non-Communist unions. The non-Communist unions may be fortunate

[40] For several years the Rockefeller Foundation gave fellowships for a few Indonesian trade unionists to study at the International Ladies' Garment Workers' Union course for labor leaders in New York City.

enough to have one or possibly two paid union workers,[41] while the SOBSI unions in the same field may have ten to twenty on a full-time regular payroll. This large number of trained leaders may account for the fact that SOBSI is by all odds the largest and strongest federation in Indonesia. Of course, its growth has been helped by the fact that it was the first permanent federation to be organized and that it took part in the revolution.

SOBSI has also been more successful in securing leadership from the ranks of the workers. As a result, the Communist-oriented unions are apt to represent the manual workers (*buruh*) more completely than do the non-Communist unions, many of whose leaders are often white-collar (*pegawai*) or professional workers. This tendency to stratification, where the SOBSI unions are reaching more of the workers at the lower levels and the non-Communist groups are attracting the more highly skilled and office workers, is particularly true among the railroad, oil, and estate workers.

Much of the time of union leaders is given over to handling grievances, either directly with the employer or through the Ministry of Labor and the Regional and National Disputes Committees. Political connections are helpful, and training in law is useful. Some union leaders also spend considerable time on more specific political activities, such as elections, demonstrations, and demands for labor legislation.

Other union leaders have become concerned with providing food and clothing and health facilities for their members at reasonable prices. SOBSI runs a clinic at its main headquarters in Djakarta. The leaders of the PBKA railroad workers are in the forefront of this movement; in fact, jointly with the railroad administration they operate the *Badan Sosial Pusat Buruh Kereta Api* (Social Welfare Department of the Railroad Workers). This organization operates as a coöperative entrepreneur, collecting small sums of savings from the workers; these have been invested in a rice mill, a *batik* plant, a soap mill, a clothing factory, and a shoe factory. Although the United States International Coöperation Administration has helped by supplying machinery from abroad, some technical experts, and training, the local capital comes from the savings of workers themselves, and the management comes from the union leaders. There is some talk that other government unionists may join in these projects to get necessities at low prices.

---

[41] Exceptions are unions with a check-off, such as PBKA, which has funds to pay many full-timers.

In addition, this organization runs a housing department, a purchasing coöperative, a credit union, an insurance fund, and a clinic.[42]

When the government appoints labor representatives to the various disputes committees, it tends to choose labor leaders. Similarly, they are also tapped for the new Labor-Military Organization (BUMIL). Some of the same leaders were selected in 1959 and 1960 as functional representatives of labor in the National Planning Council, the Supreme Advisory Council, and the Parliament. For example, Erning Pradja, the KBKI president, was elected to Parliament in 1955, served as head of the Indonesian delegation to the ILO Conference in 1956, was appointed by President Sukarno in 1958 as a labor representative to the National Advisory Council, and the following year was chosen by the President as Minister of Labor.

Because of the number of rival federations, each leader must push the claims of his union as against all others. This makes it difficult to secure "moderate and responsible" leaders. Furthermore, as in many other countries, leadership rivalries must be recognized in studying the labor movement in general and the difficulties of trying to get the federations to work together.

STRUCTURE AND MEMBERSHIP

The structure of the trade union movement is complicated by the large number of national federations, regional organizations, and independent unions. Although union organizational charts are popular in Indonesia, it is often difficult to learn how much is actually in operation and how much is a paper plan for the future. Furthermore, the real center of power may not be exactly as shown on the chart.

The organizational structure of SOBSI, the largest federation, is not unlike that of the American Federation of Labor–Congress of Industrial Organizations. In fact, a SOBSI leader suggested that one of the reasons for the success of his organization and the AFL-CIO was the similarity of their structural form. SOBSI has two major lines of organization: one through the national unions, the other on a geographical base. SOBSI tends to give more weight to the national unions than the geographical representatives, as is the case in the AFL-CIO. Final authority is supposed to reside in the national congresses, the latest of which was held in 1959 after some delay on the part of the Minister of Defense. Actually, the executive committee and the elective officers

[42] PBKA, *Laporan Kerdja 3 Tahun, Nopember 1955 sampai achir, 1958 untuk Kongres KeV* (*Report of Work for Three Years, November 1955 to the End of 1958, for the Fifth Congress*) (Bandung, 1959). For stories on the dedication of the clothing and shoe factories, see *Times of Indonesia,* October 11, 1958, p. 3, and December 3, 1958, p. 3.

make decisions between the congresses and are very influential in determining what is decided there.

Forty national unions are affiliated with the SOBSI organization. These include such workers as those on the railroads (SPKA), on the estates (SARBUPRI), in the textile plants (SBT), on the waterfront (SBPP), and in the oil industry (PERBUM). The national unions, with headquarters either in Djakarta or various other cities in Java, have their own officers, negotiate with employers, and carry their cases for arbitration to the Central Disputes Committee. An oil case coming from PERBUM in South Sumatra would be pushed by the PERBUM officials in Djakarta.

The national unions and their locals have considerable autonomy on trade union issues within their own industry. SOBSI stresses that each of the unions should finance its own activity. This independence of each of the national unions does not preclude sympathetic support of the activities of other SOBSI unions. At the local level, however, it is the responsibility of the local of a particular national union to handle its own strike situation with the support of the national union rather than aid from other local SOBSI unions. Each of the national unions has its own regional (*Daerah*) offices and local (*Tjabang*) branches, which coördinate with the geographic arm of SOBSI in carrying out general political objectives, holding demonstrations, celebrating May Day.

SOBSI itself has real power, although it grants certain autonomy over particular economic or trade union issues to its national unions. SOBSI sets for its unions political policies which do not deviate from those of the Communist party. It issues a number of journals and pamphlets, supplies and helps train leaders. It holds many congresses and encourages affiliates to do likewise in order to indoctrinate their members and to spot potential leaders. Some claim it has to seek outside funds, since the dues of its member unions would not seem to be sufficient to finance all its activities. Although SOBSI and its affiliated unions are reported to have relatively good systems of communication, undoubtedly the great distances within Indonesia result in more local autonomy than is planned.

The structure of SOBSI is more fully developed than that of the other federations, because of its larger membership. In general, many of the other smaller federations follow the same model of national unions affiliated with the federation, plus the geographic pattern of local and regional offices. The real strength of KBSI seems to rest in a few of its large national unions such as PBKA (railroads) and PERBUPRI (estates), rather than in KBSI itself. The treasury of the railroad workers, for example, is much larger than that of KBSI.

Another form of organization used in Indonesia is the one big union to which all members belong directly. The best example of this type is the Moslem federation SBII, and the nationalist-oriented organization KBKI follows essentially this same type of organizational structure. This may have some advantages in the initial stages, where the number of members is relatively limited in a given local district or region and where there is also a crying shortage of leadership. One leader in a district can serve workers in several different trades or industries. To the extent that these organizations are divisions of the political party, unity rather than separate national unions may be more desired by the parent organization.

The main organizational line of the SBII is from the national to the regional to the local level. On the other hand, the SBII already has recognized industry differences by establishing industrial departments to handle the special needs of the workers, for example, on the estates or in the oil industry. Whether or not these departments will eventually become separate national unions is still undecided, and will probably depend on the growth of the organization. KBKI may also develop separate national unions and become a true federation. At the present time it is trying to secure the affiliation of a number of the independent unions.

TABLE 10

NUMBER OF TRADE UNIONS AFFILIATED AND NONAFFILIATED WITH LABOR FEDERATIONS IN INDONESIA

	August, 1955	End of 1957	End of 1958
Affiliated with federations			
SOBSI	39	37	40
KBSI	12	20	25
SOBRI	14	8	9
HISSBI	9	6	12
SBII	—	1	1
KBKI	3	3	3
GSBI	4	1	1
SARBUMUSI	—	1	1
KBIM	—	1	1
GOBSII	—	1	1
Regional Federations (7)	3	—	—
PPB	—	5	5
GOBNI	—	1	1
Local Federations (9)	—	—	—
Nonaffiliated			
Independent	67	128	161
Total	151	213	261

SOURCES: Ministry of Labor, *Directory of Trade Unions*, August 9, 1955; *Tindjauan Masa'alah Perburuhan*, Vol. X, No. 11–12 (March–April, 1959), p. 16.

An August, 1955, report of the Ministry of Labor included seven regional and nine local federations, many of which are located in Sulawesi and the eastern islands. (See table 10.) One of the largest covers seventeen locals of government workers employed by the local autonomous region of Jogjakarta. Not all regional government workers in Jogjakarta belong to one of the seventeen locals of this federation; in fact, a SOBSI affiliate (SEBDA) probably has a majority of the lower-paid workers.

The Ministry of Labor listed 67 independent (*non-voksentral*) national unions in 1955, compared to 84 unions affiliated with federations. By the end of 1958, 161 independent unions were registered, compared to 100 affiliated unions. A number of these unions have their headquarters away from Djakarta. One of the oldest and strongest of these independents, with members in all parts of Indonesia, is the Union of Pawnshop Workers (*Serikat Buruh Pegadaian*). There is no dual or multiple unionism among the pawnshop workers, and the union covers over 99 per cent of them. Its officers come from various political groups. A careful system of accounting brings in sufficient funds for the union to own its own building and printing plant in Jogjakarta.[43]

The Ministry of Labor further listed, in 1955, 659 nonaffiliated local unions, many of them composed of workers in one firm only. There were then a total of 1,501 national, regional, and local unions, affiliated and nonaffiliated with federations.

The role of the union member is less developed in Indonesia than in Western countries. Meetings are held to rouse them to take part in strikes and demonstrations; membership cards are passed out to the workers. Much effort is made to collect dues from members, but here a serious problem frequently arises, because not only are the wages of Indonesian workers low in relation to the cost of living, but there is competition among several unions in the same field. One union will not put much pressure on a person to pay dues for fear that he will drop out and join another union which is less strict in its collection of dues.

Some workers may be considered members of two unions at the same time. This is particularly true because it is not necessary to pay union dues to be considered a regular member. In fact, many unions indicate quite freely that they collect dues from only ten to thirty per cent of their members each month. Some workers think it wise to belong to two unions to get protection from both, and because they have friends in both. Others may be encouraged to join another union so that the first

[43] Profits from this plant are sufficient to enable it to publish its own monthly journal, *Suara Buruh Pegadaian*. The August, 1959, issue presents financial statements for the union and the printing plant, pp. 235–237.

union may have some control over its rival. The SBII has a special provision to test its membership. For a worker to be counted as a member of the SBII, he must have paid his initiation fee and the first month's dues. This is a better test of membership than just getting workers to raise their hands and receive cards from the union. However, although a careful check is made by SBII on dues from the field, there is no assurance that this system will record accurately at any time how many members are active in the union.

An exact way to find out the number of members in a union is through a check-off of dues, but there are few such cases in Indonesia, one of the most important being the PBKA (railroad workers) affiliated with the KBSI. The check-off has also been granted to the post, telegraph, and telephone workers. Other unions have tried to secure the check-off, but private management, STANVAC being an exception, has generally resisted such moves. Some unions have not wanted a check-off because it would disclose too accurately how few members actually belonged to their union.

With multiple unions, plural membership, and no exact test of membership, it is apparent that union figures in Indonesia must be scrutinized very carefully. The test of how many workers go out on strike is frequently used, but this may be faulty because a number of people who are not members of the union may decide to join the strike rather than stand out against their fellow workers. In fact, in some plants with multiple unions, if the number of members were counted in this way, the total number of those going out on different strikes would exceed the number of workers in the plant. Similarly, many estimates are made on the basis of the claims of the union leaders, which are apt to be exaggerated to try to stress the importance of their union in comparison with other groups. Many times the total claims of the union leaders in a given plant will exceed the number of workers, but this is not entirely impossible because of plural membership. On the basis of some field experience, it seems apparent that the data become less accurate as one moves from the local union to the regional, to the national, and to the confederation, since there seems to be a compounding of the optimistic estimates the higher one goes. The desire for exact membership figures is greater on the part of some Western observers than of the Indonesian leaders themselves. Fairly general agreement among union leaders,[44] management officers, and government officials, however, exists about the relative importance of competing unions.

Recent estimates of union membership range from 1.5 to 5.5 million members. (See table 11.) Although even the low figure is probably

[44] Often this does not include the union leader's estimate of his own union's strength.

much too high for the number of workers who actually pay dues in any given month, probably some two million workers are effectively influenced by the unions in that they would take part in labor demonstrations or strikes and *consider themselves* union members. On the basis of data collected between July, 1955, and July, 1957, the Ministry of Labor

TABLE 11

ESTIMATES OF INDONESIAN TRADE UNION MEMBERSHIP, 1955–1958

Federation	Conservative estimate, end of 1955 [a]	Registered members June 30, 1956 [b]	Registered members June 30, 1957 [b]	Members reported by Regional Labor Offices, end 1957 [c]	Trade union claims June 30, 1956 [d]	Trade union claims March 31, 1958 [d]
KBSI	80,000	205,687	261,483	105,884	376,997	376,000
SOBSI	750,000	1,366,769	1,502,132	1,179,694	2,661,970	2,732,909
SOBRI	30,000	39,936	43,862	116,928	125,325	281,000
HISSBI	—	4,944	8,044	16,256	180,203	260,945
SBII	150,000	275,000	275,000	84,051	275,000	600,000
KBKI	10,000	94,477	100,758	331,918	94,477	1,001,775
GSBI	—	32,737	32,777	18,175	39,327	145,300
GOBSII	—	1,347	1,347	6,298	1,347	1,347
SARBUMUSI	—	11,950	11,950	13,828	11,950	11,950
KBIM	—	—	41,672	10,290	—	41,672
O.B. Pantjasila	—	—	—	—	—	61,000
B.P.B.	—	—	—	21,475	—	—
Not affiliated	425,000	76,241	170,697	378,277	699,627	180,000
Total	1,445,000	2,109,128	2,449,722	2,295,066	4,514,991	5,693,898

[a] Estimate made by U.S. expert.
[b] Ministry of Labor, *Serikat Buruh Jg. Terdaftar (Registered Trade Unions) Period June 30, 1956, to June 30, 1957* (Djakarta, 1957), p. 30–33.
[c] Ministry of Labor, *Report for Two Years April 1957—April 1959*, p. 8.
[d] As reported to the Ministry of Labor by the unions. See *Tindjauan Masa'alah Perburuhan*, May, 1958, p. 8.

reported that membership in registered trade unions, broken down not only by federation but by industry and geographical region, totaled 2,449,722 in 1957, as compared with 2,109,128 a year earlier. (See table 11.) The increase of about 340,000 members indicates both more complete registration and some increase in total membership. There are still some indications that membership in some unions in certain industry classifications has been exaggerated. The largest group of union members was reported in agriculture (see table 12)—1,009,962;[45] in

[45] By comparison, the Central Statistical Office reported only 791,247 regular and temporary workers and employees on the nine major types of estates in June, 1956. *Wages Paid on Estates, 1956–57*, p. 7. In 1959, SARBUPRI, the largest national union in Indonesia, claimed 351,676 members out of an estimated 593,000 estate workers throughout the country.

industry, 596,115, and in the services, 275,047. Unfortunately, because of the unitary structure of some of the federations, 382,427 union members could not be classified.

From a cross-classification by federations and industries it is apparent that membership in SOBSI, KBSI, and the nonfederated unions is widely distributed in all occupations. The same may be true of SBII and KBKI, but unfortunately their membership has not been classified by industry. Although the figures indicate that SOBSI has substantially more members than all the other unions which are classified, in agriculture, mining, manufacturing, transportation, communication, and services, perhaps the most significant point to note is that it has about 530,000 members out of the total of 596,000 classified in manufacturing.

TABLE 12

NUMBER OF MEMBERS IN REGISTERED UNIONS IN INDONESIA, CLASSIFIED BY INDUSTRY, JUNE 30, 1956, AND JUNE 30, 1957

Classification	June 30, 1956	June 30, 1957
0. Agriculture	874,452	1,009,962
1. Mining	27,356	27,356
2./3. Industry	476,042	596,115
4. Building	8,377	1,377
5. Public utilities	9,082	13,496
6. Trade	15,670	22,108
7. Communication	108,406	122,834
8. Services	217,448	275,047
9. Unclassified	381,427	381,427
Total	2,109,128	2,449,722

SOURCE: Ministry of Labor, *Serikat Buruh Jg. Terdaftar (Registered Trade Unions), Period June 30, 1956, to June 30, 1957* (Djakarta, 1957), pp. 31–33.

The figures in table 13 clearly point out the heavy concentration of union membership on Java, about three-fourths of the total, excluding those not classified by regions (406,043). The Medan area of North Sumatra also has a very large group of union members (366,472), a number in excess of those reported in Central Java. In all the rest of Indonesia, only about 140,000 members were reported in 1957.

A second method which the Ministry of Labor has used to gather trade union membership is to secure reports from each of the regions (*daerah*).[46] As of the end of December, 1957, this total amounted to 2,295,066. (See table 11, column 4.) The figures for most of the unions were considerably smaller than those included in the registered membership (column 3). On the other hand, the figures for SOBRI seem

[46] The Ministry seems to favor this method and included these figures in *Two Year Report during the Karya Cabinet, April 1957—April 1959*, p. 8.

much too high, while those for KBKI and the nonaffiliated unions show a marked increase. The estimates for SBII may be too low.

The Ministry of Labor has published membership reports in a third way, based on claims made by the unions themselves without specific reference to location or industry. These range from 4,514,991 on June 30, 1956, to 5,693,898 on March 31, 1958. These figures represent the

TABLE 13

NUMBER OF MEMBERS IN REGISTERED UNIONS IN INDONESIA, CLASSIFIED BY AREAS, JUNE 30, 1956 AND JUNE 30, 1957

Area	June 30, 1956	June 30, 1957
Medan	320,631	366,472
Padang	24,233	27,891
Palembang	47,119	68,955
Bandung	328,884	415,399
Semarang	273,536	335,358
Surabaja	570,054	650,326
Makasar	20,473	26,714
Bandjarmasin	21,914	26,161
Djakarta	96,241	126,403
Unclassified	406,043	406,043
Total	2,109,128	2,449,722

SOURCE: Same as for table 12.

optimistic hopes of leaders rather than actual union membership. Almost all the figures are exaggerated, with the possible exception of the 180,000 in nonaffiliated unions on March 31, 1958.

Whatever set of figures is used, however, SOBSI is the largest federation. KBKI, SBII, and KBSI are the next most important federations. A figure of about two million trade union members would seem correct, with possibly about half of these affiliated with SOBSI.

With what figure should the total trade union membership in Indonesia be compared? Probably not the total labor force of 33 to 40 million, because it includes such a large number of farmers and other self-employed workers. A better estimate for comparison purposes is about 8,000,000 people employed as wage or salary workers in industry and government service. (Government workers are included in this category because many of them are organized, perhaps more strongly than in private industry.) Of this total number of workers, 20 to 25 per cent are trade union members.

If these percentage figures are used, there is still considerable room for trade union expansion of membership. If the optimistic claims of union leaders are used, however, there would seem to be less chance for union growth, except as there were additions to the labor force, particularly those in the industrialized sector. Since trade union membership is largely concentrated in the larger estates and plants, including government service, one further area for increase in membership is in the small plants, which are often managed by Chinese or perhaps Indonesians. Union leaders of both the Right and the Left, however, were conscious that if they pushed the small firms too hard they might put them out of business or keep them from expanding. If the unions could not secure higher wages for the workers in smaller plants, it might be difficult for them to organize such workers. In Singapore, however, some of the unions have made remarkable headway in organizing smaller shops and in securing benefits for workers in these industries. Many of these shops are owned and operated by Chinese. It is possible that the Indonesian unions may put pressure on the Chinese establishments, even if they are small in size, to provide better wages and working conditions for their employees. On the other hand, considering developments since 1958, the government may extend rules limiting Chinese ownership of undertakings. This would involve more Indonesian management, which might not be strong enough at first to increase wages.

INFLUENCE IN SOCIAL AND ECONOMIC LIFE

Because the trade unions in the prewar period and after the Declaration of Independence on August 17, 1945, played such an important part in the movements for independence and nationalism, every Indonesian government has tended to be more prolabor than proforeign management. Certainly this contrast between government attitudes before and after the revolution is important. Trade unions have had some influence on the policy decisions of the Ministry of Labor. The fact that each of the major political parties is trying to form unions affiliated with it is a clear indication of the importance attached to the labor vote. In the general elections of 1955 several trade union officials were elected to Parliament on various tickets. Every discussion of functional representation includes labor as one of the major groups, and labor is represented with 25 seats in the Parliament appointed by President Sukarno in March, 1960.

In some areas the unions have also been active in their local governments. For example, in Pakan Baru in Central Sumatra, the SOBSI trade unions in 1956 were playing a key role in the city government. A leader of the oil workers union (PERBUM) spent most of his time on government affairs. Likewise in Surabaja, the trade unions connected with SOBSI have joined with the Communist party in winning a number of local elections. Several officials of the non-Communist unions also serve in important local and provincial offices. All these office-holders reflect the importance and influence of the unions in their community. One might speculate that, as in other countries, some men were becoming union leaders in order to gain political position.

Although some labor leaders are important members of the community, labor as a class does not have a high position in Indonesian society. As already pointed out, education is considered to be the important criterion for leadership and social standing, the professions and the white-collar workers (*pegawai*) standing higher on the social ladder than manual labor (*buruh*).

Although relatively skilled workers do not have as high a social position as *pegawai,* in some cases they have enough economic power to command a considerable differential over unskilled workers. There are some who believe that the shortage of skilled workers and the surplus of unskilled workers causes a greater disparity of wages in an underdeveloped than in a developed country. The International Labor Organization reported that skilled workers in Djakarta in 1953 received Rp.10–20, or two to four times the general level of wages for unskilled workers, Rp.5–6.[47] The figures in table 14 indicate that, although wages in the building construction industry in Bandung have risen by over 60 per cent from 1951 to 1958, there has been a constant differential system, with skilled workers paid twice as much, the most skilled three times as much, and the foremen (*mandurs*) four times as much as the unskilled. Female unskilled workers in a tea factory in West Java received early in 1959 Rp.4.75 a day, and men Rp.5.75. A skilled machinist, on the other hand, was paid about Rp.20, or over four times the pay of unskilled women workers. Such a comparison of money wages is not accurate, however, since all the workers receive substantial wages in kind, especially rice, depending on the number of dependents in a family. Table 14 indicates that the payments in kind on Javanese estates for a married man with two children were slightly higher in 1958 than his money wages. Adding about Rp.5 to both the unskilled worker's and the machinist's money wages would mean that the latter received about 2.5 times as much as the unskilled worker with a family.[48]

---

[47] *International Labour Review,* Vol. 70 (1954), p. 39. Bakers and plumbers were paid Rp.10; bricklayers and carpenters, Rp.12.50; structural steel and electrical workers, Rp.15; garage mechanics, Rp.18; and motor freight truck drivers, Rp.20.

[48] Length-of-service awards further complicate the comparison. The head of an office in a government ministry reported that he had working under him several people who received higher income because they had larger families and had

TABLE 14

MINIMUM DAILY WAGES IN SELECTED YEARS, 1951–1958, IN CERTAIN INDUSTRIES IN INDONESIA

Workers	1951	1953	1955	1958
Estates on Java and Southern and Western Sumatra	Rp.	Rp.	Rp.	Rp.
Married with 2 children:				
In money	3.00	3.50	4.25	4.75
In kind	1.80	1.44	2.52	4.86
Total	4.80	4.94	6.77	9.61
Index number	97	100	137	195
Estates in Northern Sumatra				
Married with 2 children:				
In money	3.25	3.50	4.25	4.45
In kind	5.78	5.63	6.26	10.10
Total	9.03	9.13	10.51	14.65
Index number	99	100	115	160
Sugar-cane estates				
Married with 2 children:				
In money	4.00	4.00	5.50	6.00
In kind	1.65	1.65	3.20	5.70
Total	5.65	5.65	8.70	11.70
Index number	100	100	154	207
Kretek (native cigarette) manufacturing industries				
In money: males	—	—	4.00	5.50
females	—	—	3.50	4.50
Tandjung Priok Harbor				
Regular:				
In money	—	5.25	8.05	10.62
In kind	—	1.17	1.24	2.12
Total	—	6.42	9.29	12.74
Index number	—	100	145	199
Building construction in Bandung				
In money:				
Foremen	20.00	22.00	26.00	34.00
Chief *tukangs*	15.00	16.50	19.50	25.50
Tukangs (bricklayers, carpenters, etc.)	10.00	11.00	13.00	17.00
Other (unskilled)	5.00	5.50	6.50	8.50
Index number	91	100	118	155

SOURCE: Ministry of Labor.

A recent study of wages in Sukabumi, made with the assistance of N. K. Adyantaya, an ILO expert working with the Indonesian Ministry of Labor, indicated very narrow differentials for skilled over unskilled workers.

many more years' seniority than he. Being a high school or university graduate entitles a man or woman to a certain classification in the government. In colonial times the Dutch were paid at one level, Eurasians at a lower level, and Indonesians still less.

Industry		*Average Daily Wages*
Plantations	Skilled	Rp.5.36
	Unskilled	Rp.4.15
Other establishments	Skilled	Rp.7.90
	Unskilled	Rp.5.22

This means a differential of about 30 per cent on plantations, and just under 50 per cent in other establishments.[49] Of course the use of averages tends to reduce the differentials, since there are many degrees of skill in the skilled category. In some cases, however, the differentials for skilled workers may not be sufficient to induce workers to take the necessary training. Certainly the use of payments in kind and allowances for long service and size of family may tend to reduce substantially the apparent differentials.

Table 14 also indicates considerable wage differences by industry. The cigarette industry is one of the lowest paid, and many of the workers in the *batik* industry also receive low incomes. Harbor workers are better paid, and oil workers are among the best paid. Wages in large cities tend to be higher for comparable positions than in small towns or rural areas. Table 14 further indicates that the estates in North Sumatra tend to pay more than in other regions. In rice milling, woodworking shops, and rubber remilling plants, wages in Sumatra are considerably higher than in Java.[50] Furthermore, on Sumatra and Kalimantan estates more is given in wages in kind than in Java. In 1958, North Sumatra estates [51] provided each month the following:

Product	*Worker*	*Wife/husband not working*	*Each child*
Rice	18 kilos	12 kilos	9 kilos
Sugar	1 kilo	½ kilo	½ kilo
Salt	½ kilo	¼ kilo	¼ kilo
Dried fish	1½ kilos	1 kilo	½ kilo
Cooking oil	2½ bottles	—	½ bottle
Kerosene	4 bottles	—	—
Soap	3 bars	—	½ bar (of 400 grams)
Peas	½ kilo	—	—
Tea	½ kilo	—	—
Textiles	2 meters	1 meter	1 meter (40% price by worker)
Canned milk	—	—	1 600 cc. can for each child under ten

[49] *Tindjauan Masa'alah Perburuhan,* Vol. X, No. 6 (October, 1958), p. 10.
[50] *Ibid.,* pp. 19–20.
[51] *Ibid.,* p. 20; for other areas, see p. 21.

The greater scarcity of all grades of labor in the outer islands tends to make for a rather large discrepancy in wages between the low levels of Java and the higher levels, for example, in Sumatra. The money differences, however, must be corrected to some extent for the higher cost of living in Sumatra than Java. As long as population tends to increase rapidly in Java without a corresponding increase in capital investment, severe pressure will remain on wages, and the bargaining position of unskilled labor will not be strong. The really low subsistence level of most wage earners in Indonesia keeps labor in its subordinate position. Not only are wages low, but the prices of nineteen basic foodstuffs in Djakarta rose 77 per cent from a base of 100 in 1953 to 177 in 1957, and then, even more rapidly, to 258 in 1958 and to 325 by the end of 1959.[52] None of the wages included in table 14 climbed as rapidly as prices. Payments in kind, of course, helped to hold up real wages, but the evidence seems clear that real wages have recently declined in most cases.[53]

The present trend to multiple unions in a given industry is also a factor weakening the position of organized labor. Although management feels that competitive unions mean extravagant demands, labor believes that multiple unionism makes it possible for management to play off one group against the other. Government officials are not in favor of such a division, because it makes their decisions much more complex and difficult.

Some unions tend to join forces in a given area when they have to bargain with the employers. This coöperation perhaps is clearest in the estates on the east coast of Sumatra, where eleven unions coöperated in negotiation with the employers and in appealing to the P4D in Medan and the P4P in Djakarta. A regionwide decree resulted in an agreement

[52] *Statistik Konjunktur (Monthly Survey)* (December, 1959), p. 76. There is no one satisfactory cost of living index in Indonesia. Prices continued to rise in 1960.

[53] Average earnings in Sukabumi rose in 1958 at a much faster rate on the estates than in manufacturing, but these increases were less than the rise in prices:

1958	*Average*	*Plantations*	*Manufacturing*
Mid-January	100	100	100
Mid-April	111.6	112.5	105.4
Mid-July	117.1	118.4	108.2
Mid-October	125.9	128.2	110.0

Ministry of Labor, *Note on the Compilation of Index Numbers of Earnings in the Plantation and Manufacturing Industries Sectors in Sukabumi* (September, 1959) (mimeo). The Ministry of Labor has also reported substantial wage gains from the first quarter of 1957 to the fourth quarter of 1958 in a number of industries in the various provinces. In no case, however, were these gains commensurate with the price increases. *Two Year Report during the Karya Cabinet, April 1957—April 1959*, pp. 80–81.

for all estates and for all unions in that area. In the early months of 1959, the Government Estates Organization (PPN Baru) was negotiating with the various estate unions for three regional agreements. On March 1, 1958, the four large oil workers' unions signed a common contract with Standard Vacuum Oil Company which provided for no strikes or lockouts for the duration of the agreement.

As trade unions become older and more stable, it is likely that their real strength will increase in many communities even more rapidly than their membership. Conditions vary so much from section to section that generalization is difficult, but it seems likely that in the near future in most areas trade unions will have more political strength than economic power or social prestige. Certainly Indonesian unions today are larger, stronger, and more important than in the colonial period.

The Problems of Management

Just as there have been rapid changes in the labor organizations in Indonesia, so has the role of management also changed. In colonial times management was largely foreign and, with the government, tended to control labor relations. With the revolution substituting an Indonesian government for a colonial regime, foreign management was put on the defensive politically. Furthermore, some managements found it hard to move rapidly enough from the older, feudalistic, authoritarian, paternalistic attitudes to a newer, constitutional basis. After the revolution, management was no longer in an absolutely dominant position; it was subject to checks by trade unions, public opinion, government legislation, and the ruling of the Central Disputes Committee. Many managements were worried about productivity, discipline, and profits; others were simply confused by changing work patterns, the complex wage payments in money and in kind, conflicting demands of multiple unions, and the uncertain political conditions.

With the take-over of Dutch estates and other businesses starting in December, 1957, the role of foreign management was greatly reduced.[54] It has been replaced by Indonesian military and civilian management. Although the full effects of this change have not been experienced, this shift should mean that the antiforeign factor will be reduced, and that lack of experience may become the crucial problem. Because of this shift in management, the radical youth of the unions, and the rapidly changing labor relations picture, examples of organizations with democratic managements based on a community of interest with the unions still will be rare, although the government as manager

[54] There is still some foreign management in Indonesia: European, American, Chinese, Indian, and Arab.

of the former Dutch estates has tried since 1959 to introduce systems of consultation with the unions.

THE RECRUITMENT AND TRAINING OF A LABOR FORCE

Methods used by the Dutch in colonial times to hire a labor force and to control it by government regulation have had a marked effect on labor-management relations and the attitudes of many Indonesians toward work. Slavery, the "forced cultivation" system, compulsory labor service, and contracts with penal clauses have already been discussed. Traditional patterns of work developed under such systems of compulsion are apt to linger on in strange ways in a newly independent country. As already mentioned, the element of compulsion to work in the colonial period accounted for the feeling on the part of many Indonesians that *merdeka* or freedom meant freedom from work. Managements after the revolution complained in many cases about the lack of productivity of the Indonesian worker, the short work week, and the even shorter number of hours that most workers actually performed on a job. Foreign estate managers told of the carelessness of their workers and then regaled the listener with stories of how good it was in the prerevolutionary days. In those "good old days" it was possible for the manager to punish or fine the worker with little or no redress on the worker's part, while at the present time dismissal for cause often involves endless disputes.[55] Employers also pointed to the fact that Indonesia is a tropical country where many workers are not anxious to work long hours. The desire for leisure is strong in the cultural pattern, and conflicts with the work standards of modern industry. On the other hand, Indonesian leaders have stressed the danger of this position and urged Indonesians to work harder in order to increase the wealth of the country.

Modern management still faces recruiting, committing, and training problems. By and large, in Sumatra and the other outer islands all the problems are serious, while in Java and Madura, with a large labor supply, the third problem is of primary importance. In all areas there is the task of finding people with specially needed skills, and, if there are not sufficient available, of supplying the necessary training.

The estates on the east coast of Sumatra prior to 1958 hired all their Javanese labor through AVROS, an association of estates in the region. They adopted a policy of not rehiring any estate worker who applied for long leave to go back to Java, since if all the legal condi-

[55] In the colonial period, corporal punishment was frequently used. A number of estate managers were disliked so intensely by their workers that after the revolution they were attacked and some of them were killed.

tions were fulfilled this required a considerable payment on the part of the estate. This required AVROS to hire new Javanese, some of whom would not be pleased with Sumatra and might later wish to leave. Furthermore, those who went on long leave might well be among the people who might recruit labor for the plantations. This policy tended to hold a number of Javanese in Sumatra somewhat against their will because they did not want to lose their jobs—a sort of forced commitment. However, there are a number of second-generation Javanese working on the estates who are fully committed and want to remain. GAPPERSU, the Indonesian organization replacing AVROS, still faces a recruitment problem from Java, since many Sumatrans do not like to work on the plantations at what they consider to be "coolie" work.

The oil companies also have programs to recruit Javanese workers, especially through employees already on their payrolls. Such recruiting is frequently done when the worker goes from the oil fields back to Java on his long leave. The high wages in the oil industry, coupled with a variety of fringe benefits, seem to attract sufficient workers. To secure highly trained Indonesian staff employees, however, the companies have to offer good housing and educational facilities for the children. The latter is particularly difficult in some field operations where public schooling is still below the level of that in the major cities of Java. Where good facilities have been provided, the oil companies have been able to secure a permanently committed labor force, but in many of the smaller installations, particularly in Kalimantan (Borneo), the staff employees are apt to want to move after a short term of service.

Management has had to provide training for all types and skills of workers. Even though the number of graduates of commercial and vocational schools is increasing, these students often need some specialized training. Most of this has taken one form or another of on-the-job training. Some of the larger companies, however, have adopted major training programs. They have provided vocational training for those with only a primary education, and technical training for those who have had at least some high school training, and at the present time they are offering fellowships to promising young students to complete a university course of studies.[56]

The drive for "Indonesianization" necessitates further training pro-

---

[56] See Center for International Studies, MIT, *STANVAC in Indonesia* (Washington: National Planning Association, 1957), esp. pp. 70–78. Shell also has a whole battery of schools and training courses, including an academy to train professional personnel.

grams. Indonesians feel that with the coming of independence more of the higher staff positions should be open to them. One way in which this was being accomplished was through the immigration authorities, who made it very difficult for foreigners to take jobs in Indonesia, even if they had worked in Indonesia for a great many years, unless it could be clearly demonstrated that there were no Indonesians available for the positions.[57] Because of such delays, some corporations decided to train Indonesian staff employees. Many Dutch employees prior to 1957 thought twice before applying for an exit permit because of all the difficulties of reëntry.

Some companies have openly publicized their "Indonesianization" programs, others have been going about it in a quieter fashion. Frequently it involves a period where an Indonesian employee moves up from serving as an assistant to a foreigner to being a "responsible" officer with a foreign adviser. Until the adviser leaves, this new relationship involves many problems as to who is really in control. In one large oil company, some of the Indonesian staff employees refer to the program as "Americanization" rather than "Indonesianization," because, although the Dutch staff has been greatly reduced, the Indonesian staff has not increased as rapidly as the American staff. Furthermore, many of the new American staff were unfamiliar with Indonesia and the Indonesian language and were so anxious to do a good job that they may inadvertently have taken over some of the functions which under the Dutch had already been passed to Indonesian staff employees. The company looked upon this as a transition phase and emphasized that it takes time to train more Indonesians for senior staff positions. In 1958 and 1959 Shell faced somewhat similar problems as it tried to "internationalize" its staff in a short period of time.

This problem is further complicated because to hire American staff it is necessary to pay salaries comparable to American salaries. This means that in some companies there is a wide discrepancy between those hired in America, those hired in the Commonwealth, those hired in Holland, and those hired in Indonesia. Some managements have done a great deal to reduce differences in local currency payments and perquisites for staff employees hired in Indonesia and abroad. Some of these new perquisites which have gone to Indonesians at the senior level are not widely publicized, since the firm is not in a position to give the same privileges to junior staff and lower grade employees. Unions have mentioned this discrimination as one of the sources of friction in the oil companies and on the estates. The estate unions

[57] The Indonesian government, however, gave STANVAC the right to bring in specialists, subject only to a post-audit after they had arrived.

granted the fact that since independence a number of Indonesians have been made heads of certain plantation sections and been given homes and jeeps in the same manner as European managers. Basically this question of differences in pay and perquisites, however, is something which is bound to trouble Indonesian labor relations as long as foreigners are employed on foreign scales above Indonesian levels.

In the 1957–58 take-over of Dutch estates, 2,300 managers were replaced, and Indonesians had to be trained to take their places on 400 estates. An urgent need was created for management training. The *Persatuan Pengusaha Perkebunan Besar Indonesia* (P3BI) (formerly *Algemine Landbouw Syndicaat,* ALS) undertook the preparation of 130 correspondence lessons on 13 subjects, including labor relations, agricultural law, techniques of marketing, insurance, statistics, and management. The universities are stepping up their courses in business management, and special seminars are being planned for Indonesian managers. Training within industry (TWI) courses are helpful not only to labor but to management. Certainly much more needs to be done in the training field as well as in the general field of improving labor productivity.

The key question now is whether management offers enough incentive to the workers to secure quality work and higher productivity. In the colonial period employers could rely on force to secure industrial discipline. With force no longer possible, it is not surprising that many workers feel less compulsion to work hard, regularly, and carefully. Exhortation by the employers, or even by government leaders, has not been enough to improve plant morale, discipline, and productivity. Workers are afraid of, and resist, speed-up methods which they think might result in profits for the employers and more unemployment for labor. Some employers have thrown up their hands in despair, not knowing how to secure discipline without the old force.

Neither management nor labor is fully aware of the implications of the Indonesian revolution. New incentives and new methods must be devised to encourage worker discipline and productivity. Wages have usually been considered a basic incentive for all workers committed to an industrial way of life.[58] Piecework systems have been used in some cases where the work is repetitive and easily measured. But this may not result in a really high level of output, because workers fear working out of a job and because they may also be worried lest a speed-up result in a subsequent reduction in the piece rate. Here

[58] Some Balinese employers still complain that some of their workers are not fully committed to industrial life, since they prefer to have more time to dance than receive higher wages for longer hours of work.

is a place where the unions might now provide an effective voice to assure workers that they would have some protection against the abuses of incentive systems.

MANAGEMENT DEALINGS WITH TRADE UNIONS

Employer reactions to trade unions have generally been negative. Employers see their prerogatives threatened by these new organizations. The former colonial government generally offered management protection, while the Indonesian government tends to favor the Indonesian workers. Since excessive demands by SOBSI unions have often been exceeded by those of other unions, some managements say that all unions are alike. These employers further claim that none of the unions is realistic or realizes the importance of industrial discipline, increased productivity, or capital investment. Under such circumstances, collective bargaining and mutual concessions are hard to obtain. In fact, one manager said in 1956 that it was his position flatly to oppose all union demands because the union would appeal the case to the Central Disputes Committee which would tend to compromise the case on the basis of the last position of the employer and the union.

Even if management wants to get away from older, paternalistic practices, it is forced to continue many of them, especially on the estates and in the oil industry, where it has to provide housing, recreation, and health facilities for the workers, because none are available. Unions are including demands for more and better perquisites, and many employers who would like to pay just money wages are required to continue a number of payments in kind.

Most managements realize that they must deal with the unions within the framework of the present labor laws. Some have tried to foster unions within their own plant, and a number of these exist in Indonesia, although they are not the common pattern as in Japan. Other firms have encouraged their own workers to form independent unions in opposition to trade unions belonging to national federations, thus adding to multiple unionism.

A few of the larger firms are spending a great deal of time trying to develop genuine collective bargaining with their employees and their unions. How far this will be successful remains to be seen. For example, one firm which had spent months negotiating on the question of long leave with its union found that in another firm this same issue had been taken to arbitration. Obviously the decision of the government arbitration board in the case of the second company might undermine entirely the months of collective bargaining in the first firm.

A pattern established either by arbitration or agreement may serve as a model for later decisions.

One of the unusual aspects of union-management relationships in Indonesia is the fact that unions draw their members much further up into management than in many other countries. Foremen and *mandur* (supervisors) and even chief *mandur* (chief supervisors) belong to the unions. A great many office workers also belong to the union and are able to supply labor with information concerning the finances of the company. In some plants leadership for the unions comes from the junior staff and even some of the senior staff, although some companies try to insist that senior staff members should not join the union. Any supervisor who is a member of the union thinks of himself as part of the labor force and not of management. One of the basic problems facing many managements is the lack of a sufficient number of trained, loyal supervisors. This is undoubtedly an important factor in accounting for the low level of productivity. Furthermore, Indonesian managers may need incentives to improve efficiency as much as workers.

Labor relations have become so complicated since the revolution that firms have expanded their industrial relations departments. Some of the important functions to be handled are training, health services, housing, fringe benefits, wages in kind, and labor disputes. In a number of these fields, particularly in handling negotiations with the unions and the government arbitration boards, the large firms have developed Indonesian staff employees to act as spokesmen. Although this is helpful in many cases, sometimes the Indonesian company officials also find it difficult to get along with the Indonesian workers. At the Dolak Merangir plantation of Goodyear in August, 1956, the unions struck against the allegedly arbitrary action of the first Indonesian (Batak) who had been made head of the labor department. The company supported its new manager, but later transferred him to other tasks.

The pressure of independence and the new unions has also created management organizations that specialize in labor relations. From 1950 until 1958 AVROS became the central organization of the rubber producers on the east coast of Sumatra for handling labor recruiting and negotiating with the unions and governmental agencies. The individual estates felt that they were not large enough units to meet the new and growing unions. If they had no central organization, the unions might play off one estate against another. Even the large oil companies believe that the unions are in a position to try to gain an advantage first from one company and then another. For this reason there has been considerable circulation of information about labor relations among the oil companies. Suggestions have been made for a meeting of all the oil companies with the unions. Thus far, because of differences in company policies, this has not been the rule. Other firms have formed trade organizations, one function of which is to deal with the unions. In fact there is a rather sizable list of such employer organizations in Indonesia.[59]

TABLE 15

MEMBERSHIP IN
Jajasan Badan Permusjawaratan Urusan Sosial Pengusaha di Indonesia
(FEDERATION OF EMPLOYERS' ASSOCIATIONS IN INDONESIA), 1958

Employers' organization and/or enterprise	Number of enterprises	Number of workers
Persatuan Pengusaha Perkebunan Besar Indonesia (former A.L.S.) (Plantations)	333	255,790
GAPPERSU (former A.V.R.O.S.) (Rubber)	271	218,881
ASSI (Sugar)	60	97,729
BEBTO (Tobacco)	11	1,949
Gabungan Perindustrian di Indonesia (former IB) (Industry)	146	65,000
PERIMPI (former VIGI) (Wholesalers)	173	15,000
OVEIP (Exports)	141	10,000
Raad van Brandverzekering Mij. (Fire Insurance)	12	1,288
Persatuan Pengusaha Pelabuhan (P. 3) (Harbors)	41	11,000
Ikatan Pertenunan di Djakarta (IPEDE) (Textiles)	25	2,000
Gabungan Perusahaan Korek Api (GAPEKA) (Matches)	6	4,500
BABO (Estates)	17	800
Ex VWHI (Shipping Agents)	25	36,000
Gabungan Perkebunan di Indonesia (Estate Owners)	17	4,358
Bank Industri Negara (Management)	29	26,669
GAPO (Autobus)	95	1,200
Individual membership	61	125,772
Total	1,463	878,254

SOURCE: *Monthly Bulletin* of the Federation of Employers' Associations, No. 2 (May, 1958), p. 2.

Although many of these groups help their members with labor relations problems, they in turn have organized a special group to give their members advice on labor relations. This is known as the Central Consultative Bureau for Social Affairs of Employers, or *Jajasan Badan Permusjawaratan Urusan Sosial Pengusaha di Indonesia.* As table 15 indicates, its membership consists of sixteen associations made up of 1,463 estates or enterprises and 61 individual firms employing over

[59] The Ministry of Labor listed 37 such organizations in 1958—of which 29 had head offices in Djakarta—plus several large estates and industrial federations. *Tindjauan Masa'alah Perburuhan,* Vol. X, No. 11–12 (March–April, 1959), pp. 17–19.

875,000 workers.[60] This organization has become Indonesianized and is now known simply as the Federation of Employers' Associations in Indonesia. It does not engage in collective bargaining, nor does it handle specific cases at the P4P, but it provides information to employers and discusses with government officials the employers' points of view on basic labor issues. It includes Indonesian, Chinese, and other foreign employers, and publishes special releases and a *Monthly Bulletin* in both Indonesian and English (formerly Dutch).

Management is now undoubtedly a short factor in Indonesian economic development.[61] It has the enormous task of recruiting and training a labor force, including more personnel in the management group itself. It has the even more crucial task, if Indonesia is to develop, of introducing new systems of incentives geared to the current situation in the country, to raise the level of productivity. This will undoubtedly require a less negative and a more coöperative attitude toward the unions. So far the clashes have largely been between foreign employers and Indonesian workers. Although the anticolonial issue is being buried, there is no certainty that there may not be clashes between Indonesian employers and Indonesian trade unions. Unless the workers through their own organizations believe the new incentives are mutually beneficial, they may resist them, just as scientific management was at first attacked in the United States.

The Role of Government

The government is a key factor in labor relations in Indonesia today. It hires a large number of workers, and the standards which it sets in government positions in turn affect local labor markets and local labor conditions. Although there are no general minimum wage laws, the minimum levels established for unskilled government workers in turn set local wage patterns, at least the lower level. Furthermore, the government tries to prevent price increases, especially in rice, to keep real wages from falling.

In the second place, it has instituted a certain amount of labor legislation which tends to protect the rights of the workers. Third, the government has established a system of disputes committees which results in almost universal compulsory arbitration rather than direct

[60] In 1956 this organization reported 1,723 members and 836,288 workers. ILO, *Report of the Committee on Freedom of Employers' and Workers' Organizations* (Geneva, March, 1956).

[61] See Frederick Harbison, "Entrepreneurial Organization as a Factor in Economic Development," *Quarterly Journal of Economics*, Vol. LXX, No. 3 (August, 1956), pp. 364–379.

collective bargaining between management and labor to settle the terms of the labor contract. Fourth, starting in 1957 the military arm of the government has taken an increasing part in labor affairs. In March, 1957, a State of War and Siege was declared, and in August, 1957, a specific strike ban was issued for essential industries. Starting in December, 1957, when a few unions began taking over Dutch properties, the government itself, as in 1945–46, decided that the take-over must be in its hands, and military administrators were appointed by regional commanders to supervise the operations. In 1958 the government established four new organizations consisting of civilian officials and representatives of the army to take over and run the former Dutch properties.

Finally, the government of Indonesia, and particularly the Parliament, is made up of people from a variety of political parties, each interested in promoting its own trade union. Furthermore, the Minister of Labor is a key figure, much more so than the Secretary of Labor in the United States. One former Minister of Labor became a Prime Minister and head of the Constituent Assembly. Several Cabinet ministers and members of Parliament have been associated with important trade union groups. The present Minister of Labor is the head of KBKI, the Nationalist-oriented federation of labor.

THE GOVERNMENT AS ENTREPRENEUR OR INITIATOR OF DEVELOPMENT

The government of Indonesia is a large employer of labor. The number of government workers was estimated in 1958 at about 1,800,000, including all national, provincial, and local government workers as well as those employed by government corporations, such as the railroads, public utilities, and government-owned estates—not including those businesses taken over from the Dutch. In spite of recommendations by some finance ministers to cut the number of bureaucrats in order to reduce government deficits, government employment has not declined, and in fact is apt to increase as the government takes over various business enterprises. As mentioned above, although the Five Year Plan, 1956–1960, called for a modest series of proposals rather than an overall program like the one in India, and although parts of the program were pushed aside because of political and security problems, a new National Planning Council was appointed in 1959 to work out a comprehensive plan. In the meantime the government has started a program of shops to distribute rice and cloth to the people. Whatever plan is proposed, one of the critical questions will be the foreign investments needed to supplement the meagre supply of domestic capital.

Since independence, the Indonesian government has followed a somewhat contradictory policy on foreign investment. On the one hand, it has been afraid that foreign investments might mean more, or new types of, imperialistic, colonial controls, and there has therefore been a tendency to avoid foreign capital. Old foreign investments, primarily Dutch, were supervised closely so that only a fraction of the profits might be repatriated. The take-over of Dutch properties starting in December, 1957, of Kuomintang Chinese in 1958, and of mainland Chinese in rural trade in 1959, has not been encouraging to private foreign capital. On the other hand, a number of high government officials have recognized the necessity for foreign capital in a country where savings and investment are as low as in Indonesia. These officials have talked about encouraging foreign capital. President Sukarno himself made a statement favoring foreign capital while he was in the United States in 1956, and a bill to protect foreign investment was finally passed by the Parliament late in 1958. Thus far, outside of the oil industry and one or two other exceptions, there has been little private foreign capital going to Indonesia since 1949.

Undoubtedly one of the factors which made some foreign concerns reluctant to make new investments in Indonesia has been the unsettled labor conditions. Labor conditions by themselves are not the only or even the most significant factor. Employers have cited such other issues as high taxation, difficulties in repatriation of profits, complex problems in foreign exchange controls, difficulties in importing essential capital goods and equipment at reasonable prices, and the long delays involved in securing entrance visas for foreign management experts. Unsettled financial conditions, inflation, and restriction on monetary movements have also played their part. In certain sections of the country insecurity problems are serious, and in others the problems of squatters and land tenure make it difficult for estate managers to make long-term investment and commitments.

The current level of wages in Indonesia is not usually a serious problem for most foreign employers, if they could be assured of a reasonable level of output. The problem is not the seven-hour work day, but the fact that a number of people work less than a full day. Without any assurances on labor productivity, although money wage rates are low in relation to wages in other countries, the employer argues that labor costs are high. Labor disputes and strikes have been annoying, but their number and duration have declined substantially.

In judging whether there will be sufficient foreign investment in Indonesia, no one factor will be crucial. The general feeling of foreign investors is a great deal more significant. Labor problems may be a contributing factor to uncertainty, but by and large they are not the controlling factor. The reluctance of many foreign investors and the lack of a large, indigenous group of Indonesian employers, make the government turn to foreign government loans.

The United States, through the Export-Import Bank, has lent over $100 million to Indonesia, and has made grants since 1950 for technical assistance and lent money to purchase rice and other agricultural surplus crops against repayments in rupiah. Indonesia has also received grants from other European countries, the Colombo Plan, and the United Nations, and more recently has signed loan agreements with China and the Soviet Union. Mr. Khrushchev, during his 1960 visit to Indonesia, agreed to loans of $250 million in addition to the $100 million formerly agreed upon with the Indonesian government. The reparations agreement with Japan also provides for both development grants and loans.

The level of productivity is an important factor for all government development enterprises. One of the largest of these is the new cement plant at Gresik in East Java, near Surabaja, financed by the Bank Industri Negara and an Export-Import loan. The cement plant was constructed by an American engineering firm, Morris and Knudsen, which signed a contract with the Mineworkers' Union stating that it was hiring workers only for a temporary period of construction, and that when the construction was over the contract with the laborers would be terminated on payment of dismissal compensation. Already in 1956 there were signs that the union was anxious to continue to hold the same number of positions after the transfer of the finished plant to the operating agency of the Indonesian government. If this demand of the Mineworkers were secured, the plans of the government to provide cement at lower costs and lower prices to the Indonesian economy would vanish. The manager of the cement plant was conscious of this problem, but union pressures on government plants are apt to be great. This problem of excess manpower was also an issue in the privately owned cement plant in Padang, Central Sumatra, which was taken over by the government. The government as an employer, therefore, faces the problem of the number of workers it will employ. Certainly the large number of employees attached to all government bureaus does not augur well for a low-cost, small work force in government enterprises. Here is an area of real conflict between the "job-conscious" unions and the government.

Another major conflict arises in the Indonesian government's attitude toward strikes. In general the government is prolabor, but believes it must prohibit strikes in time of emergencies, while the unions want to preserve the right to strike. Workers in plants taken over from the Dutch and in certain other establishments supervised by the government are subject to the general strike measures discussed in the next section, but in 1956 the government ruled against strikes of railroad workers, stressing their role as government workers. Labor disputes of government employees are not handled by the regular Central Disputes Committee, and government workers cannot engage in regular forms of collective bargaining, since their wages, hours and working conditions are set by legislation. This, of course, does not keep the unions from agitating for improvements in the scale of government salaries. In 1956 the pay for government workers was raised, but many of the unions felt that this was inadequate to meet the rising cost of living. Some increases were given in 1957 to higher ranks, but in 1958 the pressure was strong for increased salaries for all government workers in the face of rising prices. The government will always find itself in a predicament as inflation caused by internal emergencies or by stepped-up development plans creates pressure for higher wages and salaries.

Since 1945 the government has done nothing to discourage unionization of government workers, and union membership is high among them. Each department may have its own union or group of competing unions. The railroad workers are divided into two major unions, and the workers on government estates belong to one of a dozen or more unions to which private estate employees belong. Although these government unions are limited in their bargaining and strike activities, they still play an important part in the Indonesian labor scene. Many of their members give leadership to other unions, and they exert pressure on Cabinet officials and political parties to take prolabor stands.

REGULATORY POLICIES

Indonesia is a country with relatively little labor legislation but a good deal of labor regulation. The most important labor laws in Indonesia are the Labor Code (Conditions of Employment), the Labor Disputes Acts of 1951 and 1957, the Workmen's Compensation Law, and the Collective Agreements Law. A number of specific bills have been proposed but not adopted because it was frequently difficult under the Provisional Constitution of 1950 to secure the necessary Cabinet clearance, the Parliamentary committee approval, and final passage by Parliament. In the meantime, decrees or circular letters were frequently used by the Ministry of Labor to cover such subjects as the voluntary registration of unions, holidays, time off for election, and notification by employers of mass dismissals of ten or more workers. The decisions of the Regional Disputes Committee, *Panitya Penjelesaian Perselisihan Perburuhan Daerah* (P4D), and the Central Disputes Committee, *Panitya Penjelesaian Perselisihan Perburuhan Pusat* (P4P),[62] are perhaps even more important in the labor relations field because these decisions cover a number of items not yet subject to specific laws. For example, the Central Disputes Committee has handed down binding decisions requiring employers to give one to four months' notice before dismissal, except for cause. Similar decisions have been made on almost all problems facing management and labor. In fact these decisions are generally a substitute for the system of free collective bargaining in the United States and Western European countries.

Although some Dutch colonial labor legislation dated back to the nineteenth century, it was not until after the institution of the Ethical Policy in 1901 that such protective measures were adopted as the appointment in 1904 of labor inspectors to supervise labor recruitment and labor contracts, the passage of the Factories Act of 1905 to prevent accidents, and the gradual cession to the Labor Bureau of greater responsibilities, such as the enforcement of regulations concerning child labor, the employment of women at night, safety standards in hazardous industries, and workmen's compensation. Although considerable new or improved legislation was passed in the 1930's, Indonesians felt that much of it applied to Dutch employees rather than to all labor. For example, special regulations were passed for estate assistants, most of whom were foreigners. In general the provisions of the Civil Code applied to European employees and to a few higher-paid Indonesians and other Asians who held jobs similar to those of Europeans. Only a very brief section applied to Indonesian workers. At the outbreak of World War II, several military ordinances tightened the provisions included in the penal code of 1923 against strikes or picketing which were against the public interest, and a tripartite Commission of Labor Affairs was formed to advise on labor problems and to issue binding decisions in labor-management disputes.

During the struggles with the Dutch, the Republic of Indonesia began to develop its own labor legislation. After the granting of sovereignty and the formation of a unitary state, the government had to adopt labor legislation for the whole of Indonesia.

In Law No. 1 of 1951, Parliament determined that the Labor Code

[62] P4D is the abbreviation used by Indonesians rather than PPPPD. The D stands for Regional. In P4P the last P stands for Central. Both of these abbreviations are used widely in labor circles.

of 1948 should become the law of the land for all of Indonesia.[63] This particular act is still in the process of development as the Ministry of Labor applies certain sections to more and more groups of workers. In general the law provides for a seven-hour day, a forty-hour week, with a weekly day of rest and holidays free.[64] It requires monthly days of rest and maternity leave of 3 months for women. It sets limits on the employment of children under 14, youths 14 to 18, and women. It provides for two weeks' vacation, and more recently the three months' long leave sections have been applied to certain large corporations by the Central Disputes Committee. The law also requires that places of work and workers' living accommodations meet certain sanitary and hygienic standards to be established by the labor inspectors. Although penalties are provided for violations and the Ministry of Labor is charged with enforcement, it is impossible, with the present staff, to secure complete compliance. The unions insist, however, that the larger firms at least meet the standards provided by the Labor Code.

By all odds the most important of the 1951 labor regulations was Emergency Act No. 16, promulgated by the President on October 22, 1951, which established the basic pattern for handling labor disputes and which remained in operation until June, 1958, when Law No. 22 of 1957 came into operation.[65] The act did not prohibit strikes but regulated carefully the handling of disputes with a view to minimizing the number of strikes.

Basically the administration of labor disputes was handled at three levels, the local, the regional, and the national. In addition, there were special provisions for voluntary arbitration, which were not frequently used, and for *ad hoc* investigating committees which might be appointed to study particularly difficult cases. Although the act planned to have as much of the work as possible done at the local level where the disputes originated, in practice a great majority of the cases were appealed to the national level. The Ministry of Labor, in most of the key cities, had a chief of the industrial relations department whose obligation it was to be informed about all impending labor disputes

[63] An English text has been published by the ILO Legislative Series of Indonesia, 1951-1. The author also has had access to a compilation of *Labor Legislation of the Republic of Indonesia 1951–1957*, prepared by N. V. Standard Vacuum Petroleum Company (Djakarta, December, 1957).

[64] Government Regulation No. 4, 1951 requires employers to secure permission from the Labor Inspection Service for longer working hours.

[65] This Act was preceded by an ordinance of the Ministry of Defense dated February 13, 1951, prohibiting strikes and lockouts in vital undertakings, because early in 1950 the number of strikes, especially on the estates, grew so rapidly that the Cabinet became worried that they were disrupting the economy.

and to offer his services as a mediator. If either of the parties was not satisfied at the local level, he had to file the dispute with the Regional Disputes Committee (P4D). For three weeks after filing of the case, or longer if the P4D so ruled, no strikes or lockouts were legal. A Ministry of Labor official headed the P4D; the other six members were representatives of other ministries. They themselves, or their deputies, went to the scene of the dispute and tried to mediate it. They could also issue recommendations, but these were not binding on the parties. Unfortunately, most of the disputes were not settled by these recommendations, since one side or the other, more frequently labor, usually felt it to its advantage to appeal the case to the Central Disputes Committee (P4P) in Djakarta. The P4P from 1951 to 1958 handled 8,500 cases, or over one-third of the more than 22,000 disputes referred to the Ministry of Labor.[66]

When the case arrived at the P4P in Djakarta, it was generally turned over to one of the three major divisions: agriculture, manufacturing, or other industries. The case might be specifically referred to a representative from one of the seven ministries included on the P4P. Although each case was handled on its merits, there was a tendency for P4P, in the light of existing law, agreements, usage, equity and the interest of the state, to look to previous cases and to establish certain rules which became widely accepted practices. Furthermore, P4P tended to lump together cases of a similar character and hand down one general ruling. For example, rulings were handed down for all the estates and all the unions on the east coast of Sumatra. In East Java, although separate decisions were made for each of the estate unions, the decisions were based on the same principles.

Individual discharge cases received a great deal of attention from the local officers, regional boards and even the P4P. This resulted in delays in handling the major disputes, which often involved a variety of issues. In such complicated cases the P4P might make a ruling on certain of the issues and then, to study other complex points, would appoint an *ad hoc* investigating committee made up of representatives of the various ministries particularly concerned in this dispute. This investigating committee reported to the full P4P before a final decision was made. For example, the P4P established a study committee on

[66] There was considerable divergence between the number of cases settled at the local and regional levels in various areas of Indonesia. For example, the industrial relations officials in Jogjakarta were able to handle a number of cases at the local level before referring them to the regional headquarters at Semarang. On the other hand, the Medan regional office in North Sumatra referred about 95 per cent of their cases to Djakarta for solution.

pensions in the 1956 estates dispute on the east coast of Sumatra. A second board was set up to study the issue of yearly bonuses. In some cases, therefore, before one dispute was settled in its entirety another might have begun. Labor relations were in a state of constant flux, with no real periods of quiet.

The decisions of the P4P might be in the form of a simple recommendation, but, since it was known in advance, because of the long preliminary stages, that one side or the other would not accept a mere recommendation, most of the decisions of the P4P were binding in character. This meant that most labor disputes in Indonesia were really settled by compulsory arbitration rather than by collective bargaining. The P4P could appeal to the courts for enforcement of its decisions. There was a tendency prior to 1957 not to take illegal strike cases to the public prosecutor.

Although cases were handled individually and conditions changed, these decisions developed into a system of industrial jurisprudence which in many respects supplements the Labor Code. One cannot understand labor legislation in Indonesia without a knowledge of the major P4P decisions.[67]

In the light of the above machinery, what has been the record on (a) disputes not resulting in loss of work, and on (b) strikes or work stoppages? These results should be studied in two parts, from 1950 to 1956, and then from 1957 on, after the emergency strike ban was in effect. Table 16 shows that the number of disputes rose from 180 in 1950 to 3,891 cases officially filed with the Ministry of Labor in 1956.[68] Strikes also tended to increase from 1950 to 1956 (1953 actually being the highest year), but the number of workers involved has decreased and the number of working hours lost by strikes has declined markedly from 54 million hours in 1950 to less than 7 million in 1956. These trends reflect the greater experience of unions and management in labor relations, the use of shorter strike techniques, and the increasing effectiveness of the mediation and arbitration machinery. Furthermore, although over 3,100,000 workers were involved in labor disputes in 1956, the number of workers actually on strike was less than 11 per

[67] The Board sends its decisions to the management and labor participants, while important cases are reported in the newspapers. The Ministry of Labor issues mimeographed books containing the cases in serial order, but these are not for general circulation. They do, however, index the disputes by the contestants and in terms of the major question involved, such as individual discharge cases, mass dismissals, wages, bonuses, vacation pay, and other topics.

[68] The 1953 change in the definition of disputes, to include only those which were submitted to the Ministry of Labor, may account in part for the decrease in number of disputes from 1952 to 1953.

cent of those involved in disputes. The three largest causes for disputes and strikes were wages, discharge, and special allowances.

In comparison with 1956, the figures show a rise in 1957 in both the number of disputes and the number of workers involved. The strike figures, however, indicate a very marked decrease in 1957, if the mil-

TABLE 16

NUMBER OF DISPUTES, WORK STOPPAGES, AND WORKERS INVOLVED IN INDONESIA, 1950–1959

Year	Disputes	Workers involved in disputes	Work stoppages	Workers involved in stoppages	Working hours lost through work stoppages
1950	180	—	184	490,539	54,489,897
1951	2,754	—	541	319,030	26,039,398
1952	4,003	—	349	132,963	6,152,377
1953	1,823	1,268,480	280	419,580	4,812,090
1954	2,963	2,304,747	347	157,582	2,385,730
1955	3,697	3,488,747	469	238,872	4,097,803
1956	3,896	3,111,957	505	340,203	6,968,931
1957	4,131	5,057,478	151	62,024 [a]	863,257 [a]
1958	3,350	2,975,922	55	13,578	98,060
1959 [b]	2,052	1,577,437	65	26,245	217,316

SOURCES: Ministry of Labor, *Ekonomi dan Keuangan Indonesia*, Vol. VIII, No. 7 (July, 1955), p. 458; *Tindjauan Masa'alah Perburuhan*, Vol. X, Nos. 9–10 (January–February, 1959), pp. 44–49.

[a] In addition, 1,030,083 workers went out on strike and 7,218,706 hours were lost at the end of 1957 in the protest movement concerning West Irian.

[b] Provisional figures from Bank Indonesia, Bulletin No. 20, 1960, tables 55 and 56.

lion workers who lost over seven million manhours of work in the short protest strikes against the Dutch position in West Irian are excluded. The 1958 figures show a further decline to a negligible amount of 98,000 hours of work lost through strikes. On the other hand, there were 3,350 disputes involving about three million workers.

Ever since the Emergency Act No. 16 of 1951 was promulgated, plans had been under way to amend the law or to put it on a permanent basis. A number of proposals were made, including a specific bill which was discussed by the Parliamentary Section of Labor in 1956 after receiving Cabinet approval. Some specific provisions were disliked by organized labor, some by management, and some by certain legislators. At that time several general criticisms about the 1951 Act and the proposed amendments were also voiced. A few labor leaders, management spokesmen, government officials, and foreign advisers suggested that the system should be completely changed to get away from compulsory arbitration. One labor leader conceded that this would not reduce disputes in the first year or two but argued that, after a period of trial and error, unions would be forced to take more responsible positions, to carry through collective negotiations, and to reach amicable decisions. One representative of a large estate group had a similar idea, although he recognized that many of the smaller estates would fear such a decision because during the first year or two conditions might become so intolerable that they would have to go out of business. Similarly, some of the smaller unions did not like this proposal because only the stronger unions could withstand the strikes which might develop. Furthermore, the smaller unions might not be able to secure recognition by the employers. Some labor advisers suggested that to avoid multiple unionization, P4P, like the NLRB in the United States, should have the power to hold elections and to determine who represented the majority of the workers, the group which secured the majority being given exclusive bargaining power. Such a suggestion has been attacked in Indonesia as undemocratic, since it would eliminate the smaller unions. Furthermore, some of the non-Communist unions have opposed such a measure on the ground that it would play directly into the hands of the largest labor group, SOBSI. No such radical change was politically feasible, since the initial disruption to the economy might be so great that the Cabinet in office would fall. It was much safer for the government to continue to use its power of compulsory arbitration, even its right to forbid certain strikes, to preserve a quasipeace in industrial relations and to allow production to continue.

Parliament finally passed a new law, the Settlement of Labor Disputes Act No. 22 of 1957, which was promulgated on April 8, 1957, and came into effect in June, 1958. The present law includes most of the features of the 1951 Act, with three major changes: an attempt to have more cases settled at the local and regional level, a plan to include worker and management representatives on the committees, and the right of the Minister of Labor to veto the decisions of the P4P.

The first change provides that all possible steps must be taken by the union and the employer to settle a dispute themselves before referring it to the Labor Relations Office of the Minister of Labor for mediation. Moreover, if either labor or management wants to take action against the other it must give written notice to the Regional Disputes Committee (P4D) specifying that negotiations have been attempted through a government mediator, or that the other party has refused to negotiate, or that twice in the last two weeks the requesting party has tried in vain to induce the other party to negotiate. Such action may be taken only after official confirmation from the chairman of the P4D, which shall be given within seven days after receipt of the notice. In addition to the right to make recommendations in the 1951 Act, the P4D is given the right to make binding decisions at the regional level in certain cases involving local issues and individual discharge cases. This has relieved the national P4P of a great many time-consuming disputes which have only local significance.

The second new provision involves functional representation of labor and management as well as the government at both the regional and national levels. The original proposal of five government, three labor, and three management representatives was modified to five, five, and five, with the further provision that five deputies be appointed to represent each group. This has made it possible to have a wide representation of both trade unions and employer organizations, which might have been politically difficult if a smaller number had to be chosen. In Djakarta the Central Disputes Committee has been divided into two subcommittees: one handles cases arising in agriculture, in commerce and on the docks; and the other takes industry and other cases. Each committee includes some regular members and some deputies, so that for all practical purposes the deputies have as much voice as the regular members. All the appointments were made by the President on the basis of slates prepared by the Ministry of Labor on recommendations from labor and employer organizations. Once sworn in, all members and deputies are supposed to consider the public interest, not to grant special favors, and not to represent their own particular organization.[69]

In the third place, the Minister of Labor may within fourteen days of a P4P decision suspend or reverse it, "in case he considers such necessary to ensure public order and to protect the State's interest." As finally provided in Article 17, this veto power of the Minister of Labor can be exercised only after consulting the ministers having representatives on the P4P. Although up until January, 1960, this veto had not been exercised, there is the possibility that important cases might be appealed to the Minister of Labor, thus introducing another layer in public mediation and arbitration of labor disputes.

During the period just before the dispute goes to the government and while it is being mediated, or handled by the P4D, a special inquiry committee, or the Minister of Labor, or while it is being sub-

[69] Government Regulation No. 51 of 1957 covers the appointment and discharge of the chairman, members, and deputy members of the Central Settlement Committee. See also Government Regulation No. 50 of 1957 and Regulations of the Ministry of Labor Nos. 6 and 7 of 1958, which provide for various procedural rules governing P4P, P4D, and their secretariats.

mitted to outside arbitration, neither labor nor management may change the labor conditions or take any retaliatory action such as a strike or lockout. Although the new law encourages more decisions at the local and regional levels and prescribes relatively short periods for normal consideration, in important cases strikes may be postponed for a long time until a final decision is reached.

Experience with the new machinery indicates a great reduction in the load of the Central Disputes Committee (P4P), because the regional committee (P4D) can issue binding decisions which cannot be appealed unless the issue involves more than one region or industry. The case load has also been reduced because of the emergency situation in the country, with workers knowing that they have no right to strike. Of the 102 cases before the P4P from January to July, 1959, about half (52) dealt with wages, other important topics being dismissals, labor relations, and housing.

The new tripartite boards seemed to be working together quite harmoniously. More than 90 per cent of the cases heard by P4P the first year were decided unanimously. In general the new law was preferred to the old one, but some observers were skeptical about how much the change in labor relations could be attributed to the administration of the new law and how much to military and political conditions within the country.

One of the most important of these conditions is the strike ban instituted in 1957 as part of the emergency security measures which gave military commanders broad authority in their respective territories. In order to implement the joint statement of the War Administrator and Minister of Labor of October 10, 1957, stating that workers as a functional group should assist and coöperate with the government in its efforts to solve national problems, the Chief of Staff, General Nasution, issued orders on November 6, 1957, establishing a Central Labor-Military Organization, *Badan Kerdja Sama Buruh dan Militer* (BKS *Bumil*). On December 12, 1957, after the break with the Dutch in Indonesia, representatives of fourteen labor organizations, consisting of eleven of the federations of labor and three special groups of bank employees, civil servants, and workers of foreign-owned concerns, signed a charter of coöperation with the military administrator. Because of the importance of the struggle for West Irian, the working program dated January 13, 1958, gave top priority to coördination with the West Irian Liberation Front. *Bumil* was to see that in the firms taken over from the Dutch the workers did their duty, that no sabotage took place, and that the plants were kept in good running condition. *Bumil* was also to make suggestions as to how to absorb workers who had lost their employment as a result of the West Irian struggle. Each of the fourteen labor groups appointed a permanent and an alternate member to the labor consultative council which was to advise the military commander on matters in the labor field. The chairman, vice-chairman, and heads of financial administration and information bureaus were military men, but the security, the economic, and the social affairs divisions were each headed by three union representatives. In addition to the central organization, *Bumil* established regional (*Daerah*) offices in such cities as Semarang and Medan, and subregional offices in cities like Jogjakarta and Balikpapan. In each place a military man was in charge of *Bumil* with representatives from all the labor organizations in the region. Its charter provided that *Bumil* should not enter into the internal affairs of the unions, and that all expenses would be charged to the military organization.

Since one of the purposes of this organization was to provide industrial peace, some of the unions began to appeal their labor disputes to *Bumil.* This brought *Bumil* into conflict with the regular arbitration machinery of the government. The issue was resolved by maintaining the jurisdiction of P4P and P4D over regular dispute cases. Though P4P itself has no direct representation at *Bumil,* the Ministry of Labor maintains a liaison officer. There is no question that the military commanders have been active in preventing strikes and political demonstrations.[70]

Labor has tried to gain concessions from *Bumil,* and the latter has kept strong unions in line. Some of the smaller unions have used their positions in *Bumil* to try to secure more prestige. One union official was frank enough to admit that he appointed one of his officers to *Bumil* so he could draw a salary, since it was hard for the union to collect dues because there could be no strikes.

Some of the top military leaders, however, had hoped their organization might lead to a united labor movement. On certain broad labor issues like higher wages, all the union groups were united, but on political issues, groupings tended to follow along ideological lines. Although a number of informal meetings have been held among non-Communist trade unions with a view to securing greater unity, most of these efforts have resulted in *ad hoc* working coöperation rather than unity.

President Sukarno and his followers are interested in forming a new

---

[70] In 1960 at Palembang a PERBUM leader was jailed for an illegal strike of wax-workers. *Times of Indonesia,* February 16, 1960, p. 4. SOBSI was barred from demonstrating against the explosion of the French atom bomb in the Sahara, *ibid.,* February 25, 1960, p. 4.

National Front which would include the military and all political and functional organizations. In July, 1960, the Minister of Labor held a conference of all the leading labor unions and numerous government bodies to discuss a draft regulation for the establishment of an all-embracing Labor Front (*Organisasi Persatuan Pekerdja Indonesia*, OPPI). SOBSI refused to approve the plan, while a number of specific modifications were proposed by other labor leaders.[71] Despite the backing of the President and his Minister of Labor, it appears that voluntary unity among all labor groups is not to be realized in the immediate future.

The government is ubiquitous in the field of labor relations. It is a large employer of civil servants, it manages a great variety of business, it provides for tripartite labor disputes and arbitration machinery. Through the military it has established the Labor-Military Organization. The President, with the assistance of his Minister of Labor, who is head of one of the largest federations of labor, is trying to establish an all-embracing Labor Front. Labor representatives have been appointed to the new parliament and major councils of the country. In a labor dispute today a union may deal with a government organization such as the estate organization PPN *Baru*, which is composed of both civilian and military officials, and then appeal the case to a tripartite body on which the unions, the employers, and the government have an equal voice. The employer group may be able to appeal to the military commander, as may the representatives of the union. The union may also seek help from the labor members of Parliament or the National Planning Council. The extent to which collective bargaining between management and labor can be carried on in this atmosphere is difficult to judge. It is likely that some collective bargaining will continue, with frequent appeals to government agencies. As long as a state of emergency exists in Indonesia the military will play an important part in labor relations. As long as President Sukarno pushes for a "guided economy," the civilian government will continue to become more actively enmeshed in labor problems.

Conclusions

Industrial relations in Indonesia reflect a transition from a colonial to a nationalist economy, in which older autocratic and paternalistic attitudes and policies still linger on. The country is trying to move from an agricultural economy with raw material exports to a more

[71] Government of Indonesia, Department of Labor Affairs, *Conference on Presidential Draft Regulation on the Establishment of the Indonesian Workers' Association Organization, July, 1960* (Djakarta, 1960) (mimeo).

commercialized and industrial base, but as yet no plan of rapid economic development has been implemented. The labor force of 35 to 40 million persons out of a population of about 90 million is made up largely of farmers and other self-employed individuals. Only about eight million people are employed by others, including the government, for wages or salaries. Population densities vary so much that there is surplus labor in Java, Madura, and Bali, while there is a relative scarcity of labor in Sumatra, Sulawesi, and some of the other islands. In all areas the number of skilled professional and managerial personnel is very small indeed.

Trade unions were born with the rise of nationalism; they were part of the active phase of the revolution against the Dutch from 1945 to 1949; and they still are one of the major protest forces in the country. These relatively new organizations, with the vigor and enthusiasm of youth, have risen in importance since 1945. They face a series of problems, including multiple unionism with various political and ideological ties, a shortage of experienced and trained leaders, lack of an active and educated dues-paying rank-and-file, and an insufficient appreciation of the necessity of productivity and economic development.

Management is no longer predominantly foreign, as it was in colonial times and even up to 1957. The remaining foreign managers face real difficulties in adjusting to their new political and social position and in adapting their labor relations practices to current conditions. More and more, management is becoming "Indonesianized." Whatever the nationality, whether private or government, management faces the key problems of eliminating older practices based on force, of training more supervisors, and of finding incentives which will tend to stimulate workers to higher levels of productivity. The scarcity of sufficient trained managers is a real bottleneck to industrialization and economic development.

The government is an ever-present factor in labor relations in Indonesia, as in many other newly nationalistic economies that have overthrown colonial control. The government has its own labor problems as a large employer, both in its regular departments and in various types of enterprises. It has formed new organizations to run the estates and other enterprises taken over from the Dutch. It has organized a Ministry of Labor, and some labor legislation has been adopted, the most important providing for tripartite arbitration of labor disputes. This system has tended to be a substitute for free union-management negotiations, although there is some evidence of increasing use of collective bargaining, subject always to appeal to arbitration. It is unlikely in the near future that the government will take its hands off labor relations or give up its power to arbitrate disputes or to declare strikes illegal in times of emergency. Nor will the military give up its power in the labor relations field as long as a state of emergency exists.

The future of labor relations in Indonesia is dependent upon the economic, social, and political developments of the country. Indonesia is passing through the long, second stage of its revolution, the more difficult phase because, unlike the active phase where almost all the people rallied against the colonial power, there is no great positive area of agreement. Sukarno is trying to have a "guided democracy" with an increasing number of national controls over all phases of life. There are indications that not all of the federations of labor are willing voluntarily to join his proposed Labor Front.

The great danger in Indonesia is drift in which there will be some attempts at political stability and some measures for economic development, but no concerted and coördinated effort to achieve these twin objectives. Such a drift may lead to more and more regional revolts, military coups, serious shortages, and further economic deterioration.

If, as many people hope, political problems can be resolved and a good deal of effort is put forth in the field of economic development, the government, the unions, and management may be able to replace older policies such as low subsistence wages, low output, and employment of extra workers, with new industrial relations practices geared to increasing the level of production and the standard of living of the people. During this period of concentrated effort to secure economic development, however, some checks on wage-price policy may have to be introduced by the government, as in other developing countries. In the long run, the gains from political stability and economic development would seem to hold out the most hope for an increase in the standard of living of labor, farmers, and the rest of the people of Indonesia.

Chapter IV — Brazil, Argentina, and Chile

ROBERT J. ALEXANDER

The "ABC" countries have traditionally been the leaders of South America. Politically, militarily, and economically they were in the vanguard of the region through the nineteenth century and the beginning of the twentieth. Since World War I they have led in the industrialization of the continent; this brought in its train the development of a modern system of labor-management relations. However, striking differences in institutions and practices have evolved in each of these nations.

The purposes of this chapter are twofold: to seek to explain the differences in the systems of labor relations in the three countries, and to note the effects of these systems on the process of economic development. After a short look at the general characteristics of economic growth, we shall pay some attention to the labor side of the equation, noting the problems of recruitment and training of workers and the extent of unionization among them. We shall then look at the employers' situation, including the selection and training of management personnel, the tendencies toward employer paternalism, and the organization of the employers for collective bargaining. Thereafter, there will be a brief survey of the way in which relations between the employers and their workers' organizations are conducted, and, finally, an attempt to draw together some conclusions about the material.

The Economic Background

Argentina, Brazil, and Chile were until recent decades primarily the producers of raw materials and foodstuffs for the large industrial countries, and imported manufactured products. They still depend largely on the export of mineral or agricultural commodities for the bulk of their foreign exchange, and industrialization has not gone far enough in any of the three countries to make it self-sufficient in manufactured goods, particularly producers' goods.

BRAZIL

The economic history of this nation is a story of recurring cycles of production of key export commodities. Starting soon after the beginning of colonization with the brazilwood (the product from which Brazil got its name) cycle, there came booms in diamonds, sugar, rubber, and finally, in the latter part of the nineteenth century, coffee. The coffee period, which still continues, saw Brazil obtaining virtually a monopoly on the production and export of this product. Attempts, largely unsuccessful, to limit production, and the entry of many new producers into the world coffee market, have in recent years reduced the relative importance of Brazil as a producer of the coffee bean. However, the country is still heavily dependent upon coffee as its principal foreign-exchange earner.[1]

Remnants of all the cycles of production are still to be found in Brazilian agriculture, which varies markedly from one part of the country to another. In the Amazon valley, in the far north, agricultural production is largely confined to the collection of rubber, brazil nuts, and oleaginous nuts in the wild jungles, and some small subsistence farming. Farther south and east, in the area of the "hump" of Brazil, sugar is still the principal product, as it was in colonial times. The area has been badly hit by drought in recent decades, and there is also a growing desert region in the northeastern area.

Farther south, the large state of Baía is one of the world's principal producers of cacao, though in recent years it has failed to keep up with modern techniques and has fallen behind West Africa. Grazing is also a major agricultural industry in Baía, and the principal type of agricultural production in neighboring Minas Gerais.

The area around Rio de Janeiro has a diversified agriculture, which is even more notable in the state of São Paulo. The latter is not only the largest coffee-producing area in the world, but in recent years has also become the largest grower of sugar in Brazil, and the country's

---

[1] The extent to which Brazil is still dependent on coffee exports is demonstrated by a note in *Hanson's Latin American Letter* of September 28, 1957, that as a result of a drop in Brazilian coffee exports from 16.8 million bags in the year ending June 30, 1956, to 15 million bags in the year ending June 30, 1957, "Brazil saw its net reserves of gold and exchange drop by some 30 per cent and its net reserve position reduced by June 30 to *less than eight weeks* (italics Hanson's) minimum essential import requirements for economic stability."

principal source of cotton. A number of other agricultural products are also grown successfully, notably truck garden crops, cultivated largely by the sizeable Japanese element in the state. In recent years coffee growing has spilled over into the state of Paraná, to the south of São Paulo, as well as into Goiás to the west. In the two southernmost states of Santa Caterina and Rio Grande do Sul, grains and cattle are the two principal sources of agricultural wealth. The chief restriction on the expansion of these types of cultivation is inadequate transportation facilities.

The great hope of Brazilian agriculture in the future consists of the two western states of Goiás and Mato Grosso, in the watersheds of the Paraná and Amazon rivers. This area, which until recently has been almost inaccessible because of lack of adequate transport and communications, is a region of rolling plains and low plateaus which some have compared to the Great Plains of the United States and to the Argentine pampas. As population moves into the area and a road network is developed, this can become the country's breadbasket.

Different types of cultivation and their historical development have generated varying social systems and customs in the regions of Brazil. The isolated and itinerant Indian or mestizo rubber or nut gatherer of the Amazon Valley, eking out a precarious existence along the edge of the mighty stream, is vastly different from the Negro peasant of northeastern Brazil. In the northeastern section, the slave plantation system of colonial and imperial Brazil was most deeply rooted. This has left its imprint on the racial strain of the inhabitants and on the still strong, though rapidly diminishing, paternalistic pattern of relations between the owner of the *fazenda* and his workers. Down through the nineteenth century, the fazenda was largely self-sufficient, virtually the center of the world so far as most of those living on it were concerned. The plantation owner provided, well or poorly, for virtually all the wants and needs of his workers. Until 1888 these workers were most likely his slaves, and the traditions of the slave era linger on.

The workers in the cacao industry of eastern Brazil are in somewhat the same situation as their brothers farther north. The paternalism of slave days persists there, too, though the owner of the cacao fazenda is less conscious of his responsibilities than his sugar-growing counterpart to the north, and, if anything, the situation of the cacao worker is more miserable than that of the northeastern sugar worker.

In the Rio de Janeiro–São Paulo area, the agricultural wage earner finds much less of the slave tradition in his relations with his employer. In recent decades his standard of living has probably been going up fairly steadily, under the pressure of the forces of industrialization and the tendency to drift to the city to improve his lot. In the very far south, the agricultural worker is a man with more independent traditions, and there is a greater degree of small land ownership. The situation of the worker on a wheat fazenda or of the gaucho on a cattle ranch in Rio Grande do Sul is more comparable to that of similar workers across the borders in Uruguay or Argentina than to that of the Brazilian sugar or cacao worker.

Mining is of growing importance in Brazil. It is centered largely in the state of Minas Gerais which, as its name indicates (Minas Gerais means "great mines"), has one of the world's greatest concentration of minerals. Not only is there a major deposit of iron ore, but copper, bauxite, molybdenum, titanium, gold, diamonds, semiprecious stones, and a great variety of other minerals are also to be found. The exploitation of some of these has barely begun. In the south, in Santa Caterina and Rio Grande do Sul, the country's only important sources of coal are to be found. This coal is of low quality and the veins are narrow and difficult to exploit.

Petroleum is also of increasing importance. The principal oil field now being exploited is in the state of Baía, though in recent years there has been intensive exploration activity by the government oil monopoly, Petrobras, in the Amazon valley, and some operating wells have been discovered there. The Brazilians are perhaps excessively optimistic about the possibilities of oil in the Amazon region.

ARGENTINA

This nation is one of the world's principal producers of meat and grains. It became Great Britain's largest supplier of these commodities during the third quarter of the nineteenth century. In turn, the British invested very heavily in the Argentine railroad system, primarily to get these products to the ports of Buenos Aires and Rosario. The upshot was that Argentina became the richest of the South American countries, and the standard of living of its inhabitants rose a great deal higher than that of any other country on the continent.

The cattle ranges of Argentina were tended by the successors to the fabulous gauchos, made famous in song and story for their independence, their violence, and their valor. The cowboy of the fenced-in plains had some of these qualities, but he also developed a feeling of loyalty to and identification with his "patrón" which in many cases survived even the Perón experience.

The wheat *estancias* of the pampas were cultivated largely by immigrants from Spain and Italy who streamed into the country between 1870 and 1914. Many of these, who came to be known as *golondrinas* or (swallows), came from Europe during the harvesting season (the opposite of that in their native Italy and Spain) and returned home during the Argentine winter. But hundreds of thousands of them ultimately made their homes in the New World, and their descendants are the rural peons of present-day Argentina. These workers came to be largely dependent upon their employers for housing, medical care, whatever education their children received, and virtually every other need.

Grain and meat are still the principal agricultural products of Argentina, though in recent years the country's exports of these staples have declined and the growing population of the cities is eating a larger part of the production. In addition to wheat and meat, the Argentine pampas produces flax, sunflowers, and other oil-producing crops. In the subtropical north are grown sugar and cotton (largely for internal consumption), *yerba maté* (the bitter Argentine tea), and coffee. The semiarid western edge of the pampas grows grapes, from which some of the finest wine of the Western Hemisphere is made. In the cold south, sheep raising is the principal occupation.

Mining has never figured prominently in the Argentine economy. In contrast with the munificence of minerals which the Chileans have discovered on their side of the Andes, the Argentines have found relatively few such resources east of the Great Divide. There are considerable quantities of low-grade coal, the exploitation of which was increased during the Perón period; and there are some copper, bauxite, gold, and other minerals, but not in sufficient quantities to make mining a major part of the economy.

Oil production has been going on in Argentina for more than forty years, principally in the southern part of the province of Buenos Aires and in Patagonia. There are also deposits of oil in the northern province of Salta, and it is presumed that there are important resources in some other parts of the country. However, production has been unable to keep up with demand, and, as in Brazil, increasingly large amounts of valuable foreign exchange have been spent on the import of petroleum products.[2] During the latter half of 1958 the government, headed by President Arturo Frondizi, made a number of contracts with foreign oil companies for the purpose of obtaining their aid in exploiting the subsoil resources and overcoming Argentina's deficit in petroleum.

---

[2] Perón, *La Fuerza es el Derecho de las Bestias* (Santiago, Chile, 1956), pp. 158–164.

CHILE

Although agriculture is still the occupation of a million Chileans, it has been unable to keep up with growing demand, and in the last quarter of a century Chile has been converted from a net exporter of agricultural commodities to a net importer. Agriculture has been vastly overshadowed by the mining industries, principally nitrates and copper.

Chile runs for nearly three thousand miles down the Pacific coast of South America, and is divided into three distinct areas, approximately equal in length. The northern third is a desert, created by the Humboldt current, which runs a hundred miles offshore and forces the prevailing winds to drop their moisture out at sea. This area is the main center of the mining industry. The southern third of the country consists in part of a series of islands, largely uninhabited, which are characterized by torrential rains most of the year round. There are tremendous untapped forests in this region. Farther south, in Chilean Patagonia and on the island of Tierra del Fuego, the largest industry is sheep raising, and Punta Arenas, the world's most southerly city, is the center of a large packing industry.

The Central Valley, running from about one hundred fifty miles north of Santiago to Puerto Montt, where the valley runs into the sea, is the principal agricultural area of Chile. Here wheat, corn, and vineyards predominate, while in the Santiago region and in the far southern part of the valley dairying is also important. The land of the Central Valley is held by a small number of large landowners and much of the arable land is not cultivated, since the landholders make a comfortable living through exploiting a relatively small amount of their holdings through old-fashioned methods and very cheap labor, and have little incentive to use more modern techniques or complicated agricultural machinery. In the southern part of the region, however, German farmers have led the way in developing better methods.

Mining is the source of most of Chile's foreign exchange. In the 1860's and 1870's, Chilean and English entrepreneurs began exploiting the nitrate resources of what were then the Peruvian and Bolivian provinces of Tarapacá and Antofagasta. In 1879, in the War of the Pacific, Chile seized these two provinces from her neighbors, and thereafter nitrates provided quick riches for many Chileans and most of the country's foreign currency earnings for a quarter of a century. Chile had a monopoly on the world's supply of natural nitrate and it was not until the Germans, cut off from Chilean supplies, developed the process of extracting nitrogen from the air during World War I, that the Chilean nitrate industry ran into hard times.

The 1920's were a period of permanent crisis for Chile, because of the collapse of sales of its principal export. It was not until the development of copper mining on a large scale in the middle 1930's that this crisis was partially overcome. At the present time, copper, produced mainly in the three big mines of El Teniente, Potrerillos, and Chuquicamata, provides the great bulk of Chilean foreign currency earnings, with nitrates producing most of the rest. The Guggenheim interests own the two biggest nitrate companies, a third important one being owned by Chileans; in the copper mining industry, El Teniente belongs to Kennecott Copper, the other two to the Anaconda interests.[3]

Chile also has other important mining industries, largely for domestic use. Some three hundred miles south of Santiago, in the neighborhood of Concepción, are the richest reserves of coal in South America, while a bit to the north of the capital are extensive iron ore resources, first exploited by Bethlehem Steel for export but now used largely to supply the Chilean steel industry. Chile also has a small production of gold and some other minerals, and the possibilities for further expansion of mining are generally considered good.[4] In the far south, the Chilean Development Corporation has tapped what have so far proved to be modest petroleum resources in Patagonia, helping to solve the country's pressing need for more fuel.

THE PATTERN OF MANUFACTURES AND COMMERCE

There has been considerable industrial progress since World War I in all three countries. The same fundamental factors influenced this development in Brazil, Argentina, and Chile. They all experienced the dislocation of their economies resulting from World War I, the Great Depression, and World War II, when they were cut off from their sources of supply of manufactured goods. They all witnessed political changes which favored industrialization. Profound alterations in public opinion encouraged the growth of manufacturing.

During World War I the three countries found that the markets for their exports were disrupted. Shortages of shipping, the need of the warring powers to concentrate on the import of goods necessary for the war effort, and the blockade of the Central Powers were re-

[3] A good discussion of the economic history of Chile can be found in George Wythe, *Industry in Latin America* (New York: Columbia University Press, 1945), pp. 196–224.

[4] A discussion of Chile's mineral resources, particularly of iron and coal, can be found in Carlos Sanchez Hurtado, *Evolución Histórica de la Industria Siderúrgica Chileña e Ibero-Americana* (Santiago, Chile: Editorial Nascimento, 1952).

sponsible. Although there was a relatively quick recovery of markets after the first year of the war, the permanent impact of the conflict on Chile's nitrate sales was disastrous and was felt as soon as the conflict ended, when wartime demands for nitrates disappeared.

More serious was the effect of the war in cutting off the three nations from their sources of supply of manufactured goods. The industrial powers were too busy concentrating their efforts on turning out war material to spare sizeable resources for production of goods to sell to Latin America. In the face of their inability to import manufactured goods, and in particular consumers' goods such as textiles, clothing, and processed foodstuffs, the three nations turned to the production of these goods.

The great depression had very dramatic effects on the industrialization process. The crisis in the industrial nations meant that those countries cut down drastically their imports from Brazil, Argentina, and Chile, and as a result the latter did not have sufficient foreign exchange to buy necessary manufactured goods. This factor in itself favored industrialization. Its effect was intensified by the more or less accidental discovery by the Latin American countries of the virtues of foreign exchange control as a protective device. In an attempt to allocate the scarce foreign exchange supply during the depression, most Latin American nations—including Brazil and Chile, though not Argentina—attempted to ration their foreign currency. Those goods which were considered "unnecessary," or relatively so, could only be obtained by the expenditure of large amounts of local currency to get the foreign exchange necessary to purchase them. This had the effect of extending protection to such industries.

Even more important than these events in furthering industrialization, however, was the fact that the Great Depression convinced large segments of public opinion in all three countries of the need for building up manufacturing industries. The governments of Brazil and Chile sought by a wide variety of measures to encourage the growth of factory industry within their borders. In Argentina, this development of public opinion did not make itself felt until the advent of the Perón era in 1943. The reason for this was that Argentina was governed during the 1930's by a series of dictatorships and semidictatorships which depended for their support largely on the rural landholding aristocracy. This rural oligarchy was strongly opposed to industry, fearing that the growth of manufacturing firms producing goods competing with those Argentina traditionally imported from Great Britain would engender retaliation by the British against Argentine exports of meat, wheat, and corn. The administrations in power between 1930 and 1943 not only refused to protect Argentine industry, but signed treaties with the British giving special consideration to their products in the Argentine market. It was not until the Perón revolution shifted power from the rural aristocracy to the cities that industrialization received positive government encouragement in Argentina.

In Brazil and Chile, this transfer of power with the resultant change in the attitude of the government had taken place much earlier. In Brazil, the revolution of 1930, which put Getulio Vargas in the presidential palace, marked the end of rule by the rural aristocrats of the states of São Paulo and Minas Gerais, among whom the presidency had alternated for a number of years. Vargas came from the progressive southern state of Rio Grande do Sul, and he gathered around himself groups which were anxious to further the industrialization of the country. In Chile, the control of the rural aristocracy was first loosened in the close-fought election of 1920, which put Arturo Alessandri in La Moneda, the Chilean presidential palace. However, this victory was incomplete and it was not until the Great Depression and the return of Alessandri to the presidency in 1932 that the government began to take an active interest in sponsoring industrialization. Particularly after 1939, when the Popular Front government of President Pedro Aguirre Cerda established the Chilean Development Corporation, the government carried out an intensive program consisting not only of protection for Chilean manufacturing but also of government investment in factory industry.

By the end of World War II, all three countries had governments which were giving strong encouragement to the process of industrialization. Popular opinion had shifted to a position of strong support for this program. There are few politicians in any of the three countries who would now seek office on the basis of opposition to the growth of manufacturing.

SOURCES OF THE ENTREPRENEURIAL CLASS AND CAPITAL ACCUMULATION

Although there are no statistics available for comparison, it is the author's observation that the industrial entrepreneurial class in the countries under consideration has striking similarities. Little capital and few individuals have come into manufacturing from the most important preindustrial wealthy class, the landowners. The merchants, a second element of the preindustrial aristocracy, have been of somewhat more importance, but have not been the principal source of either entrepreneurship or capital for industrialization.

In Brazil and Chile, the rural landlord class has been both unwilling and unable to contribute to industrialization. Conspicuous consumption has been a tradition in both groups, and they generally spend virtually all of their incomes. They have failed to mechanize or otherwise build up the capital equipment of their own agricultural enterprises, let alone put funds in urban manufacturing. There is sociopsychological opposition to investment in industry, even if individual landlords had an inclination to do so. The rural landowner in both countries constitutes a caste, the prestige of which arises partly from association with the land. Members of the agricultural group tend to lose status if they invest in industry.

There have been exceptions to this situation in both Brazil and Chile. In the southern part of the Chilean Central Valley, where the land was cultivated first by German immigrant farmers instead of by would-be Spanish gentlemen anxious to live off the work of Indian or semi-Indian peasants, there has been a greater tendency both to invest heavily in the improvement of agriculture and to put some of the excess funds into industry. In the southern states of Brazil, where the old colonial plantation system was never established and where the land was first opened to cultivation by German, Italian, and Portuguese farmers, the same situation prevailed. Even in other sections of both Brazil and Chile the traditional aversion of the rural landlord to have anything to do with industry has been breaking down in recent years, though it is still a powerful influence.

The Argentine agriculturalist has not invested in industry until recently for other reasons. The agriculture of the Argentine pampas, which was developed to provide wheat and meat for Europe, has required the investment of large amounts of capital for its own prosperity. Thus the Argentine landlord tended to plow some of his profits back into the building up of his estancia. At most, he would contribute funds to some industry closely allied with his basic agricultural interest, such as flour milling or slaughtering. A bit farther north, agriculturalists contributed to the development of sugar refining and other industries to process the local agricultural products.

The Perón experience gave Argentine rural landholders a greater interest in industrial investment. The Perón government took into its hands a monopoly of the purchase and sale of the principal agricultural products and followed a policy of paying very low prices to the farmers, while obtaining the highest prices possible in foreign markets. At the same time, Perón enacted social legislation for rural workers, forcing up production costs. Caught in this squeeze, many small farmers gave up completely and went into the cities to find jobs in well-paying factory industries. Larger landlords tended to invest in manufacturing rather than in improvement of their estancias, which brought only a very small return at best during the Perón period.

The preindustrial merchant class, particularly the richest portion of it, engaged in the export-import trade, was somewhat more receptive than the large agriculturalists to investment in industry. However, the merchants constitute at best only a secondary source of capital funds and entrepreneurial personnel. They were accustomed to doing business in quite a different fashion from that which would be successful in manufacturing, selling relatively small amounts of goods at very large price markups and seeking the most rapid turnover possible. A factory which took months to build, and sometimes needed years to become profitable, did not hold very much attraction for them.

However, one finds examples of some small merchants who were engaged in selling goods directly to the consumer switching to the manufacture of some of the things they were handling. The most spectacular instance is the Matarazzo complex in Brazil, founded by Francisco Matarazzo, an itinerant Italian peddler, who began his industrial career manufacturing some of the lard he sold in the interior of São Paulo state. He went on to build up the largest industrial empire in Brazil, making and selling a wide range of commodities from canned goods to chemicals, from meat to cement.

Most industrial enterprises in the three countries had their origins in the workshops of artisans and were built up through plowing back profits over a considerable period of time. A large proportion of these artisans were immigrants who arrived in the New World poor but enterprising, and who did not have either the prejudices of the local aristocracy against working with their hands or the fatalistic acceptance by the local working class of the impossibility of rising in the economic and social scale. For instance, in Brazil, immigrants from Portugal loom particularly large among industrialists of the northeastern region, while Italian and German immigrants were more important in the southerly states.

The immigrant artisan, generally more skilled and a better businessman than his local counterpart, arrived before or just after World War I. He lived abstemiously and used the greater part of his income for buying machinery or expanding his workshop. He began to employ others, often foreigners as well, and before long his workshop became a small factory. With the great impetus given to industrialization during the last three decades, many of these small factories grew into large manufacturing enterprises.

In Brazil there is a special class of entrepreneurs: groups of politicians and their friends closely associated with the Vargas administration used their influence with the government to fill their pockets. The foreign exchange operations of the Banco do Brasil were particularly useful for this purpose. Much of this ill-gotten wealth found its way into financing manufacturing industries. A somewhat similar development, though on a more modest scale, took place in Argentina during the first years of the Perón administration.

Most industrial firms are closely-held corporations, a majority of them family firms. For a variety of reasons, including tax laws, it has been convenient to give industrial firms corporate form in recent years, but this has not meant that there has been much generalization of ownership. Perhaps an extreme case is that of the Matarazzo firm in Brazil, which is strictly a family enterprise. One of the rules of the firm is that anyone who wants to sell his stock in the enterprise must first offer it to other current stockholders, and cannot sell any of it outside of this group until he has done so.[5]

The stock exchanges of Argentina, Brazil, and Chile reflect the state of industrial corporations in the three countries. Government securities remain the principal items traded on all of these exchanges. Corporate stocks are of relatively small but growing importance, and they are traded only for a short while during the stock exchange day. Undoubtedly the exchanges are of more importance in Argentina than in either Brazil or Chile as a source of new capital and a medium for the purchase and sale of already issued stock.

The stock exchanges have begun to tap the savings of the potential small investor. The largest element in this class is probably the professional man—doctor, lawyer, engineer—who is reported in both Argentina and Brazil to be the best buyer of industrial stocks offered for public sale. A considerable number of resident foreigners, including employees of foreign firms and diplomatic personnel, are also active purchasers of stock, especially in Brazil.

ROLE OF FOREIGN INVESTORS

Foreign investors have played an important role in the industrialization of the three countries. Before World War II, European investors, principally British, but some others from France, Germany, and Italy, had financed the construction of public utilities and transportation facilities. The railroads of Argentina and Brazil and some of the smaller

[5] Interview with Carmino Urcioli, Labor Relations Director of S/A Industrias Reúnidas F. Matarazzo, in São Paulo, April 23, 1956.

lines in Chile were constructed by British and French investors. Gas, electric, and other public utilities were also largely financed by Europeans.

Foreign investment has recently been of increasing importance in the field of manufacturing, while it has decreased relatively in railroads and public utilities. The Brazilian and Argentine governments repatriated foreign investments in railroads after the last war. In Brazil and Chile new government-owned and -financed electric power facilities have reduced the relative importance of the foreign firms, though none of the latter has been bought out by the governments.

Private foreign investors constructed rubber factories, chemical plants, automobile assembly plants, food processing firms, and a variety of others. The United States government, through the Export-Import Bank, helped to finance the construction of iron and steel plants in all three countries. Although in key industries foreign firms have been of considerable importance, the great bulk of industrialization has been undertaken by local entrepreneurs. The role of foreign firms has probably been larger in Chile than in the other two countries, least important in Brazil, and somewhere in between in Argentina.

Foreign firms have been increasingly anxious to enter into partnership with local interests. This not only provides needed local currency capital, but also serves as some protection against antiforeign feelings. In Chile it is not infrequent for a foreign firm to bring in capital equipment, provide technical personnel, and make available patents as its contribution to a jointly-owned enterprise. In Brazil and Argentina some of the foreign firms already located in the country have sold local stock issues to increase their capital.

ROLE OF THE GOVERNMENT IN ECONOMIC GROWTH

Finally, mention must be made of government as a source of capital funds. The governments have assumed most of the burden of expanding public utilities and other facilities needed by the growing manufacturing industries. In all three cases, they have pioneered in developing the iron and steel industry, though in Chile the government sold out part of its interest in the Compañía Acero del Pacífico in 1955.

In addition to these direct investments, each government has established a development bank or corporation for the purpose of aiding private interests to develop various industries. The first of these was the Chilean Development Corporation, established in 1939, which played a crucial role in expanding the country's industries. It bought stock in new firms, helped reorganize old ones, and loaned money to still others. The Industrial Development Bank established by the Perón regime in Argentina carried a large part of the burden of financing capital expansion in industry. The National Development Bank of Brazil, established in 1952, devotes its principal attention to railroads and public utilities, but also helped finance a considerable number of other industries.

These government development organizations serve another very useful purpose. They help to channel foreign funds, particularly from foreign government lending institutions such as the Export-Import Bank and the International Bank for Reconstruction and Development, into local private industry. The international lending institutions demand government guarantees for their loans, which are provided through the development banks and corporations.

The governments of Argentina, Brazil, and Chile do not participate in the accumulation of capital for industrialization because of any ideological bent toward state intervention. President Juscelino Kubitschek of Brazil made this point when he was reported by the *New York Times* of June 18, 1958, as saying that the Latin American governments intervened in economic development because private enterprise was unable to do the job alone, and only the governments of the respective countries could push economic growth as rapidly as desired.

LOCATION OF INDUSTRY

One further fact should be stressed concerning the pattern of development: the geographical concentration of manufacturing which characterizes all three nations. In Brazil, there is overwhelming concentration in the state of São Paulo, which produces half of the country's national product, though there are significant centers of industry in Rio de Janeiro, Minas Gerais, Rio Grande do Sul and Pernambuco. In recent years there has been a tendency on the part of some firms with headquarters and main factories in São Paulo or Rio to establish branch plants in provincial capitals, particularly in the eastern and northeastern states.

In Argentina, the principal concentration of manufacturing is in the Greater Buenos Aires region, which contains almost a third of the country's population and possesses the most important packing houses, textile plants, metallurgical works, and chemical firms. Smaller manufacturing centers are located in Rosario, Córdoba, La Plata, San Nicolás (center of the new steel industry in the province of Buenos Aires), Tucumán, Mendoza, and other provincial cities. The great majority of Chilean industrial establishments are located in and around the capital, Santiago. With the establishment of the Huachipato steel plant near Concepción, this latter region gives promise of becoming the second principal manufacturing center of the nation.

CULTURAL FACTORS

The concentration of industry in a comparatively small number of cities emphasizes one of the outstanding social and cultural facts about Brazil, Argentina, and Chile, the striking difference between city (particularly the large city) and countryside. The cities are modern —and, in the case of São Paulo and Buenos Aires in particular, very modern. The countryside, in contrast, is in many areas still little changed from colonial times. This is especially true in Brazil and Chile.

Rural eastern and northeastern Brazil are heavily influenced by the traditions of slavery. Relations between employer and employee are those of master and servant. Transportation facilities are primitive, electricity is largely unknown, health and educational conditions are backward. Even in the more southerly regions of Brazil, the contrast between the city and the country is marked. This contrast is less sharp in Argentina, where transportation facilities are more extensive and agriculture is better equipped.

All three countries have a majority of Catholics among their citizenry. Usually the Church's influence in politics and economic affairs is relatively small. In Chile and Argentina there is a long tradition of anticlericalism, and the Masons are influential in politics. In Brazil, too, Catholic Church influence is normally not great, though the fact that it can obtain what it very much desires was demonstrated in 1946 when it succeeded in getting a prohibition of divorce written into the country's new constitution. In the field of labor relations, the influence of the Church is minimal in all three countries, though during the last decade the Catholic Falange party has been achieving some influence in the Chilean organized labor movement.

The Organization of Labor

RECRUITMENT OF AN INDUSTRIAL LABOR FORCE

Since the beginning of rapid industrialization in the 1930's, new recruits for the industrial labor force have generally come from the countryside, as well as from among the children of older industrial workers. Mass immigration into Brazil and Argentina had declined to a trickle by the advent of the Great Depression. Chile had not had mass immigration since the years following the revolutions of 1848, and so it, too, has largely depended on bringing workers from the countryside to augment its urban labor force.

Methods of recruiting workers are relatively simple. Most new industrial workers acquire their jobs by presenting themselves at the factory gates and asking for employment. In Argentina, white-collar workers and some industrial workers are sought through classified advertisements, for which the newspapers *La Nación* and *La Prensa* are particularly well known. Some labor unions, notably the printers and hotel and restaurant workers, run their own hiring halls, and employers seek new employees through them. However, this system is apparently not used in any manufacturing industry. Although a national employment service was organized under Perón, it never became a major source of recruitment for Argentine industry. In the other two countries such services are rudimentary at best. Private employment services are similarly in their infancy in all three nations.

Employers are beginning to become more selective in choosing their employees. In Brazil, the Fundação Getulio Vargas runs a service in Rio and São Paulo for the selection of skilled workers, as well as of various types of management personnel. There are also several private firms which offer the same services to industrial employers, particularly foreign firms.[6]

In many instances, employers are particularly anxious to give jobs to children of their older employees. They feel that youngsters brought up in the homes of industrial workers will already be acquainted with much of the terminology, routine, and other aspects of industrial employment. They are able to learn on the job in a very short time things which it had taken their fathers years to understand.[7]

Most employers with whom this writer has talked have agreed that the Brazilian, Argentine, and Chilean workers have been fast to learn and to adapt themselves to the conditions of modern factory industry. Within approximately a generation, all three countries have developed a reasonably efficient industrial labor force, in spite of the difficulties involved in turning illiterate agricultural workers, unused to the discipline of the modern factory, into literate and efficient industrial employees.

Industrial employers and government have become increasingly interested, in recent years, in training skilled workers. In Brazil, the government authorized the National Industrial Employers' Confederation and the National Commercial Employers' Confederation to establish the National Service of Industrial Apprenticeship (SENAI) and the National Service of Commercial Apprenticeship (SENAC), re-

---

[6] Interview with Robert F. E. Suchanek, Director of Mechanical Tests of Instituto de Seleção e Orientação Profissional, of Fundação Getulio Vargas, in Rio de Janeiro, April 2, 1956.

[7] Interview with Ramón Videla Montalba, Labor Relations Chief of Grace Co.'s Chiguayante textile plant, in Chiguayante, Chile, February 14, 1947.

spectively. SENAI and SENAC, which have now been operating for more than fifteen years, have set up wide networks of training institutions for skilled workers in their respective fields. Some of these are resident training schools, others are day schools, and, in the state of Rio Grande do Sul, SENAI has the policy of coöperating with existing educational institutions in expanding their services for industrial workers and their children.

However, SENAI and SENAC have been inadequate to meet the needs of Brazil's expanding industries. The former had only some 35,000 students in training in 1956, and plans were afoot to expand the operations of the organization into a system of training of workers within industry, in order to handle hundreds of thousands instead of tens of thousands of workers.[8] In addition to the SENAI and SENAC, the Brazilian Government itself operates industrial schools as part of its regular educational system, and these handle approximately the same number of students as those registered with SENAI.[9]

Perón's administration used SENAI as a model in establishing a government-sponsored apprenticeship system in Argentina. This was the first attempt on the part of the Argentine government to aid the country's industrial employers to improve the quality of their work force. Like its Brazilian counterpart, however, the Argentine industrial apprenticeship system is inadequate for the job it is attempting to deal with.[10]

In Chile, there are two institutions which have borne the principal brunt of training the country's skilled industrial workers. One of these is the Universidad Técnica Santa María, a private school which in recent years has received extensive government aid. For the last quarter of a century it has been training young men for jobs as skilled workers and foremen, and a few selected men for engineering.[11] The government's main institution is the Universidad Técnica del Estado, which was established in 1955 to bring together all of the scattered government schools operating in this field. It coördinates a system of industrial schools for the training of craftsmen and another for training foremen and engineers.[12]

[8] Interview with Paulo Novaes, Subdirector of Serviço Nacional de Aprendizagem Industrial, in Rio de Janeiro, March 21, 1956.

[9] Interview with Francisco Montojos, Director of Industrial Education of Ministry of Education, in Rio de Janeiro, April 5, 1956.

[10] Interview with Ing. Carlos Burundarena, Director General of Apprenticeship, in Buenos Aires, May 22, 1956.

[11] Interview with Julio Hirschman, Vice Rector, Universidad Técnica Federico Santa María, in Valparaiso, August 13, 1956.

[12] Interview with Roberto Toledo, Chief of Department of Research, Universidad Técnica del Estado, in Santiago, August 14, 1956.

The Chilean system of skilled worker training is probably more nearly adequate to its task than are those of Brazil and Argentina. However, in none of the three countries are these institutions sufficient. Most skilled workers still learn their jobs by working alongside older workers. Such training is, for the most part, informal, and the quality of the workers turned out is not sufficient to industry's requirements.

THE DEVELOPMENT OF LABOR ORGANIZATIONS

The organizational forms and functions of the trade union movements in Argentina, Brazil, and Chile are strikingly different. The variations are to be explained principally by the political histories of the three countries. The dictatorship of Getulio Vargas emasculated the labor movement and converted it into little more than a subsidiary of the Brazilian government. The Perón dictatorship greatly modified the labor movement of Argentina, though its lasting effect was considerably less than in Brazil. In Chile, the nature of the country's political democracy has to a large degree determined the structure and functions of the trade unions there.

BRAZIL

The Brazilian labor movement is still profoundly influenced by the dictatorship of the late Getulio Vargas, which dominated the nation from 1937 to 1945, the so-called "Estado Novo" or New State. This was an attempt on Vargas' part to establish a corporate state on the model of Fascist Italy and Portugal. Although the New State officially came to an end with the overthrow of Vargas in October, 1945, the form and activities of the trade unions remain largely those established during the dictatorship.

The upshot of the Vargas experience was that the labor movement was reduced to impotence during exactly the period when economic development was gaining momentum. Although subsequent to 1945 the unions acquired more independence and power, they were still generally weaker than in either Argentina or Chile. They were thus less able than they might have been to demand a larger share of output for the workers. Capital accumulation was probably hastened by this fact.

At the time of Vargas' seizure of power, the labor movement of Brazil was still very weak. It had begun among immigrant workers in the major cities in the 1890's, largely under anarcho-syndicalist inspiration and direction. In 1909 the trade unions had reached the point where it was possible to establish the country's first central labor organization, the Confederação Operária do Brasil, which continued in existence until the late 1920's.

The labor movement grew rapidly during the First World War, under the impetus of wartime demand for labor and rising prices. During the latter years of the war and in 1919, there was a series of widespread strikes, including a general walkout of textile workers in the northeastern city of Recife which received international attention at the time. After the Russian Revolution, a number of the younger anarcho-syndicalist labor leaders were attracted by Communist success, and, after a long controversy with their older comrades, established the Communist party of Brazil in 1922. Throughout the rest of the 1920's the labor movement was torn by a series of internecine struggles between the anarcho-syndicalists and the Communists, with the latter becoming the predominant element by 1929.

The government was exceedingly hostile to the labor movement during all of this period. One minister of the interior won dubious fame by his comment that "the trade unions are a problem for the police," which fairly aptly summed up the attitude of the governments of the time.[13]

The Revolution of 1930 put Getulio Vargas in the presidency. One of the first acts of the new ruler was a decree authorizing legal recognition of trade unions. Both anarchists and Communists fought bitterly against the new regulations. Because in the one case they were ideologically opposed to government interference in labor relations, and in the other they felt that government interference would be disadvantageous to them, the anarchists and Communists both tried to prevent labor organizations under their control from seeking legal recognition, and denounced government-approved unions as "yellow" and "scab" organizations. However, the number of legally sanctioned labor groups grew rapidly, and by 1935 the great majority of the trade unions enjoyed government recognition. Collective bargaining was becoming the rule in the larger cities and towns.

A final blow was dealt to radical influence in the labor movement by the collapse of an attempted Communist-led revolt in November, 1935. The unions were purged thereafter, and brought under closer government supervision. This process was completed when in 1937 Vargas established his New State. This provided in theory for the establishment of unions for every group of workers, employers, and members of the free professions throughout Brazil. Parallel organizations of employers and workers were to be set up for every indus-

---

[13] Interview with Ecgard Leuenroth, one-time secretary-general of Confederação Operária Brasileira, in São Paulo, September 2, 1946.

try or specialty in each locality, and in each state. On a national basis, there was to be a series of confederations to encompass the various state federations.[14]

As a matter of fact, this elaborate structure was largely abortive. The employers were a good deal less than enthusiastic about joining government-controlled organizations, and generally were not coerced into doing so. When they did form groups as provided by the corporate state structure, they generally did not adapt the jurisdiction of their organizations to the pattern set up in advance in the New State's bible, the Consolidation of Labor Laws.

The effects of the New State were principally manifested among the workers. Trade unions existing in 1937 were forced either to adapt themselves to the new system or go out of business. Such adaptation consisted of accepting the names and jurisdictions established by the government, and submitting themselves to rigid control by the Ministry of Industry, Commerce, and Labor over elections, finances, and relations with employers. During eight years of the New State dictatorship, Vargas brooked no "subversion" in the trade unions. The Ministry of Labor had the right to nullify the election of elements hostile to the corporate state and the Vargas government. When an official showed independence of judgment which would appear to make him dangerous to the regime, his union was "intervened" by the Ministry, and he was ousted from office.[15]

The unions were tied financially to the government. The New State established the "imposto sindical" or trade union tax of one day's pay a year, which was automatically deducted from the worker's wage. Of this money, 60 per cent was paid to the local "sindicato" (union); 15 per cent was turned over to the federation to which this local union belonged; 5 per cent went to the confederation to which the federation belonged. The remaining 20 per cent went into the so-called "trade union social fund," administered from Rio under close government control for purposes which were never adequately disclosed. The trade union tax was deducted each year by the employer and placed in a special account in the Banco do Brasil. It could be withdrawn by the labor organizations only with the countersignature of a Ministry of Labor official.[16] Payment of the trade union tax did not automatically make a worker a member of the union. An additional

[14] *Consolidação das Leis do Trabalho* (São Paulo: Edição Saraiva, 1955), Title V, Ch. II.

[15] Interview with Pedro Viadero, President, Sindicato dos Trabalhadores nas Industrias Gráficas de São Paulo, in São Paulo, August 22, 1946.

[16] *Consolidação das Leis do Trabalho,* Title V, Ch. III.

dues payment was necessary for membership, and only those who paid dues were able to use the union's social services. During the New State period, only a few hundred thousand workers bothered to become dues-paying union members. In subsequent years the number increased considerably, but even by 1959 it was doubtful if most Brazilian unions could count much more than 10 or 15 per cent of the workers for whom they presumed to speak as actual dues-paying members.

This New State system was all part of a scheme to destroy the role of the trade unions as the principal defenders of their members. Vargas' intention was to make the workers turn to the government for the adjustment of grievances, and to eliminate the potentially dangerous trade unions as an avenue of protest. To this end, strict government control over union jurisdiction, elections, and finances was supplemented by two other measures: the establishment of a system of labor courts, and the virtual abolition of collective bargaining.

The unions were converted into social welfare organizations. To obtain legal recognition, a union had to prove that it had such extensive welfare services for its members as infirmaries, dental office, schools, and libraries. If more than one group within a given jurisdiction sought recognition, preference was given to the one which had most services, regardless of the relative membership of the two groups. Most funds originating from the trade union tax were supposed to be spent on these welfare projects.[17]

Theoretically, the *sindicatos* were authorized periodically to request wage increases and other improvements in working conditions through the medium of the government labor courts. In fact, few such requests were made during the period of the Vargas dictatorship. There was no room for independent collective bargaining between the unions and the employers.

Late in 1944, the Vargas government, under pressure of prodemocratic sentiment stirred up by approaching victory in the war, began to allow freer elections in the unions. During the months that followed, the labor movement displayed a vigor it had not had for more than a decade. Strikes were frequent, some collective agreements were signed, workers streamed into the unions. This state of effervescence in the labor movement continued for about a year and a half after the overthrow of Vargas in October, 1945. During this period the leadership of most local unions was in the hands either of supporters

[17] Interview with Celio Dinardo L. Lacerda, head of Registration Section of Trade Union Organization and Registration Service of Ministry of Labor, in Rio de Janeiro, April 5, 1956.

of the deposed President (who were now organized into the Brazilian Labor Party) or followers of Communist leader Luiz Carlos Prestes.

This era came to a close early in 1947. The Supreme Electoral Court declared the Communist party illegal, and the government of President Eurico Dutra, which had been elected at the end of 1945, quickly followed this up by intervening in virtually all unions led by members of the Communist party (as well as many which were non-Communist but militantly led) and restored all the rigor of the New State legislation regarding unions. Meetings were again submitted to police surveillance, no elections were held for the duration of the Dutra administration, and a number of unions were kept under "intervention."

This state of affairs continued until the reëlection of Getulio Vargas to the Presidency in 1950. His campaign for reëlection raised great hopes among trade unionists, virtually all of whom supported him. His second administration was marked by a relaxation of controls over labor. Elections were once again free; the government intervened in few unions.

However, Vargas' prestige fell rapidly among the workers during his second administration. This was due largely to continuing inflation and his apparent inability to stop it and to resolve other pressing problems. When, in August, 1954, the Army sought to have Vargas go on "a long vacation," he committed suicide, leaving behind two notes picturing himself as a victim of "the enemies of the workers" and "foreign imperialists." His dramatic death served for a while to restore his prestige sufficiently so that two former associates, Juscelino Kubitschek and Vargas' former Minister of Labor, João Goulart, were able to be elected President and Vice President, respectively, in the elections of October, 1955.

During the presidency of Juscelino Kubitschek, who was inaugurated at the end of January, 1956, there was continuing relaxation of government control over labor. This particularly benefited the Communists since, with the death of Vargas, his Brazilian Labor party, the principal non-Communist force in the labor movement, lost much ground. It was wracked by personal and ideological rivalries and did not develop leadership capable of giving it new direction. In many areas, it was successfully infiltrated by the Communists.[18]

By 1959, all functioning labor organizations in Brazil were still those recognized under the New State laws, which themselves remained largely intact. The lowest-echelon trade union group is the "sindicato" covering the workers of a given trade or industry in a city or town.

---

[18] Robert J. Alexander, *Communism in Latin America* (New Brunswick, N.J.: Rutgers University Press, 1957), p. 134.

The principal functions of the local *sindicato* are three in number. In the first place, they administer the extensive welfare schemes paid for by the *imposto sindical.* Second, many *sindicatos* present annual requests to the labor courts for wage increases and changes in working conditions, while a few unions now negotiate collective agreements on these matters with the employers. Finally, some of the better organized and more militant unions handle grievances of their members with the employers, rather than taking such matters to the labor courts.

The second level of Brazilian labor organization consists of groups on a statewide basis, *sindicatos* of a specific trade or industry, such as a federation of textile workers or a federation of metallurgical workers. In some states in which the total number of unions is small, the unions are grouped together in one or two federations, one of industrial workers, another of commercial workers. The highest echelon of labor organizations is the confederation. At the end of the New State, no confederations had yet been organized, but in the late 1940's three such organizations were established on a nationwide basis: the National Confederation of Industrial Workers, the National Confederation of Commercial Workers, and the National Confederation of Land Transport Workers. The federations and confederations established under the *Estado Novo* framework were very much under the control of the Ministry of Labor during the late 1940's and early 1950's.

However, in 1953, the federation and confederation leaders had a violent quarrel with the then-Minister of Labor, João Goulart. As a result, the top-echelon union leaders suddenly realized that for their own tenure in office they would have to develop closer contact with the rank-and-file. Some of the federations became increasingly active in helping their affiliated unions to work out collective agreements or obtain favorable labor court decisions. The Textile Workers' Federation of São Paulo is outstanding in organizing new unions in this state where workers remain generally unorganized.[19] The Paper Workers' Federation of the same state also carries on organizing activities. It also negotiated a unique agreement with the employers of the industry which establishes a joint labor-management welfare scheme for the state's paper workers.[20]

The confederations also became more militant. The National Confederation of Industrial Workers, covering all the country's manu-

[19] Interview with Fernando Garcez, President, Federação dos Trabalhadores nas Industrias Téxtais de São Paulo, in São Paulo, July 8, 1954.

[20] Interview with Olavo Previatti, President, Federação dos Trabalhadores nas Industrias de Papel de São Paulo, in São Paulo, April 27, 1956.

facturing workers, was particularly active. It established "delegations" in every state to work with local union officials in handling grievances, aiding in the elaboration of demands before regional labor courts, and helping organizational activities. It also carried on a vigorous campaign for changes in existing labor legislation, to loosen the government's control over the labor movement. All of this was in striking contrast to the previous situation of these highest-echelon trade union groups, which had seemed to do little but collect their share of the trade union tax and occasionally provide legal help in presenting a case before the Superior Labor Tribunal.[21]

However, by the beginning of 1959, the bulk of the Brazilian trade union movement still remained very much under the influence of the Ministry of Labor, because of the trade union tax and the Ministry's authority over union jurisdiction, elections, and finances. Although there had been a considerable development of collective bargaining in some parts of the country in the years since the Estado Novo, most problems which in Chile or Argentina were resolved via the negotiation of collective agreements and through grievance procedures were handled in Brazil through government labor courts.

ARGENTINA

The effect of the Perón dictatorship on the labor movement in Argentina was almost as significant as the impact of Vargas' New State on that of Brazil. However, Vargas destroyed the union movement that existed before he came to power and substituted a government-dominated system of unions, while Perón merely took over the labor movement and adapted it to his own needs. Vargas left a working class without experience in conducting its own affairs, whereas Perón left behind a labor movement which still had a powerful voice in the nation's affairs, and had accumulated experience in dealing with employers.

The Argentine labor movement is one of the oldest in the Western Hemisphere; its origins go back to the middle of the nineteenth century. By the 1880's, anarchist-controlled labor organizations were spreading rapidly among the artisans who made up the bulk of the urban labor force, while a union patterned on the United States railway brotherhoods had gotten a foothold among the country's railroad engineers and firemen.

Anarchist influence in the trade union movement reached its apogee during the first decade of the twentieth century, when most unions

---

[21] Interview with Diocletiano Hollanda de Cavalcanti, President, Confederação Nacional dos Trabalhadores na Industria, in Rio de Janeiro, March 8, 1956.

were affiliated with the anarchist Federación Obrera Regional Argentina. The FORA and its affiliates believed in "direct action," by which they meant the submission of demands to the employers, to be followed by strike action if these were not accepted immediately. They refused to sign collective agreements on the ground that such accords limited the independence of the labor movement. Strikes, many of them violent, some of them national general walkouts, were exceedingly numerous during this period.

The anarchist influence was increasingly challenged by Socialist and syndicalist elements. The former established the Unión General de Trabajadores in 1902, which merged with dissident elements of the FORA in 1909 to form the Confederación Obrera Regional Argentina. The CORA was soon captured by syndicalists, whose model was the French CGT of that period, and who became for a dozen years the principal rivals of the anarchists in the labor movement.

In 1910 the anarchist influence in the labor movement was violently curbed as the result of the government's temporary outlawing of the FORA when it attempted to organize a national general strike against the celebrations organized to honor the first century of Argentine independence. Thereafter, the syndicalist elements were the most powerful group in the trade unions. They voluntarily dissolved the CORA in 1914, affiliating their unions to the FORA, but this attempt at unity failed when the anarchists withdrew the following year.

From 1915 to 1922 Argentine labor enjoyed one of its most flourishing periods of activity and organization. The syndicalist faction of the FORA, known generally as FORA IX (of the Ninth Congress), grew rapidly and succeeded in organizing a number of new groups, including the unskilled railroaders, some of the packinghouse workers, and even some agricultural laborers. The anarchist FORA V (of the Fifth Congress) grew less rapidly.

Another attempt to unify the labor movement failed in 1922, when, after participating in a congress to merge the two FORA's into a new group known as the Unión Sindical Argentina, the anarchists again withdrew, maintaining their small group intact. The new group was not the equal in strength or membership of the old FORA IX, because the powerful railroad workers' unions refused to affiliate with it.

The railroaders, other than engine personnel, had meanwhile been organized into the Unión Ferroviaria, which from its inception was the country's largest union. This, like the older organization of engineers and firemen, La Fraternidad, was patterned after the United States' railway brotherhoods, and devoted its energies both to collective bargaining and to fraternal and welfare activities on behalf of its members. Both railroad unions were under Socialist party influence.

In 1926 the Socialist-oriented unions formed still another central labor group, the Confederación Obrera Argentina, which affiliated with the International Federation of Trade Unions. The backbone of the COA consisted of the two rail unions and the Confederation of Commercial Employees.

A wide degree of unity in the labor movement was finally achieved in September, 1930, when the USA, the COA, and a number of independent unions joined to form the Confederación General del Trabajo (C.G.T.). From that time until the downfall of Perón, the CGT represented the great majority of the organized workers of Argentina. Although it suffered splits in 1935 and 1942, these proved to have only a minor impact on the organization in the long run.[22]

With the advent of the Great Depression, the tempo of Argentine industrialization quickened. At the same time, the stream of immigrant workers from Spain, Italy, and Central Europe was shut off. Increasingly, urban workers were recruited from among migrants from the Argentine countryside and the sons and daughters of immigrants. Neither group was very receptive to the old ideas of anarchism, socialism, or syndicalism, the country folk not knowing the meaning of these terms, and the second-generation Argentines tending to reject them as part of the "foreignness" of their parents. Yet both groups were receptive to a kind of native radicalism which Perón was to provide.

Other developments also tended to pave the way for Perón. One was the bureaucratization of the labor movement, reflected in an increasing divorce of leadership from rank-and-file, and a growing apathy on the part of the average trade unionist toward his organization's affairs. Another was the failure of the unions to organize the unskilled workers in the packinghouses, in the factory farms of northern Argentina, and in the smaller cities and towns. Finally, no government between the two world wars paid much attention to the needs and aspirations of the Argentine worker, and the country lagged behind others of Latin America in the enactment of labor and social security legislation.[23]

However, among the organized workers there existed a well-established system of collective bargaining. The patterns were varied; some contracts, such as those on the railroads, were national in scope. Many others, such as those of commercial employees, hotel and restaurant workers, and printers, were regional or local in coverage. In all instances, grievances were handled by direct negotiation between unions

[22] Interview with Sebastian Marotta, one-time Secretary General of Federación Obrera Regional Argentina IX, in Buenos Aires, November 28, 1946.

[23] Robert J. Alexander, *The Perón Era* (New York: Columbia University Press, 1951), pp. 7–11.

and employers; in some areas, as on the railroads, there was complicated machinery for this purpose. Some unions, again notably the railroaders', had developed extensive systems of social security for their members, including medical and hospital care and retirement systems.

Perón did not destroy this pattern. He extended it, centralized it in Buenos Aires, and created a major role for the government in the process. His objectives were political, not economic. He sought to impress upon the unionists that he was their great benefactor and that without him the workers would suffer severe setbacks. He sought to bring completely under his dictatorial government's control all major and most minor decisions in the labor-management field.

Perón got his chance as the result of a military coup d'état in June, 1943. Between November, 1943, when he became Secretary of Labor in the military government, and October, 1945, when his power was finally solidified within the military group, Perón succeeded in winning the support of the great majority of organized workers and their trade unions. He intervened actively in collective bargaining negotiations, urging and finally demanding that they be conducted in the Secretariat of Labor. He exerted great pressure on employers to give concessions to the unions. At the same time, he established by decree a great amount of social legislation, setting up an ample social security system, strengthening factory laws, and otherwise bringing Argentine labor law into line with that in neighboring countries.[24]

The result was the growth of the Peronista political movement based on the trade unions. Even many union leaders who were suspicious of Perón found themselves compelled to go along with him, under pressure from their rank-and-file.[25] Others, who refused to join Perón, were crushed by means of a decree-law of October, 1945, which provided for legal registration of unions and permitted only legally registered organizations to engage in collective bargaining with employers. In a number of cases, such recognition was refused to unions led by officials hostile to Perón, and new Peronista unions were created and promptly recognized.[26]

On June 4, 1946, Perón was inaugurated President of the Republic, a post he held until his overthrow in September, 1955. During that period, Perón, with considerable help from his wife, Eva Duarte de

[24] *Ibid.*, pp. 20–32.

[25] Interview with José Argaña, Assistant General Secretary, Confederación General de Empleados de Comercio, in Buenos Aires, October 30, 1946.

[26] Interview with Alfredo Fidanza, Secretary General, Sindicato Obreros de la Industria del Calzado, in Buenos Aires, October 28, 1946.

Perón, tamed the trade union movement and brought collective bargaining completely within the control of the Ministry of Labor and Social Welfare. It became impossible for anyone critical of the regime to attain office on the national or regional trade union level. Who was to be elected was decided beforehand in the ministry, its regional "delegations," or the presidential palace. Only on the local shop steward level was it possible for non-Peronistas to be elected, thus providing a safety valve for the expression of discontent. Even here, if a shop steward became too obnoxious to the authorities, he was removed.[27]

The labor movement was highly centralized under Perón. Those unions accustomed to conducting their collective bargaining on a regional or local level in the pre-Perón period had had a federal form of organization in which most power rested with local or regional units. However, the Perón regime reorganized these unions to provide virtually dictatorial power for the center, leaving the local unions little to do but collect dues and process grievances. By the end of the Perón period, even the dues-collecting process was put in the hands of the national organization through a national checkoff system.

One important vehicle for this process of centralization was the Confederación General del Trabajo (General Confederation of Labor), which was captured by Perón in the middle of 1944. Soon after he became President, the C.G.T. took upon itself the right, not specified in its constitution at that time, to "intervene" a national union or even a local union which was not conforming to the Perón political line, ousting its elected officers and appointing an intervenor to run the union's affairs until it was deemed to be safe, or elections could be properly arranged. Some unions stayed under this type of intervention throughout most of the Perón period.

The CGT established "delegations" in each province, and subdelegations in the more important cities and towns of each province. Their purpose was to keep an eye on the trade unions in that part of the country, in coöperation with the local delegation of the Ministry of Labor, and if need be to "intervene" in a recalcitrant organization. This process of intervention by the CGT and its regional delegations was finally made legal by a revision of the confederation's constitution.

Those unions which had not been members of the CGT at the time of the June, 1943, coup were forced to join it. One of the last to do so was the Federation of Packinghouse Workers which, in spite of the fact that it had virtually been organized by Perón, maintained a strongly independent position and refused to join the CGT on the

[27] Interview with Luis Cerutti Costa, labor lawyer and Minister of Labor in Lonardi government in 1955, in Buenos Aires, May 18, 1956.

grounds that it was too closely controlled by the Ministry of Labor. This did not prevent the CGT, in the middle of 1950, from intervening in the Packinghouse Workers' Federation, after which the intervenor affiliated the group with the CGT.[28]

Perón and his Evita converted the labor movement into an integral part of their political machine. During the early 1950's, each union adopted a standard preamble to its constitution which declared its objectives to be fulfillment of the program of "justicialismo" of General Perón, and proclaimed loyalty to him to be the first duty of every Argentine worker.

Perón was overthrown in September, 1955, and successor governments found the trade unions one of the most difficult problems they had to deal with. A large portion of the membership remained loyal to Perón and willing to lend itself to political maneuvering by his partisans. The government of General Lonardi, who assumed power with the ousting of Perón, adopted a policy of gradualism. It did not "intervene" the CGT or its affiliated organizations, though it did force the resignation of Hugo di Pietri, last Peronista secretary general of the CGT, and called for general union elections within 120 days. Attempts by Socialist and syndicalist unionists to seize the headquarters of a number of important unions and oust their Peronista officials were thwarted except in a few cases.[29]

With the ouster of General Lonardi by a coup d'état early in November, 1955, the CGT leaders called a revolutionary general strike which brought a complete alteration of governmental policy toward labor. In order to break the strike, the new President, General Pedro Aramburu, decreed intervention of the CGT and all of its affiliates. Naval Captain Laplacette was made intervenor in the CGT itself.[30] For a year and a half most unions remained under control of military intervenors.

Revisions were made in the Law of Professional Associations, the Peronista statute providing for official recognition and control of the trade unions. The most important change provided for the possibility of dual unionism in a given industry or trade, whereas the Peronista law had permitted only one union in a field.[31] The Aramburu government also changed the Law of Collective Negotiation to provide for proportional representation of all recognized unions in a given jurisdiction in collective bargaining with employers. However, in negotiations

---

[28] Alexander, *The Perón Era*, pp. 84–102.

[29] Interview with Luis Cerutti Costa, previously cited.

[30] Interview with Raul Migone, Minister of Labor, in Buenos Aires, July 10, 1956.

[31] *La Prensa*, Buenos Aires, May 24, 1956.

provided for in a decree of February, 1956, only unions already in existence at the time were to participate; in future negotiations the dual union provision would become applicable.[32]

Most unions had been restored to elected leadership by the middle of 1957. However, attempts to reconstitute the CGT proved abortive. With the election of a new president, Arturo Frondizi, and his inauguration on May 1, 1958, the new regime pushed through Congress a law virtually reëstablishing the Peronista Law of Professional Associations, calling for only one legally recognized union in each field and only one CGT, and providing for new elections in all unions within ninety days. This law was strongly opposed by anti-Peronista groups in the labor movement, since the majority of workers in most unions were still loyal to the deposed dictator.

Despite this law, the General Confederation of Labor had not been reëstablished by the end of the first year of the Frondizi administration. The labor movement was badly split among a strongly pro-Peronista group of unions popularly known as "the 62," an equally vocal anti-Peronista coalition of unions, "the 32," and a third element composed of Communist-controlled unions, generally referred to as "the 19."

It was not until May, 1961, that the CGT was finally turned over once again to the workers. At that time the government ended its intervention in the Confederation, turning over the organization to representatives of twenty of the largest unions in the CGT, ten of them Peronista-controlled, ten led by anti-Peronistas. Communist union leaders were not included in the new leadership of the Confederation.

The disturbed economic situation of Argentina during 1958 and 1959, and President Frondizi's measures to deal with it, provoked a series of strikes. Oil workers, railroaders, packinghouse employees, bank clerks were among the groups involved. There was also a threat of a general strike in October, 1958. This walkout was thwarted by the Frondizi government, which also acted energetically to quash the partial strikes mentioned.

Labor unrest continued during the first months of 1959, after the enactment by the Frondizi regime of a stabilization program involving severe austerity measures, designed to bring a halt to the inflationary spiral which had been increasingly intense since the fall of Perón. As part of this stabilization effort, President Frondizi sought to freeze wages, while allowing prices to seek their "normal" level. This aroused particularly violent unrest among the workers, and the government was increasingly firm in its suppression of strikes which it felt en-

[32] Interview with Raul Migone, previously cited.

dangered the political status quo. The government, meanwhile, continued to interfere in the internal affairs of the unions, notwithstanding Frondizi's statements before his election that he wanted to end all such intervention.

In spite of changes in the labor movement brought about after the fall of Perón, the framework established during his dictatorship remained largely intact. Most industrial and transport workers and much of the white-collar class belonged to trade unions. The rigid pattern of centralization which had characterized the national organizations during the Perón period was modified during the succeeding years, and a number of national unions, including the Commercial Workers' Federation, the Hotel and Restaurant Workers, and the Printers' Federation, had once again become more or less decentralized. It seemed possible that in some of these unions the local groups would again become the collective bargaining agents of the workers, instead of the national unions which had done the negotiating during the Perón period.

CHILE

Chile's relative freedom, the penchant of the Chilenos for politics, and the existence of a myriad of small parties constantly forming new alliances and breaking old ones, go far toward explaining the current state of the Chilean labor movement. Political democracy resulted in early recognition by government and employers of the legitimacy of trade unionism, and provided the background for development of a system of collective bargaining which, on balance, has been successful. At the same time, the extreme degree of political consciousness of urban Chileans and the numerous political parties struggling for influence in the unions have been a constant source of dissension in labor-management affairs, and have made it virtually impossible to maintain for long a united labor movement.

Although workers' mutual benefit societies are of a much older vintage, the first trade unions appeared in the 1890's, particularly among the nitrate miners of the north. Their early leadership was anarchist and Socialist. The country's first central labor organization, the Gran Federación Obrera Chilena, was organized in 1909 under very conservative auspices. However, during World War I many thousands of workers, most of them under Socialist leadership, streamed into the GFOCh. In 1917 the Socialists gained control of the organization, changed its name by dropping the first word, and rebuilt it as a highly centralized group. Meanwhile the anarcho-syndicalists had succeeded in bringing most of the maritime workers into an organization which they christened the Industrial Workers of the World. The Chilean

IWW was in close touch with its North American counterpart, and received financial and organizational support from it.

In 1920, Chile experienced a political revolution of major magnitude. In the Presidential election of that year the victor was Arturo Alessandri, a young lawyer of middle-class background, whose election resulted in transferring political power from the rural landholders to the city. Alessandri had the backing not only of most middle-class elements in the cities, but of the new and still small industrial and mining working class as well.

Alessandri sought throughout the first four years of his administration to achieve the passage of a Labor Code which would not only give juridical recognition to trade unions, but would also greatly extend the factory laws and other protective legislation and establish the basis for a social security system. His struggle was finally won in September, 1924, just before he himself was forced out of the Presidency by a military insurrection.[33] The Labor Code, as first enacted in 1924, and finally codified in 1931, established certain peculiarities which have plagued the labor movement ever since. The law extended government recognition to trade unions, but established a comparatively narrow jurisdiction for each individual union. The Labor Code recognizes two types of labor organizations, the so-called "sindicato industrial" and the "sindicato profesional." The former covers the manual workers of one particular plant, all of whom belong to a single organization. The *sindicato industrial* has certain special privileges such as sharing the profits of the firm. The *sindicato profesional* can include members of a particular craft or can include the white-collar workers of a particular firm, or the manual workers of a number of establishments if each individual plant is too small to have twenty-five workers, the number required for a *sindicato industrial.*[34] There was no provision for national unions, because Alessandri and others feared the political potentialities of these organizations.

As in Brazil, the older Chilean unions fought the development of the legally recognized organizations. By 1924, the majority of organized labor was in the Federación Obrera Chilena, which in 1922 affiliated with the Red International of Labor Unions at the same time that the Socialist Labor party joined the Communist International. A minority of the workers' groups were still under anarcho-syndicalist control.

[33] See Robert J. Alexander, *Reseña del Movimiento Obrero en la América Latina* (Washington: Pan-American Union, 1950), pp. 22–23.

[34] *Código del Trabajo* (Santiago: Editorial Nascimento, 1942), Titles II and III.

[35] Alexander, *Communism in Latin America,* Chapter X.

Both Communist and anarcho-syndicalist union leaders sought in the beginning to prevent their organizations from seeking legal recognition. Even to this day, there are important unions, including those of workers employed by government-owned enterprises or those under anarcho-syndicalist leadership, which do not enjoy legal recognition, though they have *de facto* recognition from both government and employers.

The tide was turned in favor of the legally recognized unions by the one dictatorship which Chile has suffered in the present century, the government of General Carlos Ibañez from 1927 to 1931. During this period, Communist and anarchist leaders of older unions were severely persecuted, while the government strongly encouraged establishment of legal unions. At the same time there grew up in these legal unions, which by the end of the Ibañez administration had joined together to form the Confederación Nacional de Sindicatos Legales (National Confederation of Legal Unions), a leadership hostile to the Communists and the anarchists. Two years after the fall of Ibañez, these elements banded together in the new Socialist party.

The 1930's were marked by a gradual growth of the labor movement and the expansion of collective bargaining in urban manufacturing industries. However, a large proportion of the urban labor force as well as most mine workers did not as yet enjoy the effective right of collective bargaining.

The trade union movement continued to be split politically. The Communists had revived the Federación Obrera de Chile after the fall of the Ibañez dictatorship in 1931. The anarcho-syndicalists formed a new group, the Confederación General de Trabajadores. The Socialists dominated the Confederación Nacional de Sindicatos Legales. Some of the white-collar workers' organizations were under Radical party influence.

Some degree of unity in the labor movement was achieved in December, 1936, at a convention attended by delegates from all three existing central labor groups. Out of this convention came the Confederación de Trabajadores de Chile (CTCh), although after some hesitation the anarcho-syndicalists decided not to affiliate their unions to the new group and so kept the Confederación General de Trabajadores alive.

The election in 1938 of President Pedro Aguirre Cerda, candidate of the Popular Front (composed of the Radical, Socialist, Communist and several smaller parties as well as the CTCh), brought new support to organized labor. The trade unions during the next few years received positive encouragement from the government and grew rapidly. Such industries as coal, copper, and nitrate mining, which had had company-controlled unions, finally recognized legitimate labor organizations and began to bargain collectively. Trade unionism and collective bargaining also became all but universal in manufacturing and transportation.

The main difficulties facing labor after 1939 were political. With the fall of Ibañez in 1931, organized labor was politically divided. The Communists still had influence among the miners, some construction workers, and a few other groups. The anarchists were strong among maritime workers, printers, shoemakers, and construction workers. The new Socialist party was influential among railroaders and industrial workers, while the Radical party had considerable power among unions of white-collar workers, particularly government employees.

Political division of labor has continued down to the present day. Although most unions, except those under anarchist control, joined the Confederation of Workers of Chile in 1936, the CTCh was an uneasy alliance at best, constantly threatened with political splits. A definite break finally took place early in 1946 when Communist- and Socialist-dominated central labor groups, each with the name Confederación de Trabajadores de Chile, were formed. It was not until 1952 that the majority of the unions, this time including the anarchist-controlled ones, joined to form a new organization, the Central Única de Trabajadores de Chile (Central Union of Workers of Chile—CUTCh). However, by this time internecine warfare among different political factions in the labor movement had resulted in many organizations staying entirely outside of the CUTCh, while an important group of unions had in fact become employer-dominated.

The CUTCh was from the outset largely under Communist control. The Communists have consistently had three advantages over their opponents. They possessed a propaganda machine which could, and frequently did, crucify any trade union leader who stood out strongly against their influence. They have had a corps of paid functionaries who spend all their time on trade union affairs, a luxury which the other political groups in the labor movement, less amply supplied with funds than the Communists, have not been able to afford. Finally, they have constantly used the siren song of "working-class unity" and "unity of the Left" to confuse their opponents and prevent unification of non-Communists in the labor movement against them. The Communists were successful in convincing other groups that the Communist party was the most representative working-class and Left party. This is only understandable if one realizes that the concept of a political life divided sharply between "Left" and "Right" is as strongly entrenched in Chile as it is in France.

These advantages have made it possible for the small Communist tail to wag the large trade union dog for more than a decade. By 1957, the real strength of the Communists among rank-and-file Chilean trade unionists was very small. They controlled little more than the coal mining unions, one faction of the construction workers, and a scattering of other organizations.[35]

The CUTCh finally split in August, 1957, when non-Communist elements walked out of the second congress of the organization and set up their own Preparatory Committee for a Democratic Trade Union Center. Under this committee's auspices, a congress was held in November, 1958, at which a new central labor body, the Confederación Nacional del Trabajo, was established. It affiliated with the International Confederation of Free Trade Unions early in 1959.[36] Although it represented only a minority of the labor movement by the middle of 1959, it was the first organization openly to challenge Communist control of organized labor in almost a decade.

The intensely political nature of Chilean trade unionism has been a disturbing factor in labor relations for several decades. Strikes are not infrequently called more for the consolidation of the political group in control of a given union than because they are justified economically. General strikes "in solidarity," or in protest against some measure of the government, have been almost routine and have done much damage to the labor movement and to relations with employers. Undoubtedly political rivalry in the unions has made grievance negotiations more difficult than they might otherwise have been.

From time to time, too, the political orientation of the unions has brought repressive retaliatory action by government. Thus, in 1946–47, when President Gabriel González Videla was governing with a cabinet which included three Communist ministers, the administration refused to recognize some regularly elected representatives of certain unions, and chose rather to deal with *ad hoc* committees of workers from these organizations which were dominated by the Communists. A few months later, when President González broke with the Communists, his administration was equally partial to anti-Communist union leaders and pushed through Congress the so-called Law for the Permanent Defense of Democracy, which outlawed the Communist party and permitted him to exile to distant parts of the country Communist trade union leaders.

Again, during the second administration of General Carlos Ibañez

---

[36] *Inter-American Labor Bulletin*, Washington, D.C., May, 1959.

[37] Interview with Edmundo Mendez, Chief of Social Organizations Section, General Directorate of Labor, in Santiago, July 31, 1956.

(1952–1958), the government generally evinced a hostile attitude toward the unions controlled by his political opponents. Clashes between the government and the unions were frequent, and the Ministry of Labor so interpreted the Law for the Defense of Democracy to veto candidates in union elections whom it labeled "Communists." [37] This action highlighted a significant fact about Chilean labor relations: that the law is rather strict toward the unions, but is seldom enforced in full.[38]

The Labor Code provides that the government may intervene extensively in union electoral and financial affairs. Until passage of the Law for Defense of Democracy, the Ministry of Labor could oust any union official who had been convicted of a crime; with the passage of that law, membership in the Communist party was added to the list of crimes. In the field of finance each union must submit its budget six months in advance of the beginning of the fiscal year, and at the end of the year must submit an accounting of how funds were spent. If discrepancies between the budget and the actual expenditures are too great, erring union officials may be subject to criminal prosecution. It should be added that this part of the Labor Code has rarely been enforced.

Politics have made difficult the maintenance of a strong central labor organization in Chile, and have also raised difficulties for the establishment and continued life of national industrial unions. As a result of political divisions, it has been impossible for more than a decade to maintain a national textile workers' organization; the miners have been split into two divergent groups for almost that long; the construction workers are split into several organizations.

However, there have been a few successful national industrial union groups. Outstanding is the Confederation of Copper Workers of Chile, established by the unions in the Big Three tin mines in the early 1950's. Its position was strengthened in 1956 when the Copper Workers' Statute officially recognized the organization and its status as bargaining agent for the miners. The Maritime Confederation is another successful national labor group, including most of the local unions of seamen and dock workers as well as many fishermen. It is more loosely organized than the Copper Workers' Confederation, but does an important job of coördinating the activities of its affiliated unions. The Federation of Bakers is perhaps the oldest national trade union industrial group, dating from the 1930's. It is the collective bargaining

[38] In July, 1958, the Law for the Defense of Democracy was repealed, over the veto of President Carlos Ibañez, thus putting an end, for the time being at least, to this type of government intervention in the unions.

agent for bakers in Santiago and some provincial cities. The largest of the national organizations is the Railroad Workers' Industrial Federation. It processes grievances for workers of the State Railways, helps to manage their large coöperative, and carries on lobbying, though the Federation is not allowed to negotiate collective bargaining contracts, since State Railway workers are considered government employees.

COMPARISON OF LABOR ORGANIZATIONS IN THE THREE COUNTRIES

The form and functions of the trade unions thus reflect the political experience through which each of the nations has passed. Brazil's unions speak for virtually all the country's industrial and transportation workers and most commercial workers, though only a small percentage of the labor force actually pays dues. In Argentina, the Perón era resulted in almost universal unionization of urban workers as well as many agricultural employees, and established the general pattern of checkoff of union dues by the employer. In Chile, most industrial, mining, and transportation workers are also organized, with compulsory checkoff of union dues provided for by law in the case of "recognized" unions.

The Vargas dictatorship in Brazil converted the unions into little more than appendages of the Ministry of Labor, made them conform to a predetermined corporate state organizational pattern, and withdrew from them virtually all collective bargaining functions. Only since the fall of the New State have the unions been groping toward a greater degree of independence from the government and the development of a bargaining relationship with the employers. In Argentina, Perón centralized the labor movement, transferred power from local to national officials, and put overriding power in the CGT, which was itself completely subordinated to the Ministry of Labor; but the Argentine unions did not lose their right to bargain collectively, though it was closely supervised by the government. Subsequent to the ouster of the dictator, the centralization of the labor movement was relaxed and the control of the government somewhat modified. In Chile, the law provided for a trade union structure based on the plant union and the local craft union, and gave the Ministry of Labor extensive control over union finances and elections, although such control has only been exercised sporadically.

The trade union movements of all three countries have been intensely political. In Brazil, the chief rivals for influence since the end of the New State have been Vargas' Labor party, the Communist party, and the Ministry of Labor, which has been particularly influential among the leadership of federations and confederations. In post-

Perón Argentina, the fundamental political division in labor has been between the Peronistas and the anti-Peronistas, though many parties have sought to gain influence in the labor movement. In Chile, the very large number of parties which characterizes the country's democracy has been reflected in the existence of half a dozen different political groups inside the labor movement, which has made the achievement and maintenance of a united trade union movement exceedingly difficult.

In all three countries, the control of the government over the labor movement is marked. In the New State days it was virtually absolute in Brazil, though it has been reduced somewhat since then. In Perón's Argentina, the Ministry of Labor, as well as Perón and his wife, constantly intervened in the internal affairs of the labor movement, choosing the principal officials of the CGT and its affiliated unions. The Perón regime also enacted legislation giving the state a considerable degree of legal right to intervene in the unions. In Chile, the Labor Code provides for very extensive intervention by the government in the unions' affairs.

The Problems of Management

RECRUITMENT AND TRAINING OF MANAGEMENT PERSONNEL

The development of an adequate managerial force has been one of the key problems of economic growth in Argentina, Brazil, and Chile. It has been necessary to recruit adequate personnel to manage industries as well as to raise their productivity. The managers are also faced with special problems in dealing with their workers, and in Brazil and Chile this has led to extensive systems of employer paternalism. Finally, employer elements have established organizations to represent their interests both in dealing with workers' unions and in more general fields.

As has been the case with wage labor, the development of the economies of Brazil, Argentina, and Chile has tended to outrun the methods of recruiting and training managerial personnel. The entrepreneurs who started the large-scale industrialization of these countries were largely their own top managers. Relatives, friends, and long-time associates in business tended in the first instance to occupy the other more responsible managerial positions. In any case, these early managers were largely self-made men, who had little formal training in management techniques and had learned to deal with problems as they came along.

In many instances native managerial talent was supplemented by immigrants. One frequently finds Italians, British, Germans, Central Europeans, and Spaniards in the position of plant manager and other supervisory capacities. But generally speaking, it was not until recently that the managerial class began to become acutely aware of its own deficiencies. Only since World War II has there been serious interest in improving management techniques and increasing the efficiency of the firm. It is as though the industrialists had reached a plateau where, after a mad rush to climb up through the first stage of development and expansion, they now looked around and felt the need to rearrange their entrepreneurial equipment for the next long hard pull toward industrial maturity.

The most spectacular example of this interest has been the Chilean Institute for Rational Administration of Firms (ICARE), established in 1953, with a broad program dealing with problems of technical efficiency, managerial training, labor productivity, and human relations. In addition to coöperating in surveys and reorganization efforts of a number of firms, ICARE has developed a broad program of training managerial personnel. This has been topped off by a series of executive training programs for selected management people, run for six weeks every winter in the resort town of Viña del Mar.[39]

In Argentina, the Instituto Argentino de Relaciones Industriales, established during the Perón period, is roughly comparable to the ICARE in Chile, though of a somewhat more limited scope. It maintains a School for Personnel Directors and a psychological testing service for the use of its members in hiring and promoting employees. It also has subsidiary organizations of personnel officers, industrial engineers, and safety engineers. It has issued a number of publications, including a monthly magazine *Relaciones del Trabajo*.[40] The insistence of employers on tying wage increases to productivity increases during collective negotiations after the fall of Perón is further indication of their interest in the problems of labor productivity and efficient management.

In Brazil, the growing tendency toward more careful selection of personnel, particularly in administrative categories, is an indication of the same interest. So is the wide employer support which has been given to the new School of Business Administration in the University of São Paulo, the first institution of this kind to be established in any of the three countries.

---

[39] Interview with Enrique Barriga, Manager of ICARE, in Santiago, August 7, 1956.

[40] *Memoria y Balance al 31 de Diciembre de 1954* (Buenos Aires: Instituto Argentino de Relaciones Industriales, 1955).

Managerial personnel, however, is still chosen on a rather haphazard basis in most instances. There is no doubt that personal influence and friendship play a large role in giving a young man a chance to enter a plant. There are no such things as the huge executive training programs which have developed in the United States. For one thing, the relatively small size of industries would hardly permit such extensive training programs. For another, the industrialists have not evolved that far in their thinking. Finally, few firms would be in a position to administer such programs even if they wanted to install them. Managerial personnel is likely to consist rather of people trained in engineering than in "human relations" or "management." Problems of relations with the workers are likely to be handled by someone with legal training, partly because of the important role which the law plays in these matters.

EMPLOYER PATERNALISM

Employers of these three countries have special problems to face, which arise from the fact that they are building industry in hitherto underdeveloped economies. They are frequently faced with the problem of hiring a worker from the countryside who is illiterate, unaccustomed to the strict discipline of the factory, and almost unacquainted with a money income, and of converting him into a disciplined, responsible industrial employee. One method which Latin American employers have used has been paternalism, but there are interesting differences in the approach of the employers of Argentina, Brazil, and Chile. In Argentina, there has been relatively little development of paternalistic institutions; in Brazil, the employers have been somewhat reluctant to engage in paternalism individually, but have developed an important system through their collective organizations; in Chile, paternalism by the individual employer is most general.

The lack of employer paternalism in Argentina is due to a number of factors. The early industrial working class was drawn largely from among immigrants whose intellectual attainments and range of experience were considerably greater than was true for the early industrial workers in Chile and Brazil. The Argentine educational system has always been more nearly universal than that of either of the other two countries. Finally, when after 1943 the industrialists began drawing their labor supply from the relatively backward agricultural masses of Argentina, the Perón government was in the process of seeking to channel all action on behalf of the workers through its own hands and those of its closely controlled labor movement, and had little sympathy for paternalistic efforts by employers.

In Brazil, the extensive system of employer paternalism had its origin right after World War II and was quite frankly designed to help adapt the workers to the new industrial economy and to prevent them from turning to the unions and the Communist party. The system is centered in the Social Service for Industry (SESI), and the Social Service for Commerce (SESCI). These organizations, which are independent but subsidiary branches of the national confederations of commerce and industry, have a varied program which differs greatly from state to state. Three philosophies are noticeable in the administration of SESI in the various states. One looks upon SESI as a source of political patronage, for the purpose of electing to office people who will speak for or be sympathetic with the viewpoint of the industrialists. The second regards SESI as a vast charitable and welfare organization, designed to keep the workers reasonably well satisfied and quiet through providing them with medical and dental aid, low-cost grocery stores, schools, and libraries. The third regards the Social Service of Industry as a means of making it possible not only for the workers but for the community as a whole more easily to adapt to the changes brought about by the advent of an industrial society.

Chilean paternalism, unlike that of Brazil, is generally expressed by the individual employer. Many employers maintain clinics and even small hospitals for their employees, even though all industrial workers are covered for medical purposes by the government's social security system. Some operate low-price company stores or aid their workers in maintaining coöperatives. Many provide housing. Most employers find it necessary from time to time to lend money to their workers. A few have extensive educational programs which they run or help their workers run.

There is a tendency among Chilean employers to reduce the amount of paternalistic activities. This is particularly notable in the mining regions, where the companies are attempting to substitute wage increases for subsidized company stores and in general to become less responsible for the private lives of their employees. However, for some time to come the Chilean employer will continue to provide a large variety of services for his workers.

EMPLOYER ORGANIZATIONS

The urban employers early became aware of the need to establish organizations to defend their interests, both in dealing with organized labor and to treat with more general problems. In some cases these organizations were established in conformity with labor legislation, in others they were of more spontaneous development.

In Brazil, the Consolidation of Labor Laws of the Estado Novo called for the establishment of local "sindicatos," federations, and confederations of employers to parallel those of the workers. However, employers were hesitant to form organizations provided for in the Consolidation of Labor Laws. They did not want to submit to the strict control by the government which the Consolidation provided for, and tended to look upon organizations established under the Consolidation as government tools rather than true defenders of their own points of view and interests.

Since the collapse of the New State, the employer groups provided for in the Consolidation have become more widespread, since virtually all government intervention in their internal affairs has ceased. The government itself has increasingly insisted on dealing with only legally recognized employers' organizations, the labor movement has grown more militant, and employers have felt the need for institutions to defend their interests. However, the employers' groups do not conform strictly to the pattern provided for in the Consolidation of Labor Laws. Although the lowest-echelon groups, the *sindicatos,* usually have their jurisdiction set forth in the law, this is not the case with the federations of employers' *sindicatos.* Where the law provides for each separate group of employers, textile manufacturers, chemical manufacturers, etc., to establish appropriate state federations, the employers in each state have established only two federations: of industrial employers and of commercial employers. The government has not insisted on the strict application of the law, and has given legal recognition to these groups. On a national basis, employers' organizations are brought together in the confederations of commerce and industry.

In Argentina, there was an extensive pattern of employer organizations before Perón. As with the workers' unions, the Perón regime merely extended and generalized this pattern. As a result, virtually all employers now belong to "cámaras," representing their industry or branch of commerce. These are united in a complicated series of national industrial associations and regional employers' groups. Their function is both collective bargaining and more general defense of members' interests. Under Perón an attempt was made to bring all employers' groups together in a single confederation, the so-called Confederación General Económica (CGE—General Economic Confederation). In the last months of the Perón regime, a law was passed forcing all employers to belong to the CGE affiliate in their trade or industry and make a compulsory contribution to it. However, the Aramburu government felt that this was a political organization for the support of the Perón regime and dissolved it late in 1955. By the middle of

1959 no organization had been voluntarily established to take its place.

In Chile, most employer organizations are purely voluntary. Only a handful of employers have established "sindicatos" as provided for in the Labor Code. However, almost every group of employers has an organization. The most powerful is probably the Associación de Industriales Metalúrgicos, the metal industrialists group, established in the early 1950's. On the more general level, there are the Sociedad de Fomento Fabril, representing all industrial employers; the Confederación Nacional de Comercio, to which most large mercantile employers belong; the Unión de Comercio Minorista, to which smaller merchants are affiliated; and the Cámara Nacional de Navegación, among shipping interests. No government compulsion is exerted to make employers join any of these. The groups do not generally engage in collective bargaining, which, under Chilean law, is conducted by the individual firm, though in some cases the employer groups advise their members in the negotiation of collective agreements.

Collective Bargaining

Just as the nature of the workers' and employers' organizations has been much influenced by the political experiences of the three countries, so have the methods by which the employers deal with the unions. The Vargas Estado Novo abolished collective bargaining in Brazil, and the succeeding years have resulted in only a partial reëstablishment of this form of management-labor relationship. In contrast, in both Argentina and Chile, collective bargaining is the generalized pattern, though the methods by which it is conducted differ greatly in the two countries.

During the New State, Vargas substituted a system of labor courts for collective bargaining. Both individual workers' grievances and collective demands for wage increases and other changes in working conditions were handled by these courts instead of through direct negotiations between the parties. As a matter of fact, virtually no collective demands were made even to the labor courts during the New State period. In 1959, most grievances are still being handled through the labor court system. In contrast to the situation during the Vargas dictatorship, most important unions regularly present demands to the labor courts for wage increases and other modifications of working conditions, which are resolved by so-called "collective decisions" of the courts. The employers' role in these proceedings is limited largely to presenting written and oral argument, through counsel, to the courts. In an increasing number of cases, demands are being presented informally to the employers, and are being negotiated directly between the union and the employers' association, with the Ministry of Labor merely giving its approval to the agreement thus reached, and by doing so making it legally binding on all employers and workers within the jurisdiction of the respective unions.

In such major cities as Rio de Janeiro, São Paulo, Porto Alegre and Recife, the development of independent negotiation between workers and employers has gone particularly far. Many of the important unions in these cities are resolving individual grievances through direct negotiation with the employer, and are only going to the labor courts if negotiation fails. Strikes for wage increases are becoming common, particularly in São Paulo. Many employers are also anxious to process grievances in direct dealing with their workers. They feel that the labor courts tend to be prejudiced in favor of the workers, and in many cases prefer to deal directly rather than submitting matters to the decision of an "outsider."

In Argentina, a pattern of collective bargaining had been general in unionized industries even before the advent of Perón. Under the dictatorship this pattern was universalized and centralized. Those industries and trades in which collective bargaining had been conducted on a regional or local basis were generally made to conform with the basis of national negotiation preferred by Perón. Furthermore, the government, which had played virtually no role in collective bargaining before the Perón era, was given an important part in the procedure, since all negotiation had to be conducted in the Ministry of Labor, which also had to approve of the agreements reached. Subsequent to the fall of Perón, although the Aramburu government tried to step out of the collective bargaining picture and turn this problem completely over to the workers' and employers' organizations, it was only partially able to do so. The habits established during the dictatorship proved to be too strong.

In Chile, collective bargaining is also the pattern. Chilean labor law provides for negotiation to be conducted between individual plant unions and the employers. The great majority of collective agreements are so negotiated. However, in a number of industries, including baking, copper mining, textiles, and the maritime trades, an informal process of consultation among the employers' organizations on the one hand, and groups of unions on the other, has grown up. In the copper industry, this was formalized in the Copper Workers' Statute of 1956.

In both Argentina and Chile, individual worker grievances are largely handled through direct negotiation between the employer and the union. In the former, the Perón regime established a final court of appeal for grievances in the Ministry of Labor. In Chile, by contrast, grievances are likely to be dealt with by the government only when they present the serious danger of a strike in a basic industry.

A system of shop stewards legally protected from dismissal is universal in Argentina. These stewards generally take up a grievance with a foreman. The second stage of the grievance procedure provides for the shop committee of the plant to present a complaint to the management. The third step is in the Ministry of Labor, where both union and employer have permanent representatives on a grievance committee presided over by a ministry official.

In Chile, grievances are handled largely through direct negotiations between employers and the unions. Most unions have shop stewards who in some cases are recognized by the employers. If the employer does not recognize the legitimacy of the first-step grievance being presented by the shop steward, the steward's job is limited to reporting the case to one of the directors of the union who possess legal immunity from dismissal. Grievances are handled in widely different ways in Chile, depending upon the firm and the union. In some cases there are periodic meetings between the union directors and the management. In others, the door to management is always open to the directors, who spend most of their time in collecting, reporting, and negotiating grievances. In one case, the copper mines, there is a special statute which specifies how much time they must be on the job.[41]

INFLATION AND EMPLOYER-UNION RELATIONS

Since World War II, inflation has been increasingly acute, and wage increases have thus been the principal subject of discussion in negotiations between employers and the unions. Indeed, in Brazil wages and closely related problems have been virtually the only matters dealt with in the "collective decisions" of the labor tribunals and in collective bargaining agreements. Much the same thing has been true about collective contracts in Chile.

Prices were already rising rapidly in Brazil by the end of World War II. Between 1944 and 1954, the cost of living in Rio de Janeiro increased, on the average, approximately 10 per cent a year.[42] The unions reacted to this continuing increase in the cost of living by presenting demands to the regional labor tribunals for wage boosts, or by entering into direct negotiations with the employers to the same

---

[41] Interview with Eduardo Delfín, President, Confederación de Trabajadores del Cobre, in Chuquicamata, Chile, August 18, 1956.

[42] *Datos y Cifras*, publication of Inter-American Regional Organization of Workers, Mexico, D.F., May–June, 1954.

end. It became the normal thing for a militant union to make such demands regularly every year, and increases were generally roughly equivalent to cost-of-living rises. In addition, the unions kept up constant pressure on the government to increase legal minimum wages, which in some parts of the country tend to be the prevailing wage levels. There were adjustments in minimum wages in 1944, 1951, 1953, and 1956.

In Chile, too, inflation has been steady since the end of World War II. In the face of the steady rise in the cost of living, the unions regularly demanded wage increases each year, and the tendency was to grant wage boosts more or less equivalent to the rise in prices during the previous twelve months. At the same time, government fixing of minimum salaries for white-collar workers operated on the same principle of annual revisions of salaries to bring them into line with price increases during the previous year.

In January, 1956, the government of President Carlos Ibañez enacted a price stabilization law. In conformity with that law, the government decreed that no collective agreement could provide for a wage increase in excess of 50 per cent of the previous year's price rise. At the same time, the system of annual revision of minimum salaries for white-collar workers was suspended. During the following two years, wages tended to lag considerably behind prices, but price increases were significantly less than in the years immediately preceding the enactment of stabilization legislation.

Inflation did not become a major problem in Argentina until 1949. During the previous four or five years there had been a pressing world demand for Argentina's grains and meat in world markets, and the country was able to get exceedingly high prices for them. This general increase in national income made it possible for the Perón regime for several years to force up money wages, at the same time using part of its profits on the sale of Argentine products abroad to subsidize the principal articles of prime necessity produced and sold within the country.

However, by 1949 price increases began to outrun wages. With an index number of 100 representing the price level of 1942, prices had increased by 1949 to 237, rose to 297 in the following year, and reached 563 by 1952.[43] According to the United States Department of Commerce, Argentine real wages rose 34 per cent between 1943 and 1949, but thereafter the trend was reversed, and by 1952 real wages in general had fallen to a point only 13 per cent above the 1943 level,

[43] Cámara Argentina de Industrias Metalúrgicas, "Convenio No. 97 Actualizado para Empleados y Obreros de la Industria Metalúrgica," Buenos Aires, 1954.

and real wages of skilled workers were approximately the same as those of 1943.[44] Price increases after 1949 reflected the reversal of the Perón government's policy of subsidization of key consumption goods, made necessary by the end of the postwar bonanza in international trade and the reduction in the government's profits from that trade.

With the increase in the impetus of inflation, the Perón regime sought to restrict wage rises after 1948. By the end of the Perón period, the government had virtually taken the fixing of wages into its own hands. This policy was continued by the governments succeeding Perón. In February, 1956, the Aramburu administration decreed a 10 per cent general wage increase. Between February, 1956, and the inauguration of President Arturo Frondizi in May, 1958, prices of fifteen articles of prime necessity had risen approximately 60 per cent,[45] and President Frondizi decreed a general 60 per cent wage increase over levels of February 1, 1956.[46] Prices continued to rise even more rapidly after this decree.

With the exception of the 1944–1949 period in Argentina, it is likely that wage increases in the three countries since World War II have done little more than keep up with the increase in the cost of living, if they have done that much. Although groups of workers with particularly strong bargaining power or political influence may have enjoyed real wage rises, it is unlikely that this has been true for most workers in the three countries.

From the point of view of the owners and managers of industry, inflation has by no means been all bad. It has allowed them to pass on to the consumer increased costs arising from collective bargaining and from labor and social security legislation. It has also provided them with a certain margin of virtually automatic profit, arising from the fact that between the time they purchase their raw materials and labor and the time they actually get their products on the market prices have risen appreciably. It is perhaps significant that Chilean industrial employers did not give any great degree of support to the efforts of President Ibañez to halt that country's inflation in 1956 and thereafter.

Summary and Conclusions

It is impossible to state with any finality the effect of the systems of labor-management relations on the economic development of Argen-

---

[44] Cited by Arthur P. Whitaker in *The United States and Argentina* (Cambridge: Harvard University Press), p. 205.

[45] *La Vanguardia*, Buenos Aires, June 5, 1958.

[46] *La Vanguardia*, Buenos Aires, May 29, 1958.

tina, Brazil, and Chile. However, certain general ideas about these systems and their effects on economic growth can be suggested:

1. Whatever differences there have been in economic development or in the nature of labor-management relations in the three countries, are not due to any significant differences in the sources of capital accumulation or in the nature of the entrepreneurial class. In all three cases, the industrial entrepreneurs came principally from the artisan class, which tended to build small workshops into factory industries. A second source of industrial entrepreneurship was the merchants, while the agriculturalists, the dominant group in preindustrial society, made relatively little contribution to the ranks of the industrial enterprisers.

The government played a significant role in mobilizing capital for development. This role was largest in Chile and smallest in Brazil, but important in all three nations. The governments not only built up important public utilities needed for economic growth, but also invested to a greater or less degree in the actual industrialization process.

Foreign investors, too, made significant contributions to economic growth. Private firms established numerous industries, and international lending agencies helped the development of both public utilities and manufacturing establishments, through loans to the respective governments.

2. We may note that the differences in the labor-management systems are largely the result of the varying political histories of the three countries. In Argentina, a system of national unions and national collective bargaining agreements is the direct result of the Perón experience. The decentralized labor movement and local collective bargaining characteristic of Chile is due to the nature of the country's labor law and the diversity of its political parties. The widespread substitution of decrees of government labor tribunals for collective bargaining in Brazil is the heritage of the New State experiment of Getulio Vargas.

3. Labor costs have been higher than would otherwise have been true in these three countries because of the prevalent type of labor-management relations. Both collective bargaining in Argentina and Chile and the labor tribunal set-up in Brazil gave the workers greater bargaining power over money wages than they would otherwise have had. At the same time, the policies of the governments in the fields of social security and labor legislation added to the costs of production of industry. Employer paternalism in Brazil and Chile have had the same result.

4. Inflation played an important role in offsetting the cost-increasing

effects of collective bargaining, the labor tribunals, social security, labor legislation and employer paternalism. It allowed employers to pass these costs on to the general public, and to keep real labor costs lower than they would otherwise have been, since wage increases have generally lagged behind rises in prices. Real wages have increased but little since World War II in the three countries. Inflation also provided an incentive to the industrial entrepreneurs by providing them "inflationary profits."

5. It is fair to say that in spite of inflation, the labor-management systems of these three countries provide considerable benefits for the workers. They have given them a relatively high level of health protection, through social security systems, employer medical schemes, and union clinics. There has been a certain degree of protection against the risks of old age, through social security and some employer paternalism.

Workers in Argentina, Brazil, and Chile have gained considerably in terms of personal self-esteem as a result of the development of trade unionism and an orderly system of labor-management relations. This is an intangible benefit which it is impossible to quantify. But it is clear to this writer that the labor-management systems existing in all three nations have tended to assure the worker that he will not be considered merely a "factor of production," but will be treated as an individual, with certain prescribed rights and duties.

The labor-management systems evolved in the "ABC" countries of South America have thus helped to prevent some of the worst abuses to which workers were subject during the early phases of the industrialization of Great Britain, the United States, and the Soviet Union. Perhaps if Brazil, Argentina, and Chile had not had machinery whereby the workers could at least partially defend their own interests, it might have been possible for these nations to industrialize more rapidly than they have done. However, whether consciously or not, the people and leaders of the "ABC" countries chose to have their economies grow somewhat less rapidly, but under more humane conditions, than was true in at least some of those nations which industrialized before them.

Chapter V | *Israel*[1]

IRVIN SOBEL

The Histadrut: Political and Social Maturity Prior to Economic Development

In no other nation of the world has the labor movement played as important and even dominant a role as in Israel. In fact, its very existence as a society and independent state has been attributed by many authorities to its labor movement, the Histadrut. The Histadrut, termed the "wonder child" of the world social democratic trade union movement by the late Professor Selig Perlman,[2] and a huge monopoly and octopus by its ideological detractors, has been a highly controversial entity during its entire history, but even its most unrestrained critics would never deny its significant achievements and importance.

The Histadrut is a unique labor organization in every sense. It is at the same time both a labor movement with a strong socialist orientation and a major entrepreneur and owner of industry headed by a de-

[1] This essay is based upon research undertaken on the Histadrut, sponsored through a Ford Foundation Faculty Research Fellowship during the year 1956–57. Unfortunately, the Sinai Campaign and the evacuation of Americans from Israel caused some postponement of the research and, although I returned to Israel for five months in 1957, completion of the data-gathering and interviewing for this essay and that on "Management in Israel" awaited a return trip during the early summer of 1959. The coöperation of everyone in the Histadrut and Israeli government made this essay possible, but I would especially like to thank the late Dr. Ezra Hayut of the international department of the Histadrut and Mr. Yehuda Shohamy, then of its trade union department, and now in Mapai. However, all conclusions and deficiencies are my own. I would like to thank the Ford Foundation for its willingness to make adjustments to accommodate my special situation due to the Sinai Campaign interruption.

[2] Selig Perlman, "The Labor Movement: A Theory" (unpublished manuscript, 1949), p. 6.

termined and powerful managerial wing. The trade union and industrial sectors are intertwined with a broad network of consumer and producer coöperatives and collective farms, the latter constituting the original focal point of organizational strength and basic ideology. Unlike other Western labor organizations, which developed after the industrialization process had been set in motion and the labor force committed, recruited, and structured, the Histadrut saw its role as an industrializer and economic developer.

The Histadrut can only be understood in terms of the confluence of two forces: *Zionism,* aimed at the establishment of a Jewish state, and *Socialism,* as interpreted, adapted, and modified by the Eastern European intellectuals who founded the Israeli labor movement as a branch of a world Labor-Zionist movement. These two forces produced a labor movement dedicated not only to fashioning an independent Jewish state, but also to modeling it along certain basic lines which might be described as equalitarian and coöperative—or, at least, as a society in which private enterprise would at best have a limited role. The three basic features of the Histadrut—colonization, nationalization, and its social ideals—evolved out of the perceived "calling" of the early leaders and members of the organization.

Before the state of Israel existed, there was a need to establish an economic basis for its eventual functioning; after independence, a need to intensify the rate of economic development. As the largest voluntary organization in the society, embracing over half of the population and more than four-fifths of the wage-earning labor force, the Histadrut was the only entity large enough to assume many functions normally assumed by a modern national state. It therefore created diverse institutions which extended to many phases of its members' lives.

The Histadrut evolved under different historical circumstances than have other labor movements. There existed, both prior to its formation and even until quite recently, no well-entrenched employer class, and both employers and workers had been mainly drawn from the same economic, religious, and intellectual environments. For that matter there was no well-articulated labor class; in fact, the early Israeli "working class" were essentially middle-class intellectuals in their native countries, who emigrated to Palestine to participate in building a state. It was believed necessary to transform oneself from middle-class to worker status, and from intellectual to builder and farmer. Thus, as a precondition of a national transformation, hundreds of thousands of personal transformations would have to take place. The Histadrut in consequence felt impelled to assume educational and training functions, first to create the ideological frame of mind for such basic personal changes, and then to provide the technical competence necessary for performance in what was a new cultural environment.

Despite the strong and apparently rigid ideological convictions of its founders, pragmatism animated the organization from its very inception. Ideology generally gave way to national developmental needs, and certain institutional forms and methods perhaps more ideologically compatible to the original founders have consistently been abandoned in favor of more operationally feasible methods considered less desirable philosophically.[3] The specific forms and ways in which coöperation developed can be related more to necessity than to any philosophical preconceptions. Nevertheless, the Histadrut, given its strong intellectual orientation, has always been characterized by an attempt to rationalize given developments by either associating them with some social doctrine or even founding a new one. Early coöperation, for instance, developed simply out of the existing poverty of the early pioneers and pioneering organizations, and their need to pool what limited amounts of capital, fertile land, operational knowledge, medical resources, and even defensive strength they had available in order to survive.[4]

The traditional trade union function and activities, while important, never constituted either the main or even the central core of the organization, although there was a need for some organizational entity strong enough to assure that whatever employment opportunities existed in the non-Arab sector went solely to Jewish labor. Without such employment, immigration, the lifeblood of the future state, would have been impossible. In the absence of any governmental force willing to establish those social conditions and that type of social legislation which would constitute the base upon which the new state could be founded, collective bargaining was seen as necessary to create the desired conditions. Thus, by the time the state of Israel was established in 1948, the Histadrut through its collective agreements had already achieved virtually all those conditions generally obtained through social legislation in advanced industrial societies. Despite this strong emphasis upon bargaining, the movement maintained a broad unitary point of view, and separate national functionally-oriented trade union groupings did not emerge on any scale until recently.

This broad point of view is all the more remarkable because, from

[3] The tendency of the producers' coöperative form to be displaced in favor of wholly owned Histadrut plants is indicative of this pragmatism.

[4] The Kibbutz or collective can more easily be explained in these terms than by any preëxisting social philosophy which made this form mandatory.

its outset, the Histadrut was characterized by intense political factionalism, and is the membership base for the three major labor-oriented political parties in Israel. Despite these internal difficulties, the Histadrut has been able to organize approximately 80 to 85 per cent of the eligible labor force, a proportion which is undoubtedly the highest in the world. The approximately 30 per cent of Israel's economic activity generated in the labor and coöperative sector is also another unparalleled achievement.

It is not the purpose of this brief introduction to create the image of perfection, unblemished success, and total economic and political adequacy, or the nonexistence of major organizational problems. Histadrut's organizational diversity causes basic contradictions and strains —as, for example, the differing views and functional orientations of its managerial and trade union wings. Forms, techniques, operational practices, and even basic functional groupings which were successful either in the earlier preindustrial or beginning industrialization periods must now be changed, and in some cases abandoned, in the light of altered circumstances.

Organizational relations with the political leadership of Israel, and the willingness of the labor movement to subordinate its position to that leadership—the great majority of whom originated out of the Histadrut, and out of a labor party whose major voting strength is still in the Histadrut—is another problem area still in flux. The relations of Histadrut to the state, which is now not only assuming more developmental functions but also taking over functions which the movement previously performed, and policy of which is increasingly more favorable to private enterprise, constitutes another possible source of contention. The growing strength, determination, and competence of the private sector and its managers is increasingly being manifested on the Israeli labor scene. Internal differences, ideological disparities, and personal rivalries, all glossed over by the apparent unity which is characteristic of nationalist movements in the preindependence and early independence periods, are coming to the surface and have to be reconciled. The Kibbutz movement—the early locus of the Histadrut, and the source of a disproportionate share of its leadership and idealism—is itself beset by internal cleavages and is just able to hold its own numerically, despite the considerable rise in the population. Poorly educated and only recently literate Oriental workers, with no ideological preparation, constitute a rapidly increasing proportion of the total labor force and of Histadrut membership.

THE HISTADRUT: AS A LABOR FORCE DEVELOPER

The young men and women who emigrated to Palestine in the early part of the twentieth century, and who constituted the vanguard of the Second *Aliyah* ("going up," or emigration) were predominantly from Russia, Poland, and Romania, and were mainly of middle-class origin. They were sons and daughters of shopkeepers, independent craftsmen, tradesmen, or merchants who were dissatisfied with the narrowness of ghetto life as well as desirous of escaping anti-Semitism, which militated against them economically, politically, and socially. Socialistically inspired by Poale Zion (Worker of Zion) ideology, they believed that the only way a Jewish society could evolve was by a process of "normalization" of the work force. Normalization meant that Jews would become farmers and industrial workers as well as artisans, shopkeepers, managers, and professionals. In other words, the basic goal was to approximate the same occupational proportioning which would prevail in a normal—and, it was hoped, advanced—national state. Since Jews had traditionally been barred from both agriculture and heavier industrial sectors in Eastern Europe, at both the worker and managerial levels, this desire for proletarianization became linked with an ideology which amounted to almost a deification of manual labor. This conscious act was carried out by these young intellectuals at the price of hardship and at times great personal sacrifice. But they constituted the foundation of an embryonic state to be, became the source of much of its eventual leadership, and established the Kibbutz movement and ultimately the Histadrut.

This process of voluntary development of a manual labor force, a process which required and emphasized ideological recruitment and commitment, continued until the 1930's, when involuntary refugees from Nazi Germany began to constitute the major source of immigration to Palestine; and it came to a halt at the beginning of World War II. Current policy is enforced by necessity, mainly involuntary, and exercised upon immigrants many of whom came from preindustrial cultures.

Much of this voluntary recruitment, commitment, and training took place in the earlier era under the auspices of the Poale Zion movement, and then, after the establishment of the Histadrut, under the combined sponsorship of the Histadrut, the worldwide Labor Zionist movement, and the Jewish Agency. Since potential immigrants had to be recruited abroad, the relatively undeveloped private sector played a limited role in the process of labor force development.

Of equal importance in influencing the pattern of labor force evolution was the Histadrut's role in economic development, for in promoting and sponsoring the Kibbutz and Moshav movements, and later in organizing producer coöperatives and in developing its own industry, the Histadrut influenced the occupational and industrial structure to which immigrants had to adjust. There was a reciprocal relationship between Labor-Zionist policies toward recruitment and development of that type of labor force which would be appropriate for a national state, and the development of Histadrut economic activities. Because of its success in recruiting and training individuals abroad, mainly in agriculture through its affiliate Hechalutz (Pioneer, the Poale Zion organization for preparation for immigration), and then in obtaining immigration certificates for these recruits, the Histadrut was pressed to find employment for the new immigrants (*olim chadashim*). This influenced the Histadrut's early emphasis upon Kibbutzim, Moshavism, building and construction work, and producer coöperatives.

After the establishment of the state of Israel, the responsibility for building a modern labor force was shared by the state, the Histadrut, and the Jewish Agency. The Histadrut became somewhat less important in the process by virtue of three related developments: the taking over by the state, in 1953, of the "Labor" school trend; the transfer of the Employment Service from the Histadrut to the state in 1958–59; and the increasing tendency for the state to develop its own training institutes and organizations. Nevertheless, the Histadrut still plays a vital role.

The successive waves of immigration brought somewhat different types of population, with different characteristics. The Second *Aliyah* (1904–1914)—which gave birth to the Kibbutz and its organization of watchmen (Hashomer)—and the Third *Aliyah* (1919–1923), both of which contributed the current founding fathers of Israel, were Russian-Polish in origin. The Fourth *Aliyah,* which took place in the 1930's, was composed primarily of German refugees, who were in general professional-, administrative-, and business-oriented individuals. They were much less influenced by the Histadrut, although some who were influenced by Social-Democratic ideology later became leaders in the (currently governing) Mapai party.

During the first two years after the establishment of the state of Israel, the new immigrants were former concentration-camp inmates, generally Eastern European in origin. They were succeeded by Oriental (Sephardic) Jews from North Africa and Asia, followed by Poles and Hungarians in 1956–57. Israeli data, giving a breakdown of the population by place of origin, show that at the end of 1956 approximately one-third of the population was native-born, and two-thirds were born in countries outside Israel. Of those born abroad, 26.2 per cent of the immigrants were Asian, 17.5 per cent North African, and 56.3 per cent European; Polish, Romanian, Russian, German, and North American Jews, in that order, constituted the great bulk of the latter category. The proportion of Histadrut members of Oriental and African origin is much higher. Native Israelis constitute only 12.2 per cent of Histadrut membership.[5]

The impact of this attempt to create a more normally distributed labor force can be inferred from the data in table 17, which indicate a striking difference between the occupational structure of the Israeli

TABLE 17

OCCUPATIONAL AND INDUSTRIAL DISTRIBUTION OF JEWISH IMMIGRANTS, 1920–1928, UNITED STATES AND PALESTINE

	Per cent in Palestine	Per cent in United States
Agriculture	44	5
Industry	—	24
Service	30	42
Trade	20	24
Other	5	5
Total	99	100

SOURCE: Walter Preuss, *Die Judische Arbeiterbewegung* (Vienna: Fiba-Verlag, 1936), p. 286.

Jew and his counterpart elsewhere. If we compare the occupational distribution of Jewish immigrants to Israel with those who migrated to the United States during the 1920–1928 period, the effect of this restructuring process is even more apparent. Since the great bulk of Jewish immigrants, both to the United States and to Palestine, were Eastern European in origin and came largely from the same societal elements, these data are the more striking.

The magnitude of the impact of the Poale-Zion and Histadrut upon occupational and industrial recruitment and structuring can also be inferred from other available data. However, some brief explanation of the immigration policy of the British mandatory government is necessary before the meaning of the data can be fully explored. The British government attempted to limit immigration by requiring entry certificates. Those who did not have financial means, savings, or property, were able to enter Palestine only if they could obtain work certificates,

[5] Statistical Department of the Histadrut, unpublished data.

limited by the British government and issued through the Jewish Agency. By recruiting young intellectuals and workers through the Labor-Zionist movement of which it was the Palestinian branch, and giving them mainly agricultural and, in some cases, manual training through *Hechalutz* establishments in the various European countries, the Histadrut maintained constant pressure through the Agency upon the mandatory government.

About 150,000 of the 385,000 working-age immigrants came into Israel with work permits during the mandatory period and were registered by the Histadrut employment exchanges. Another 84,000 mainly with work certificates, were registered at the Aliyah Center.[6] Approximately 45 per cent of all immigrants were recruited in this fashion, and well over half of these had *Hechalutz* training. Some of those who came in as immigrants without a work certificate, many of whom were never part of the *Hechalutz* movement, were also recruited and trained by the Histadrut.

TABLE 18

Proportion of Immigrants Moving to Urban and Farm Areas by Place, Type of Certificate, 1931–1940, and by *Hechalutz* and Non-*Hechalutz* Affiliation

	Certificated		Uncertificated		Combined immigration	
	Hechalutz	Other	Hechalutz	Other	Hechalutz	Other
City	20.4	45.9	25.7	72.1	24.6	60.2
Farm settlement	29.1	25.7	47.5	17.4	42.6	21.1
Farm Kibbutz	42.3	4.4	21.9	1.1	27.0	12.6
Unknown	8.2	24.0	4.9	9.4	6.1	5.6
Total	100.0	100.0	100.0	100.0	100.3 [a]	99.5 [a]

Source: W. Preuss Statistical Department, Vaad Hapoel of Histadrut, *The Workers Aliyah 1919–1947* (unpublished data).
[a] These totals are as indicated in the source.

The data in table 18 indicate the impact of Histadrut and *Hechalutz* upon the labor force. They show a much greater proclivity among certificate holders and *Hechalutz* members, whether or not certificated, toward agricultural activity. If one were to add the approximately 60,000 to 70,000 illegal immigrants, the great proportion of whom came from among those same intellectually and ideologically recruited groups predominant in the *Hechalutz* movement, the role and influence of the Israeli labor movement appears even more dominant in the prestate era.

[6] Many of these were registered in both places.

Other Histadrut activities also influenced the training of the Israeli labor force. Before the establishment of the state of Israel, under the British mandatory system, no compulsory educational system was set up, and the Jewish community had to form and support its own schools. Three basic school systems or "trends" evolved: religious, labor, and general Zionist. Approximately 45 per cent of Jewish youth were educated in the labor trend, which was sponsored and financed by the Histadrut.

Agricultural schools and colleges under Kibbutz Federation auspices provided and continue to provide the major portion of trained agricultural technicians and specialists. Approximately 60 per cent of the new immigrants received Hebrew training from the Histadrut cultural department's language schools, with some of these, generally Asian and North African immigrants, having to be taught to read and write. A network of twelve trade schools encompassing various standard trades, and training about 1,000 skilled craftsmen annually, is administered by the Histadrut, although the state provides some of the financing. Vocational on-the-job training is carried out in the place of work by the national unions, and perhaps 6,000 to 7,000 workers are trained annually through formal on-the-job programs. Close contact is also maintained with the after-work training programs in the schools carried out under the sponsorship of the Working Youth organization (*Naar Oved*).

The two major focal qualifications for entry of immigrant workers—64 per cent of whom in the past decade have had no occupation, and 70 per cent no specific skills—have traditionally been building and agricultural work. Here recent immigrants not only receive substantial amounts of direct training from the national unions in these fields but become acclimated to work and industrial discipline.[7] The Histadrut, through Solel Boneh and the Kibbutz and Moshav movements, is also a major employer of these two types of workers.

It would thus be impossible quantitatively to estimate the influence of the Histadrut upon the evolution of a modern labor force, but it was dominant before the foundation of the state, and even after independence is still of major significant. However, given the changes in education, the transfer of the Employment Exchange to the state, the assumption by the state of more and more training functions and all of the responsibility for organizing immigration, as well as the growing importance of the private sector, the predominant role of the Histadrut will undoubtedly pass on to the state. The very magnitude of the

[7] The Building Workers and the Agricultural Workers are among the two largest unions in the country.

immigration in the postindependence period, with the great majority of immigrants suddenly uprooted from their own countries and generally lacking in training, ideological commitment, a sense of work discipline, and even a previous modern work history, would have made the assumption of this entire task by any one organization well-nigh impossible.

The cumulative impact of the Histadrut upon the labor force thus has been and continues to be extremely impressive. In 1949, for example, 43 per cent of all manual workers, 50 per cent of agricultural laborers, and 79 per cent of all Kibbutz and Moshav members had been recruited abroad and received training before emigration from *Hechalutz*. Another large proportion had either been recruited and obtained work cretificates, or had been placed or trained, through Histadrut sponsorship.

However, the Israeli economy is still characterized, and, according to many Zionist ideologists, plagued, by a much larger than normal percentage of workers in the tertiary sector, especially for a country at its level of economic development. Approximately 50 per cent of the total labor force is engaged in tertiary activity, with large numbers in petty trade, personal services, administration, and professional areas such as law and medicine. These proportions are among the highest in the world and approach those in U.S. tertiary sectors. Israeli economists hope that through continued rapid industrialization and the intensification of rationalization already begun in trade and distributive services, the Israeli labor force will be "normalized."

THE HISTADRUT: ITS HISTORY

Eighty-seven men and women representing 4,433 Jewish workers throughout Palestine gathered in December, 1920, at the Technion in Haifa. They came determined to effectuate the unity of the Jewish workers in Palestine into one movement. Despite the similarity of their basic goals and even ideals, political differences had previously made this unity seem unattainable. Out of this conference the *Histadrut Haklalit Shel Poale Erezt Israel* (General Confederation of Jewish Workers of Israel) was formed. The organization was the direct result of at least a half century of attempted worker colonization in Palestine; the efforts of the Jewish Socialist movements in Eastern Europe, which evolved from the belated impact of the Age of Enlightenment upon Eastern European Jewry; political Zionism, which became an active force and united Eastern Europeans and world Jewry; and the Balfour Declaration, which for the moment was interpreted as making what had previously been a dream a reality. This fifty year prehistory molded the Histadrut, its specific institutional forms, and its philosophy.

Jewish life and thinking became revolutionalized when the influence of the Age of Enlightenment was belatedly felt in Eastern Europe. The *Haskalah*, a movement aimed at secularization of the Jew and the Europeanization of Jewish life and thinking, was the end product of this new idealism. The movement was influenced by the ideals of the French Revolution and translated into the Russian milieu of the ghetto, with its prevailing discrimination and anti-Semitism, the restriction of the Jew to a few nonagricultural areas known as the "pale of settlement," and was later modified by a newer Western European ideology, Marxism.

For a while it seemed as though Jews, given the influence of the Age of Enlightenment and the reforms of Alexander II, would be integrated into Russian society, and that social barriers would be overturned. The first Jews affected by these changes, beginning in the 1850's, went to Russian universities, became professional and administrative leaders, and were thoroughly Russianized. Societies such as ORT (Society for Agriculture and Artisanship) and OPE (Society for Spreading Education) appeared in the 1870's and helped create a great desire for education, training, and assimilation into every walk of Russian life. The 1880's saw the dashing of these hopes; repression became even more intense, the new industrialization largely excluded the Jew who was an artisan and merchant, and even the Russian revolutionary movements such as the Populists or Narodniks, led by otherwise liberal idealists, displayed anti-Semitic overtones.

Second-generation *Maskilim* (intellectuals of the *Haskalah*), influenced by Marxism and utopian socialist ideology, were preponderately socialist. However, their socialism was basically humanistic and idealistic, if not romantic, and contained a substantial admixture of Old Testament, prophetic sociology, and ethics. The latter influence was all the more remarkable because these young intellectuals saw religion not only as a barrier to the secularization and reawakening of the Jew, but as a higher conservative force which led to a type of Confucian resignation and pacificism which they considered as "the opiate of the Jewish masses." These groups ultimately formed the Jewish labor movement (which proclaimed the right of the Jewish people to freedom and equality not only as individual citizens but as a national group), and paved the way for a new Hebraic and Jewish literature, the secularization of the Jew, and a radical reëvaluation of Jewish ethical and religious values.

Out of the anti-Semitism and the displacement resulting from early industrialization, there developed in the 1880's the first active, if rather embryonic, Zionism, which spurred the first *Aliyah* (of 1882–1903). This wave of immigration had as its intellectual inspiration such early social philosophers as Moses Hess and Leo Pinsker, the author of *Auto-Emancipation*. Pinsker's position was that the Jews were a ghost nation in that they were not rooted in a national homeland. Civil and political equality, the goal of the *Haskalah*, would not raise them in the eyes of other people, and the only possible solution was creation of a Jewish nationality based in Palestine and populated by individuals rooted in their own soil.

Movements such as the *Hovevei-Zion* (Lovers of Zion) began to spring up, and in 1882 a group of 500 young intellectuals called the BILU (House of Jacob Rise and Go Forth) left from Odessa for Israel. Although without funds, they received some help from their sympathizers, and were trained at *Mikve Israel*, the first Jewish agricultural school in Palestine, and finally after great hardship in attempting to compete with Arab labor were settled on a tract of land in Gadera bought by sympathizers. Others joined early settlements at Rishon Le-Zion, where wheat was sown in soil suited for vineyards. The pogroms of 1894 stimulated further immigration and interest, especially by Barons Rothschild and Hirsch, who began to subsidize the settlements by extending credit to buy land, purchasing grapes at artificially high prices, and forming a company to organize wine cellars at Rishon Le-Zion (First in Zion) and Zichron Yaacov (Memory of Jacob). Rothschild organized the ICA (Jewish Colonization Association) in 1898, which began to encourage settlement by granting subsidies and reselling land on credit. Citriculture was established in Judean hills and in the Sharon, while cereals were cultivated in Galilee. All in all, fifteen Jewish villages were established.

Despite the idealism and equalitarianism of the BILU and its belief that labor coöperatives were the only means of transforming an urban group into rural dwellers as a potential base for a new society, the first *Aliyah*, in which immigration averaged about 1,000 annually from 1882–1903, did not provide the economic base for either mass settlement or immigration. The settlers soon forgot their ideals and, encouraged by the Rothschilds, opposed hiring other Jews as laborers in agriculture. This policy, if followed consistently, would have inhibited the amount of immigration, the absorptive capacity of the country, and the development of an agricultural worker movement. Even Gadera, the site of the early idealistic colonization by the original BILU, where the settlers had originally visualized themselves as the vanguard for bringing in other Jewish workers and the start of a rural coöperative agriculture, was transformed into a colony of private, ofttimes wealthy, farmers.[8] The first union of Jewish agricultural workers, whose program anticipated that of the Galilean and Judean agricultural organizations by twenty-five years, and which in 1900 formed the Society of Land Workers and Provident Funds for Jewish Workers, was broken by an organized expulsion from all Rothschild colonies, whose managers argued that "Jews are not cut out to be farm workers."

When the first young socialist-inspired Zionists began to arrive in Palestine in the early 1900's, they found a Jewish community of about 50,000 which lived mainly in the cities and engaged in petty trade, minor business, and artisan activities. The land had suffered from centuries of neglect and had to be reclaimed before even the most meager standard of living could be expected. The early failures and the loss of idealism, even on the part of the BILU settlers, convinced Zionists in general, and especially the Labor-Zionists, that Palestine would be an expensive undertaking, requiring a Zionist or national land purchase-and-redemption organization as a prelude to systematic colonization. It was felt necessary to insist that those who obtained this land either hire Jewish labor or organize agricultural labor coöperatives. Privately-owned land, it was contended, would lead to speculation and the exploitation of cheap Arab labor, and would negate "normalization" of the working Jewish population. As a result, the Jewish National Fund was set up by the World Zionist Congress of 1901 as the custodian and supervisor of all Jewish land, in order to establish a national land reserve and to provide the agricultural and absorptive base for the new Jewish homeland. Thus what was to become the Labor-Zionists' and subsequently the Histadrut's first overriding goal, *Kibbush Avodah* (Capture of Work), resulted from the desire to increase the tempo of immigration and became one of the major reasons for national (Jewish National Fund) ownership of land.

The two most important movements of the Eastern European Jewish masses, Zionism and socialism, were formally born in the same year, 1897. The first Zionist Congress gave birth to Zionism as a political

---

[8] The charter of the BILU bears a utopian-socialist stamp. If my translation of the document, dated 1882 and in Hebrew, can be accepted, it reads as follows:

> "To return sons of Israel to the lands of their fathers. To establish an agriculture and industry on the basis of man's own toil, of those who will with their own work, blood, and sweat find their and their family's living. A society is to be founded in which all belong, and their settlements are to be the possession of all of them. One treasure for the sake of all, and even individual belongings will be the possession of the Society as a whole."

As a result of the charter, Baron Rothschild sent a message to "expel all those nihilists" from his holdings.

movement, while an Assembly in Vilna founded the first Jewish socialist movement, the "Bund." These movements were in violent opposition, but each profoundly shaped the other. The Bund was forced to become more nationalistic, while Zionism increasingly became more socialistic. Since Jews were discriminated against in Russia, Zionist competition forced the Bund to consider the "Jewish Question," for even the Russian revolutionary movement had previously not been overly sympathetic to their presence. While the youthful Bundists believed that under true socialism there would be no anti-Semitism, the influence of national aspirations was strong enough to force them to demand "autonomy" for the Jew, not only in the Russian Social Democratic Labor party but ultimately in the multi-nationalist Russian socialist state.

Almost simultaneously, three anti-Bund Labor-Zionist parties emerged in Russia: the Zionist-Socialist party (Z-S), the Poale Zion (Workers of Zion), and the Sejmists or Jewish Socialist Workers party. The three parties exhibited different degrees of Marxian influence, as well as differing on the issue of Palestine versus Uganda as a base for Jewish colonization. The British had offered Uganda to Theodore Herzl, the founder of Zionism, as the site where a Jewish national homeland could be established. Early Jewish willingness to emigrate to Israel, and the ability to link national and historical aspirations, made the decision in favor of Palestine an academic one. The Bund and the Labor-Zionist movements were intense rivals for the loyalty of the younger non-religious or secularized Jewish population.

While these ideological conflicts were taking place in Russia, the pogroms and the economic displacement of the Russian Jew were intensified. Young Jewish Labor-Zionists began arriving in Palestine, hoping to start the process of nation-building by becoming agricultural laborers and workers. Two political groups soon emerged, and not only is the history of the next fifteen years dominated by these groups, but a unified labor movement did not come about until these two entities were able to achieve a *modus vivendi.* The first group was the Poale Zion, with its Marxist wing led by Borochov and the right wing led by David Ben-Gurion and Itzhak Ben-Zwi, currently the two dominant figures of Israeli political life. The other important group, the Hapoel Hatzair (Young Worker), anti-Marxian and hostile to the international socialist labor movement, was a highly utopian party which stressed coöperation.

The differences between the two parties in their practical programs were minimal, but so important was abstract ideology to these young idealists that the two groups were intense rivals for a quarter of a century. In actuality, the Marxist wing of the Poale-Zion, while vociferous—especially in Russia, where the Bund was an omnipresent rival—was never dominant in Israel, where practical realities, the absence of either a developed capitalist or laboring class, the individuality of the Jewish worker, and the need for all forms of coöperation made the Marxian model and dogma highly unrealistic. Thus the dominant Poale Zion figures in Israel, although using Marxist terms from time to time, were of the right wing and were equally influenced by Owen, Fourier, the Revisionists, LaSalle, and the Biblical prophets.

Obtaining employment for these vanguards, especially in agriculture, still remained the basic problem and was never settled satisfactorily prior to 1920, thus retarding the whole Zionist movement and the evolution of a working class. The boycott against Jewish workers continued, employment was difficult to come by, and were it not for the communal mode of living of the young workers, their sharing of proceeds from whatever work was available, and support, meagre as it was, from Poale-Zion movements in Eastern Europe and the United States, they would have starved.[9] Nonetheless, although these difficulties retarded development, they created the pressures which led to the establishment of the Kibbutz and the Moshav as the only means of mass employment and mutual defense, the nationalization of the land, mutual aid, and employment services to assure that work was given to Jewish labor.

The original discrimination had an economic basis, for the young Jewish workers were inexperienced and lacked skill, and could not survive on the pittance paid the Arab fellah. Even after this productivity differential disappeared, employment still remained a problem. One source of employment was the organization of a coöperative paramilitary force of watchmen for Jewish settlements, the *Hashomer* (watchmen) who replaced Bedouins who were sometimes inclined to loot.

The factors which contributed to the formation of the Histadrut can be summed up as follows: the Kibbutz movement which began with Degania in 1911; the agricultural worker unions; the attempts to form unions of urban workers; the establishment of the sick funds and the wholesale coöperatives (Hamashbir); World War I and the Jewish Legion which culminated in the formation of Achdut Haavadah; and finally, the Technion Conference in 1920.

While the ideas of social justice and coöperation were linked with

[9] The majority of Russian Jews who emigrated to the United States were members of the Bund prior to their departure. These Bundists, although there were a few Poale-Zion sympathizers such as Joseph Schlossberg and Max Pine, were instrumental in founding the ILGWU, the Amalgamated, and other clothing workers' unions. At first this hostility hindered any substantial support from the United States, but after 1918 these differences were increasingly forgotten.

the idea of a reconstructed Jewish state, the conditions of pioneering and of implementing agricultural settlement in Palestine made coöperatives necessary. The Chalutzim were ill-equipped individually for pioneering, the soil was barren and stubborn, the natives were hostile, and there was little capital for individual pioneering.

The Jewish National Fund Settlement Department, under Dr. A. Ruppin, secured in 1908 three small tracts of land of approximately 2,500 acres. Ruppin's plans included an apprenticeship period in which the young workers would train under agricultural experts, followed by group settlement in fully settled villages. Trainees could also, with credit, be subsequently settled in another tract of Jewish National Fund land. The "Kinnereth" farm was to be run by a manager during this period, with trainee-workers receiving a minimal wage and a share of the profits. A young group of workers called the *Romni,* who had already established themselves as a commune in Hadera, started to work the farm, but, disliking the manager, they refused to renew the work contract on the land and asked to be allowed to farm an adjacent bit of JNF land for themselves. Dr. Ruppin granted their request, and the first collective settlement, Degania, was founded. Its success was followed by the establishment of another modified collective at Merhavia, under the guidance of Dr. Franz Oppenheimer, a noted German economist and socialist theoretician. This farm featured coöperative work and living, with a wage based on productivity on a plot of land given to members of a family. Hashomer collectives were established at Rishon Le-Zion (*Avada*), Hadera, Segera (Legion of Labor), and Yizreel (*Tel Adash*); and at Gan Shmuel in 1917. In addition, an agricultural contracting coöperative, *Ahava,* was founded in 1913, this organization being the forerunner of the Histadrut agricultural contracting agency *Yahkim-Hachal.* These groups were numerically small, and were originated by the respective parties, yet internally they operated in the same fashion. The Poale-Zion organization of 1910 founded *Kapai,* a fund for settlement, and although the amounts obtained now appear microscopically small, since they were secured by pooling donations from relatively poverty-stricken Poale-Zion members in Russia and later in the United States and Great Britain, they were basic to the survival and success of the Kibbutz movement. The small groups, called Kvutzoth, as contrasted with the larger units which emerged later and which are called Kibbutzim, provided the base for the agricultural workers' union and ultimately the Histadrut.

From 1887 on, small groups of agricultural workers had attempted to organize. These organizations had advocated mutual aid, employment exchanges, and the use of Jewish labor. Because of the boycott against

Jewish farm labor and the strength of the Rothschild organization, they had no basic impact. *Hahoresh* (the Plow) was organized in Galilee, under Hapoel Hatzair auspices, but no permanent organization evolved until 1911, when separate unions of agricultural workers were organized in Galilee and Judah, the former consisting primarily of Hapoel Hatzair members, and the latter Poale-Zion. There are no subsequent records of any Galilean conferences, but permanent mutual aid funds resulted from both organizations. In various years, resolutions requesting sick funds, general funds for productive purposes, employment exchanges, diversity of agriculture, nationalization of all Jewish land, and equality of all workers were passed. Although the workers were ostensibly engaged in agriculture, the difficulty of securing work, the slow pace of development and land acquisition which inhibited the evolution of the Kvutzoth, and the seasonal nature of the work, all caused frequent abandonment of agriculture and movement to the cities either permanently or to participate in building and urban development work. Ben-Gurion and Ben-Zwi both write of their work as building laborers in Tel Aviv, which began as an all-Jewish suburb of Jaffa, and the latter also functioned as a member of a stonecutters' commune in Jerusalem. In fact, probably only one-fifth (about 2,000) of the pre-World War I labor immigrants remained in Palestine, the rest being driven out by working and employment conditions.

Meanwhile city life expanded somewhat, and there were substantial numbers of urban settlers, artisans, businessmen, and professionals. Over 5,000 Jews were located in Jaffa and Haifa, while a large but predominantly religious population lived in Jerusalem. Strikes took place at the Stein plant in Jaffa in 1905. Continued strikes of the printers, who were first organized in 1897, against the publishers of religious books in Jerusalem characterized this relationship. Strikes were broken in 1902 and 1909, but the organization was able to survive. Another strike which failed was that of the workers in the wineries in Rishon Le-Zion. Most of the workers were boycotted and left the country.

One year after the establishment of agricultural workers' organizations, first in Judea and then in Galilee, both organizations adopted suggestions for a mutual medical fund. Membership was restricted to workers, who were obligated to pay small monthly fees and to perform ward services once a month. The sick were entitled to full medical care but no convalescence payment. Such funds were instrumental in maintaining that small laboring population which remained in Palestine during World War I, when physical starvation and disease were predominant features of daily life.

The agricultural workers fought starvation in an organized fashion.

A home was founded for all suffering members, families were given shelter, bread, and even legal defense. In 1916 the Hamashbir (Co-operative Wholesale Supply Organization) was established to supply bread, food, and other needed staples to workers and their families and to collective farms. *Hamashbir* means suppliers. Farms and farm communities abandoned by their owners were reactivated by worker squads. Farm collectives were established and supplied by Hamashbir during this critical war period.

The second *Aliyah* was coming to an end by 1914. An increasing number of nonlabor immigrants settled near the seashore and in towns which grew rapidly in size. Tel Aviv, an all-Jewish suburb of Jaffa, was founded. Jaffa's Jewish population increased to 12,000, Haifa's to 3,000, and Petach-Tikvah to 3,000, in addition to settlements in religious centers such as Safed and Jerusalem, which had the largest continuous Jewish population.

The war stopped economic activity and development. The Jewish population diminished from 85,000 to 55,000, the great majority expelled from the country as enemies since they were still regarded as legal citizens of a hostile state, Russia. The country became a battle-field, with Judea in British hands and Galilee and Shomron in Turkish hands. Atrocities against Jews by the Turks increased, despite the formation of an auxiliary Jewish regiment to support the Turkish Army.

Even before the Balfour Declaration of 1917, ostensibly granting the country to Jews as a national homeland, voluntary movements for forming a Jewish Army to support the British and to liberate the country began to arise. The Poale-Zion were active in forming a Jewish Legion, but Hapoel Hatzair, with some exceptions, refused to participate. One regiment formed in 1915 fought in the Dardanelles, but real enthusiasm was displayed only after the Declaration of 1917. Three regiments, one American, one Palestinian, and the third British, were established. Poale-Zion leaders and members joined the Legion in large numbers, and as a result of their discussion and interaction the necessity of uniting Jewish labor into a single labor movement, and hopefully a single party, was given top priority.

Three major groups were involved: the Poale-Zion, Hashomer-Hatzair, and the Independents, who were mainly either newcomers or non-Palestinian Legion members. The latter group demanded unity and insisted that no basic difference existed between the parties. In January, 1919, an organizational meeting of the Conference of Agricultural Workers was held, in which the majority (Poale-Zion and Independents) endorsed a resolution to establish a unified party. Hapoel

Hatzair under A. D. Gordon rejected the idea.[10] The majority groups met in March, 1919, at a so-called "General Labor Conference" and merged with some dissidents from Hapoel Hatzair into the Achdat Avodah (Unity of Labor) party, which they designated as a nonparty workers' organization.

The issues which divided the two groups were abstract and theoretical, involving symbols rather than realities. One group regarded itself as dedicated to labor as an individual method of self-realization rather than as a class symbol, more deeply rooted in the soil, and closer to the traditional Hebraic ethical spirit. The other, theoretically Marxian-oriented in the class struggle and a part of the international labor movement, differed at best only slightly in its daily activities and in its operational framework of collective farms, sick funds, and mutual aid activities. The Poale-Zion was actually under the influence of its conservative "Palestinian" wing, led by Ben-Gurion, but although the interparty differences had ceased to exist, the ideological conflicts and the slogans lingered on. However, the December, 1920, conference, although not unifying the two rivals, did generate a spirit of compromise which enabled them to form a unified labor movement and merge their separate coöperative wholesale, sick funds, and contracting institutions.

Of the 4,333 workers who voted for the 87 delegates at elections held one week before the conference, 1,863 were members of Haachaut Avodah, 1,324 belonged to Hapoel Hatzair, 842 were newcomers organized by Hechalutz, which was established during World War I, and 303 were a group of extreme left-wing Poale-Zion workers augmented by Communist Poale-Zion comrades from Russia. Of the newcomers, a large proportion were members of Zeire Zion (Youth of Zion) who looked to Hapoel Hatzair for spiritual guidance, but not having been involved in the previous ideological hostility they took an independent position for unity at any price. The unity that was achieved allowed the political parties to maintain their separate existences, but unequivocally determined that the Histadrut would be the only organization which

---

[10] A. D. Gordon, the intellectual leader of the Hapoel Hatzair, was middle-aged upon his arrival in Israel, but nevertheless spent twenty years in back-breaking pioneering work. He saw in the evolution of a Jewish coöperative society the national outcome of a return to the soil and a reidentification with nature. An idealistic utopian primitivist, he believed that man can only gain happiness through a return to the soil and nature. The Jews needed individual self-fulfillment and discovery which would come only from labor, and society cannot be changed by a mere materialist change such as socialism without first changing human nature. He thus rejected the class struggle; if anything his views were anarchistic. He raised or elevated labor to an ideal or theology, and argued that only through a creative union with the soil of Palestine would historical rights be revived.

could conduct all the affairs falling within the spheres of activity deemed trade union and coöperative (*viz.*, Kupat Holim, Hamashbir, and Kapai); until then these activities had been separately conducted under the auspices of the political parties, causing duplication and conflict.

In the period between the first and the second conference, questions concerning the inclusion or exclusion of various areas of activity and authority within the framework of the organization were answered through deliberation, negotiation among the members of the Executive Secretariat, and decisions made in the process of the work itself. The second general conference adopted the basic constitution of the Histadrut, which was given more final form at the third general conference. The first members of the Executive Secretariat, each with equal authority, were Y. Ben-Zwi, David Ben-Gurion, A. Kaplan, and J. Sprinzak.

The purpose of the Histadrut was defined as follows: "To unite all workers who live on their own work, not exploiting the toil of others for the object of building up a workers' community in the country." Membership is open to all male and female workers who subsist on their own earnings without exploiting the labor of others and who agree to abide by the rules and decisions of the organization. Thus professional, clerical, and self-employed workers were members of the organization from the outset, and the Clerks' Association, which had a history of incipient but not continuous organization, joined with the Agricultural Workers as a separate autonomous trade union.

The Histadrut was authorized to form trade unions on the basis of trade and occupation. No worker can be a member of a trade union without belonging first to the Histadrut. Thus the Histadrut is not a federation of trade union bodies differing in wealth and power. It is an organization of workers, each holding direct membership in the general federation. The Histadrut is not a political party and is open to every Jewish worker regardless of political affiliation or religious belief. The conventions and councils of the organization are composed of groupings organized according to party lines, with relative numerical strength determined by proportional representation.

The functions of the Histadrut were defined as follows:

1. To found and develop collective and other farm holdings and also workers' groups for industrial activity.

2. To organize contracting works and establish labor exchanges for the placement of Histadrut members.

3. To organize trade unions on an impartial basis, without regard for party and religious affiliation.

4. To assist in raising labor productivity in any branch of agriculture or industry.

5. To furnish professional and technical training for the workers' community.

6. To supply commodities on a coöperative basis. This, of course, gave sanction to Histadrut operation of Hamashbir.

7. To maintain mutual aid institutions open to all members on an equal basis. Kupat Holim was thus brought into the Histadrut sector, with membership in the organization conferring automatic rights of participation in the sick fund.

8. To provide care and assistance for new immigrants and to aid in organizing immigration abroad.

9. To establish cultural and professional institutes and to encourage education. Courses were to be given in Hebrew instead of Yiddish.

10. To make contact and establish relations with other organizations, parties, and institutions inside and outside the country would involve close connection with Jewish labor organizations in other countries and with the international Socialist movement.[11]

The four strands of activity which are still characteristic of the Histadrut, and which the founders deemed necessary if the organization were to perform its "historic mission" as a developer of a society along desired lines, provide the basic framework for the constitution. These form distinct but interrelated functions: education, economic development and coöperation, trade unionism, and mutual aid. They were from the outset the organization's response to the necessity not only of evolving a modern labor force, but also employment opportunities under the desired social conditions for the working population that it hoped would soon follow. The original conception of the Histadrut was relevant to a period in which political independence was lacking, and enabled the working community to enjoy some major measure of self-government in every sphere but the political.

THE COUNCILS AND CONVENTIONS OF THE HISTADRUT

The forty-year history of the organization is perhaps summarized by the actions taken at its nine national conventions and its national councils, generally held twice yearly. These general meetings have made the basic decisions, ratified the actions taken, approved the formation of specific institutions, and hammered out the policy which

[11] Much of the constitution needs revision, and in addition a great many changes which have taken place in councils and conventions have been imperfectly incorporated into the constitution. The current changes in the economy and the stresses within the organization all cause the need for constitutional revision. A committee has been reviewing the constitution, but so far a complete revision has not taken place.

the General Secretary and the Central Executive Committees have administered.

The first convention authorized immediate steps for the establishment of a Workers' Bank, to be headed by a commission of three. The first general council, which met almost immediately after the organizational convention, established offices for encouraging immigration and finding employment and centers for private and public contracting work. Trade union organization was to be based upon work councils to be established in every plant, institution, or working place. The second national council authorized the issuance of 10,000 shares at one dollar each for the establishment of the Workers' Bank, the shares to be purchased by members of the Histadrut. The Council decided to establish producers' coöperatives, an organizational form which was originally the one preferred by most of the Histadrut leadership.

The third council gave its endorsement and support to the Moshav (Smallholder Agricultural Settlements) movement. This form, which was ideologically more compatible to many settlers who were unwilling to join a collective farm (Kibbutz), not only broadened the base for agricultural settlement and colonization but enabled the Histadrut to increase its recruitment efforts abroad. Subsequent councils protested against the mandatory government's restrictions upon immigration, and set up an equalitarian system of pay, based on the size of family, for all Histadrut employees regardless of rank. This equalitarian pay system continued for approximately thirty years, was the source of much controversy, and is still advocated by the more equalitarian-minded left wing of the Histadrut. A common organization of Jewish and Arab workers, on the basis of national sections within the trade unions, was also advocated.

The second convention, held in 1923, gave the Executive Committee of the Histadrut the right to adjust and settle disputes between trade unions and local labor councils and between the central office for contracting and its branches. Agricultural colonization and the organization of new coöperatives and collectives were to be administered by the Agricultural Workers' Association. Of great importance was the formation of urban and rural local labor councils, which were put in charge of all Histadrut local functions. The Histadrut, despite the opposition of the Hapoel Hatzair, decided to join the Socialist Amsterdam Trade Union International, and recommended that each individual national trade union join its appropriate International Secretariat. However, the most important action taken was the establishment of *Hevrat Ovdim,* the Jewish Workers' Coöperative Society for Colonization, Industry, Contract Work, and Supply, whose membership was made coextensive with that of the Histadrut. *Hevrat Ovdim* was to be the owner of all coöperative organizations, funds, and credit and supply institutions, and was empowered to control, plan and coördinate all labor economy activity in compliance with the general goals of the Histadrut.

The ensuing councils passed resolutions establishing the Histadrut Labor Exchange and an unemployment fund. The latter fund was to be used mainly to create jobs which would expand employment rather than pay unemployment insurance. The council also decided to establish a strike fund, to be financed not only by 10 per cent of all membership fees but also out of profits from Histadrut institutions as well. Succeeding councils expelled the Communist faction and their representatives, but allowed individual members to appeal to the Histadrut High Court for reinstatement. The establishment of a daily paper to be edited by Berl Katznelson, which was intended to assume the role of spokesman for the organization, was authorized in 1925. This paper, *Davar*, has been published continuously since 1926 and currently has the second-largest circulation in the country. The same councils endorsed the first collective agreements between Histadrut and employer representatives, establishing basic wages in various trades, the eight-hour day, employer contributions to the medical fund (*Kupat Holim*), accident insurance, and recognition of the local labor council as the representative of workers. Only through such collective agreements could the assignment of all work to Jewish labor be assured, since these agreements were subsequently to require that all vacancies be filled through the Histadrut labor exchanges. As the more class-conscious Marxian-oriented groups had traditionally opposed collective bargaining and the collective agreement as symbolizing a recognition of the employer class, this policy represented some modifications of positions previously taken. The twelfth council also decided to establish a workers' insurance company. *Hassneh* subsequently became an important instrument financing Histadrut economic undertakings.

The third convention met against a background of increased restriction of immigration by the mandatory government, substantial unemployment, the imminent failure of the Histadrut contracting organization, and a substantial slowing down, if not reversal, of economic growth. The convention demanded more rapid agricultural colonization and greater settlement effort, ratified the principle of collective bargaining, put the local trade unions under the control of the local labor councils, and set up the Employment Exchanges.[12] The convention also decided to form a sports organization for Histadrut members,

[12] In 1934 the Histadrut exchanges were converted into General Labor Exchanges of all workers' organizations, also servicing members of the *Hapoel Hamizrachi* (Religious Workers) and the Revisionists. The Histadrut remained dominant in the new system.

established a Central Cultural Commission, and set up *Ohel* (tent), a dramatic group for presenting plays in Hebrew to be given especially in Kibbutzim and Moshavim.

After the 21st council, held in October, 1928, David Ben-Gurion was elected General Secretary, replacing the previous four-man Executive Secretariat. By this time the differences between the two major parties had almost been obliterated, and the organization felt that conditions were such that there would be little objection to a single executive. Ben-Gurion continued in this post until 1933, when he entered the Executive of the Jewish Agency and became its dominant leader.[13] It was during this period that a new left-wing doctrinaire Marxian party, *Hashomer Hatzair* (Young Watchman) oriented in its own network of Kibbutzim, the Kibbutz Artzi Federation, was formed.

The council ratified the establishment of *Nir*, a financing company for labor colonization under the control of the Agricultural Center, and requested that the possibility of establishing an agricultural contracting organization be investigated. Later on, such an organization, known as *Yahkim*, was founded. The 24th council decided to encourage intensified colonization in the Hadera region.

In 1931 it was decided to increase the number of Histadrut (Labor Trend) elementary schools and to require that Histadrut teachers enter the teachers' organization as a separate section. The Histadrut had unsuccessfully attempted since its formation to induce the Teachers' Association to join it. The teachers, including university professors, remained outside the Histadrut until 1949, but since joining as an autonomous national union they have been among the most militant groups within the Histradut.

The April, 1932, council (the 27th) decided to consolidate all fees into one dues payment. Nonworking member wives were to be entitled to all social benefits through the payment of a slight additional fee. A decision was made to establish an unemployment fund (*Hoser Avodah*) when member contributions from additional assessments reached the sum of $5,000. This fund was designed to find jobs and to make loans to a public works agency which was later established jointly by the Histadrut and the Jewish Agency.

The fourth convention of the Histadrut, held in 1933, two years after the combination of the two major political groups, was held under different circumstances than in 1927, at which time one-third of the Histadrut members had been unemployed. There had been an expansion of building, artisan, and small industrial undertakings since 1926, when 70 per cent of the members had been engaged in agri-

[13] *Achdut Haavada* and *Hapoel Hatzair*, the two political parties, combined in 1931 to form *Mapai.*

culture. Only 44 per cent were so classified by 1932. The German immigration, which was just beginning in 1933, was primarily urban, and the resultant growth of the urban economy and urban building spurred by German entrepreneurs was sufficient to induce revival of *Solel Boneh,* the contracting agency, and permanently to shift the economic base of the Histadrut from agriculture to industry.

Histadrut economic policy, although never abandoning its agricultural base, from this period on was to be increasingly geared to the development of an industrial sector, and Histadrut planners henceforth were to speak of Israel as a potential Switzerland.[14] The conventions authorized negotiations with the Industrialists' Federation for a national collective agreement. Organizational objectives were to be: (1) the participation of employers in a mixed labor exchange; (2) workers to be hired only through the medium of labor exchanges; (3) labor committees to be elected in every enterprise; (4) the establishment of a "permanent" category for workers employed longer than six months; (5) a fortnight's notice before discharge; and (6) boards of conciliation and arbitration to review discharges of permanent employees. All but the first of these demands were ultimately gained.

Immediately after the fourth convention, David Ben-Gurion resigned to take his post as head of the political department of the Jewish Agency, and was succeeded by David Remez.[15] Ben-Gurion's accession to power in the Agency meant that the policy of this organization, which was the representative of the World Jewish Congress, would be more closely linked with the Histadrut, not only in regard to Jewish National Fund land policy toward Moshavim and Kibbutzim but subsequently in regard to joint economic activity in such organizations as *Bizur* (Public Works), *Mekorot* (Water Development and Irrigation), and *Nahshon* (Shipping). Agency funds were basic to the establishment of these entities, and later on to the establishment of El-Al, the Israeli airline, and Zim, passenger and freight shipping. It should, however, be understood that by this time the Poale-Zion was the largest organization in the World Jewish Congress, just as the Histadrut was the strongest single organization in Palestine.

The great bulk of council activity and the majority of resolutions

---

[14] The Gordonians, who still comprised a substantial segment of the population, were basically agricultural utopians prepared to accept farm-village coöperative activity, with village activity predominantly organized by producer coöperatives. Thus these changes were dismaying to the more militant faithful who had elevated agriculture and labor into a theology.

[15] Ben-Gurion succeeded Chaim Arlosoroff, also a Labor-Zionist, in the Jewish Agency Executive. Arlosoroff, a hero of the labor movement and one of its political leaders, was killed, presumably by the Revisionists, a rival political group with fascistic tendencies.

between the fourth and fifth councils dealt with protests against British immigration and tax policies and the unfavorable attitude of the mandatory government toward the Histadrut. An attempt was also made to induce the British administration to give Jews more jobs in the mandatory government. The 35th council, by a small majority, endorsed the idea of partition and a binational state. The 36th council, held in early 1938, ratified the establishment of *Bizur* and *Nahshon* as joint undertakings with the Jewish Agency. The policy of interorganizational Labor Exchanges, with joint participation of Histadrut, Hapoel Hammizrahi, Revisionists, and the Agudath Israel, was also endorsed. It was during this period that the Haganah, a military force, began to be organized mainly in Kibbutzim and Moshavim by Major Wingate. The encouragement and sponsorship of illegal immigration, aided by Labor-Zionist organizations abroad, became a reality. The 40th council, which met in December, 1938, decided to attempt to induce the trebling of enlistment by Jewish workers in the British Army through provision of mutual aid to dependents of service personnel. It was simultaneously decided to strengthen the Haganah, but at the same time to coöperate with the British as though the "White Paper" which reduced immigration had never been issued. Nevertheless, the council decided to continue illegal immigration in order to save Jews from falling into Nazi hands, and it protested against any British attempt to restrict such movement of persons.

The 45th council recommended price controls in Palestine and decided to encourage linking wages to the cost of living. Such agreements subsequently were signed with the Manufacturing Association, and since early 1942 have continued to be an integral part of Israeli collective bargaining experience. TNUVA, the Histadrut agricultural marketing and processing agency founded in 1926, was especially lauded for its attempts to keep agricultural prices down.

The fifth convention, held in April, 1942, took place at a time when the British were retreating before Rommel in Libya and Egypt, and many Palestinians feared that the Nazis would soon overrun the whole area. The convention voted to use all overtime pay to establish aid funds for families of Jewish service personnel. Two members, Golda Meirson (now Meir) and Aron Rubinovitz, were added to the Secretariat, the former to take charge of trade union activities, and the other for other departmental work.

The 47th council decided to increase the number of volunteers to the Allied forces by 10,000, and a subsequent council, although not giving up the right to strike, acceded to the establishment of a government mediation board.

Economic development proceeded at a rapid pace during World War II. Industrial expansion was intensified by the cutting off of manufactured articles from Great Britain and the need to serve as a major supply and repair depot for the entire Middle East. Israeli merchants became producers, and the number of firms in the Histadrut sector owned by *Solel Boneh* expanded appreciably.

The sixth convention met in two sessions, the first in 1944 and the second in January, 1945. The first session reported on the genocide of the Jews in Europe and the need to rapidly intensify immigration in the postwar era. The convention attempted to reunite Hechalutz, which had been split by the establishment of Hashomer Hatzair in 1927, and for the first time advocated national unions organized on an industrial basis. The Left Poale-Zion split the coalition and later, together with the Hashomer Hatzair, was to found the Mapam party in 1948.

During 1946–1948 virtually all decisions concerned independence, and until the War of Independence was successfully terminated, in 1948, few relevant decisions regarding normal Histadrut activity were made. The 61st council hoped for the materialization of trade unions organized along national industrial lines, provided that these unions clearly remained organizationally subordinate to the Histadrut. Productivity and efficiency councils and committees were authorized in all plants and institutions, private, governmental, and Histadrut.

The eighth convention, which met one year after the establishment of the state of Israel, immediately began to discuss policy to meet the mass immigration which had already begun. The convention called for the adjustment of economic policy in every sphere in order to absorb immigrants as rapidly as possible. Immigrants were to be admitted to full membership in the Histadrut and were to be given all the medical and social services consonant with membership without charge. The Histadrut was given a mandate to accelerate its economic undertakings in city, town, and agricultural settlements. The convention called for an intensification of construction of housing of all types. The organization also decided to take the initiative in increasing productivity and, jointly with the government and the Manufacturers' Association, subsequently founded the Productivity Institute. Despite the dominance of the Mapai party in both the Histadrut and government, the convention encouraged an independent trade union wage policy and reaffirmed its freedom to strike and its opposition to compulsory arbitration. It did, however, despite the opposition of the left, endorse governmental mediation and conciliation. The convention, at that time unwilling to risk protracted controversy over what was obviously a divisive issue, decided to continue in the World Federation of Trade Unions, but agreed to send "observers" to the conference which was to establish the International Confederation of Free Trade Unions. Three years later, despite the opposition of the left, the Histadrut joined the ICFTU, and soon thereafter left the Communist organization, World Federation of Trade Unions.

The 66th council approved a basic departure from previous Histadrut equalitarian wage policy, by linking wage incentives to the productivity movement which it had initiated by its sponsorship with employers of joint productivity councils. Hereafter wage incentives were to be incorporated, whenever possible, into Histadrut collective bargaining agreements. For the first time trade unions were to be opened to Arab workers. Succeeding councils finally ratified the abandonment of the system of equal family pay for all Histadrut employees in favor of the current system of salary differentials according to professional grade and functional role.

The era between the seventh and eighth conventions witnessed almost a trebling of Histadrut membership and a considerable expansion of organizational efforts in every phase of economic, trade union, political, cultural, and mutual aid activity. The meeting took place after an election in which the two left-wing parties, Mapam and Achdut Avodah, challenged Mapai over virtually every phase of organizational policy. Mapai received about 58 per cent of the vote. However, before the election the party had to modify its previous wage policy to permit a general wage increase of about 10 per cent.

Despite the impressive gains in ownership of industry, number of members, and trade union activity, substantial concern was evidenced by both Histadrut members and leaders. These revolved about the extent to which the new membership (a large proportion of whom were Oriental Jews) was ideologically oriented and absorbed within the organization, and whether these groups were truly capable of sustaining the ideals of the organization and, ultimately, providing its leadership. Mordecai Namir,[16] who had become General Secretary following the resignation of Pinhas Lavon in 1950, and who himself resigned early in 1956 to become Minister of Labor, indicated in his summary report that workers in Histadrut plants neither felt nor were treated differently, and evidenced no more real responsibility than workers in private enterprise. To those who still believed in a "workers' commonwealth" which would give every worker a stake in the conduct of his own affairs, this admission indicated some leadership soul-searching. Histadrut or Mapai wage policy—which was heavily influenced by the

[16] Mr. J. Sprinzak was General Secretary from 1945–1949, when he resigned to become Speaker of the Parliament.

efforts to keep production costs down, had geared wages to the cost of living, and had permitted real increases only under valid incentive systems—came under attack. These attacks became more bitter when, as a consequence of professional worker strikes, substantial wage increases were granted these groups in 1955–1956. Worker groups supported by Mapam were restive and ultimately forced the Histadrut executive to request a smaller but still substantial general wage increase for all workers.

Other problems were concerned with the extent to which Histadrut industry was efficiently planned, and whether, as alleged by the opposition, major Histadrut enterprises had become huge empires with monopolistic privileges. There was a great deal of discussion about the high proportion of the labor force in the service and trade sectors, and the failure of the agricultural sector to increase proportionately.

The convention voted to intensify cultural and educational activity among the immigrants, to establish plants in new development areas, to form a professional workers' department, and to encourage the participation of workers on management boards. Subsequent decisions reactivated the employment fund. Following the convention, Pinhas Lavon returned as General Secretary, a position he held until his recent well-publicized conflict with Mr. Ben-Gurion.

Subsequent Histadrut decisions established the professional department, provided funds for religious activity in workers' settlements,[17] and agreed to the nationalization of the Employment Service, provided "Histadrut" principles were observed in the distribution of work. Mr. Lavon raised questions about the efficiency and the low rate of profitability of Histadrut enterprises (about 3 per cent on investment), and declared that all planning of Histadrut enterprises should be centralized in a small secretariat which would constitute its control organization. Histadrut enterprises would thereafter avoid those sectors of the economy where private enterprise was performing satisfactorily, and would concentrate upon developmental activity or areas which were too risky for the private sector. He also indicated that all of the central economic organizations such as *Solel Boneh*, TNUVA, and Hamashbir would be reorganized and decentralized. An industrial union department was to be established as a type of roof organization for the growing national unions in the industrial sector.

---

[17] This decision met with disapproval from many groups in Histadrut, who felt that this was an undesirable concession to expediency to compete with *Hapoel Hamizrachi* for membership. As earlier stated, virtually all of the original Labor-Zionists were deeply antireligious, and this concession involved an ideological and ethical sacrifice.

These problems were given increased urgency by Mr. Lavon in a speech before Mapai in May, 1958, which provided the rationale for reorganization of the movement's basic economic undertakings. Professor Abba P. Lerner, a distinguished economist and economic adviser to the Israeli treasury during this period, had insisted that the cost-of-living increases were extremely inflationary and that the cost-of-living index was faulty in many respects. An early January, 1959, meeting of the executive adopted a Mapai proposal in opposition to any general demand for a wage increase in the negotiations which were to cover the next two years.

TABLE 19

MEMBERS OF THE HISTADRUT AS A PROPORTION OF THE TOTAL EMPLOYED POPULATION, AND HISTADRUT AS A PERCENTAGE OF TOTAL POPULATION

Year	Number of Histadrut members	Total Jewish workers	Histadrut workers as a per cent of all workers	Histadrut population as a per cent of total population
1925	9,000	17,000	52.9	—
1930	20,200	27,300	74.0	—
1935	53,000	70,000	75.7	—
1940	89,000	120,000	74.2	35.7
1945	113,600	152,000	74.7	39.7
1948	138,750	190,000	73.0	42.6
1950	186,400	247,000	75.5	36.7
1955	365,220	425,000	85.9	51.7
1959	475,434	—	87.0	58.7

SOURCE: Statistical Summaries by the Institute of Social and Economic Research of Histadrut.

The ninth conference, held in 1960, approved the National Union of Industrial Workers and reaffirmed the linkage of wages to productivity and the need for responsibility in wage policy to avoid inflation. The proposed change in computation of the cost-of-living index was approved by a straight party vote. The convention endorsed the formation of the Afro-Asian Institute of Economics and Coöperation, a school designed to train union leaders in the newly emerging countries of Asia and Africa. This school is financed jointly by the AFL-CIO and the Histadrut. Opposition was expressed to any nationalization of the health service, except where the nationalization takes the form of a government supervisory and subsidizing body which will merely establish criteria for the existing autonomous and separate sick funds.[18]

[18] The Histadrut feels that *Kupat-Holim* is one of its prize assets in attracting and maintaining membership. Many of the new immigrants join Histadrut as a result of being given three months' free medical service by *Kupat-Holim*. The

This history and record was accompanied by a steady growth in membership, both numerically and in the proportion of the labor force organized by the Histadrut (table 19). From 4,333 members in 1920, membership increased slowly to 9,000 in 1925, when more complete statistical data became available. The data in Table 19 understates the official membership of the Histadrut by about 50 per cent since nonworking wives of members are entitled to membership in the Histadrut and have access to all of its benefits. Approximately two-thirds of the membership consists of working members, while the remainder consists of nonworking wives.

STRUCTURE OF THE HISTADRUT

Basic institutions such as the Kibbutz and Moshav movements and Hevrat Ovdim have their own histories and records of development. It would be impossible in an essay of this size to describe all the activities, institutions, or structural forms of an organization as complex as the Histadrut. However, by concentrating on its salient features, an understanding of its essential characteristics, basic problems, and prospects is possible. Attention thus will be focused upon (1) the structural and power interrelationships within the organization; (2) the role and present status of Histadrut agriculture; (3) the economic and coöperative sectors of the economy affiliated with Hevrat Ovdim; (4) the Histadrut as a trade union and collective bargaining organization, and its wage policy; (5) and the organization's party structure and its current relations with the Israeli government.

The structure of the Histandrut is nominally a highly centralized one. Membership is in the organization and not in any of the semiautonomous groups which are granted their authority by it and are accorded privileges only to an extent compatible with central organizational goals. However, the various constituent entities have periodically been able to exercise power with only a modicum of supervision from the center. As internal differentiation proceeds with the great expansion of the organization, new balances are constantly being struck between federal and central principles and between more particular and universal interests.

All men and women workers over eighteen years of age who live on the earnings of their own labor and who abide by the discipline of the

---

organization is violently opposed to nationalization of the Health Service, despite its sizable annual deficit (5 to 7 million Israeli pounds). The Histadrut feels that the deficit has been incurred as a result of giving free service to Army dependents, immigrants, and other governmental workers, and that it should get a much larger government stipend than it now receives.

Histadrut may be members. Included in the membership ranks are skilled and unskilled industrial workers, agricultural workers, and all members of Kibbutzim and Moshavim. Wives of members engaged in their homes as housewives are also full members of Histadrut.

Histadrut membership fees are paid in the form of a tax according to a progressive scale ranging from 3 to 4½ per cent of wages. Revenue from membership fees is divided according to an automatic system in which 57½ per cent is allocated for the various social, mutual aid, cultural, organizational, and administrative services of the Histadrut, while the remaining 42½ per cent goes with employer contributions to the *Kupat Holim* (health fund).

The aims and purposes of the Histadrut cover four major fields of activity: trade union, economic, mutual aid, and cultural. All of these activities are functionally incorporated into the structure of the Histadrut. The policy-making bodies of the Histadrut are the convention and the councils. The convention is the highest authority and meets on the average of once every four years. The convention elects the council, which meets twice yearly and is the highest Histadrut authority between conventions.

The Histadrut is not a political party, and in fact is composed of members from at least seven political groups, and it theoretically takes no political action. However, since many aspects of policy involve issues which are debated from the point of view of the competitive parties, politics play a basic role in the organization. Election to the various policy-making and governing bodies is based upon the proportion of votes obtained by each political party. Mapai, since its formation, has always received a majority of votes cast in the Histadrut elections, and thus a majority of the members of the executive bodies have always been Mapai members. Since strict party discipline prevails, voting always follows the party pattern.

Any group which receives the support of at least 100 members is entitled to submit a list of candidates for election to the 801-delegate convention. Prior to each convention every Histadrut worker votes for his favored list by secret ballot. Each of the seven parties is represented at the convention by a number of delegates precisely proportional to the number of votes it receives. The convention elects the 281-member council, which meets twice yearly, on exactly the same proportional basis.

The Executive Committee of the Histadrut, comprising 91 members, is elected by the council, again on the same proportional basis. The Executive Committee, a large proportion of whose members are full-time Histadrut officials, meets every two weeks and is responsible for executing policy determined by the convention and councils. It appoints from its own membership the Central Executive Bureau, which consists of thirteen members and is responsible for the daily conduct and management of the organization's affairs. Since all of the other executive organs are cumbersome and unwieldy, and either meet too infrequently or do not possess the requisite information, organizational management and control have become synonymous, especially since party discipline makes support of Central Executive officials, generally higher officials of the party, mandatory. Each member of the Central Executive is responsible for the daily administration of one or more of the departments and institutions of the organization. The following are the departments responsible to the Executive Committee; they again illustrate the great variety of Histadrut activity: trade union; education and culture; Arab; mutual aid; organizational; international; financial; employment; legal; municipal; travel; vocational training; *Hevrat Ovdim;* and professional workers.

The executive branches of the Histadrut at the local level are the local labor councils, which are responsible for the conduct of affairs impinging upon their own areas. They are linked to the Histadrut Executive through the organization department, which exerts supervisory power over them.[19] They are elected by the same proportional party system, and the secretary of the local labor council is a member of the party or party coalition receiving the greatest number of votes. All local councils give representation to the trade unions and other Histadrut bodies within the locality. A considerable proportion of the members of the local councils, always including the secretary, are full-time officials.[20]

Histadrut enterprise plays an important role in every sector of the economy and a central role in two basic branches, agriculture and heavy industry. Although estimates are hard to come by, there probably were at the end of 1959 about 2,500 coöperative societies attached to and under the supervision of *Hevrat Ovdim.* Altogether the Histadrut economy generates over 25 per cent of the national income and

[19] The local secretary is generally approved by the Histadrut Executive, acting through the organization department.

[20] The Histadrut also has judiciary organs. The Supreme Court of Honor is the highest judiciary body, which has its counterpart in local courts in each locality. Any individual may bring before these courts claims related to a breach of ethics by an individual or institution. The council also elects a central control commission with the authority to examine the activities of all institutions in light of their budgets and rules regulating their activities. Similar councils also exist at a local level. Audit unions of various categories examine the records of all Histadrut firms.

about 30 per cent of total employment.[21] Undoubtedly, had any strong or even moderately developed private employer groupings existed in Israel, the objectives and the operations of the labor movement would have been different. But in the absence of any important body of employers to provide employment for immigrants, the labor movement, the only established organization of any size, began to undertake developmental functions.

Understanding the history and structure of the economic undertakings is necessary to any current assessment of the role of the organization as an economic developer. Two basic but differently organized sectors of the Histadrut economy will be analyzed. These are the industrial and distributive sector, and Histadrut agriculture. A large segment of the industrial sector is structured around firms owned, managed, and administered by the Histadrut, while the agricultural sector is characterized by coöperative organizations. The latter assume two basic forms, the Kibbutz (Collective) and the Moshav (Small-Holders Settlement).

THE INDUSTRIAL AND DISTRIBUTIVE SECTOR OF THE HISTADRUT

Histadrut's device for organizing its economic activity is *Hevrat Ovdim*, which is the acknowledged central society of its industrial and coöperative enterprises. The control of any given coöperative society is exercised by any one of seven audit unions. Each coöperative is assigned to an audit union, in which all the founders' or voting shares are owned by *Hevrat Ovdim*. By the device of the audit unions, the needs of *Hevrat Ovdim*, representing the labor movement, and the requirements of the law are simultaneously met. However, the control which the Histadrut is able to exercise through this device over strong coöperatives, such as those in transportation, is extremely limited.

In respect to commercial companies directly owned by the Histadrut, *Hevrat Ovdim* acts as a holding company. Companies in this category, the most important of which are *Solel Boneh, Koor*, The Workers Bank, *Hamashbir*, and TNUVA, are completely controlled by *Hevrat Ovdim*, which holds all the founders' shares and a substantial proportion of the owners' shares. Notwithstanding this supposed direct control, the amount of integrated planning which the *Hevrat Ovdim* has been able to exercise is extremely limited, and at times the larger central firms have functioned almost autonomously. The companies which the *Hevrat Ovdim* owns do not distribute their profits to it, other than a small proportion necessary for the organization's upkeep, but instead

[21] *Statistical Abstract No.* 3, General Federation of Jewish Labor in Israel, December, 1959.

use them for reinvestment and expansion. Members of the Histadrut, who are the nominal owners of *Hevrat Ovdim*, cannot by its constitution get any part of its profits. It is this ability to reinvest a large part of its earnings and its freedom from the requirement of paying dividends which constitute the major economic advantage of Histadrut's entrepreneurship.

INDUSTRIAL SECTOR: SOLEL BONEH AND KOOR

Industry in Israel grew out of a variety of sources, but in the absence of housing for new immigrants—intensified by the increasing difficulty, especially after 1920, of living in predominantly Arab areas, and the absence of any substantial public works—one basic economic activity has always been construction and building. Out of this sector, which generally has provided about 10 to 12 per cent of total employment in the economy, there developed most of the basic Histadrut industry.

Even before the formation of the Histadrut, the Agricultural Workers' Union had signed a contract to build roads for the mandatory government, and soon afterward the Histadrut unified all labor building activities in an office of public works. As the field expanded, with substantial building of Jewish quarters in the new city of Tel Aviv, and in Haifa and Jerusalem, all the various coöperative societies, working under the office of public works, were merged into *Solel Boneh* (Paving and Building). This enterprise gravitated increasingly toward the direct employment of its own labor force rather than operating through coöperative workers' groups. Poorly financed, ill-advised in its extension of credit, affected by a severe decline in economic activity, and relatively inefficient because it was used to train immigrant workers and acclimate them to work discipline, *Solel Boneh* failed in 1927. Three separate Histadrut contracting offices, one for each of the three urban centers, continued the work and finally, with the increase in economic activity in the 1930's associated with German immigration, the *Solel Boneh* was reactivated. This time, profiting from previous mistakes, it recruited efficient technical staff and skilled workers, and introduced the latest construction techniques. Its operations included various public works, fortifications in anticipation of the war, the Port of Tel Aviv, and a number of new settlements. By World War II it was the largest contractor in the Middle East and was busily engaged in building airports, fortifications, and military roads, as well as continuing its original urban and rural construction activities.

In the course of its development, *Solel Boneh* went beyond public works and building and began to launch, or to acquire from private investors—who were frequently only too glad to get out without loss of capital—diverse industrial enterprises for the production of building material. These entities, which when broadened and diversified formed the basis for penetration into the heavy industrial sector, were combined into a subsidiary holding company, Koor Industries and Crafts Limited. At one time (1945–1946) *Solel Boneh* was responsible for 70 to 75 per cent of all construction activity in Palestine. Today that proportion, even though the organization has trebled in size, has declined to about 35 to 40 per cent. In 1959 about 6,000 persons were employed directly by Koor (and approximately 20,000 by *Solel Boneh*).

This steady growth and expansion was not only the result of building and public works activity performed by *Solel Boneh* during the early years of statehood, but also of an aggressive expansion policy, made possible partly by German indemnities which supplied capital goods to Israel, and made available through partial governmental development loans. This expansionist policy of Hillel-Dan, former head of Sol-Koor, and one of the entrepreneurial giants of Histadrut, led to the formation of such controversial enterprises as the Steel Mills and Middle East Tube company at Acre. Histadrut detractors attributed some of the expansion to the use of the organization's considerable political power to coerce private capital into a controversial 51-49 per cent agreement, such as that with Alliance Tyre.[22] These impressions were factors in the decision ordered by Mapai which led to the splitting of *Solel Boneh* into three separate units. These three separate units are: (1) Koor, (2) the *Solel Boneh* Building company, which was merged with *Shikun*, the Histadrut Housing Coöperative company, and (3) a new branch for foreign contracts and construction of port facilities. Within recent years, *Solel Boneh* has again been engaged in building airports and roads in Middle Eastern countries for the United States Air Force. It has also secured substantial contracts to provide technical aid and supervise building in countries such as Liberia, Ghana, Nigeria, Burma, and Nepal, to name a few.[23] The diversity of the industrial sector of the Histadrut, now under Koor, is illustrated by the data in table 20.

[22] It is almost impossible to sort out the rumors about coercive pressure by Histadrut upon private enterprise. In many cases the Histadrut was asked to take over private enterprises (called cold nationalization) that were failing, and I myself know several cases where the Histadrut refused to take over firms despite pressure from localities and Histadrut workers to save jobs. In some cases the Histadrut was approached by private groups to go in on a joint basis with them, in other cases there seemed to have been hints from Histadrut officials that things would go better for the particular undertaking if the "partnership" were consummated.

[23] Israel is an important source of technical assistance to the new and emerging societies in Africa and Asia who have been influenced by the Israeli pattern of development. Israeli Moshavim and Kibbutzim are used for training purposes, and *Solel Boneh* is one of the major sources of mobilizing technical aid.

TABLE 20

EMPLOYMENT BY FIRMS IN KOOR ENTERPRISES, 1959

Category	Employment
Metal works	
Vulcan Foundries	500
Vulcan Engineering	160
Merkavim (bus bodies)	270
Hamat (metal and machine tools)	600
Middle East Tubes	300
Steel Mills (starting employment)	500
Siltam	150
Shipyard and ship repair	
Hayama	250
Ogen	100
Electronics	
Tel Rad (telephone and telephone exchange)	100
Yizrom (light bulb and fluorescent lights)	90
Vulcan Batteries	33
Tadir (quartz crystals)	26
Rubber	
Alliance Tires	350
Hamgaper (rubber footwear)	210
Gamid (mechanical plant)	40
Glass	
Phoenician	575
Safety glass	25
Phoenikia (glass instruments)	55
Ceramics	
Harsa	300
Lapid	130
Cement	
Nesher	750
Haifa (old and new plants)	
Ramle	
Yuval Gad (pipes)	722
Paints	
Solgon	26
	6,362

SOURCE: Confidential.

THE COMMERCIAL SECTOR: HAMASHBIR HAMERKAZI

The most important organization in Israel in the field of trade and commerce is *Hamashbir Hamerkazi* (Israel Coöperative Wholesale Society, Ltd.). The society is the leading supplier of its own members and owners, the agricultural settlements and consumer retail societies, and of various other Histadrut firms such as the producers' and service coöperatives. Founded in 1916 to supply workers in agricultural settlements, and later establishing retail branches in various cities, it soon began to market agricultural produce for the Kibbutzim and Moshavim, which it in turn supplied. *Hamashbir* was reorganized in 1929 and at that time became a wholly owned subsidiary of *Hevrat Ovdim*. *Hamashbir* supplies Kibbutzim and Moshavim which buy centrally and in bulk, and consumer coöperatives located in workers' areas in the cities and suburbs, at a price of 7 to 8 per cent over cost. The variety of goods supplied by *Hamashbir* runs from agricultural implements to clothing and writing materials.

In order to cope with its supply problems, and confronted with what it regarded as high and monopolized prices for goods produced by private enterprise, *Hamashbir,* like many coöperative movements in Western European countries, began to manufacture its own supplies either by the development of its own factories or through the purchase of private firms. *Hamashbir* also has an import subsidiary to conduct its import operations. Holdings of *Hamashbir* include *Shemen* (edible oils), footwear factories, foundries (*Hamalchim*), paper factories, ice factories, textile firms, seed classification, sugar processing, and cleaning plants.

Affiliated with and served by *Hamashbir* are an estimated 425 coöperative retail societies with about 500 to 600 thousand registered customers, employing over 3,000 workers. Each society is a separate, independent entity, and although no dividends are given to customers and funds are reinvested, additional funds have generally had to be supplied by *Hamashbir.*

A considerable amount of criticism of the consumer coöperative movement has been engendered by the low relative efficiency of these stores, partially induced by their limited average size and their resultant high operating expenses. This has caused *Hamashbir,* which has also been criticized for overexpansion, managerial deficiencies, and exploiting its monopolistic rights in Kibbutzim and Moshavim, to revise its managerial structure and to enter into directly-owned supermarkets in order to compete with similar private stores. *Hamashbir* has also lost its monopolistic privilege with Kibbutzim and Moshavim. Consonant with the attempt in Israel to rationalize trade in order to reduce the size of the work force in the trade and service sector, *Hamashbir* has organized and now directly owns *Hamashbir-Latzarkon,* a chain of department stores in the large cities. These organizations, while profitable, have not yet been notably successful.

TNUVA was established for the coöperative marketing of agricultural produce in the urban market and the processing of milk. Its activities include some light industry deemed necessary for its marketing effectiveness. Organized in 1926 as a marketing agency for all produce of collective and coöperative settlements, TNUVA in 1956 employed 2,600 workers in various phases of its operations. TNUVA markets about 70 per cent of all the produce sold in Israel. The organization is currently processing milk and soft fruit drinks, and is engaged in canning vegetables for export purposes.

Dissatisfaction with TNUVA's administration, especially the prices paid,[24] led not only to organization pressure but also some violation of regulations by individual units, especially Moshavim, which began to market through the private sector. One rationalization was that private marketing firms which specialized in individual crops were more efficient and, therefore, paid higher prices. As a result TNUVA was decentralized in 1959 into five divisions, each one for a major product type (milk, eggs, food, vegetables, fruit, and fish) and the TNUVA monopoly was terminated.

PRODUCER COÖPERATIVES

The organizational form deemed most consonant with the ideology of the earlier founders of the Histadrut was the producer coöperative. Such coöperatives have been organized mainly in the handicraft, service, and transport areas, peak organization periods being 1925–26 and 1933–35, by groups of worker-entrepreneurs who secured aid either from the Workers' Bank or from the Coöperative Fund. The separate coöperatives are supervised by the *Merkaz-Ha Coöperativa* (Coöperative Center) which attempts to administer them in accordance with the coöperative spirit and to supply them with technical, managerial, and marketing services. Large numbers of coöperatives were organized after independence as a device for the absorption of new immigrants. Despite these aids and subsidies, failures are frequent, and the producer coöperative form, notwithstanding substantial effort to found new firms, is not a growing movement. In 1956, there were 278 coöperatives employing some 12,000 workers, over half of them in the transportation field.

In 1955–56, deemed fairly typical, twenty of 281 coöperatives failed. Reasons cited for failure were managerial deficiencies, conflicts among members, failure to depreciate machinery and equipment adequately, the poor working condition of equipment, and inadequate financing. In a few cases firms were refinanced, with the Histadrut becoming either the sole owner or assuming a 50 per cent share.

Successful coöperatives have been reluctant to admit new members

---

[24] TNUVA contended the prices paid were average, which caused them to pay established Kibbutzim less than premium prices in order to give new Kibbutzim, frequently with inferior produce, the established price.

unless substantial payments are made, so that a large proportion of the labor force of these organizations is hired and, by definition, presumably exploited. Most coöperatives, however, are less successful and are finding it increasingly difficult to remain competitive as the economy industrializes and becomes more complex.

Among the most controversial Israeli groups have been the bus coöperatives. From a large number of individual coöperatives, each one serving its own area, consolidation began, and aided by the inadequacies of other forms of transport and a relatively developed road system, these entities grew until they controlled virtually all inter- and intracity bus transportation.

Egged, which combines three societies (*Eshed, Don, Hameshaker*), now has over 6,000 employees, of whom approximately 50 per cent are hired workers. This high proportion of hired workers, which is highly embarrassing to the Histadrut leadership; the relatively large payment necessary to become a member coöperator; the necessity of obtaining huge loans for new equipment, attributed by many to poor depreciation policy, to the members' taking what Israelis regard as overly high salaries, and to strikes for higher fares against the authority of the Histadrut and the government in 1956—all have contributed to public disfavor and a desire for nationalization.[25] A compromise proposal by Pinhas Lavon, then General Secretary of the Histadrut, was to form a new public corporation in which the present workers would have 40 per cent of the stock, the government 40 per cent, and the Histadrut and municipal governments 10 per cent each. This compromise was rejected by the bus coöperatives, but public opinion and government policy will ultimately force some adjustment.

This by no means exhaustive list of the Histadrut economic sector is illustrative of the broad patterns of growth and development, and the present status of this segment of the economy. Its significance and the value of its activities in the development of the Israeli economy can only be inferred, but perhaps a few statistics will provide some basis for generalization. In 1955, 148,500 of 371,000 Histadrut members (approximately 40 per cent) were employed in their own sector. While employment in Histadrut undertakings rose to 177,000 by 1959, the proportion of its membership employed in its own sector declined to 37 per cent. The 285 per cent increase in employment within the Histadrut sector since 1949 approximates the national rise in population. In the same year, 1955, the Histadrut sector contributed approximately 30 per cent of total investment in the economy.

---

[25] "Rich as a member of Egged" is a frequent statement heard on the street.

Investments of 183 million Israeli pounds in 1956, translated into dollars at a rate of 2.5,[26] would indicate that the Histadrut sector has recently contributed at an annual rate of $75 million to total investments in the economy (table 21). These funds come from reinvested earnings and from Histadrut financial institutions. Approximately 60 per cent of this amount originated from the Workers' Bank, the second-largest in Israel, and its American affiliate for financing Histadrut

TABLE 21

INVESTMENT IN THE HISTADRUT SECTOR AND IN THE ECONOMY, 1955, IN ISRAELI POUNDS

	Histadrut	Total for country	Histadrut percentage
Settlement and farms	73	150	48.7
Industry and crafts	23	90	28.5
Housing and building	52	210	24.8
Transport and hauling	23	60	38.8
Trade and commerce	5	15	33.3
Services	7	75	9.3
	183	600	

SOURCE: Institute for Economic Research, Histadrut, unpublished data.

economic activity, *Ampal; Gmul,* the Workers' Provident Fund, administered by the Histadrut; and *Hassneh,* the largest insurance company in Israel. The Workers' Bank and *Hassneh* are also linked to *Hevrat Ovdim.* The remainder of the funds (about 40 per cent) come from governmental developmental loans. While comparable data are not available for the entire ten-year decade following statehood, it has been conservatively estimated that investment in the labor sector approximated 550 to 600 million dollars. From an economic standpoint, the most important function of the Histadrut in Israel's economic development has been in its ability to pool savings in small amounts from diverse labor sources, and mobilize these funds for economic development. The reinvestment policy of Histadrut industry, which has few individual stockholders, undoubtedly results in a greater proportion of self-financing than would be forthcoming from private firms of similar profitability. The Kibbutz, which will be discussed subsequently, constitutes an even more highly effective form for inducing voluntary sacrifice and a high level of saving.

Recent years have witnessed some challenge to the Histadrut by

[26] At the black market rate of 40¢ the Israeli pound.

the private sector and an increasing degree of soul-searching both within the Histadrut and in Mapai about the health of the labor economy and, especially, the extent to which it has been efficient. It was also felt that the emphasis upon expansion and growth after independence should be modified in favor of greater efficiency and structural consolidation.

Several reasons for dissatisfaction were expressed. Within the Histadrut it was felt that the large organizations had become power centers and empires accountable only to themselves, and that each of the large firms was proceeding on its own, deciding to build new plants and expand with little or no supervision from *Hevrat Ovdim.* It was also contended that the heads of the large groups negotiated directly with government for developmental loans, and that competition, duplication, and waste were rife within Histadrut enterprise. *Hevrat Ovdim,* it was insisted, had lost its planning, decision-making, and over-all review functions. It was felt that *Hevrat Ovdim* was too large and unwieldy a body and met too infrequently, and that a permanent executive secretariat with some power was needed. The individual holding companies were considered empires of their current leaders, who had literally founded these organizations and were instrumental in their growth, as they neither had decentralized managerial structure nor provided an acceptable framework for efficient day-by-day management.

In a speech before *Hevrat Ovdim* council in August, 1957, Pinhas Lavon expressed extreme dissatisfaction with the low profitability of Histadrut enterprise. This low rate of profit (about 3 per cent of investment in 1956) created concern because member funds such as the Workers' Provident Fund (GMUL) and the Workers' Bank are all invested in Histadrut industry. As early as 1953, Mordecai Namir had stated that workers in Histadrut enterprises behaved, acted, and felt no differently in their own enterprises than in the private sector, and that this tendency, if unchecked, would mean that the goal of workers' self-government would be increasingly frustrated, especially since the producers coöperative form had increasingly been giving way to the Histadrut wholly-owned firm.

The criticism that Histadrut had been overzealous and had tried to expand in order to eliminate the private sector, and had thus retarded economic growth by its effect upon this grouping which comprises 40 to 45 per cent of the total economy, was met by Mr. Lavon's announcement that Histadrut was going to restrict itself to developmental projects mainly in new settlement areas, and would not enter fields or activities either in the developed communities or where the private sector was operating adequately.

Mapai was politically concerned, since there was a great deal of adverse comment from both within and without the party that Histadrut enterprise was given favoritism in development loans and in German indemnities, and that this had led to ill-advised activity such as the construction of the steel mill at Acre, which the right-wing opposition alleged could never hope to be economically viable. Many Israeli economists contended that the economy's only hope for ultimate economic independence would be to develop smaller fabricating industries with a high proportion of value added, through the use of Israeli labor and local raw materials. The comparatively low value added, the high imported capital requirements, and the low exporting capacity of Histadrut basic industry (Sol-Koor) were all cited[27] as supporting reasons for questioning the feasibility of *Solel Boneh* and Koor's economic policy and the government's attitude toward it.

In a speech before the Mapai party conference in May, 1958, Mr. Lavon, cognizant of this criticism, announced that the fetish of big basic undertakings was over, that concentration in *Solel Boneh* was undesirable, and that deconcentration and decentralization would take place in all Histadrut enterprises. The monopolistic privileges held by TNUVA and *Hamashbir* were also to be terminated. He stated that the bus coöperatives should be organized along lines already indicated, and that worker representation on management boards would be instituted in order to bring the Histadrut sector back to the original aspirations of its founders. The party voted for a reorganization of all labor-controlled undertakings, and for the nationalization of the bus and transport coöperatives.

What has been evident in the past few years is the somewhat decreasing importance of the Histadrut in the developmental sector of the economy. The newly-organized large enterprises such as the Copper Mines at TIMNA, and the Dead Sea Chemicals, Fertilizer, and Magnesium development, have been under direct government ownership, and private enterprise has been assigned a more important role in the recent plans for the economic development of the Negev. Private enterprise, especially larger-scale American, British, French, and South African firms, have been increasingly willing from 1957 on to invest in developmental activity in Israel, and have been granted a larger proportion of developmental loans and concomitant favorable tax consideration. At a party seminar in May, 1959, there was some controversy between Pinhas Lavon and Levi Eshkol, Minister of the

[27] For instance, of Koor-estimated 1959 turnover of $81 million, only $6 million were exports, mainly concentrated in two firms, Alliance Tyres and Nesher Cement.

Treasury, especially when Eshkol stated that the government might sell some of its successful plants to private individuals on the model of the contemplated Volkswagen works sale.

Any attempt to give a comprehensive account about the effects of the Histadrut upon the economic development of Israel would be highly tentative, because no one can definitively answer the question whether the organization adversely affected the development of the private sector. Undoubtedly the Histadrut performed functions and engaged in activity that would not have been attractive to private industry, and both before independence and after performed functions which no other nonstate organization could have performed. Certainly in a period in which economic forms were fluid the private sector did not develop at a rate consonant with the necessary degree of absorption, if the goal of a state was to be realized. It is equally apparent that the Histadrut, through its banks, investment policy, provident funds, and contact with other groups abroad, was able to pool and combine small amounts of worker funds and mobilize them, together with the comparatively much greater amount of savings forthcoming from the Kibbutz than would have been available from predominantly private agriculture, into an impressive total. This ability to induce and mobilize small savings and to induce sacrifice is undoubtedly the Histadrut's unique achievement to economic development.

Despite the shortcomings and obvious deficiencies of Histadrut enterprise, invidious inferences should not be made about its relative efficiency, since the relevant comparisons are between Histadrut industry and that of the private sector and not with our more advanced industrial system. Histadrut industry is somewhat larger and more efficient than its private counterpart,[28] has pioneered in new managerial and technical procedures, and has been slightly more innovation-minded. Increases in manhour productivity,[29] profitability, and exports have been substantial. *Hamashbir* and TNUVA both have bene-

---

[28] During World War II many tradesmen, cut off from their supplies, began to manufacture on a limited basis. They still retained, however, a cost-plus high-profit mentality, and mainly considered the industrial part of their activity as a temporary adjunct of their mercantile function. After the formation of the state of Israel they continued as a cartel-minded, tariff- and protection-seeking interest group. However, there are signs of increased vigor in the private sector due to the influence of foreign capital, and even to the evolution of new and younger better-trained management in private firms. Many of these young managers were trained in and held high rank in the Israeli Armed Services, a highly efficient entity.

[29] Over-all output per manhour has been increasing at a comparatively rapid rate of 7½ to 8 per cent annually in Israel. The rate of increase (about 10 per cent) due to its greater degree of mechanization is somewhat higher in Histadrut industry, but is lower in the services.

fited through the challenges provided by the termination of their monopolies.

The changing attitude of Mapai and the state toward Histadrut enterprise, and the continued growth of the private economy, will undoubtedly reduce the proportion of economic activity generated through the labor economy, even though labor-owned industry will continue to show numerical growth. In the past five years, while employment in the Histadrut sector has risen by about 30,000, the proportion of total Histadrut membership employed in its own activities has declined from 40 to 37 per cent. Nevertheless, the Histadrut economy will be a factor of major importance in Israel for many years to come.

THE AGRICULTURAL SECTOR OF THE HISTADRUT

Originally the Histadrut was based far more upon agriculture than upon industry. Mass settlement in agriculture, using the Jew as an agricultural laborer, dates from the foundation of the early worker settlements which started shortly before World War II and accelerated afterward. If the Histadrut and its early institutions had any roots, it is in the Agricultural Workers' Union, then composed mainly of either current or would-be collective farmers. In fact, if one were asked to select the most unique of the many unique aspects of the Histadrut, one would select its agricultural farms, especially the world-renowned Kibbutz. Israeli agriculture outside of citriculture is predominantly either collective or coöperative. Out of the Kibbutz, and to a lesser extent the Moshav, there originated a disproportionate share of the leadership of the Histadrut and later on the state. Of the total land area under cultivation in the country, about 1,200,000 acres, 70 per cent, is worked by collective and coöperative agricultural societies within the labor economy. The relative share of the population represented is approximately 10 per cent of the two million people in the country.

All settlements must lease their land from the Jewish National Fund, since Israeli agriculture is based upon nationally owned land. Financing is provided by the Jewish Agency Settlement Department, which furnishes long-term loans for the housing of settlers, the development of the land for crops, and the acquisition of mechanical equipment. The groups brought to the land have been organized by Histadrut and held together and given training by the organization prior to their undertaking land settlement. Frequently groups were organized for two to three years before obtaining land, and were provided employment and training during that period. In addition to funds and loans granted by the *Keren Kayemeth* (Fund for Redemption) and *Keren Hayseod* (Foundation Fund) administered by the Agency's settlement department, Histadrut agencies such as *Nir Shitufi,* the agricultural counterpart to *Hevrat Ovdim,* the Workers' Bank, and even *Hamashbir* and TNUVA grant loans and carry the settlement's credit.

There are three types of agricultural coöperative settlement in Israel under labor movement asupices. These are: the Kibbutz, or collective settlement; the Moshav, or coöperative smallholders' settlement; and the Moshav Shitufi, which combines the leading features of the other two types.

The distinguishing feature of the Kibbutz in respect to its social and economic organization is the complete abandonment of private property. All assets are collectively owned, and even consumption goods are theoretically collectivized. All members work without payment, and their entire needs are taken care of by the group, also without payment. Children are the responsibility of the group and are looked after by members trained for that task, thus freeing the women from domestic duties (even kitchen and mess halls are communal) and increasing the supply of labor. Kibbutzim range in size from small groups of 50 to 75 people to larger groups such as Givat Brenner, with a population of about 2,000. Larger groups frequently undertake wide ranges of economic activity, and many own and operate industrial enterprises.

The Kibbutz movement prior to statehood had the larger population and was growing more quickly than the Moshav. Since statehood, the growth relationships have been reversed, and currently the Kibbutz movement is almost a static one. Meanwhile the Moshav movement has continued to expand, although recently at a declining rate.

The Moshav is a form in which marketing of produce and supplies, use of equipment, and provision of community services are undertaken coöperatively. Each family independently farms its own allotment, and the income of the family, after deduction for the joint services, is determined by the amount of produce it delivers to the marketing office of the Moshav. More extensive coöperation in production is now taking place, however, since the recent development of industrial crops such as sugar beets, sugar cane, cotton, and peanuts, is increasingly making a plantation type of organization more rational. Each family has a limited amount of land, determined by its size and the fertility of the soil, but averaging about 7½ acres per family. Mixed farming is the rule, and although the degree of mechanization in the Moshav movement is substantial it is not as high as that found in the Kibbutz sector.

The central Moshav movement, jointly with the Jewish Agency, initiates new settlement. The movement itself was begun in 1921 by Dr. Eliezer Jaffe, who felt that the Kibbutz form was not the most suitable for all immigrants, some of whom preferred more individual latitude, income proportional to effort, family life, and wives performing the usual household functions. This form was the one envisaged by Dr. Ruppin and the Zionist Settlement Organization when they began to purchase land through the Jewish National Fund. A modification called the Moshav Shitufi, which combines collective farming and individual family living, has not been overly popular, even though this form is older than the Moshav. Members of new Moshavim frequently work outside the Moshav in order to pay expenses until they have acquired the necessary agricultural skills and the soil at their disposal is sufficiently developed to provide them a livelihood.

The Moshav has been far more attractive to the postindependent immigrant than the Kibbutz. The reasons are various, but they may be related to the long period of ideological orientation necessary for successful Kibbutz adjustment and the need of the state and the Histadrut to settle immigrants—a large proportion of whom came to Israel because of lack of any other alternative and not as a matter of conviction—as quickly as possible. The looser coöperative framework makes some common security and mutual aid possible without stifling the family orientation of the members, and enables a better balance between individual initiative and group responsibility. Judged by other criteria such as output per man economically active, the higher initial cost of settlement imposed by the Moshav method, and ability to plow earnings back into expansion and development, the Kibbutz is still a more economically efficient form.[30]

In 1923, the first conference of Kibbutzim in Palestine was held to discuss special problems and to unify some functions which might better be performed at a federation level. Three years later a second conference was held at which it was decided to form the *Hever Hakvutzot ve Hakibbutzim* (Association of Collective Settlements).

[30] Both forms have their ideological proponents, but I believe the statement is unquestioned by most. The much greater contribution of the Kibbutzim to Israeli leadership and culture has also been mentioned. The proponents of the Moshav contend that this is the result of the differential maturity of the two movements. However, this contention must be rejected since there are a number of highly mature, well entrenched Moshavim, whose contribution in these areas, although substantial, does not compare with the Kibbutzim. The variation can be attributed to differences in ideological motivation and in zeal, as well as the much more substantial effort by the Kibbutz to encourage cultural activity among its membership in order to relieve the monotony of life and to build up the organic unity of such communities.

The purpose of the Association was to expand and consolidate the movement and to afford mutual aid in intersettlement affairs. In a grouping which was always ideologically intense and diffuse it would have been unrealistic to expect that any unitary movement could last very long without splintering. Some settlements soon seceded, primarily because of political differences and because they wanted to evolve organic unity of all those Kibbutzim who believed in a political movement characterized by "Marxian" democratic centralism. These Kibbutzim affiliated with the Marxist Hashomer Hatzair party in 1928 and founded the Kibbutz Artzi movement. Soon afterward, other settlements seceded because of differences as to size, economic structure, rigidity of organizational bonds, and as to whether a Kibbutz should attempt to organize industry to diversify its activities and employment, and formed *Kibbutz Hameuchad*. Within the *Hever Hakvutzot* there remained only those units which intended to remain small, and which adhered to the original form of the *Kvutza* as exemplified by Degania, which was founded by the followers of A. D. Gordon.

The tasks of these federations are: to regulate the movement of immigrants or new applicants toward existing settlements or to form new ones; to set up economic enterprises for all communal settlements affiliated with them; to maintain advisory institutions, agricultural clubs for the exchange of practical experience, and general education and cultural institutions common to all affiliated settlements; to represent the affiliated settlements before government and the Jewish Agency; and to establish separate funds for financing old or new settlements.

This basic framework of settlement groupings continued unchanged until statehood, when the Hashomer Hatzair and the left Poale Zion (a leftist splinter group from Mapai) combined to form Mapam as a left-wing Marxist labor party. For five years Mapam was the chief rival of Mapai, which with statehood and the responsibility of government has moved steadily to the right. This political change had no effect on *Kibbutz Artzi,* which was already ideologically homogenized, and upon *Hever Hakvutzot,* which was always oriented to Mapai, even though no test of political affiliation had ever characterized this group. Conflict broke out in *Kibbutz Hameuchad* settlements which had previously never been differentiated along political lines and whose membership was divided between Mapam and Mapai in approximately a six-to-four ratio. Party differences separated families and friends of many years and led to the secession of a number of settlements, which combined with those already in the *Hever Hakvutzot* federation to form *Ihud Hakkibutzim ve Hakvutzot.* In addition, some Kibbutz members, finding themselves in the minority, moved from Kibbutzim in which they had lived all their lives to new Kibbutzim whose members were now of the same political party.

In 1953, when roughly 50 per cent of Mapam seceded over both the refusal of the party to take a firmer stand against Communist Russia and the rigidity with which it held to Marxian doctrines which no longer seemed relevant to any Israeli problems, and formed *Achdut-Avodah*, the *Kibbutz Hameuchad* federation joined the latter political party. Today the Kibbutz federations are virtually identical in membership, basic problems and day-to-day operations, but this does not in any way mitigate the deep-seated ideological infighting.

Political disunity, the preference of more recent immigrants for the Moshav, the slower occupation of new land after 1952, and the mechanization of the Kibbutz under the spur of efficiency and increasing difficulty of recruiting new members, coincident with the increase in land area of the average Kibbutz, has brought the rate of population increase in the collective farms almost to a halt. This retardation of growth has caused consternation both in the Kibbutz movement and among many Israeli idealists. The movement was considered the source and inspiration of the labor movement, and has provided a large proportion of Histadrut and state leadership. At one time or another most Israeli leaders of the labor parties have been affiliated with a Kibbutz, even though their affiliations in some cases were short-lived and mainly designed to provide them with a political base. The Kibbutz provided early managerial training for many of the leaders of Histadrut economic institutions and contributed a major proportion of Israeli artists, writers, and composers. In fact, so important has been the Kibbutz movement and experience in putting its brand upon Israel and its current institutions that most observers call Israel's particular brand of coöperation "Kibbutz Socialism."

Today many of the established Kibbutzim are big business organizations, with relatively high standards of living which many of the older groups deplore. A more or less permanent managerial, technical, and skilled group has developed as these agricultural units have literally been industrialized. This functional separation within and outside the Kibbutz, despite its absolutely equal distribution of income, has meant that the old equalitarian ideology has been somewhat modified in practice. Another disturbing feature to the older idealists has been the need of many Kibbutzim, unable to recruit an adequate number of new members, to hire labor at market prices which generally are lower than the value of the day's work, thus making the Kibbutz, according to its own doctrine, an exploiter of labor. The Kibbutzim have attempted to solve this problem by hiring labor from contracting offices established by their federations and paying these firms the value of the day's work, hoping thus to avoid the stigma of exploitation.

Despite this failure to grow numerically, the Kibbutz movement is most vital and is still able to induce its sons and daughters to stay in the movement. With Israeli agriculture industrialized and mechanized, and with crop surpluses a problem for some types of agricultural output, this reduced proportion of the labor force in agriculture and in the Kibbutzim is consonant with trends observed all over the world where agriculture has been rationalized. But even allowing for this, although the Kibbutz movement will still continue to play a vital role quite out of proportion to its numerical size, it will from the standpoint of the proportion of the labor force engaged in collective agriculture be less significant. This constitutes the so-called crisis of the Kibbutz.

The economic importance of the Kibbutz and Moshav movements to Israeli development can be inferred from the following data. The turnover of these sectors of the economy reached half a billion Israeli pounds in 1959, or about 200 million dollars, approximately 12 to 14 per cent of national income. In the same year, an estimated 95,000 of the 177,000 workers in the Histadrut sector, of whom approximately 5,000 were employed in Kibbutz industry, were workers affiliated with either collective or coöperative farms.[31] Investments of about 30 million dollars annually in the agricultural sector, of which 55 to 60 per cent comes from internal sources, indicate the significance of these agricultural forms as saving devices.

Since 1937 a major proportion of new investment in the agricultural sector has originated from reinvested earnings.[32] Prior to 1937, due to the low agricultural prices which prevailed in the world economy, the absence of any agricultural protection in Palestine, the use of the Kibbutz and Moshav to absorb less skilled immigrants, and the huge proportion of activity devoted to clearing and soil renewal, collective and coöperative farms—despite their low standard of living and the great degree of sacrifice engendered—were, with the exception of a few highly efficient ones, unprofitable. Had it been necessary for these entities to have paid for their land, and had a large proportion of the costs of soil development and preparation not been written off, they would not have been paid off as quickly, if at all. Despite some costly practices, caused mainly by the heavy costs of mechanization and the

---

[31] *Statistical Abstract No.* 9, Economic and Social Research Institute of Histadrut, December, 1959, p. 10.

[32] G. Muenzner, *Jewish Labor Economy in Palestine* (London: Victor Gollancz, Ltd., 1945).

absence of adequate long-term credit, which forces the Kibbutz treasurer to borrow on the short term for long-term purposes at high costs, there is no doubt that Israeli agriculture is not only highly efficient but that this efficiency is an outcome of the deep commitment induced by both agricultural movements, especially the Kibbutz, which has resulted in sacrifice and a high rate of voluntary saving.

HISTADRUT TRADE UNIONS

Some trade and industries had been organized into countrywide unions even before the founding of the Histadrut. The Agricultural Workers' Union, the Railroad, Post and Telegraph Workers, and the Clerks and Office Workers were all founded in 1919. However, although the Histadrut constitution advocated the organization of trade unions, there were many ideological pressures and practical realities which insured that this provision was interpreted to mean local unions controlled and supervised by the local labor council.

The failure of industry to develop on a large scale, which meant that in many areas there were no workers of a given industry or only one plant in the entire county, and the lack of desire to build particularistic power centers which might run counter to the more global orientation of the organization, were the major factors inhibiting the growth of strong national trade unions. However, despite this and some ideological opposition to the use of the trade agreement as a basic policy, practical realities connected with the need to maximize employment of Jewish labor forced the Histadrut to bargain collectively, through their local labor councils, aided by the trade union department and, where relevant, the Histadrut trade union sections.

The sixth convention in 1945, which anticipated rapid industrialization in the postwar era, adopted a resolution to establish nationwide unions of factory, construction, transport, and maritime workers on an industrial basis. In keeping with that decision, the Building Workers organized in a countrywide union in April, 1946. They were soon followed by the nurses and chemists, who formed separate sections within the Clerks' Union, and by the printers and teachers of the Labor Trend.

Notwithstanding the absence of organization centered around strong national unions, the Histadrut had by Independence in 1948 secured working conditions and social benefits which even by American standards were highly advanced, and an average wage equal to Central European standards. The resultant wage rates and social benefits were substantially above the real productivity of workers, and the Israeli government and the Histadrut are still attempting by wage restraint and by encouraging increases in productivity, through the negotiated joint productivity councils, to bring productivity into line with real wages and social benefits.

Provident funds continue to provide, just as our negotiated pension systems do, amounts in excess of government social security benefits. Currently social costs as a proportion of total wage costs approximate 15 to 18 per cent of wages in agriculture and construction, where the labor force is more inclined to be a casual one; 25 to 30 per cent in the private industrial sector; and 30 to 40 per cent in Histadrut and government industry. Histadrut has frequently used its own industry as a lever to establish precedents for higher social benefits.

At the end of 1958, there were 36 national trade unions, mainly industrial, organized into an Industrial Workers' Federation, with heavy and light branches. These 36 unions aggregate 330,000 members, with several large unions providing the great bulk of the membership. The Clerks have the largest membership, 55,000, followed by the Hired Agricultural Workers with 50,000, the Building and Public Workers' Union with 33,000, Government Workers with 30,000, Metal Workers with 25,000, Workers in Histadrut Plants with 25,000, Teachers' Union with 18,000, Food and Bakery Workers with 15,000, and the Textile Workers with 13,000. Two independent groups of workers, the Poale Mizrachi (50,000) and the Arab Workers (10,000) belong to the Histadrut trade union department and are members of the appropriate trade unions.[33] However, they are not full members of the Histadrut. About 88 per cent of all Israeli workers belong to the trade union department of the Histadrut.

In performing its trade union functions Histadrut acts as a general union as well as representing the particular interests of workers in a given industry. The worker's prime affiliation is to the Histadrut, which in turn allocates him to a national trade union, which is an administrative creation of the Histadrut and a unit of its trade union department. The Histadrut is the authoritative center and can effectively centralize as much of basic wage policy formulation as its Executive desires.

At the local plant level, the Histadrut members elect a work committee by direct personal election. The committee is recognized as the sole representative of the workers by management. Specific arrangements provide for representation on the committee of special categories of employees, such as clerks and professionals. The work or workers'

[33] The Poale Mizrachi is a political party of religious workers. One labor group attached to the Herut Party and numbering approximately 45,000 is totally independent of Histadrut.

committee is headed by a secretary who may in a large plant be a member of the local labor council, but in any case is always subject to its discipline.

At the level of the labor council, which encompasses all workers in a locality and is the worker's basic unit of affiliation in the Histadrut, there generally is a secretary representing all the workers in a particular industry in that local area. This local official, who is generally a paid official of the labor council, is also the local representative of the national trade union.

Since the local secretary of workers in a particular industry is an official of the local labor council, and the council not only must approve any strike and use of strike funds, but also has the power of discipline over local members, it is the labor council through its head which has the preponderance of power and authority over the local unit of the national union. This power discrepancy is intensified because the secretariat of the national union, although nominally elected, are actually appointees of the Histadrut trade union department, and in most cases have no previous base in the industry and very rarely have risen through the ranks of the particular work groups. When the employer is not a member of the National Manufactures' Association, the local labor council, acting through its branch secretary, negotiates the basic agreement; and even where national agreements exist, since they have to be interpreted and implemented with special consideration for each plant, the local council has considerable latitude, especially where there is a strong and vigorous head who wishes to modify or alter the trade agreement.

The smaller size of the Israeli economy, the presence of few large employers in any industry, the centralized structure of the Histadrut, and certain historical necessities, have all facilitated centralized bargaining through the Manufacturers' Association and, presently, the Industrial Workers' Division of the trade union department. Acceptance of the central bargain is a precondition to negotiation at the industry and plant level. Basic agreements negotiated at the Association-Histadrut level include such important matters as the determination of the cost-of-living allowance, the establishment of joint production councils, the eight-hour day, the establishment of pension and provident funds, the procedures for dismissal of redundant and inefficient workers, and the establishment of committees for arbitration.

These nationwide agreements are incorporated into the agreements between the national trade union and a particular industry. Each important industry is represented in the Manufacturers' Association by a section for that industry, such a section being headed by a paid official who, with a committee of leading manufacturers, negotiates a basic agreement for that industry. Where the industry is not a national one, where either no national trade union or section of the Manufacturers' Association exists, or where the enterprise has chosen not to belong to the Manufacturers' Association, the local labor council is the negotiating body.

The local secretary, who is ostensibly the local head of the national trade union, but who in reality is primarily an employee of the local labor council, then acts in conjunction with the work committee not only in negotiating local details pertaining to specific plans but in administering and enforcing the contract. This structure, and the dual role of the local secretary of the trade union, have contributed to a tug-of-war between the organizational department, which administers the local labor councils, and the trade union department, whose primary relations and concerns are with national unions. Strong council leaders have sometimes refused to let local firms and work committees be a part of national agreements, thus reducing the importance of the national union—and, as a consequence, the anomalous position of the secretary has caused conflict between the two power centers. Sooner or later this tug-of-war will be reconciled and, if the Histadrut continues its current adjustment to industrialization—which has already increasingly tended to differentiate functional groups as other trade union centers have—the tug-of-war will be reconciled in favor of the trade union department and the national unions.

Although collective bargaining relations, as in all countries, run the gamut from excellent to poor, strikes have been comparatively unusual in the Israeli economy and strike losses have rarely exceeded one-third of a man-day per year.

The relatively small incidence of strikes can be explained by the great strength of the Histadrut relative to the employers, and the importance of strike benefits which employers generally must pay if they lose the strike. Interestingly enough, the three years in which strike losses were highest indicate conflict within the Histadrut. These have been generally manifested in differences between Histadrut managers and trade union-oriented officials and between Mapai and Mapam, the latter generally taking a workers' or trade union's point of view. For instance, a large proportion of the 1956 manhour losses can be explained by a strike of the Egged coöperative against government regulation of fares and against the Histadrut Executive, which did not support its demands for higher fares. In 1957, the Ata strike between the Haifa Labor Council and the Ata Textile Company, the largest employer in

Israel, accounts for a substantial proportion of man-days lost due to labor disputes.

Ata has pressed to be allowed a freer hand in making redundancy and efficiency dismissals, issues which constitute a frequent source of conflict in Israeli industry, both Histadrut and private. The Histadrut, like many other labor movements, developed a classification of "permanent worker," and despite the fact that it nominally allowed employers to determine the size of their work forces, local work committees frequently have made it difficult, if not impossible without a tremendous amount of negotiation and the payment of substantial indemnities, to dismiss redundant and inefficient workers. Such dismissals were difficult to execute even when the labor force was plainly excessive due to mechanization. Ata wanted permission to dismiss 116 workers before it would sign a wage agreement, and the Haifa Labor Council refused to negotiate on that basis even though the Manufacturers' Association-Histadrut national agreement, to which Ata [34] did not subscribe, had already provided for procedures to govern such dismissals. The power issue between the national trade union and the local labor council was also involved in the dispute. More important was the desire for Histadrut management and major segments of the Executive to make similar dismissals, especially in their Vulcan and Nesher plants in Haifa where shutdowns of shorter duration over the same issue had already taken place. Mapai was concerned because its economic policy geared to increasing exports favored increasing productivity and efficiency. The confluence of these forces caused the strike direction to be taken away from the Haifa Labor Council and be passed on to the Histadrut Executive. The Executive settled on the basis of the Manufacturers' Association formula, and subsequently both redundancy and efficiency dismissals, while still requiring negotiation and final resort to arbitration, have become less controversial and easier to effectuate, both in private and Histadrut industry.

WAGE POLICY

Histadrut wage policy has always been geared to providing even the lowest-paid worker a Western European standard of living. This goal plus the incorporation of certain social benefits and adjustments, such as the cost-of-living, family, and seniority allowances, which are added to the base wage, constitute the outstanding characteristics of Histadrut wage policy. This policy results in high minimum wages which are

[34] Ata is regarded as the bellwether of Israeli industry. Hans Moller, its owner and president, is considered Israel's leading industrialist. This account of the strike somewhat oversimplifies the issues.

well above productivity for the lesser skilled elements of the labor force, and a highly compressed wage structure, which at least until recently was consonant with the movement's basic equalitarianism.

Recent events indicating divergent interests between unskilled and more highly skilled workers and between manual laborers and professionals, the latter also organized within the Histadrut, have created somewhat conflicting pressures upon the Histadrut and even upon Mapai. These pressures have been intensified by the need better to allocate the labor force, enhance efficiency, and make Israeli products competitive in world markets, all of which have since 1955 operated to necessitate some widening of wage and salary differentials.

The high minima and social benefits, in the face of relatively underdeveloped industry and a market of limited scope, have meant that unless production costs were to get completely out of line, substantially higher wage rates could not be paid to the more skilled workers. In addition, at least until statehood, the Israelis had to reverse the normal occupational structuring, for there was an oversupply of doctors, lawyers, and administrators, and an undersupply of agricultural workers, building workers, taxi drivers, and even ditchdiggers.[35] Thus the normal wage structure, assuming that this reconversion were to be attained, had to be modified if not reversed in favor of what in other societies would have been the lower-skilled elements. However, since statehood, this condition no longer prevails, but despite this the wage structure continued to narrow between 1948 and 1955, due primarily to the operation of the cost-of-living allowance, which only applied initially on the first IL80 of wages and subsequently, as inflation continued, to a wage of IL125. This limit adversely affected both highly skilled workers and professionals. In addition, sharply rising progressive income tax rates also operate against middle-income and professional groups.

The narrowing of wage differentials since 1939 is illustrated in table 22. Similar tendencies would have been observed if the interindustry wage structure had been compared, for there was a discernable narrowing of wage differentials between the highest- and lowest-paying industries.

Between 1955 and 1958–59, wages and salaries were put on a new base, since by this time the total increase in the cost of living index was about 250 per cent, thus making the old base relatively meaning-

[35] A somewhat apochryphal Israeli story concerns the lady who fainted in a bus in the late 1930's, and five males, all dressed in working clothes, sprang to comfort her, each one saying he was a doctor. The bus driver stopped, saying it was his bus and therefore the lady was to be his patient.

less. Wage differentials in the industrial sector have recently remained relatively constant, with some selective widening in favor of skilled groups taking place since 1955. However, wage differentials such as in construction, where the lowest daily rate is IL7.590, and the highest daily IL9.140, are undoubtedly among the narrowest in the world. Family allowances averaging 2 to 3 per cent of wages, and seniority benefits of approximately 3 per cent, also tend to equalize total wage payments. In addition, the labor grade in which a worker is placed all

TABLE 22

INDEX OF WAGE DIFFERENTIALS IN SELECTED OCCUPATIONS AND INDUSTRIES, BETWEEN THE HIGHEST AND LOWEST PAID WORKERS, 1939–1948, 1951, 1953, AND 1955

Industry	1939	1948	1951	1953	1955
Furniture	160	122	109	113	115
Building carpenters	133	119	131	113	115
Locksmiths	133	140	131	124	118
Building workers, general	133	123	131	116	118
Shoemakers	150	128	119	124	123
Printing	167	116	118	121	123
Bakers	127	116	114	107	108

CONFIDENTIAL SOURCE: Ministry of Labor.

too frequently reflects seniority and not skill, thus constituting another irrational element in the Israeli wage structure. Since 1957–58, under pressure from the Productivity Institute and joint production councils, there has been some use of job evaluation in Israeli industry, thus helping to rationalize the system of labor grades. It is estimated that in industry about 30 to 35 per cent of all workers operate on incentive systems, generally of a proportional nature. The average bonus for the workers involved is approximately 15 to 20 per cent, and the share of incentive earnings to total earnings in all industry amounts to approximately 5.5 per cent.

It is in interskill and occupational differentials that the range of differences between the lowest-paid Israeli workers and the highest-paid technical or professional groups is perhaps the narrowest in the world. A professional man, doctor, production engineer, manager, top-rated civil servant, Histadrut executive, or university professor rarely nets more than 60 to 80 per cent above the salary of an unskilled industrial worker. These differentials are at variance with labor market needs, for due to the rapid industrialization and expansion of the

Israeli economy many of these professional groups are currently in extremely short supply.

The comparatively low wages paid the more highly educated and those assuming greater responsibility have made these groups, some of whom are organized in the Histadrut, highly volatile, and the results have been frequent strikes of teachers, university professors, government clerks, and Histadrut doctors, and the creation of a professional department in the Histadrut. The strike of professors and civil servants in 1955–56 forced the Histadrut to increase their salaries substantially, on a deferred increase plan, but this increase made the industrial workers restive and made a substantial wage increase for these groups (10 per cent) necessary. This increase temporarily forced the Histadrut and Mapai to abandon their policy of wage restraint followed since Independence.

Since statehood, the Histadrut has attempted to link wages to changes in the cost of living, and in the last few years has even attempted to limit the rate of increase through the already-discussed 3 per cent rule.[36] It has been opposed to any general wage increases, as government economic policy, which Mapai members of the Histadrut Executive must adhere to, has been one of wage restraint so that productivity will ultimately catch up with wage rates and social benefits, making Israeli products more competitive in world markets. Since any attempt to spread wage differentials between the highly skilled and the unskilled would be internally disruptive, the Histadrut, given its policy of avoiding a general wage increase, has been forced to walk a tightrope, but has permitted some selective adjustments, especially under the pressure of either strikes or threats of strike by the more highly skilled and professional groups, which are currently the most militant entities in the organization.

In analyzing the wage system which has resulted from Histadrut policy, certain basic deficiencies, which the organization recognizes and is attempting to rectify—albeit slowly rather than dramatically—are apparent. These are:

1. The whole system of differentials is haphazard and does not reflect actual labor market conditions.

2. The small differential between the lowest- and highest-grade worker encourages the hoarding of skilled workers by firms who use these workers for activities requiring lesser degrees of training and competence.

[36] The cost-of-living allowance overstates the real increase in prices, since the base period was one characterized by extreme austerity and poor quality goods, while currently there are abundant supplies and thus choices of all goods and services. This permits switching to cheaper, better, and more attractive consumer goods.

3. The high minima, although designed to aid the less skilled groups and the new immigrants, actually discourages their employment.

4. The automatic elements, especially the cost-of-living bonus and social benefits, are too large a proportion of the total wage. These by and large are unrelated to skill and labor market factors.

5. The cost-of-living bonus, which was given automatically, was a factor of inflationary pressure, distorting the structure of costs and prices, and especially operated against those industries and firms where labor costs constitute a large proportion of total costs. However, recent changes point to amelioration of this problem.

POLITICS AND POLITICAL ACTION IN THE HISTADRUT

The Histadrut, although formally titled a general federation, is not in reality a federation of autonomous trade unions—since, as we have already observed, the Histadrut was the first to organize and the majority of national unions emerged much later. If anything, it is a federation in another sense—namely, a federation primarily but not exclusively of political parties claiming either a working-class membership or a working-class ideology. Four so-called working-class parties, and three more generally based parties, have some membership in the Histadrut. Histadrut functioning is based upon the highly competitive collaboration of seven parties: Mapai, Achdut Avodah, Mapam, General Zionists, Progressives, Communists, and the Religious Workers (*Haoved Hadati*), with Mapai consistently, since its formation in 1931, constituting a clear majority of the membership.

Originally the Histadrut was a confederation of working-class socialist parties only, but since the accession to membership of workers from the "new dealish" Progressive party, and especially since the participation of members of the anti-socialist General Zionist party, it has lost its all-socialist complexion as a confederation of parties which have only "worker" membership. It was in reality never entirely a Zionist movement, since the much-despised Communists, who were always avowed anti-Zionists, have periodically been in the fold. Despite their presence, the anti-Communist, if not anti-Marxist, focus is evidenced by the resignation of the Histadrut from the WFTU and its secretariats, to joint the ICFTU.

All discussion of issues in conventions, councils, and the executive boards is based upon party positions, and every individual member of these bodies operates as a disciplined party spokesman or representative. Representation in all the decision-making bodies is determined on a political basis through which each party receives the number of delegates proportionate to its national vote. The local labor council is selected by the same political system of proportional representation.

So far the political character of Histadrut has not been productive of too much disruption, nor has it unduly forced Histadrut to compromise its goals in order to get assent. As long as Mapai has maintained an absolute majority, it has been able to govern effectively. If this majority were ever lost, the indecision generally indigenous to coalition government could be disruptive. However, especially before elections the dominant party, Mapai, may have to modify certain positions, such as its support of wage restraint, or its traditional opposition to encouragement of religion, in order to secure its mandate.

TABLE 23

HISTADRUT ELECTIONS, PERCENTAGES BY PARTY, 1955 AND 1959

Party	1955 percentage	1959 percentage
Mapai	57.7	55.4
Achdut Avodah	14.6	17.0
Mapam	12.5	13.9
Haoved Hazioni (Progressives)	5.3	5.8
Communists	4.1	3.5
General Zionists	3.8	2.8
Haoved Hadati	2.0	1.0

SOURCE: *Israel Digest*, January, 1959.

After unification of *Achdut Avodah* and *Hapoel Hatzair* into Mapai in 1931, the party was able to obtain approximately 80 per cent of the vote in all Histadrut elections held before statehood. Since statehood, due to splintering off to form the other left-wing parties, as the data in table 23 indicate, Mapai has had a clear but somewhat reduced majority.

In the 1959 Histadrut election Mapai lost votes to Achdut Avodah and Mapam in many of the established labor centers. The losses can be attributed to its stand against the bus drivers, its position in regard to efficiency and redundancy dismissals, which especially displeased some older workers, and to dissatisfaction with Mapai wage restraint policy. On the other hand, Mapai ran much stronger than expected in new immigrant centers. However, Mapai lost five labor councils to coalitions headed by the Achdut Avodah and Mapam.

Since statehood, the locus of political decision-making has moved away from the Histadrut. With the establishment of the state the Histadrut has become less important to the parties as a source of power, patronage, and authority. Today most important decisions are made outside the Histadrut, in party headquarters, and the party caucus passes the decisions along to members on the Histadrut Executive. Even when the party members in Histadrut feel that the decision taken is antithetical to their Histadrut interests, they obey.

The labor parties have increasingly diverged in their official positions. Of the three non-Communist parties, Mapam is stridently Marxist, although this is incompatible with its Kibbutz roots, which would be anathema to most doctrinaire Marxists. Achdut Avodah is a more utopian and Kibbutz-oriented party than a Marxist one, and is pro-Western in its foreign policy orientation, while Mapai, although frequently sloganizing in class-oriented terms, is a social democratic party consistently moving steadily rightward. Responsibility as the governing party of the country, the need to make decisions based on such stern economic indicators as the balance of payments, and the presence of a strong managerial and administrative wing, have all moved this party to the right, despite its base in the Histadrut and among workers. The Progressives, a "liberal" party of German professionals and intellectuals, do not differ substantially from Mapai, except in their slogans, and were it not for the benefits of a separate apparatus, which in coalition governments confers certain advantages to a small party whose votes are needed to form a majority, the basic differences between the two groups might be reconciled. The General Zionists, although having some workers enrolled, are largely a middle-class managerial and entrepreneurial group, especially strong among the citrus grove owners who are the only important private grouping in Israeli agriculture.[37]

Today Histadrut leadership is increasingly subordinate to Mapai leadership, and recent Mapai decisions which have led to reliance upon government enterprise in large-scale developmental industry and in the taking over of labor exchanges are reducing the importance of Histadrut. The party apparatus as a vehicle of upward mobility is becoming more and more separate from the Histadrut apparatus. The growth of a considerable and powerful group of younger leaders who, like Dr. Giora Josephtal, Minister of Development, have had no ties, connections, or positions with the Histadrut, or who like General Moshe Dayan have expressed some skepticism about the organization, also highlights the changing scene. Policy statements which have not always considered Histadrut attitudes, made by governmental (but former Histadrut) leaders such as Levi Eshkol and even Ben-Gurion, are other indicators of the same trend. Much of this change was inevitable with statehood and with the assumption of national responsi-

[37] The Progressives and the General Zionists united in 1961 to form the Liberal party. The combined party registered a minor increase in the number of parliamentary seats in the 1961 elections.

bility by the party and its leaders. But Histadrut with its mass membership is still a major political power center, and if Mapai or any party were to lose its base in the labor federation, it would experience great difficulty. This alone will continue to make the Histadrut and its leadership important political factors.

Summary and Conclusions

This all-too-brief development and analysis of the Histadrut and its history has perhaps raised more questions than it has answered. Perhaps no immutable conclusion can ever be stated for an organization as fluid as the Israeli labor movement, especially when new problems, structural forms, and ideological adaptations are constantly taking shape. To attempt fully to assess them or to predict the future course of the organization would be hazardous. Nevertheless, some brief comment about the Histadrut and its direction of possible change is warranted.

The Israeli labor movement, based on Labor-Zionist ideology, was not only a major factor in bringing about statehood, but also in developing rapidly a comparatively modern society based on certain social ideals and values. As a device for attaining ideological commitment, which resulted in the ability to mobilize capital from sources which ordinarily do not make such developmental contributions, the Histadrut is a unique entity. In addition, through its mass membership and its majority status in the Palestinian community and therefore its leadership in the Jewish Agency, it was able to recruit and mobilize capital from sources all over the world, and not only utilize these resources for economic development, but also direct growth along certain sociopolitical lines. The unique and predominant role of the labor movement in the absence of either a government or a developed employer class in recruiting, committing, structuring, and setting the rules for the labor force, was also a basic factor in economic development and in attaining an independent statehood. Thus as an ideological mobilizer, organizer, pragmatic institution-builder for mobilizing savings, and labor-force developer, and in the range and variety of its social welfare goals and mutual aid institutions, the Histadrut undoubtedly qualified as the "wonder child" of western social democratic-oriented trade union movements. This development was all the more remarkable because the organization attained many of its major social goals through collective bargaining without having founded strong national trade union centers.

But to claim that these attainments were costless, and accomplished without some adverse effect upon the private sector, which either was unwilling to come into Israel under the existing circumstances or which found the comparatively high wage and social costs difficult to sustain, would also be impossible. The wonder child is now an adult, and is faced with the inevitable problems and responsibilities of greater maturity. The Histadrut is currently confronted with the consequences of rapid growth and the problems arising out of its diverse and prolix organization, with its many contradictory facets and divergent functionally-oriented interest groups. These can no longer always be cemented by the unifying tendencies of an all-pervasive nationalistic spirit. Some readjustments in attitude and policy, arising out of the increasing strength of the private sector and the growth of a more universal organization than the Histadrut, namely, the state, are and must continue to take place.

There are problems and conflicts between efficiency and the social goals of the organization. These are between the managerial and trade union wings in the Histadrut, and especially between Mapai managers and Mapam or Achdut Avodah leadership, who always support the workers' point of view, except in those Kibbutz Artzi industries where Mapam managers predominate. The diverse and contradictory interests of professional, administrative, and salaried groups, which would like to widen wage and salary differentials, and the manual workers, who would like to maintain the relatively equalitarian status quo, also necessitate some juggling by Histadrut leadership. Given the universal desire for higher standards of living which pervades the membership, clashing with Mapai party leadership desire for wage restraint in the interest of economic independence, the majority Mapai leadership of the trade union movement must constantly exercise great care.

Problems of major importance have arisen in regard to the large numbers of more recent immigrants who lack the strong ideological commitment toward Labor-Zionist ideals or even toward Israel. The Histadrut must not only integrate these groups into the organization but ultimately bring them into leadership positions. This need is especially important because the Kibbutz movement, once the basic source of leadership, idealism, and ideology is no longer an expanding one.

The development of large power centers in the Histadrut economic sector also raises questions which are of importance to the organization's future. Ideologically, the problem of the hired worker in the Histadrut plants, and the sometimes parochial view taken by the bus coöperative, disturbs many of the Histadrut's idealists. While the reorganization of *Hevrat Ovdim* and the larger companies paved the way for elimination of "empire building," the need to centralize and consolidate organizational funds in order to maximize development still awaits present and future leadership.

Relations with the state and with Mapai are also undergoing revision. Histadrut leaders obviously recognized that the state would ultimately assume many of the functions formerly assumed by the organization in the preindependence period, but they were not prepared for the resultant growth of new centers of power within Mapai or for Mapai leaders, who originally had attained their important positions from their Histadrut base, increasingly disregarding the organization's position or taking a view more favorable to non-Histadrut groups. Certainly the state's interest in such functions as *Kupat Holim,* which the movement's leadership always felt affected the loyalty of the membership, was never contemplated. Many Histadrut members and leaders have not yet completely adjusted to an era in which it will no longer be predominant and its word will no longer be "law."

Nevertheless, these problems are the result of the rapid growth and unparalleled diversity of the organization and its willingness to assume functions which other union centers have traditionally shied away from. Given its long historical record of pragmatic adaptation, and the ability of its Mapai majority to discipline itself, even at the expense of some temporary unpopularity, in order to solve basic problems, these difficulties not only do not seem insurmountable, but in a comparative sense appear much less productive of future decline or trouble than in other national labor movements.

Chapter VI | Turkey[1]

SUMNER M. ROSEN

Background

Turkey began the intensive phase of her economic development under more favorable conditions than many countries now engaged in industrialization. The basic economic setting is good, the endowment of land and resources is ample, and the population is well below any limit set by natural resources. Although the interior had long been neglected under the Ottomans, industrial and commercial activity flourished in the coastal cities under foreign auspices before World War I, so that industrial activity was not new to Turkey, even though carried on under the quasicolonial conditions of the "Capitulations," and largely by foreigners and non-Moslem minorities. The principal areas of foreign investment and development were railroads, public utilities, mineral extraction, and light industry.[2]

The War of Independence of 1919–1921 involved considerable economic destruction. At the same time, its positive achievements were enormous. It resulted in the establishment of a homogeneous and highly nationalistic state led by capable and energetic men, with Turkey's national hero, Kemal Atatürk, at their head. The new government was able to eliminate the burdens of foreign domination which

[1] The material on which this study is based was gathered in Turkey, largely between 1953 and 1955. The assistance of the Ford Foundation is gratefully acknowledged. The conclusions are the exclusive responsibility of the author. While much of the factual data refers to the pre-1960 period, recent study confirms the conclusion that events since that time have not materially altered the validity of the findings herein contained. (February, 1962)

[2] Alfred Bonné, *State and Economics in the Middle East* (London: Routledge and Kegan Paul, 1948), pp. 324, 435.

had distorted the domestic economy and inhibited its growth. It set the stage for economic growth, with a program of reform without a modern parallel, the objective of which was to transform—to modernize and Westernize—every aspect of the individual, social, and political life of the population. The reforms introduced and vigorously applied during the 1920's and early 1930's included the disestablishment of Islam and the secularization of the state, the suppression of the religious orders and schools, compulsory reading of the Koran in Turkish rather than Arabic, the prohibition of the fez, the imposition of the Gregorian calendar, the replacement of religious law with European legal codes, and the reform of both the alphabet and the language. Atatürk himself led the program of reforms, and the tribunals of the Republic enforced them with ruthless efficiency. Their goal, as Atatürk said again and again, was "to bring the people of the Turkish Republic into a state of society which is entirely modern and civilized, in every sense and in every way." [3] Though this goal is still some distance from achievement, the effect of the reforms was to prepare the people psychologically for further changes, to accustom them to innovation, and to enlarge the numbers of those dedicated to promoting progress. The basis for industrialization on a wide scale was established.

Moderate steps toward more vigorous industrial activity were taken during the first years of the Republic; the government nationalized several existing facilities which had been established by foreign capital before 1914, and enlarged the capacity of the railroads and some industries, including munitions factories. An effort to stimulate the growth of the private sector included bank credits, tariff protection, tax concessions, and other measures. There was considerable growth; the number of enterprises covered by the Law for the Encouragement of Industry rose from 342 in 1927, when the law was passed, to 1,397 in 1933; by then the total capital investment was £T63 million, and the number of workers employed 62,954. The industries principally represented were textiles, mining, wood products, and food processing. At the same time a large number of handicraft shops existed; the 1927 census estimated them at 65,000, employing more than 250,000 masters and workers.[4]

These results, though encouraging, were too slow to satisfy the ardent desire of Turkey's ruling group for a rate of economic growth

---

[3] Quoted in Geoffrey Lewis, *Turkey* (New York, 1955), p. 91.

[4] Bonné, *op. cit.*, pp. 276–277; Arnold J. Toynbee and Kenneth P. Kirkwood, *Turkey* (New York, 1927), pp. 227–229; John Parker and Charles Smith, *Modern Turkey* (London, 1940), pp. 101–104; *The New Turkey* (London: *Times* supplement, 1938), pp. 62–63; Cahit Talas, *La Législation du Travail Industriel en Turquie* (Geneva, 1948), pp. 56–59.

commensurate with the speed with which social, legal, and cultural life was changing. The impact of the depression dramatized the weakness of those countries which relied on the production of raw materials, and stimulated the desire for a rate and scale of industrial development far beyond anything which earlier policies could be expected to produce. The examples of fascist Italy and Communist Russia encouraged those who felt that centralized and planned industrialization was needed.

The result was the policy of étatism, under which Turkey embarked in 1933 on a five-year plan of industrial growth. Étatism meant three things: (1) planned targets achieved under state control and with public funds; (2) the creation of heavy industry and mining facilities sufficient to achieve substantial self-sufficiency in the energy and capital goods necessary for consumer goods production; and (3) the creation of special instruments of the state to combine the functions of investment, management, and distribution. These special instruments were called State Enterprises: the most important of them are the Sümerbank, carrying on a variety of industrial enterprises, and the Etibank, charged with mining and electric power production.[5] Beyond these principles, étatism contains little in the way of an economic ideology, despite its superficial resemblance to socialism or fascism. Étatism was incorporated into the program of the single party in Turkey, the People's Party (CHP) created by Atatürk. Thus the identity of the party and state policy, which had earlier been established in the cultural and social fields, was extended to the economic area in the 1930's.

The purposes of the state's economic policies were not only to achieve a specific set of economic targets. The state had the further duty of preserving and extending the spirit of national solidarity; as the 1935 Congress of the CHP expressed it: "Every economic enterprise shall harmonize with united national work as well as with the general interest. This harmony is also the principle in the union of work between the employer and worker." [6]

Under étatism and the one-party regime, economic growth, financed in part with Soviet, British, and German credits, was considerable. Industrial production doubled between 1929 and 1939, and many of the long-term social costs of industrialization were met, including some which are not reflected in industrial indices. Assets of Sümerbank, for example, rose from £T7.4 million in 1933 to £T85 million in 1939;

[5] They are named for the Sumerians and the Hittites, early residents of Anatolia, to emphasize present Turkey's supposed historic legacy.

[6] Quoted in Parker and Smith, *op. cit.*, p. 240.

its own physical plant vastly expanded, and it made funds available for other investments as well, through its banking facilities. Both Sümerbank and Etibank, as well as other state holding and operating companies, have continued their growth throughout the postwar period. By 1955 Sümerbank had built seven cotton mills, two thread mills, a paper and cellulose plant, a rayon plant, a cement mill, a hemp and twine mill, a firebrick plant, and the large iron and steel mill at Karabük. Etibank has invested heavily in expanding and modernizing the coal-mining fields in the Eregli region, and has built or improved several large lignite mining facilities, large dams, and power plants.

Although these organizations are nominally autonomous, in practice they are subject to political control by Cabinet ministers, and operate as part of the centralized apparatus of government.[7] As the level of industrial activity and the size of the industrial labor force increased during the 1930's, the dominant trends in the emerging industrial sector were clear and well established. A comprehensive and all-powerful state apparatus, without political opposition though functioning under the parliamentary system, had successfully undertaken and led a series of formidable changes in the social and economic life of the country. Turkey's rulers had repudiated much of the past, and imposed a rapid succession of modernizing and Westernizing policies which culminated in the ambitious attempt to create a viable modern economy, planned and directed by Turks, and intended to guarantee the vigor, solidarity, and cohesion of the new Turkish society which Atatürk had made possible by his military victories.

Post-War Economic Developments

The period since 1945 has seen a great acceleration of economic growth in Turkey and enlargement of its scope. Like the Ottomans, Atatürk had neglected agriculture; his death and the onset of the war prevented any serious attempt to deal with agriculture in the intensive and thoroughgoing way that the industrial problem had been tackled. Since 1945, and particularly since the beginning of U.S. economic aid in 1947–48, the major economic changes which have occurred have been among Turkey's peasants. The creation of a network of roads has brought hitherto isolated villages into the market economy. High prices and easy credit have stimulated a large increase in the area of cultivated land, mostly at the expense of meadows and pastureland; between 1948 and 1956 the total acreage under cultivation rose by 70 per

[7] A. H. Hanson with the assistance of Mumtaz Soysal, *The Structure and Control of State Enterprises in Turkey* (Ankara, 1954).

cent, after having been virtually unchanged in previous decades.[8] U.S. dollar credits made possible a mechanical revolution in much of Turkish agriculture in this period. In 1946 there were only 1,356 tractors in Turkey, about 30 per cent more than before the war. In 1957, by contrast, the number of tractors was over 43,000, and an estimated 14 per cent of the cultivated land was under the tractor, as compared with less than 1 per cent before the war.

While the impact of the tractor and other new mechanical devices was limited in large part to particular crops and areas, it nevertheless created new and unprecedented patterns of landholding and sharecropping wherever it took hold. The prevalence of small holdings in most of Turkey, and the absence of large-scale tenancy, prevented the dislocations which accompany mechanization from being serious; there is little evidence that the stability of Turkey's rural society has been widely undermined, or that large-scale depopulation of the land has taken place. Nevertheless, the displacement of even a small fraction of Turkey's rural population has meant extremely rapid growth of the cities, which were relatively small to begin with. A combination of factors has so far prevented the explosive growth of a displaced urban proletariat. The capacity of industry to employ larger numbers has increased, and many of those displaced have become migratory workers, subsisting on temporary work in agriculture and, to some extent, in the cities as well. The rapid growth of the urban populace creates chronic and at times serious tension. Large areas in the major cities are occupied by squatters' huts, and those who joined in the orgy of anti-Greek destruction in Istanbul in September, 1955, included large numbers of this new segment of the population—submarginal, resentful, uprooted people venting their frustrations.

Turkey's cities have grown faster than her population. Between 1950 and 1955 the total population grew by 15.1 per cent, while the population in cities of 25,000 or more grew by 38.0 per cent, and the number of such cities rose from 32 to 41. By 1960 there were 59 of these cities with a population of 5.6 million, equal to 20.1 per cent of the total population. This sharp increase contrasts with the relative stability of the urban proportion of the total population between 1927 and 1950.

Large cities, those with 50,000 population or more, also grew rapidly. There were 11 of these in 1950, 17 in 1955, and 28 in 1960. The population of these 28 cities had reached 4.6 million, 16.5 per cent of the total population. Cities of 100,000 or more numbered 11 in 1960, compared

[8] *Monthly Bulletin of Statistics*, Nos. 34, 35–36, December, 1956, January–February, 1957, p. 169.

with 7 in 1955; their population numbered 3.3 million, 11.7 per cent of the total population.[9]

The pressure of urban growth has forced the state to continue its role as the principal creator of new investment and jobs in industry. The platform of the Democratic party, which attained power in 1950, stressed the role of private enterprise in industrial growth. Its leaders announced their intention of curtailing the further growth of the State Enterprises and, eventually, of selling the individual plants and installations to private capital. While the private sector has grown to unprecedented dimensions since 1950, the state has been unable to relinquish its major role, and still employs a majority of the total labor force in manufacturing and mining.

The period since 1952 has been characterized by serious inflationary pressures. High levels of investment have not been accompanied by equally high rates of saving or taxation; in fact, the largest part of the national income, that derived from the land, is almost wholly tax exempt. The provision of generous credits to agriculture, minimum prices set by the government often well above world prices, and the growth of money and credit have all contributed to the inflation. The bulk of Turkey's imports have been for capital goods and raw materials; her deficit on current account has been very large throughout the postwar period. Finally, very large outlays for defense, estimated at 40 per cent of her national income,[10] have added greatly to inflationary pressures. Official cost-of-living indices have doubled between 1952 and 1959, while the unofficial wholesale price index of the Istanbul Chamber of Commerce has risen by 17 to 18 per cent each year since 1955, a rate faster than the rise in previous years.

There has been little attempt in this period to assure that limited resources were used to achieve balanced growth. As much as 30 per cent of the total investment between 1948 and 1954 went for housing, much of it built for speculative purposes by private persons and designed for upper income groups. Only 15 per cent was devoted to industry and energy, despite the clear need for accelerated growth in these sectors.[11] In addition to structural imbalances, the course of economic expansion in recent years has been marked by shortages of both consumer goods and raw materials, short-term bilateral trading agreements, grandiose campaigns to reduce markups and punish "profiteers," emergency arrangements to fund and refinance

---

[9] Central Statistical Office, *Census of Population,* 1950, 1955, 1960.

[10] Lewis, *op. cit.*, p. 175.

[11] Nejat Bengül, "Problems of Economic Development in Turkey" (typewritten), 1958.

foreign indebtedness, and other symptoms of stress and inadequacy.

Politics and Economics

The year 1945 marked the beginning of a new and critical phase in Turkey's political evolution as well as in her economic development. By the deliberate decision of Atatürk's successors, multiparty government was introduced, with the legalization of opposition parties. To Turkey's rulers this marked the next phase in her development as a Western state and member of the free world. Atatürk had experimented briefly with the idea of an opposition, in 1924 and again in 1930, but had quickly abandoned the idea as premature.[12] Although the experiment which began in 1945 suffered from several setbacks and false starts, it was not repudiated. Among the several parties which were founded, that organized by several prominent dissidents from the CHP, which called itself the Democratic party, made the greatest headway. After a vigorous period of organization and campaigning, the Democrats scored a stunning victory in May, 1950, and unseated the CHP which had ruled for a quarter of a century. Thereafter, until the government was overturned in 1960, national life was dominated by the interaction of rapid economic change and deep, often bitter, political partisanship and rivalry for advantage.

Two effects of this interaction stand out. The progress of economic development was substantially affected by considerations of political advantage, both in the choice of investments and in the methods of financing. At the same time, various institutions typical of a free society, notably a free press and free trade unions, gradually developed, giving effective voice to various points of view among those affected by economic change.

Étatism and the quasidictatorship of the Atatürk period made it possible for the state to impose its will on the population, even in such sensitive matters as language, dress, and religion. Long-range plans in the industrial and mining fields were developed and carried out by a bureaucracy which had the power and the funds to do the job assigned to it. The concentration on industry, mining, and power made comprehensive and coördinated schemes feasible, and the special instruments available—the State Enterprises—were well suited to achieve their tasks. The political control exercised by the state enabled Turkey's rulers to insulate the bulk of the population, the peasants, from the "revolution of rising expectations" which plays so great a role

---

[12] Lewis, *op. cit.*, pp. 84–86, 101–105.

in generating high levels of demand and inflationary pressures elsewhere. The relatively modest levels of investment needed, the availability of foreign credits, and the ability of the government to impose taxes of whatever level necessary, combined to free Turkey's rulers of the need to cope with inflation or to meet sharply rising consumption needs. Thus the program of industrial development proceeded smoothly until interrupted by World War II; it laid a strong foundation for further growth without disrupting the economic or social life of the majority of the population.

By contrast, the period after 1950 saw substantially higher investment levels, but with far less coördination and control than before. Many schemes received costly commitments of resources more for the effect they would have on political advantage than on their logical priority. Much of the resources available for investment were left in private hands, with distortions which have already been mentioned. Pressure to achieve and keep the political initiative dominated the plans and decisions of the government and its agencies, whose former autonomy had been virtually eliminated. As for financing, the bulk of the population received substantial and repeated increases in money incomes along with virtual exemption from taxation, while the government attempted to meet rising consumption needs by expanding the production of consumer goods from domestic industry, and by devoting considerable amounts of scarce foreign exchange to the purchase of consumer goods and raw materials for domestic consumer-goods production. And since the pace of investment did not slacken, there was no alternative to massive deficit financing, with consequent inflationary pressures.

The introduction of political freedom removed a lid which had silenced protest for a generation, during which the most profound changes had been imposed on every aspect of life, and the accumulated frustrations and resentments of the transition had been denied legitimate expression. The introduction of political freedom and party rivalry provided the mechanism for the expression of grievances; the rival parties freely exploited these grievances in their struggle for power. While relatively few persons enter the struggle themselves, the issues which are debated affect everyone, so that all groups participate vicariously in the perennial debate, and are zealously courted by the active partisans.

The unions have become an important arena for this struggle. It is ironic that, while the Trade Union Law of 1947 prohibits unions from engaging in partisan political activity, there is nothing to inhibit the political parties from carrying on their own activities among the unions. The result has been a serious impairment of the unity and coherence of the unions, and division of individual unions as well as union organizations into partisan cliques. The fact that there is little in the way of fundamental principle to divide the major contending parties does not prevent bitter partisanship, since the stakes—the exercise of power—are high. When those in power felt themselves threatened by their rivals, the temptation was irresistible to manipulate and intimidate various key groups, such as the press and the unions, in order to reduce or remove the threat. The result was that, instead of a coherent debate on economic policy, in which the various interests affected could present their views for a balanced set of policies, discussion of economic questions degenerated into a competition to win political points by exploiting the anxieties, fears, and ambitions of key groups in the population. And since the peasants dominate the electorate, no economic policy, however sound, could be seriously proposed which would alienate them from the party in power.

The Structure of Industry and the Labor Force

Approximately 77.5 per cent of Turkey's labor force is in agriculture and related activities. The remainder, according to figures compiled in the 1955 census, is distributed as follows:

Activity	*Employment*
Mining and quarrying	58,000
Manufacturing	726,000
Construction	195,000
Utilities	13,000
Transportation and communication	177,000
Commerce	326,000
Services	511,000
N.e.c.	714,000
Total	2,720,000

SOURCE: U.S. Department of Labor, Bureau of Labor Statistics, *Foreign Labor Information,* "Labor in Turkey," February, 1959, p. 4.
N.e.c. = not elsewhere classified.

Only about 25 per cent of this total constitutes an industrial labor force. In addition to those in commerce and services, there are large numbers of workers employed in handicraft or small-scale enterprises among those shown in manufacturing and transportation and communication. This is seen by an examination of the numbers subject to the national labor law, which covers all workers in establishments of ten or more workers, plus those in large cities of 50,000 or more population in establishments employing 4 to 9 workers. This is shown below, excluding the nonindustrial categories, as of December 31, 1957:

Activity	*Employment*
Mining and quarrying	92,578
Manufacturing	331,966
Construction	181,643
Utilities	17,634
Transportation and communication	13,538
Total	637,359

SOURCE: Ministry of Labor.

Coal mining in the Zonguldak-Eregli area is by far the largest single mining activity in Turkey; about 20,000 men are employed there at one time, though the total labor force is almost double that, due to the unique system of employment, long in use, in which two groups of underground workers alternate every 40 days. Other important mining activities are iron, lignite, chrome, copper, and manganese. The state monopolizes the production of coal and copper, while manganese production is entirely in private hands. In recent years state-owned mines have accounted for approximately two-thirds of the production of lignite, half the iron ore, and one-third of the chrome.

Manufacturing employs the largest segment of the industrial labor force. It can be divided into three groups:

1. Large-scale methods of production predominate in textiles, tractors, tires, railroad equipment, shipbuilding and repair, soap and chemicals, glass, sugar refining, rubber, paper, cement, bricks and tiles, and primary metal processing. Several of these are represented by single state-owned plants, and a few by single private plants built with foreign capital.

2. Large-scale methods of production exist, along with substantial handicraft and small-scale production, in food processing, metal fabrication, printing and publishing, machinery, and leather processing.

3. Small-scale and handicraft methods predominate in clothing, wood products, furniture, and various nonmetallic mineral processing.[13]

The growth of recent years has been primarily in the large-scale sector. Except where foreign capital has entered a hitherto untried field, as in the tractor and tire industries, growth has occurred along existing structural lines. Although Turkish capital is entering industry in steadily growing quantities, native entrepreneurship still foregoes the new and risky.

---

[13] 1950 Census of Industry; see Central Statistical Office, *Statistical Résumés No. 10*, July, 1953, pp. 2–3.

This is one reason why the state continues to play a major role in industrial activity. It operates the only existing plants manufacturing paper, rayon, shoes, steel, glass, sugar, and cement, and produces more than half the textiles; in 1953, the state employed slightly more than half of all workers employed in plants with ten or more workers,[14] though the private sector has grown slightly faster as a whole. In some regions, notably around Izmir and Adana, the growth of private industry has been spectacular in recent years, but the state still plays a major role where the level of technology is advanced, the degree of investment heavy, or the risks of loss great. The cement industry has been built under state auspices, state-owned steel capacity is being enlarged, and even the Sümerbank textile capacity has been increased, particularly for higher-quality cotton and woolen fabrics.

Labor and Economic Development

Turkey's economic development has followed a path somewhat different from that of many countries now undergoing rapid economic change. Instead of having to deal at once with the problems of industrialization, political freedom, and the transformation of cultural and social patterns, Turkey was able to achieve significant progress along some of these lines before having to face the challenge of others. The economy is no longer in the first stages of transformation from subsistence agriculture, but possesses a significant industrial and urban base; the industrial labor force, though small in proportion to the total population, is significant in numbers, and includes a high proportion of fully committed urban industrial workers. Recruitment, training, housing, discipline, and other fundamental aspects of industrial work have been, on the whole, well understood and successfully dealt with. Legal and administrative provisions for workers' welfare have been created, many of them well in advance of the need, under étatist planning. An industrial base, and the core of an industrial labor force, could be built in the 1930's on the basis of the political and cultural revolutions which were already in their period of consolidation.

The problems which have faced Turkey's rulers and employers in recent years stem rather from a change in the magnitudes involved, a drastic acceleration in developments already under way. The challenge of the postwar period was one of adapting existing institutions and, where necessary, devising or permitting new ones, to supplement earlier methods. It became necessary to understand and deal with a new phase in Turkey's economic progress, or to risk serious delays and the appearance of important barriers to further balanced growth.

[14] Alec P. Alexander, *Economic Change in Turkey, 1948–1955* (unpublished Ph.D. dissertation, University of California, 1957), p. 141.

Unfortunately, there was little or nothing in the étatist system which could give the needed guidance. The economic growth of the prewar period took place almost completely within the structure of the state enterprise system, and was largely confined to the industrial sector. It was aided by the systematic educational and propaganda work of the People's party organization, which was comprehensive, energetic, and well financed. It built on the new pride of nationalism, to which industry gave such important symbolic meaning. The authoritarian character of the regime was softened by a comprehensive paternalism which could deal with the physical, economic, and social problems involved in the transition from the village to the factory city, from rural to industrial life. At the same time, the government could adopt policies looking to the long view, without being overly troubled by short-run political reaction. It was in this atmosphere that the state gradually elaborated the forms of management, control, and welfare appropriate to each stage of the industrialization process, achieving steady and relatively painless progress and growth.

World War II interrupted this progress and imposed severe economic hardships. At the end of the war, the system which had worked so well before began to shown signs of rigidity; it was difficult to recapture the sense of purpose and progress which had been present earlier. At the same time, the scope of the problems to be dealt with widened immeasurably, with the extension of the industrial revolution to the agricultural sector, along with an acceleration in the rate of growth of industry. The system was dealt a final blow with the introduction of political freedom and the emergence of a multiparty system. Free unionism, a free press, and partisan political competition for power emerged almost simultaneously to confront the étatist machinery with a challenge to which it was unable adequately to respond.

It is true that economic progress continued during the first decade after World War II, sometimes with spectacular success. At the same time, it was not balanced progress, and symptoms of serious imbalance began gradually to emerge and to play a greater role in determining economic, and ultimately political, decisions. It is in this process that we can see unfolding the interaction of economic, political, and institutional forces which are the heart of the problem of economic development.

What has happened in Turkey since 1950 has been fundamentally a gradual loss of control over the forces which have been released by rapid and widespread economic change. This has led those in power to concentrate on symptoms rather than causes, to attempt to deal with immediate grievances and complaints rather than to seek to recapture control of the entire process. In the partisan political atmosphere which has prevailed, and as the goal of control became less and less attainable, the consideration which gradually but inevitably took precedence over all others was the desire of those in power to benefit from their power and to preserve it as long as possible. At first, this was a goal which could be achieved by a combination of tactics—favoritism to some groups, promises to others, subtle pressure on still others. As inflation gradually increased in its scope and pace, and as it became more and more clear that major economic decisions with regard to investment priorities, taxation, foreign exchange allocation, credit, and fiscal policy were being made with increasing irresponsibility and without regard to any system of coördinated long-term priorities, dissatisfaction mounted to overwhelming proportions. Beginning in 1953–54, a pattern of coercion and intimidation gradually emerged and took precedence over other methods, until finally the system of parliamentary government, as well as the rule of law itself, was placed in serious jeopardy.

A serious paradox is at work in this process. Atatürk and his associates had successfully created a unified and purposeful society, committed to progress and Westernization and devoid of serious internal fissures or class divisions. This had been achieved by adapting to political and economic life the model of successful action represented by the military system; étatism became its civilian equivalent. When this system became outmoded because of the magnitude of economic change involved and because of the relative sophistication of the populace—particularly its urban segments—a new model was required which would widen significantly the channels of participation, of initiative, and of decision-making in order to preserve balance and prevent excessive rigidity and overcentralization. But faced with the challenge of political survival, those in power found themselves unable to do anything but return to the form of the older model, and to reinstitute the techniques of control and domination, though these were now clearly inadequate as well as inappropriate. The alternative to this seemed to be to abandon the central principle of étatism, which was to retain in the hands of the state the instruments of control and decision. When the Menderes regime tentatively moved in this direction in the first years after its assumption of power in 1950, the result was serious economic difficulty, as exchange reserves dwindled and as the desire of the newly prosperous for higher levels of consumption strained the productive capacity of Turkey's industry beyond its limits.

The response was a precipitate return, in the absence of a better model, to that which seemed to have served Atatürk so well, and which was in fact the only real model available. But by this time the system could not be made to work well; beyond that it was wholly inappropriate to a society with free institutions, particularly labor unions, which took their freedom seriously and expected accommodation and recognition. The result was to set the government between two contradictory sets of forces with which it was unable to deal, except by sacrificing one to the other. It elected to reimpose the authoritarian pattern, and was ultimately driven to such extremes that it could not survive. The nature and magnitude of these contradictions constitutes the focus of this study.

Management and Labor Relations

The comprehensive nature of étatist planning extended to considerations of social policy; the state enterprises have long provided substantial programs of social assistance to workers, subsidizing free supplements to wages such as housing, medical care, hot meals, education, work clothes, and similar benefits. Beginning with the promulgation of a labor code in 1936, a set of obligations was imposed by law on all employers, less comprehensive than those administered by the state enterprises but conceived in the same paternalistic spirit. Although a new generation of managers is rising in the state enterprises, and in some of the older private plants which shared this paternalistic approach, it is still true that a benevolent, though somewhat stifling, paternalism dominates the personnel policies of the state enterprises. The major change after 1950 was the use of the prerogatives and power at the disposal of these large organizations to strengthen the political standing of the party in power.

The state enterprises are inescapably identified with and wholly dominated by the regime; thus they combined a self-conscious promotion of the national interest with a responsibility to promote the fortunes of the Democrats. Where unions have achieved political influence with local Democratic organizations, this required that they be recognized and dealt with. Even then, the manager of the state enterprise saw his role as one of providing comprehensive help and guidance, and exercising firm responsibility; he expected deference and respect from his work force. In detail and emphasis, this attitude varies among the different organizations. The older ones preserve more of the earlier paternalism, while the newer ones, as well as individual plants managed by younger men, are more likely to emphasize the virtues of efficiency and cost control which their leaders have learned in their recent training abroad. But even in these cases, the need to consider the political implications of personnel policies operated to restrain such tendencies, lest workers be alienated.

The formulation and administration of personnel policies in state enterprises is the subject of a perennial tug-of-war between the central organization and the plant managers. The latter are often men of prominence in their area, where the plant they operate may be the largest industrial establishment for many miles, and are themselves vigorous practitioners of the political arts. Though they resent and resist attempts to impose policies on them, the overwhelmingly centralized character of Turkish administration and political life extends to labor policies. The result is that plant-level industrial relations are seriously inhibited, since both sides must look to Ankara on any issue of controversy, and both spend their time mending their political fences at the center. As one observer noted: "It is doubtful . . . whether relations between the Enterprises and the Trade Unions can develop healthily when questions of wages and conditions so easily and frequently become the responsibility of the Ministry's expert on labour welfare questions." [15] The state enterprise plants contain practically nothing in the way of a personnel department. The official in charge is generally little more than a record-keeper with no policy responsibilities, no training, and so little initiative that even the most trivial questions of fact from a visitor must be cleared with line management before he will answer them.

Much of what has been said of the state enterprises is true of the small group of domestic private enterprises of substantial size and considerable age which exist in some branches of Turkish industry; they have long practiced an indigenous paternalism. A larger segment of the private sector, which will continue to grow, represents a much newer entry into industrialism. Owners and managers belonging to this group tend to develop one of two sets of attitudes on labor questions. Many of them recruit their top staffs from among the technicians employed in the state enterprises, promising them higher salaries as well as more freedom of action than they have hitherto enjoyed. When they are "turned loose," these managers pursue the ideals of production and efficiency for which their training prepared them, but which suffered frustration under the inhibiting policies of the state enterprises. At the same time, they usually lack the sophistication to understand the complexities of worker psychology and industrial relations, and in general tend to be impatient with workers who are of rural origin, lack education, and represent a lower and less important stratum of society. Their actions and attitudes outrage the sensibilities of workers and union leaders, and the latter seek satisfaction through the political

---

[15] Hanson, *op. cit.*, pp. 66–67.

channels available to them. In this way, though for different reasons, this type of management, like that of the state enterprises, finds itself involved in jockeying for advantage at the political center, and in defending itself through party channels and influence. Like the managers of the state enterprises, these managers find unions an unwelcome force to be either controlled, restricted, or divided wherever possible.

A smaller group in the newer enterprises of the private sector approaches the problem of unionism and personnel relations with more sophistication. They recognize that simple production-mindedness cannot suffice as a management philosophy, and that some form of worker representation is inevitable. Such men, whose numbers are likely to grow, seek to channel the energies of unionism to achieve their own goals of effective control in the plant and political influence in the community. They understand the philosophy, as well as the techniques, of modern management in Western societies, though they continue to seek a type of control and influence which modern managers in the United States, confronted by strong independent unions, find virtually inaccessible. They are likely to coöperate with union leaders at the plant level, and may even help these leaders to achieve more access to and greater general concessions from the central government, in return for political loyalty and coöperation in the local community, and dutiful exposition of management's goals and virtues to the work force. Some are cynics, but others see in this pattern of relationships a type of paternalism more adapted to future conditions, more flexible, and thus more successful than the older model.

There is a final group of employers, the type which one labor leader has called "fossils." [16] They are largely members of the commercial group which has been attracted to industry by the promise of rising prices, high demand, and quick profits. They seldom engage in enterprises of any great size, but account for a considerable volume of employment in those industries where small-scale production is still important. Their attitudes are simple. They attempt to evade their legal obligations to their workers, most frequently by operating small establishments or nominally independent parts of an integrated production process, which are either exempt from the law or extremely difficult to police effectively. They resent unionism and resist it by every means available, since their profits often depend on their ability to exploit their labor force. They transfer the commercial frame of reference almost bodily to their industrial operations; they take a short-run view of their interests, lack any managerial talent or technique beyond

[16] Bahir Ersoy, "Labor Relations through the Workers' Eyes," University of Istanbul, *Social Policy Conferences,* Vol. 6, 1953, pp. 47–56.

the ability to gauge market demand and meet it quickly, and violate with impunity the elementary needs of their workers. The bulk of complaints made by union leaders and workers' representatives to government officials undoubtedly concerns this group of employers. It is not surprising that the most militant advocates of the right to strike among Turkish union leaders are those whose members are employed by such employers.

In summary, each of these groups of employers, for different reasons, finds strong, independent unions undesirable. To the managers of the state enterprises, unions are rivals for the loyalty of workers, and may constitute a competing source of political influence. To the newer managers, unions represent an unnecessary impediment in the path of greater production, greater efficiency, and rapid industrial growth, of the sort which seems to them so clearly in the national interest. To the merchants-turned-producers, unions are simply an obstacle to profits. Each group, however, deals differently with the unions they face. When in the late 1940's and early 1950's it was official policy to encourage unions to organize, the managers of the state enterprises usually lent an active helping hand. As this policy changed, these enterprises tended to stand aloof, to withdraw their assistance, and in some cases to induce schisms designed to promote the fortunes of union leaders favorably disposed to the party in power. They seldom, however, attempt to displace a union either overtly or under cover, though they may be able to limit its scope and its ability to defend membership interests.

Employers in the private sector are less inhibited. Those who value their reputation and their political status do not engage in outright harassment or intimidation, though they are often careful to see that potential union organization is discouraged at the outset. This approach is more likely to succeed in smaller and more remote areas than in the major cities; in the latter, employers often refuse to concede any status or recognition to unions, though they cannot prevent their formation. Because the law fails to lay any obligations on employers to recognize or deal with unions, this policy can succeed. Where unions exist and are too strong, too ably led, or too well connected politically to be ignored, employers may initiate or accept programs of consultation and discussion. Normally, however, they are alert to encourage more docile leadership or to assist the schismatic tendencies which so often exist among union members. Those employers who operate the smaller establishments for short-term profits can seldom be persuaded by any means, including political influence, to give recognition to unionism among their employees or to deal with elected leaders.

State Labor Policies

A comprehensive system for dealing with the problems of industrial employment was in preparation as early as 1924, in deliberate anticipation of the problems which industrial growth was sure to create; a government message submitting a labor bill to the Assembly stated: "Turkey will be endowed with a national industry in the near future. To give this budding industry more vigor, and to obtain the maximum output from the working masses, it is important to place the various branches of industry under the control of law, and to prevent conflicts between capital and labor." [17] This and subsequent preliminary draft bills were discussed, but no definitive bill was begun until 1934, two years after Turkey joined the ILO. Submitted in 1936, it was accepted as written and became the fundamental law of industrial relations; though it has been amended several times, it is still the major legal instrument in this area.[18]

It is notable chiefly for its comprehensive scope and Western orientation. While the industrial labor force was still small, the state created an over-all system of regulation designed to prevent problems from arising and to anticipate and deal with the various aspects of industrial relations well in advance of their appearance. It was the matured product of an expert bureaucracy, prepared at leisure and with reference to the existing standards of other nations. The presence of several expatriates from Germany who were experts in this area, particularly Professor Gerhard Kessler, stimulated the emulation of foreign practices. In addition, the government secured the services of a German-American expert, Dr. Oscar Weigert, through the auspices of the ILO, to assist in drafting the code. It represented the determination of the state to see to it that an over-all approach would in fact be taken, and that it would embody the best Western practice. As Dr. Weigert pointed out: "Besides the two original parties, employers and workers, the state now appears as a third and immeasurable powerful factor in economic life, compelling private interests to justify themselves by standards of common justice and the public good." [19] The discussions which took place in the Parliament and the press while the labor code was being considered included many statements by government spokesmen which stressed the importance of a comprehensive code to establish a framework within which the state could adequately regulate

[17] Talas, *op. cit.*, pp. 95–96.

[18] Law No. 3008 (1936), amended by Laws Nos. 5518 (1950), 5842 (1951), 5868 (1952), 6032 (1953), and 6298 (1954).

[19] Oscar Weigert, "The New Turkish Labor Code," *International Labour Review*, Vol. XXXV, No. 6 (June, 1937), p. 772.

all phases of manpower development. The code was designed to lay the groundwork on which the government would erect a systematic fabric of welfare and regulatory measures, to meet all the social and economic problems which arise with a growing industrial labor force. It gave to the state primary responsibility for assuring that timely and appropriate policies would be applied, which would smooth the path of industrial development. In the field of workers' welfare, the state would play the major role. In the area of industrial relations, the state was to serve as the dominant and decisive voice, resolving disputes without prejudice to the interests of either side, but above all in terms consistent with the national interest. Thus the state at the outset established itself as the dominant influence in industrial relations; it has preserved this claim throughout the intervening period, even while the means available to fulfill it have fallen increasingly short of what is needed.

The labor code is divided into four principal sections. Two of them prescribe standards in the areas of working hours, workers' health, and safety. A nine-hour day and a 48-hour week are established in principle, with overtime limited to 90 days per year; a daily rest period and one day of rest per week are required; the labor of women and children is restricted both as to length and type. Employers are required to meet prescribed standards of safety and health, and to submit various documents which permit the existence of these standards to be verified, including plans, sketches, and photographs of the machinery. In addition, employers must draw up a set of regulations to govern the work in their place of business, and submit these "shop rules," covering discipline, form and frequency of wage payment, shift regulations, etc., for approval to the appropriate office of the Ministry of Labor.[20] Enforcement of the prescribed standards of health and safety, and investigation of alleged violations, are the responsibility of an inspectorate, assigned to various field offices of the Ministry. A Director-General of Labor, who is the principal civil servant of the Ministry below the Permanent Under-Secretary, directs the staff of inspectors and field office personnel, which in 1954 numbered 263, 116 of them inspectors.

The two remaining sections of the code deal with industrial relations, which are divided into two classes, collective and individual. The latter rest on the central instrument of the code, the individual work contract. This legal device had been in use in Turkish industry and commerce since the nineteenth century, and had been embodied in the civil code of obligations adopted in 1926. The labor code retains the

[20] Since 1946, that is, when the Ministry of Labor was established; before then, administration of the labor code was in the hands of a Directorate of Labor in the Ministry of Economic Affairs.

individual work contract, but imposes minimum conditions and establishes administrative techniques of supervising the terms of contracts and of securing adherence to the legal requirements. In 1950, tripartite labor tribunals were created to hear cases arising out of contract disputes. The law deals only with individual rights; there is no provision for collective action in the area covered by the labor contracts. Any worker employed for 30 days or more must have his terms of employment stated in a contract. The law prescribes the terms of the contract—for example, payment of wages must take place at least once a month—as well as the conditions under which it may be cancelled, by either side, and the rate at which dismissal pay accumulates. Penalties for violating these conditions are also prescribed. In each workplace, biennial elections take place, supervised by government inspectors, to select "workers' representatives," whose functions include the representation of individual workers in cases involving their rights under the contract.

The principal function of the contract is to fix and define mutual obligations of worker and employer. It is a device for stabilizing relationships and for minimizing labor mobility. Focusing on the individual worker, it seeks to prevent the development of mass or collective discontent; when the code was passed, the Prime Minister stated: "The new Labor Law will sweep away the clouds which make possible the birth and life of class consciousness." [21] The state has never abandoned this fear, or altered the emphasis on individual relations of the original labor code. Even when unions were legalized in 1947, the labor code was not altered to admit them into the scheme of industrial relations, except in minor details.

The only matter in which collective action is permitted is wages. The labor code provides that collective wage claims may be processed through a system of mediation and compulsory arbitration; at the same time, strikes and lockouts are forbidden. Provincial arbitration boards hear "collective" disputes, defined as those involving at least one-fifth of the work force, a minimum of ten workers; their decision can be appealed to a central arbitration board, whose decision is final. Until 1958 these boards were composed of government officials and public members; since then, they have been tripartite, with labor and employer representatives sitting under the chairmanship of government officials. In addition to wages, provincial boards hear cases of alleged discrimination by employers against elected workers' representatives; they can compel reinstatement, and there is no appeal from their decisions in these cases. The selection of workers to sit on arbitration boards is

[21] Kemal Sülker, *Türkiyede Sendikacılık* (*Unionism in Turkey*) (Istanbul, 1954), p. 30.

made from these representatives in biennial regional elections; unions and union organizations play no official part in their selection.

Between 1936 and 1946, a total of ten cases reached the central arbitration board, and one author commented: "In Turkey, conflicts between the wage-earner and the employer, if not settled by negotiation, are rarely brought before the established tribunals. The psychology and state of morale of the workers, their sense of inferiority, and their frequently precarious economic situation, oblige them to resign themselves and to accept the conditions of labor imposed upon them." [22] By contrast, the period since 1950 has seen the arbitration machinery deluged with cases, and the central arbitration board had heard a total of 492 by March, 1955. Of those decided, two-thirds were in favor of the workers, and the remainder rejected. Cases were about equally divided between the public and private sectors, with the majority originating in the textile and tobacco industries. The law permits the central board to extend the terms of a decision to other workers in the same industry or area, but this power has never been used.

The legalization of unions in 1947 was not accompanied by any provision of a role for them in the arbitration process, except that when a dispute came before an arbitration board, they could submit their views and offer suggested solutions to the dispute. In 1950, their role was somewhat enlarged. In small and seasonal establishments where workers' representatives are not required to be elected, workers initiating a collective dispute may designate a union to represent them. In other establishments, a union which represents a majority of the workers may itself initiate a dispute if it has a written request to do so from one-fifth, a minimum of ten, of the workers. This change explains the great increase in arbitration cases after 1950; as the recent McNair Report of the ILO states: "This is the means, in Turkey today, whereby a large proportion of the disputes which take place are brought to arbitration." [23]

Although wage increases are often forthcoming to those who avail themselves of the arbitration machinery, it has so far affected relatively few industrial workers; about 100 to 150 cases have been decided each year in recent years, and some unions raise disputes as frequently as they can.[24] Most provincial decisions are appealed by one side or the other. It pays to appeal, since the central board often modifies local decisions, and its own awards are almost never retroactive.

Interested and objective observers agree generally that the system of

---

[22] Talas, *op. cit.*, p. 162.

[23] Report of the Committee on Freedom of Employers' and Workers' Organizations, 1956, Appendix II (Monographs Relating to States Members of the Organization), p. 1404.

[24] An arbitration decision precludes a new dispute for six months.

compulsory arbitration is seriously defective.[25] It is slow, limited in scope, and subject to the dictates of government policies. Decisions are centralized, so that they are made on the basis of formal arguments by men removed from the actual situation. The central board usually attempts to apply general criteria or national economic policies to local situations, without being able to determine whether the special facts of the case are amenable to them. The cases always involve small groups in individual plants or areas, because there are no national unions able to process wage claims for significant numbers of workers, where national data can be usefully applied, but the process of appeal, accompanied by the attempts of both sides to influence votes and decisions, removes most decisions from the local scrutiny which the local boards should be able to provide. The system is cumbersome and relatively inflexible, which makes it less useful in a period of rapid economic change. Each case, instead of being resolved by negotiation between the parties, becomes an adversary proceeding argued before strangers, on an all-or-nothing basis. In this way arbitration as practiced in Turkey is an almost insurmountable barrier to the development of a system of autonomous industrial relations. It makes the parties public adversaries instead of participants in a common relationship. It deals only with questions of wages, and because the parties depend on this public tribunal to settle such questions, they proceed more slowly than would otherwise be the case to develop the habit of direct negotiation out of which would evolve appropriate ways of dealing with such problems in industrial relations as safety protection, grievance settlement, layoff procedures, and all the other elements of what Professor Slichter long ago called "industrial jurisprudence."

The State and Workers' Welfare

In addition to preëmpting the area of industrial relations, the state has provided comprehensive programs of social welfare for industrial workers. These were included in the labor code of 1936 as statements of intention, though they became a reality only between 1946 and 1950. Various problems connected with the recruitment, training, and movement of workers are handled by the State Employment Service, established in 1946; the Workers' Insurance Organization, established a year earlier, administers programs of insurance and medical care, including accident and occupational disease, maternity, general sickness, and re-

[25] Statement by the Istanbul Printing Technicians' Union, *Akis*, July 21, 1958; Adil Ascioglu in *Akis*, April 6, 1957; Sedat Toydemir, "History and Present Status of Labor Disputes in Turkey," University of Istanbul, *Social Policy Conferences*, Vol. 4 (1951), pp. 61–66.

tirement benefits. Each of these special agencies is nominally autonomous, though in practice they are closely controlled by the Ministry of Labor. The activities of the Employment Service are financed from municipal budgets, those of the Insurance Organization from premiums paid by employers and workers. A program of unemployment insurance, also envisaged in the 1936 code, has not been introduced.

SOCIAL INSURANCE

A study mission of ILO experts which visited Turkey in 1949 found [26] that the program of social insurance generally conformed to sound Western practice, and was appropriate to Turkey's state of development. No new programs have been introduced since 1950; the emphasis has been on expanding both the coverage of existing programs and the level of physical facilities available to provide the medical and related services specified. Benefit levels have been raised on several occasions, most recently in 1957.[27] In September, 1958, 562,466 workers were covered under this program.[28]

Retirement and survivors' insurance is jointly financed by equal premiums from all workers and employers. Because coverage is permanent once premiums are paid, the total number of workers covered is the largest of any insurance program, now over 1.5 million. The number of retired workers is still small because the program is new and the average age of industrial workers is low. At the same time, total premiums paid are by far the largest of any of the insurance programs, about half the total, thus financing the expansion of physical facilities and benefits levels paid under other programs. Normal retirement is at age 60, but workers insured for as little as fifteen years can retire with a small pension. Full benefits are paid after 35 years of insurance. Eligibility requirements were fairly rigorous at the outset, but were reduced in 1954, and again in 1957, and the level of survivors' benefits raised.

In scope, the program of general sickness and maternity insurance introduced in 1950 is the most ambitious of any in force. It is jointly financed, and includes medical and maternity care, cash benefits, drugs and appliances, and free, regular medical examinations. It covers all workers under the labor law and their families; furthermore, the law requires that workers exempt from the labor law—such as defense workers and others—must receive benefits in the special schemes which

[26] International Labour Organization, *Labor Problems in Turkey* (Geneva, 1951).
[27] *Bulletin* of the International Social Security Association, August–September, 1957, pp. 370–375.
[28] *Monthly Bulletin of Statistics*, No. 61 (March, 1959), p. 7.

provide coverage at least equal to those provided in this program. The Insurance Organization, under the spur of the Ministry of Labor, has bent every effort to expand the coverage of this program to provide at least token benefits everywhere, and full-scale assistance in the major industrial areas where most of the larger installations have been built.

In addition to providing direct benefits to industrial workers and their families, the government has made use of Insurance Organization funds to stimulate the building of low-cost workers' housing in coöperation with housing coöperatives. The law permits funds from the retirement and survivors' insurance programs to be lent to such coöperatives, to meet up to 90 per cent of the total cost of land and buildings. With the accession of Hayrettin Erkmen to the post of Minister of Labor in 1953, workers' housing became a major government program, a special housing directorate was established in the Insurance Organization, and meetings were held with union leaders to dramatize the government's concern and to stimulate the formation of coöperatives. The Ministry spoke often of a target of 10,000 houses per year, and prominent government leaders, most often the Minister himself, attended various cornerstone-laying and ground-breaking ceremonies in this period. Although the stimulus to action was thus considerable, the number of houses actually built is probably quite small, and is certainly well below the ambitious targets announced so frequently in the 1953–1955 period.

This is primarily because there is practically no experience or expertise available anywhere in Turkey for mass-built low-cost housing; and the government, which has seen to it that funds in large amounts are made available for construction, has failed to provide the technical competence and capital equipment which a serious program of such housing construction would require. The coöperatives, like the contractors, have little or no knowledge of the problems involved. At the same time, the scope of the problem far overshadows the measures so far taken to deal with it. One official source [29] has estimated that there are 40,000 squatters' huts in the four major cities, and another has stated that 450,000 people live in these quarters.[30]

Directly or indirectly, the Social Insurance Organization is the major instrument for achieving the social policies of the state. Its programs deal with all the major risks and uncertainties of industrial employment, and represent an ambitious and expensive attempt to keep the

[29] Dr. Halit Unal, "The Housing Situation in Turkey—Objectives of Housing Policy," *Review* of the Ministry of Labor, Vol. 14, No. 4 (Third Quarter, 1956), p. 7.

[30] *Akis*, January 25, 1958, quoting the Minister of Labor.

initiative for dealing with them firmly in the hands of the state. The structure of the Organization provides for consultative participation, on the board of directors and at annual meetings, of representatives of workers and employers. While the requests of worker spokesmen for liberalization of benefits and coverage have, by and large, been sympathetically heard and often acted upon, their requests for a more responsible role in determining policy and participating in the direction of programs have uniformly and firmly been rejected. Even though the funds of the program come from workers and employers, the Ministry of Labor keeps the reins of control firmly in its own hands. This, in fact, is the major complaint that the unions have about these programs, and it persists despite progressive liberalization of the material benefits.

MINIMUM WAGES

The labor code of 1936 announced a commitment to the principle of minimum wages, and an amendment in 1950 provided for tripartite minimum wage commissions. The first wages were set in 1952, and their scope has grown steadily since. By 1958 they existed in 27 provinces and nineteen industries, considerably more than even in 1956. The number of industries covered varies by area, from a maximum of ten in Istanbul and Izmir to one in each of nine provinces. Each minimum wage commission comes into existence *ad hoc,* and its decisions can be appealed to a central board of government officials appointed by the Ministry of Labor. There is no information as to the number of workers covered by minimum wages, but it is probably considerable. However, enforcement is difficult in the marginal industries and firms subject to the regulations, and union complaints of violations and evasions appear frequently in the press. The level of minimum wages has tended to rise rather fast during the recent inflationary period, but some are still as low as 45 kurus per hour and 300 kurus (£T3.00) per day.[31] Higher minima are generally set in larger cities and for full-time occupations and industries. Some have been applied to such open-air agricultural activities as cotton harvesting, but most apply to industrial and related work.

STATUTORY BONUSES AND TAX EXEMPTIONS

The pressure of inflation on established wage scales in state enterprises was recognized in 1953 when a special law granted one month's extra pay to workers in certain state enterprises, in the form of a "bonus."

[31] The official rate of exchange is set at £T9 = $1. In fact, unofficial rates have fluctuated between £T6 and £T15 per $1.

In 1955 this was extended to workers in the remaining state enterprises, and in 1956 to employees of the provincial and municipal governments. This supposedly temporary expedient has been renewed in subsequent years.

In 1950 the income tax law was revised to grant exemptions to workers based on the size of their families, and in 1957 the exemptions were raised; monthly income exempt from taxation ranges from £T67.5 for bachelors to £T180 for those with five or more children. In addition, income taxes are progressive, and most industrial workers fall into the lowest bracket, up to £T2,500 per year, which is taxed at 15 per cent.

FRINGE BENEFITS

Before the introduction of comprehensive insurance schemes, workers in state enterprises received fairly elaborate wage supplements and other benefits; these persist, and are found—though usually on a much reduced scale—in many private plants. Most industrial workers receive one or two sets of work clothes a year and a daily meal from their employers. Many employers make available surplus or damaged goods free or very cheap; so-called "production" or "diligence" bonuses for regular attendance at work are frequent. The more elaborate schemes in the state enterprises include children's allowances, various bonuses on the occasion of marriages, births, and other occasions, suggestion systems, and vacations. The Sümerbank benefits program represented in 1954 an addition to the wage bill of about 25 per cent, and this is probably typical of state enterprises. Many furnish housing, education, transportation to and from work, facilities for sports and recreations, and similar types of assistance. Some subsidize credit unions, and others assist in the operation of consumer and housing coöperatives. These programs constitute a comprehensive system of state paternalism which surrounds industrial workers with a considerable cushion of security, and is calculated to make and keep them almost wholly dependent on the enterprises for many economic, physical, and psychological essentials of life. In a sense, the social security system is an attempt to reproduce this principle on a large scale, to extend paternalism to the entire industrial labor force.

THE STATE EMPLOYMENT SERVICE

This organization is charged exclusively with all aspects of labor recruitment. It benefited from extensive long-range planning and capable leadership during the early years of its existence, and from useful technical assistance from American experts during its early operating stages, so that it has been able to expand smoothly and effectively since it began serious field operations in 1950. Its annual budget is relatively small—about £T1.5 million in 1953—but its scale of operations has increased steadily. In recent years it has handled 500 to 600 thousand applications per year, and total placements have not lagged far behind. In the early 1950's, the Service concentrated on industrial and urban employment, establishing a network of offices and a competent staff trained along American lines. More recently, serious attempts have been made to deal with the large numbers of migratory agricultural workers, estimated at 250,000 to 300,000, which is particularly important in the southern cotton-growing region of Seyhan, the Aegean area around Izmir, and the fruit-growing regions around Bursa. The Service operates a system of shelters for migratory workers to provide rest, food, and bathing facilities; these have handled increasing numbers of workers, reaching 165,000 in 1956 but declining since. Once workers accept the help of the Service through these shelters, the next objective is to establish the Service as the placement agency, replacing in the process traditional channels of recruitment. The latter have often been middlemen from villages whose strategic role leads to abuse and exploitation. Their operations also prevent any reliable estimates of the size of these migratory forces, the timing and level of demand for them by farmers, and other steps needed to utilize them effectively and humanely.

The Employment Service operates various programs of training, mostly for craftsmen in urban employment—waiters, auto mechanics, longshoremen, building tradesmen, and others. Smaller programs assist rural craftsmen, such as rug weavers and peasant wives, with traditional crafts which are supplements to the major source of family income. It has also experimented with programs of mass placement for major public works projects such as dams and roads. It has recently begun programs designed to yield accurate measurements of labor force and labor market changes, but these have not yet yielded major results.

Like the Insurance Organization, the Employment Service, though nominally autonomous, operates in fact as an arm of the Ministry of Labor. It too faces the demand of unions for greater share in policies and operations, and resists them with equal firmness. Unlike the Insurance Organization, however, the Service has managed to create good relations with the unions. This is partly because it does not operate with funds paid out of wages, so the issue of control seems less a matter of principle, and partly because the areas in which it works deal with the fringes of the organized and committed labor force. Unions feel, and with some justice, that they could render useful assistance to supplement the operations of the Service, though they do not normally seek to affect major policies. Those most directly concerned with the Service are the unions of construction workers, whose members are under the perennial threat of competition from new entrants to the labor force from the villages, which are the traditional source of skilled building workers. These unions seek to protect their members by licensing systems and similar techniques, and would find their objectives much easier to achieve if the Service would impose the limitations and conditions which they wish. But the Service is only one of several channels for recruiting such workers, and could not accede to these requests even if it wished to. With the bulk of the unions representing industrial workers, the Service has established effective consultative machinery and has deliberately sought to cultivate good relations with them. It enjoys far higher status with these unions than does the Insurance Organization or the line offices of the Ministry of Labor. But unlike them, it operates on the periphery of the committed industrial labor force, where stress and scrutiny are less.

THE MINISTRY OF LABOR

Its direct role in industrial relations and its indirect domination of the major welfare programs and institutions make the Ministry of Labor the key instrument for the achievement of the state's objectives in this area. It and its predecessor agencies were the principal architects of social policies which were the counterpart of étatism. Despite the growth of industry, the Ministry itself has always been small. Its budget is among the lowest of any government agency, and its personnel, particularly inspectors, are sadly inadequate in numbers and training. It shares with other government ministries a lack of specialists and an oversupply of legally trained career bureaucrats. Its work is highly centralized; even routine decisions must often be cleared at very high levels. Its specialized staff offices, such as the Research Board, are understaffed and burdened with routine duties which leave little time for their major responsibilities. Its case load, as measured by records of inspections and complaints, rose by almost a quarter between 1954 and 1956, with no change in authorized personnel. In all important respects it is ill fitted to perform the important duties laid upon it.

Until 1953 the post of Minister was, with brief exceptions, filled by men without special qualifications for or interest in the work of the Ministry. The important work was done, with a relatively free hand, by the career bureaucrats who had filled the key posts with remarkable continuity since 1936. This small group, under the influence of Western ideas and Turkish ideals, were the real architects of social policy in

Turkey, and were able to create a comprehensive and consistent set of programs and institutions. Thereafter, the center of power shifted upward, into the hands of the Ministers themselves, and political considerations largely replaced objective long-term factors as the determinants of policies to be carried out by the Ministry and its associated agencies. In the process, the career officers of the earlier period largely disappeared from the scene. Confronted with the twin threats of growing inflationary and urban pressures on the one hand, and a union movement of increasing assurance and strength on the other, the energies of the Ministry were devoted to a determined effort to keep the initiative in social and labor matters firmly in the government's hands, and to frustrate, by a combination of manipulation and repression, the ambition of the unions to achieve responsibility and status in decision-making. In the process the government reneged, in fact though not in word, on its earlier pledges to grant the right to strike; it suspended or dissolved several union organizations; it harassed the national union organization and militant union leaders, and attempted to divide the union ranks. In these policies, the shell of étatism remained, but the substance was wholly altered.

The Trade Unions

DEVELOPMENT

Medieval Islamic guilds and their successors, called corporations (*loncalar*), endowed the handicraft occupations with stable organizations well into the nineteenth century. They regulated working life, provided effective systems of social assistance, and in large measure performed the social functions which were foregone by the decentralized and limited Ottoman state.[32] As European manufacturers began to compete with and depress the state of the handicraft arts and as foreign capital began to exploit domestic resources, notably minerals, with more modern systems of organization and capital, the corporations began to decline. The process was hastened by the adoption of a new civil code in 1860 (the *Mecelle*) which established economic relationships on the basis of individual contract, and abolished the legal prerogatives of the corporations. Thereafter systematic organization of workers disappeared, except for occasional attempts to establish societies, such as the Workers' Care Society (*Ameleperver Cemiyeti*) of 1871, which combined mutual assistance and trade unionism in brief, unstable partnership.

[32] See A. LeGenissel, *L'Ouvrier d'Industrie en Turquie* (Beirut, 1948), pp. 11–27.

Trade unionism received great stimulus during the patriotic moments which marked Turkey's evolution toward freedom and national independence. The restoration of the 1876 Constitution which marked the Young Turk victory of 1908 was followed by a series of strikes and labor demonstrations in Salonika, Istanbul, and other cities. These combined the spirit of revolutionary exuberance with an attempt to secure redress for grievances and abuses by methods which had not been permitted under the absolutism of Abdul Hamid. Some victories were won, but the Young Turk regime suppressed strikes and put the new labor organizations under rigid control in 1909, establishing at the same time a series of workers' aid societies to replace them. Turkey's defeat in World War I and the collapse of the regime saw a new revival of unionism, directed both against the occupying powers and against the pattern of the past. Several left-wing political parties were organized, advocating various socialist and reformist platforms and working to stimulate trade union organization. Between 1919 and 1923 a series of strikes occurred, including large-scale stoppages by the railroad workers, the Istanbul tram workers, and the Istanbul dock workers. Though little in the way of permanent organization emerged from these events, they demonstrated that considerable potential for action existed, and produced some capable leaders, a few of whom were active after World War II.

As the Republic consolidated its political and administrative hold, union freedom was gradually curtailed, until in 1925 and 1926 freedom to organize was restricted by law to mutual assistance societies. Thereafter little evidence of worker organization was forthcoming, except for sporadic activities during the brief periods in which the ruling party relaxed its authoritarian control. At the same time, the state gradually assumed the initiative over a greater and greater area of social policy, culminating in the labor code of 1936. Laws passed after the outbreak of World War II gave greater power of control to the central government, limiting even the small degree of organizational freedom which remained.

The end of the war and the introduction of political freedom marked the end of the phase of control, and opened the present period of union history. The prohibition of "class-based" organizations was removed in June, 1946, and immediately thereafter spontaneous centers of union organization appeared in all the large cities, and particularly in Istanbul. The freedom to engage in partisan politics led to the organization of several new parties of the Left, some of which actively stimulated and assisted these new manifestations of worker organization. These ranged from idealistic reformism to actual, though not admitted, promotion of Communism. The gap of thirty years had left a great desire to organize, but practically no experienced leadership to realize it. This gap was filled in part by those active in the new parties —journalists, lawyers, and Communist agents. The rate of organization was extremely rapid, and testified to the success of these efforts, as well as those made by groups of workers on their own. At first the government appeared to welcome it; speaking in September, the Minister of Labor, Dr. Sadi Irmak, said: "In our view the unions being organized are completely legal and legitimate. From my heart and soul I hope that they will advance both their own and the nation's welfare. We are ready to work together with the unions. I am sure that they will be valuable in achieving the goals of the Ministry of Labor." [33] The government relied on the new Ministry, and on its own political apparatus, which was well organized, well staffed, and amply supplied with funds, to lead the workers gradually into unionism. But in contrast to the conditions which had hitherto prevailed, the government and the CHP were no longer in sole possession of the stage. For several months the struggle for supremacy and influence went on between the government and the CHP, the growing opposition parties, and the activists on the Left. By November it was clear that the government was having second thoughts about its policy of freedom, and in December the police began to close existing unions and arrest both union leaders and left-wing politicians. At the same time new legislation was being prepared, dealing specifically with unionism. This legislation was passed in February, 1947, and has been in force without amendment since then. Explaining its necessity in the Assembly, the Minister justified the government's change of policy:

> Shortly after this development, in many places, among them the large cities, we found ourselves face to face with a unionist activity which quickly arose and made headway; their number approached 100. Some called themselves unions, others assemblies or associations. Yet all, it was clear, shared the motive of advancing class or collective interests and needs. Although founded to meet these needs, some shortly moved far from their duty, imposing on us the duty to promulgate a new system of law and order. For example, we saw that in some instances group interests were abandoned; advancing their personal interests and securing leadership posts occupied the energies of some who carried on political propaganda based on class or occupational interests. Others suddenly confronted us as alleged spokesmen for the whole nation, through their authority as officials of these groups; without any examination, those who represent their fellows in a particular area presumed to speak for all Turkish workers. . . . The majority of our

[33] Sülker, *op. cit.*, p. 54.

workers are patriotic and ready to work together with the state, and to rely on the guidance and help of the Ministry of Labor. It could not be a question, as in totalitarian countries, of our free étatist government arranging the union question to suit its own needs and directing unions through government officials. . . . A special law was needed to deal with this particular question.[34]

The new law restricted membership in unions to workers in the craft or industry in which the particular union was being organized, made membership wholly voluntary, permitted any number of unions to be formed in an area or occupation, forbade unions to engage in political activities, placed their funds and accounts under government inspection, required that the government approve any request for affiliation of any union or union organization to an international organization, and required that affiliation of any union to a multiunion organization receive the votes of two-thirds of the membership. Unions could organize coöperatives, operate mutual assistance funds, and, to a limited extent, participate in the settlement of disputes. The law, as these provisions indicate, envisaged single local unions under effective government scrutiny, isolated from political agitation, and limited in their sphere of action.

Union growth has been steady since 1947, as table 24 shows. Multiunion organizations are of two kinds: those on an urban or regional basis are similar to city central labor unions and state federations of labor in the United States, and are generally called *birliks,* and those on an industrial or occupational basis are called federations. A national organization, the Turkish Confederation of Trade Unions (TCTU)—abbreviated *Türk-Iş*—was founded in 1952.

GEOGRAPHIC AND INDUSTRIAL DISTRIBUTION

All 21 regional offices of the Ministry of Labor reported the existence of unions in 1955, ranging downward from a total of 76 unions with 55,165 members in Istanbul to two unions with 472 members in Edirne. Two-thirds of the total membership reported was in seven major economic areas: Istanbul, Izmir, Seyhan, Zonguldak, Ankara, Bursa, and Eskisehir. Of these, the largest recent increases have taken place in Izmir; among the smaller centers, greatest rates of growth have occurred in the Elazig-Diyarbakir and Trabzon regions.

About half the total membership is found in six industries, and half of this number are in two industries, textiles and tobacco. This is shown by table 25.

[34] *Ibid.,* pp. 58–59.

TABLE 24

UNIONS, MULTI-UNION ORGANIZATIONS, AND MEMBERSHIP, 1947–1957

Date	Unions	Membership	Multi-union organizations: Number	Multi-union organizations: Number of affiliates
1947	49	33,000		
1948	69	61,000	1	
1949	83	74,000	2	
1950	88	76,000	3	
1951	162	112,800		
1952	248	130,000	16	
1953	296	167,428 [a]	21	205
1954	344	176,262 [b]	26	179
1955	363	189,595 [c]	27	
1956	376	209,155 [c]	26	
1957	383	244,843 [c]	18 [d]	

SOURCES: *Review* of the Ministry of Labor, 1947–1955, Vol. 1, No. 2, p. 86; Vol. 1, No. 3, statistical appendix; Vol. 3, No. 1, pp. 122–123; Vol. 3, No. 2, pp. 94–95.
[a] For 266 unions.
[b] For 281 unions.
[c] Number of unions included unknown.
[d] Reduced by legal action.

TABLE 25

MAJOR INDUSTRIAL CONCENTRATIONS OF UNION MEMBERSHIP, 1954

Industry	Number of unions	Estimated membership
Textiles	38	43,417
Tobacco and cigarettes	28	29,852
Mining	16	18,091
Urban transport and utilities	20	13,012
Construction	32	10,677
Defense industry	11	10,332
Total	145	125,381 [a]

SOURCES: Ministry of Labor, interviews, questionnaire responses.
[a] For 119 of 145 unions.

More than half the total membership is in unions of 1,000 members or more. There are three large unions with a membership of more than 10,000: the Zonguldak coal miners, the Izmir tobacco workers, and the Istanbul textile workers unions. The size distribution of unions is shown in table 26.

The data on geographic, industrial, and size distribution suggest that considerable stability has characterized Turkey's union movement for several years, even though five out of every six unions now in existence were founded in 1950 or later.

TABLE 26

UNIONS BY SIZE OF MEMBERSHIP, 1954

Size class	Number of unions	Total membership	Cumulative totals		
			Membership	Industries	Cities
10,000 and over	3	36,525	—	3	3
5,500–7,000	4	26,000	62,525	5	4
3,400–4,200	4	15,039	77,564	8	5
2,100–2,300	8	18,037	95,871	13	6
1,000–2,000	33	48,318	144,189	21	18

STRUCTURE

The urban *birliks* are the older, more numerous, and more important of the two types of multiunion organization. The Istanbul association was organized in 1948, and there were six by the end of 1950, in each of the five major cities and in Gaziantep. Recent years have seen schisms among some of them, in Istanbul, Bursa, Adana, and Izmir, for partisan political reasons principally. Since 1955, alleged violations of the law, the "two-thirds" requirement referred to above, have led to the legal closing of those in three of the five major cities and in two smaller ones.

The first occupational federation was organized in 1951 by unions of waiters and hotel workers; this was followed in the same and following years by organizations of municipal transport, textile, maritime, railroad, and monopolies [35] workers' unions. By 1958 there were eleven federations reported. Except for mine workers, all industries and occupations with significant numbers of workers and unions are represented by a federation, even though there are still many unions eligible for membership in existing federations which have not yet affiliated. The dominant position in mining occupied by the Zonguldak miners' union, closely controlled by the government, largely explains the absence of a mineworkers' federation.

The virtual absence of collective bargaining and systematic plant-level relationships between unions and management indicates why the federations have so far played a limited role in union affairs. The solution to problems must be sought by political means; political organization is regional, and politics involves local influence. Therefore the *birliks,* which are the natural focus of union strength on a geographic basis, are the principal means by which the unions can

[35] The Monopolies Administration operates cigarette factories, tobacco sheds, wine and liquor distilleries, food processing plants, and related activities.

create and use the political influence they need. This also explains why the legal proceedings instituted by the government in recent years have been directed exclusively against these organizations. It is through them that the growing political strength of the unions can best be limited. This situation is unlikely to change in the foreseeable future, as long as government policies make it difficult or impossible to develop decision-making by the parties themselves. If this direction of policy should be reversed, the structure of the unions would quickly accommodate itself to the change; the existing federations provide a nucleus for the development of national unions organized along industrial and occupational lines. The initiative, however, rests not with the unions but with the government.

THE CONFEDERATION

The organization of a national confederation, in 1952, marked the high point in the growth of the unions, and appeared to be the beginning of a new phase of vigor in their life. Attempts to achieve such an organization began with the first unionizing events of 1946, and a committee was at work in 1950 drafting a constitution, but later disbanded. In 1951 and 1952, coincident with the organization of the first occupational federations, visits to Turkey were made by U.S. labor officials, ICFTU representatives, and American unionists serving as labor advisers in the Paris headquarters of the ECA. These visits provided an important stimulus to further organizing efforts. The victory of the Democrats in 1950 had been a great encouragement to unionists, and the generally favorable and permissive atmosphere of the post-election years helped to produce a substantial increase in the number of unions and union members. All these events united to create a growing conviction that the time was propitious for a major effort.

A series of meetings took place early in 1952, successively in Istanbul, Izmir, and Bursa, involving larger and larger groups of union representatives. A steering committee was appointed to draft a constitution, and a convention call was issued for September, in Izmir. There were 62 delegates present from every major union organization except the Zonguldak coal miners, plus distinguished guests from management and government. It was the highest point yet reached by the union movement in terms of prestige, achievement, and pride. The Minister of Labor himself attended and congratulated the delegates, and a substantial contribution from the Ministry helped to start the new organization on its career. The resolutions adopted included a decision to apply for affiliation to the ICFTU, a request that the right to strike be quickly forthcoming, and a series of resolutions dealing with labor law and administration. The efficient disposal of the business at hand, the presence of important guests, the adoption of the constitution, and the participation of virtually all the union organizations in Turkey, seemed to indicate that a new phase of union effectiveness and importance had indeed begun.

These hopes have largely been disappointed. The Confederation has lived almost wholly in a crisis atmosphere, has achieved nothing of substance, and has barely managed to survive. It has been unable either to develop good relations on a permanent basis with the government, or to secure the unity of the unions behind it, as their spokesman and coördinator. The successful achievement of either of these tasks would probably have made the other attainable, but with neither achieved, it has merely improvised, with a divided leadership and precarious finances.

The principal reason for this was the adoption by the government of a restrictive rather than a liberating policy toward unions in the period after 1953. A favorable government policy was important during the formative phase of the Confederation, and its disappearance demoralized union leadership. A second reason was the failure of those establishing the new organization to understand fully the internal implications of this new move, and to provide institutional safeguards to assure its success. For example, though major leaders participated in the preliminary work, none would agree to serve as one of the full-time officers. Thus, men of less prestige and importance were chosen; they could not secure the subordination by affiliated unions of regional and occupational policies and procedures to those of a new organization far away in Ankara. Given the importance of regional organizations in achieving union demands, and thus determining the status of union leaders, this reluctance to jeopardize local prestige was inevitable. Finally, the depth and universality of partisan political sympathies made it inevitable that the Confederation would find it difficult, if not impossible, to avoid a partisan identification; the leadership has often failed to realize and guard against this danger. Leaders sympathetic to the Democrats would be labeled as "yellow" unionists in the service of the government, while a CHP-oriented leadership was likely to incur the displeasure of the government, and thus to be denied the opportunity for collaboration or representation. The latter alternative held through the 1952–1957 period, and the former existed after 1957.

During the earlier period, the leadership frequently criticized the government for inaction and inadequacy on the legislative front, failure to grant the right to strike, failure to grant permission to affiliate to the ICFTU, and other matters. Such militance served both to alienate the government and to divide the unions. There were frequent charges that the leadership was exceeding the scope of its authority, and one affiliate withdrew after allegations were published by the Confederation leadership that, in the affiliate's region, the state had neglected its duties both as employer and regulator of labor life. The leaders of the affiliate could not preserve their local standing without repudiating these charges, whether they were correct or not, and made what seemed to them the necessary choice. Periodic attempts have been made, at the triennial conventions and the semiannual meetings of the Executive Council, to restore the vigor and unity of the Confederation, but such attempts cannot overcome the basic problems which divide the affiliates, immobilize the organization, and prevent a fruitful attack on common problems.

Nevertheless, the survival of the Confederation is itself an achievement which testifies that, although the conditions for putting it to practical use do not exist, it plays a valuable symbolic role in the life of the unions. It stands for their internal unity and their international status, two ideals which embody much of the meaning of trade unionism to those involved in it. Its existence has served to help preserve those ideals in the difficult times of the recent past, just as it may become the vehicle for positive achievement in the future.

THE STATE OF THE UNIONS—LEADERSHIP, ACTIVITIES, ATTITUDES, AND IDEOLOGIES

The leaders of Turkey's unions differ in many important respects from all other leadership groups in Turkish society. They are members of the working class, as a result of the legal restriction excluding nonworkers from union membership. Leadership is for them a new experience, with challenges which they often fail to master fully. Their new eminence is itself a challenge to older leadership groups in political and economic life, and they find it extremely difficult to win recognition and acceptance. Prestige normally depends on education, occupation, age, and social origin in Turkey; in all these respects union leaders are at a disadvantage. Like the unions, they are young; of 251 who furnished personal data in answer to a questionnaire in 1954, 139 were 35 years old or younger, and the modal group was 31 to 35 years of age. Only 117 were born in cities of 5,000 population or more, and only 59 in "large" cities; 50 were born in areas once part of the Ottoman Empire but now outside of Turkey; only 41 were born in those provinces which today include the largest cities and the major concentrations of industrial workers. One hundred fifty attended only primary schools, and only 15 had gone to high school or beyond. Most work at their trade full time; only 16 received any salary from their unions. This is leadership from the rank-and-file in every sense.

Most of those who admitted affiliation to a political party named the Democrats, but those who supported the then opposition would be unlikely to say so in writing to a foreign investigator. A good guess would be that practically all union leaders are politically active in some way, and that their allegiance is divided about equally between the major parties, with a few supporting religious-nationalist parties of the Right and even fewer belonging to Socialist parties. Democratic supporters tend to be more numerous in small towns and the less urbanized areas, where unionism often dates from the period since 1950, while the more prominent leaders in the major cities are usually, though not always, sympathetic to the CHP.

A substantial number of union leaders have experienced difficulties ranging from discrimination in employment to arrest and interrogation. The latter occurs fairly rarely, usually when a local prosecutor or provincial governor feels the pressure of particularly outspoken union protest on some local grievance, and responds instinctively in the pattern established during the long years of one-party rule. On some occasions, a prominent leader has been deliberately arrested or held for interrogation at the instigation of someone fairly high in the government after a particularly eloquent expression of opinion at a union meeting or in a press interview. Such incidents were designed to demonstrate the government's firmness, and though they seldom silenced those directly affected, they impressed less prominent and less independent leaders.

Interest in Western unionism, particularly that of the United States, and strong feelings of identification and solidarity with free trade unionism outside Turkey, is a widely shared characteristic of union leaders. The interest was greatly stimulated by the program of training for union leaders which was jointly operated by the United States and Turkey in 1954, under the technical assistance program, and by the periodic visits of American unionists to Turkey since 1951.

Operating amid difficulties, union leaders demonstrate substantial capacity to lead and influence their members, and to create durable, unified organizations. Many are very effective as public speakers and in private discussion, and cases of dictatorial rule are rare, though not entirely absent. When a dictator rules, those aggrieved can always organize their own union; this has happened in some instances, though political partisanship and rivalry for position were also present. There is considerable democracy in union affairs, and the rank-and-file participate actively. The unions are not very large, and bureaucratic domination is almost wholly absent; few unions can maintain even one full-time officer. The evidence of abundant devotion to democratic principles is doubly striking in a society where political democracy is new, and authoritarian traditions deep-rooted.

An elite leadership has emerged among the unions, including several men who would acquit themselves well in any international trade union gathering. Leadership positions are generally stable, and frequent turnover among the top posts is rare. Of 66 unions responding to the questionnaire, 32 had had only one president since their founding. The existence of an elite group of spokesmen and leaders of opinion is indicated both by the informal evidence of respect and influence which emerged in contact with a wide sample of leaders, and by the results of a question asking each union to name the five "best" leaders in Turkey. Each of the 21 persons who received two or more votes has a national reputation; the ten who were most frequently named include almost all the top leaders, and the one who led the list—Bahir Ersoy, of the Istanbul textile workers and the national textile federation—is the most accomplished, sophisticated, and effective union leader in the country, in the judgment of almost all observers.

The available data, which are not very complete, suggest that perhaps one union in ten had an income of £T10,000 or more in 1954, and a few had five to ten times that amount. Of 69 unions about which some financial information was available, 14 had total incomes of £T10,000 or more in 1954, and for almost all of these this was substantially more than the previous year. About 40 per cent of the unions employ some staff, usually a clerk, at least part time. The largest unions have larger staffs, including full-time organizers (Istanbul textile workers) and medical technicians (Izmir tobacco workers). The existence of mutual aid activities in several cases testifies both to the need for such help and to the influence of the pre-1945 period. Union income is wholly or largely from dues; some unions supplement this source with lotteries, balls, concerts, and other fund-raising activities, and a smaller number have received financial support from government agencies, party organizations, and employers. Many unions, on the other hand, reject such support as inimical to their independence.

The state of union finances puts ambitious programs beyond the reach of most unions, but some carry on substantial activities. These usually include some sort of social activity—cinemas and circumcision parties are the apparent favorites—and a few provide programs of training, consumer coöperatives, and informal job reference service. The major focus of union energy, however, is on the problems of industrial relations, which are met in two principal ways: direct contact with employers on grievances, and presenting complaints to the regional offices of the Ministry of Labor. The dual system of representation, by the elected representatives and by the unions, tends to exclude the latter from any integrated role in day-to-day relations with employers unless the union has been able to secure the election of its own people as representatives, or the employer voluntarily makes a place for the union. At the biennial elections of workers' representatives, intensive electioneering takes place as rival unions, and the employers in some instances, seek to determine who will win these posts. The larger and more dynamic unions have generally been able to achieve success in this effort, but the number of such cases in all of Turkish industry is not great. There is little inducement to workers to prefer the union's candidate over a nonunion man, and when the latter is supported by the employer their interests may be better served by his election.

Most unions rent their quarters, sometimes in coöperation with others in the area; these quarters are seldom comfortable, and are usually badly furnished rooms in the poorer district. A few unions own their own quarters, and some operate in quarters furnished by the employer; this is more frequent in the state enterprise plants. No more than a handful can hold their annual meetings in their own halls; usually a cinema or government building is rented for this purpose.

Most unions have a simple structure. An annual convention of members, or delegates in the case of larger unions, is the supreme governing instrument under a constitution. It approves amendments to the constitution, discusses and approves the officers' reports, adopts a budget and a program of activities, hears remarks of visiting union and nonunion dignitaries, and elects officers. The latter consist of a small executive committee and a larger executive council; the first group usually meets two or three times a week, while the second meets biweekly or monthly. These meetings are generally lively, democratic, and long.

The preoccupations of union leaders are largely local and intensely union-oriented, and the inner life of the union movement has much vigor. Leaders are extremely proud of and dedicated to their organizations, even though the tangible rewards are few. One described his relation to his union as "a love affair," a not uncommon attitude. Leaders see much of one another, both in their own localities and, less frequently, elsewhere, on occasions such as the annual meetings of the Workers' Insurance Organization. A union's annual convention is attended by most of the leaders in the area. Union delegations to Ankara are frequent, and groups of leaders often congregate at regional labor offices for conferences with the officials and inspectors of the Ministry of Labor. Such frequent interchange helps to maintain morale, to keep leaders informed about events and personalities elsewhere, and to formulate shared opinions on issues.

On occasion an issue arises which permits the unions to participate in events of general interest, and to bridge the gap which normally isolates them from most elements of the society. An example was the agitation over the Cyprus question which began in 1953 and rose in intensity, culminating in the destructive anti-Greek riots in Istanbul in September, 1955. In the plethora of organizations which sprang up in this period to express the feelings of the population, ample space was made for union participation. Though some unions saw that full-scale participation would essentially be a diversion from more germane concerns, most seized the opportunity to express their patriotism and solidarity with the rest of the country. They collected funds for the Cypriote Turkish workers and unions, sent Turkish flags and busts of Atatürk, and a delegation from Istanbul spent some time in Cyprus meeting with unionists there. In these activities the unions had found a way to break through to their compatriots, and the government had found a useful diversion for union energies. When the process overran its bounds and martial law was imposed following the 1955 riots, the unions found themselves the victims of their own fervor, with their offices padlocked, their meetings prohibited, and some of their leaders under arrest.

A sense of isolation and frustration is endemic in Turkey's unions. Though some unions have been able to establish a *modus vivendi* with employers which gives them satisfaction and a sense of purpose, most are excluded from any effective role, particularly in their dealings with private employers. They blame both the employers and the law for this; the majority seem to feel that employers are not likely to afford more scope to unions in industrial relations until they are compelled to by law or the economic strength of the workers, backed by the right to strike. Though union opinion is divided on the right to strike, there are few union leaders who do not consider it fundamental and necessary; the division is over timing and strategy. The moderates fear that granting the right to strike at this stage of union development would place the unions in an unequal struggle with employers which would lead to their growing weaker, not stronger. Others among them repudiate the militance associated with the demand for the right to strike because it alienates the fundamental source of power, the state, and weakens the unions' chances of securing more moderate and realistic concessions. The militants, on the contrary, feel that the unions must retrogress if they are not given a larger scope and more challenging tasks. They point to considerable evidence that employers cannot be educated to their responsibilities without coercion to point the lesson, and to increasing evidence that the ruling party has repudiated its commitments to enlarge the area of union freedom and responsibility.

In general, union leaders are fairly pessimistic about the likelihood that their status will improve, but show impressive sticking power nonetheless. They are more favorably impressed by the personnel policies of the state enterprises than by those of private employers, but agree that both groups operate with little influence being exerted by union requests or pressures. They are unhappy about the restrictive legal framework within which they operate; they want more autonomy and less supervision. They find the designated agencies which deal with workers' problems inadequate; the officials of the Ministry of Labor, while often sincere and devoted, lack sufficient knowledge, status, or numbers to be effective, and the welfare agencies exercise a stifling paternalism which alienates union leaders. What most disturbs them is the contrast between the potential of the unions for participation and the role to which they are restricted.

COMMUNISM AND CLASS CONFLICT

Government spokesmen frequently expressed their fear that too much union freedom might open the door to union domination or infiltration by Communism. In so doing, they used the term to symbolize the possibility of class division and class conflict, rather than any considered judgment that Communism itself constitutes a danger. At the same time, the word is so effective an epithet, and paralyzes objectivity so completely, that antiunion forces have used it deliberately, and high government officials sometimes succumbed to the temptation in their constant struggle to contain unionism within bounds acceptable to the ruling group, and to silence or discredit effective union spokesmen. As often happens in such situations, those who used the word in this way became the victims of their own propaganda. In fact, there is little evidence to support the view that Communism constitutes any real possibility for Turkey's unions or indeed for any substantial part of the population.

There are many reasons why ideologies of the Left have failed to take root in Turkey, despite frequent attempts since 1908. Those usually cited include the identification of Communism with Russia, Turkey's ancient enemy, and the supposed incompatibility of Communism and indigenous Islam. Neither of these is compelling, however. Under Atatürk, Turkey pursued a policy of friendship with the Soviets both during the struggle for national independence and again during the five-year plan; Soviet imperialism rather than ideological distaste led to their later estrangement. In fact, one of the decisive struggles within the revolutionary movement itself was whether it would be dominated by Soviet-style Communism, and the issue was settled by a military decision late in 1920, when Atatürk subdued the Communist irregulars. Thereafter, there was room for only one all-embracing ideology in Turkey, the dynamic nationalist revolution which Atatürk imposed on the nation. Its very vigor and strong, almost complete identification with the personal figure of Atatürk himself made any alternative appear to be an attack on the revolution, in the name of which the government has ruthlessly suppressed domestic Communists since the late 1920's, except for brief periods of liberalization.

Turkey's union leaders, all of whom are workers, share the fervent nationalism which Atatürk gave his people, and expend considerable energy demonstrating their rejection of Communism and class warfare by whatever means are available to them. As expressed in union newspapers, at public meetings, in the action programs of unions and multi-union organizations, and in many discussions, they are wholly pragmatic and centered on concrete economic goals and on improving their own status and role within a society whose premises they accept wholeheartedly. In his most discouraged and lonely moments, no leader contemplates accepting an ideological system which would cut him off so completely from that society. A few union officers in Istanbul call themselves Socialists, in the gradualist tradition of the British Labour party, but they have little influence. Those who most typically represent the dedicated, frustrated, and responsible leadership characteristic of the unions are adherents of the CHP and believers in étatism, Turkey's indigenous expression of economic collectivism. They have no greater goal than to represent the interests of those they lead in a system of industrial relations which recognizes the need for representation and makes it possible to work effectively.

So far none of the requisites for Communist or radical ideologies to succeed exist in Turkey. There is no predatory, rampant capitalism exploiting industrial workers and dominating the machinery of the state. No downtrodden peasantry seeks relief from the oppressive landlord. No imperial power subjugates the people to exploit the land for foreign owners. For different reasons, but with striking similarity, Turkey's union movement and that of the United States seem to share immunity to doctrines of class warfare.

Conclusions

Except for brief periods, the government of the Turkish Republic, in both the one-party and two-party eras, has rigorously and at times severely controlled Turkey's industrial worker organizations. Various types of paternalistic guidance have constituted the state's principal techniques for dealing with the social and economic problems raised by industrial development. These techniques, developed during the first stages of significant growth, have not been replaced or supplemented, though their growing inadequacy has become steadily more apparent. The prevention of class conflict determined these policies at the outset; in recent years, their retention has been encouraged by fear that freedom and autonomy would encourage the growth of independent unions able to use their strength to achieve political influence and play an independent role in the struggle for political supremacy.

Nevertheless, the period after 1945 saw considerable enlargement of political freedom in Turkey, and in this period a union movement achieved substantial organization, stability, and unity. More recently, under the stress of widespread social change, rapid economic growth, inflation, and rivalry for political advantage, the general scope of freedom was restricted, and unions experienced their share of this restriction. Meanwhile economic growth continues, the industrial structure grows larger and more complex, and mechanisms for dealing with its stresses need to be developed and, where necessary, introduced *de novo*. The evidence supports the view that the unions have reached the stage in their development where they can play a responsible and necessary role, but it is impossible to predict whether they will be permitted to do so.

What of the future? The process of industrialization and the introduction of political freedom have created a labor movement with an impressive potential, but one which has not yet achieved the momentum needed to assure its survival or further development. It finds itself in a limbo between growth and degeneration, with the decision to be made by others, who may fail to see what is at stake. All groups agree that the process of industrial growth must continue, and it is apparently possible for the state to secure whatever material sacrifice is necessary from a loyal, disciplined population. But unionism, an institution essential to social stability in an industrial society, is largely denied its place.

Turkey's industrial growth should continue, but may be interrupted or slowed down. This would quickly create such imbalances in the labor force that it is difficult to see how indigenous radicalism could be prevented from repudiating much of the achievement of the past thirty years, and dominating the unions in the process. The ensuing polarization of the society would produce precisely the results which the state has striven so zealously to prevent, and it is likely that freedom would disappear. On the other hand, freedom is not automatically ensured by the creation of a large industrial base. If decentralization of the decision-making process is not introduced at the appropriate moment, the state will have no alternative but to create a vast bureaucratic apparatus for dealing with industrial disputes; in such a system, unions would be little more than appendages of the state. The crucial decision-making period is not far off. Unless it is given the chance and the wings for flight, Turkey's union movement is likely to degenerate and decline, and the chances for a permanent flowering of freedom in Turkey will have been seriously impaired. If this happens, the tragedy will be that it need not have been.

Index

www.ingramcontent.com/pod-product-compliance
Ingram Content Group UK Ltd.
Pitfield, Milton Keynes, MK11 3LW, UK
UKHW040234290926
15471UKWH00002B/185